Digging into
Literature

Digging into Literature

STRATEGIES FOR READING, ANALYSIS, AND WRITING

Joanna Wolfe
Carnegie Mellon University

Laura Wilder
University at Albany, State University of New York

Bedford/St. Martin's
A Macmillan Education Imprint

Boston • New York

For Bedford/St. Martin's

Vice President, Editorial, Macmillan Higher Education Humanities: Edwin Hill
Editorial Director, English and Music: Karen S. Henry
Executive Editor: Vivian Garcia
Senior Executive Editor: Stephen A. Scipione
Editorial Assistant: Eliza Kritz
Production Editor: Kendra LeFleur
Production Assistant: Erica Zhang
Production Supervisor: Victoria Anzalone
Marketing Manager: Joy Fisher Williams
Copy Editor: Steve Patterson
Director of Rights and Permissions: Hilary Newman
Senior Art Director: Anna Palchik
Text Design: Jonathon Nix
Cover Design: Donna Lee Dennison
Cover art: Juniper, 2005, book carving, 27 × 25 × 17 cm. Courtesy Kylie Stillman
    and Utopia Art Sydney.
Composition: Cenveo Publisher Services
Printing and Binding: RR Donnelley and Sons

Manufactured in the United States of America.

0   9   8   7   6
f   e   d   c   b

For information, write: Bedford/St. Martin's, 75 Arlington Street, Boston, MA 02116
    (617-399-4000)

ISBN 978-1-4576-3130-6

Acknowledgments

Text acknowledgments and copyrights continue at the back of the book on pages 399–400, which constitute an extension of the copyright page. Art acknowledgments and copyrights appear on the same page as the art selections they cover. It is a violation of the law to reproduce these selections by any means whatsoever without the written permission of the copyright holder.

Rick Bass. "Antlers." From *In the Loyal Mountains* by Rick Bass. Copyright © 1995 by Rick Bass. Reprinted by permission of Houghton Mifflin Harcourt Publishing Company. All rights reserved.

Preface

Digging into Literature: Strategies for Reading, Analysis and Writing presents an innovative approach to analyzing literary and other kinds of texts. The approach is built around eight research-proven strategies that help students interpret texts and write persuasive arguments about their interpretations. In fifteen chapters, students are taken from the basic strategies for performing close readings to increasingly sophisticated interpretive techniques that enable them to involve historical and literary context, engage with literary theory, and situate themselves in ongoing critical conversations about texts. *Digging into Literature* demystifies these methods of interpretation, making the goals and practices of literary analysis available to students who have trouble "getting" what their literature instructors expect. Moreover, it empowers students beyond literature courses, extending their abilities to practice advanced forms of analytic argument.

The frustration we experienced when we first taught introductory college literature classes motivated us to write this book. We found that while most writing-about-literature textbooks provide students with an extensive vocabulary for describing and categorizing texts and their formal elements, the vocabulary did not help students understand what we meant when we asked them to make an interpretive argument about a text. Many students struggled to understand the difference between literary analysis and plot summary, and even the students who did grasp the difference often had trouble understanding why we preferred a rich, complex analysis over a simpler one.

We also felt that there was a disturbing disconnect between the types of student writing encouraged by traditional approaches to writing about literature and the kind of writing that we wanted students to try. For instance, most traditional textbooks invite students to write a "character analysis" or to explicate a single formal feature of a text, such as its plot or use of metaphor. Such student writing differs sharply from the rich and lively arguments that literary critics and English professors publish—or that we ask of our more advanced students. While advanced literary criticism investigates these formal features, it does so to extend and deepen our understanding of a text's cultural meaning and significance. Why shouldn't students experience the kind of excitement expert literary critics feel when they read or produce an interpretation that takes risks and offers a new, thought-provoking analysis of a text? Moreover, we found that our most successful students were those who seemed to recognize intuitively the need to move beyond straightforward explication and make the types of arguments that we valued in our own writing. Thus, we found ourselves rewarding interpretive skills that differed from the more traditional approaches that we explicitly taught and required.

The research of other scholar-teachers suggests that our experiences were not unique and that students struggle mightily when instructors do not make their assumptions and expectations about reading and writing explicit.[1] Accordingly, over several years we undertook our own research to fathom the nature of these common problems and to find effective ways to address them in our own teaching. (You can read more about this research in our instructor's manual, *Resources for Teaching* Digging into Literature.) What we discovered, and practiced, informs every aspect of the advice and guidance this book offers.

WHAT'S DIFFERENT ABOUT *DIGGING INTO LITERATURE?*

It demystifies the goals, values, and expectations for reading and writing in literature classrooms. Many students are left puzzled by their literature instructors' expectations for their reading and writing. They often see instructors' evaluative judgments as idiosyncratic rather than as reflections of the shared goals and values of a scholarly discourse community. *Digging into Literature* attempts to demystify these often tacit goals, values, and expectations by explicitly

---

[1] Herrington, Anne J. "Teaching, Writing, and Learning: A Naturalistic Study of Writing in an Undergraduate Literature Course." *Advances in Writing Research, Volume Two: Writing in Academic Disciplines.* Ed. D.A. Jolliffe. Norwood: Ablex, 1988. 133–66. Print.

McCarthy, Lucille Parkinson. "A Stranger in Strange Lands: A College Student Writing across the Curriculum." *Research in the Teaching of English* 21.3 (1987): 233–65. Print.

teaching students about them. Our research has demonstrated that such demystification not only improves student writing, but can also effectively address inequalities in students' prior educational preparation.

It shows how close reading translates directly into interpretive writing. Without abandoning attention to the formal features of literary texts found in other writing-about-literature textbooks, *Digging into Literature* subordinates this attention to instruction on *how* to use awareness of these features to craft an interpretive argument. Part One, "Introducing Literary Analysis" (Chapters 1 and 2) distinguishes literary analysis from plot summary and evaluation, such as one might see in a book review. These opening chapters also distinguish between persuasive literary analysis and "symbol-hunting," which adopts some of the form of literary analysis while ignoring certain substantive aspects of the primary text or its cultural context. When formalist terms or traditional literary classifications are introduced, they are combined with advice and examples that illustrate *how* these terms assist a critic in deepening interpretations. These terms and classifications appear primarily throughout Part Two, "Strategies for Close Reading" (Chapters 3 through 6), but most explicitly in Chapter 5, "Digging Deeper."

It offers an activity-driven approach to critical reading and a practical approach to critical writing. In his famous meta-analysis of writing research, George Hillocks identifies "scales"—or the process of ranking multiple essays of varying quality and discussing the evaluation criteria—as one of the instructional activities most likely to yield measurable improvement in students' writing.[2] These activities are effective because they ferret out hidden assumptions about what makes for good writing and align students' and teachers' evaluation criteria. Rather than present only "good" student writing, *Digging into Literature* provides multiple short interpretations of varying quality for readers to compare and contrast. (See, for example, the exercises that conclude Chapters 3 and 4.) We find these comparative exercises essential in beginning literature classrooms because many students initially struggle to understand why one interpretation is

---

[2] Hillocks, George. "What Works in Teaching Composition: A Meta-Analysis of Experimental Treatment Studies." *American Journal of Education* 93.1 (1984): 133–170. Print.

more persuasive or is judged as "deeper," or more plausible, than another. Moreover, such exercises provide opportunities to discuss how to improve the persuasiveness of weaker samples. Because the samples are short, they lend themselves well to in-class group work and ensure that students read the samples.

Not only does *Digging into Literature* show students how to evaluate arguments about texts, but it also shows students how to compose their own effective arguments. For each strategy discussed in the book, students are given multiple "templates" illustrating how to express various types of arguments about a text. (For example, see the list of "common words and phrases associated with genre" arguments section in Chapter 8.) The templates provide models for students who lack the confidence to assert their own arguments, helping them express their ideas in forms that are persuasive in literary studies today. Many students cite these templates as their favorite feature of the book. This practical approach carries into Part Four, "Crafting Your Essay" (Chapters 13, 14, and 15) which offers students activity-driven instruction on developing, organizing, documenting, revising, and peer-reviewing their critical essays.

It strives to make sophisticated analytic tools accessible even to beginning literature students. Literature professors we have interviewed tell us that they desire to see students insert their original perspectives into scholarly conversations. Yet few writing-about-literature textbooks do more than offer general guidance on research or documenting sources correctly. By contrast, *Digging into Literature* integrates strategies for working with secondary sources throughout the book and, in Part Three, "Strategies for Going Beyond the Text" (Chapters 7 through 12) it demystifies both why and how literary critics use literary theory, historical materials, and secondary criticism in their analyses of literary texts. For example, in contrast to other textbooks that briefly overview critical approaches to textual interpretation without clarifying what critics do with this information, *Digging into Literature* focuses on *how* to use literary theory in order to support an interpretation. Students are often interested to discover that there are different critical schools, but they tend to be mystified as to how to apply this information to their own interpretive work. In response, Chapter 10 teaches both how to use theory at the brainstorming stage and how to organize an essay that uses a theoretical lens to interpret a literary text. (The book's appendix includes several theoretical lenses that students can try on to spur such interpretations.) The metaphor of critical conversation we introduce in Chapter 1 is given concrete treatment in Chapter 11, where students are shown strategies for entering the conversation. As a cumulative finale, Chapter 12 walks students through the complex task of trying out all the strategies on a difficult text, David Henry Hwang's one-act play, *As the Crow Flies.*

It heartens and instructs novices by revealing how even experts struggle to make meaning of texts. *Digging into Literature* takes a unique approach to writing process instruction by sharing transcripts of expert literary critics "thinking aloud" as they read and write. Recent educational research suggests that observing such think-alouds—in which people make mistakes and then correct for them—can have major benefits for novices attempting new tasks.[3] *Digging into Literature* contains transcriptions of literary critics musing and hazarding ideas as they encounter unfamiliar texts for the first time and struggle to interpret them. These "transcript excerpts" appear in Chapters 3, 4, 7, 9, and 10 and illustrate how critics use the strategies outlined in the book to discover things to say about texts and develop plausible arguments about them. This "warts and all" feature makes interpretation more accessible to students by

---

[3] Some of the research appears in the following articles:

Couzijn, Michel. "Learning to Write by Observation of Writing and Reading Processes: Effects on Learning and Transfer." *Learning and Instruction* 9.2 (1999): 109–42. Print.

Higgins, Lorraine. "Reading to Argue: Helping Students Transform Source Texts." *Hearing Ourselves Think: Cognitive Research in the College Writing Classroom.* Eds. Penrose, Ann M. and Barbara M. Sitko. New York: Oxford UP, 1993. 70–101. Print.

Schriver, Karen. "Teaching Writers to Anticipate Readers' Needs: A Classroom-Evaluated Pedagogy." *Written Communication* 9.2 (1992): 179–208. Print.

Sitko, Barbara M. "Writers Meet Their Readers in the Classroom: Revising after Feedback." *Constructing Rhetorical Education.* Eds. Secor, Marie and Davida Charney. Carbondale: Southern Illinois UP, 1992. 278–94. Print.

Zimmerman, Barry J., and Anastasia Kitsantas. "'Acquiring Writing Revision and Self-Regulatory Skill through Observation and Emulation.'" *Journal of Educational Psychology* 94.4 (2002): 660–68. Print.

showing that even experts flail and stumble during the messy process of brain-storming. Moreover, these transcripts encourage students to break the habit of running with their first and most obvious interpretations and instead experiment with multiple possible interpretations, ultimately to pursue the most original and interesting ones. (*LaunchPad Solo for Literature*, an online set of reading tools discussed below in the packaging options for this book, includes annotated videos of students "thinking aloud" about a poem.)

It introduces a disciplinary perspective that will serve students well in their other college courses. *Digging into Literature* is thoroughly grounded in recent pedagogical approaches to "writing in the disciplines" (WID) that will be useful in general education courses serving nonmajors as well as literature courses intended for English majors. Nonmajors should find *Digging into Literature* a frank and revealing guide to navigating an unfamiliar discipline, providing them with analytic skills and vocabulary for negotiating unfamiliar discourse situations. At the same time, English majors will discover that *Digging into Literature* invites them to participate in the authentic genres of a real discipline, with an array of relevant strategies for brainstorming and developing persuasive analytic arguments that will prove useful throughout their experience in the major. Rather than treating student writing as a separate genre or "mutt genre" unconnected to writing practices that thrive outside of the classroom,[4] *Digging into Literature* asks students to write for the same purposes and to use the same analytic strategies found in published literary criticism. The differences between student and professional writing in this approach thus become one of degree rather than kind.

It works flexibly, with texts that you prefer and choose, in a wide range of literature courses. In courses with a heavy focus on the writing process, instructors may find the number of readings in the book, and its sampling of literary genres, periods, and authors to write about, sufficient for their needs.

---

[4] Wardle, Elizabeth. "'Mutt Genres' and the Goal of Fyc: Can We Help Students Write the Genres of the University?" *College Composition and Communication* 60.4 (2009): 765–89. Print.

Nonetheless, *Digging into Literature* is designed to allow instructors to supplement its rhetorical instruction with further readings for students to discuss and write about. As a result, it can be used effectively in courses designed to expose students to a wide array of literary genres or in courses focused on a specific literary period, theme, or issue. Because its take on "literary texts" is broad and inclusive, it can also be used in courses that ask students to write about film and other works of popular culture. Instructors may wish to supplement *Digging into Literature* with a literature anthology or a custom selection of novels, stories, plays, films, and poems. (The instructor's manual suggests many additional works that we have used with success in our own classes.)

Digging into Literature is principally for college instructors who are concerned with improving students' writing and analytic abilities and who want to introduce their students to the intellectual challenges and joys of literary criticism. Such courses, depending on the curricular emphasis and structure of the school, might range from first or second-semester composition courses using literary texts, to introductory literature courses, to the growing number of writing-intensive "gateway courses" to the English major. It is also appropriate for advanced high school English courses designed to teach students how to interpret and write about literature.

ACKNOWLEDGMENTS

Our collaboration on this manuscript has been a long journey, which began with the venting of some frustrations and the sharing of a few good ideas. Little did we know this would lead to an extensive, decade-long interrogation of what it means to teach reading, writing, analysis, and interpretation. Working together on this project has been deeply rewarding, and we know well that the book you hold is superior to one either of us could have produced on our own.

We are grateful for the insights and guidance provided by the gracious staff of Bedford/St. Martin's, especially the wise counsel and generous support provided by Steve Scipione, Karen Henry, Sherry Mooney, Vivian Garcia, Eliza Kritz, Joy Fisher Williams, Kendra LeFleur, and Michael Granger.

We also thank the reviewers of an earlier manuscript which helped us shape and refine the text you hold today. These reviewers include Sandra Allen, University of Iowa; Stephen Bernstein, University of Michigan–Flint; Schahara Hudelson, South Plains College; Stephen Mexal, California State University–Fullerton; Deborah Miller, University of Georgia; Carol Guerero-Murphy, Adams State University; Jessica Parker, Metropolitan State University of Denver; David Richter, Queens College of CUNY; Lee Rumbarger, University of Oregon; Cary Ser, Miami Dade College–Kendall Campus; Christian Smith, Coastal Carolina University; and Laura White, University of Nebraska–Lincoln.

Many colleagues have strongly supported and encouraged our work on this manuscript and the pedagogical advice it contains, sometimes by classroom-testing earlier drafts or sharing with students our research. We must thank Beth Boehm, Langdon Brown, Davida Charney, Patricia Chu, Randall Craig, Alanna Frost, Matthew Giancarlo, David Gold, jil hanifan, Dawn Heineken, Aaron Jaffe, Anne Jung, Eric Keenaghan, Karen Kopelson, Zak Lancaster, Stephen North, Annette Powell, Wendy Roberts, David Russell, Helene Scheck, and Ann Elizabeth Willey. Additionally, we are clearly, deeply indebted to the earlier work of Jeanne Fahnestock and Marie Secor.

We also could not have completed this project, nor so thoroughly have enjoyed the process of completing this project, without the love and support of our families. Our deepest thanks, then, to Ryan, Andi, and Cassie Wolfe and Bret and Jolie Benjamin.

Joanna Wolfe

Laura Wilder

GET THE MOST OUT OF YOUR COURSE WITH *DIGGING INTO LITERATURE*

Digging into Literature doesn't stop with a book. Bedford/St. Martin's offers resources that help you and your students get even more out of your book and course. You'll also find convenient instructor resources, and even a nationwide community of teachers. To learn more about or to order any of the following products, contact your Macmillan Learning/Bedford/St. Martin's sales representative, visit **macmillanhighered.com/myrep**, or visit **macmillanhighered.com /catalog/diggingintolit**.

Assign *LaunchPad Solo for Literature*—the online, interactive, guide to close reading

macmillanhighered.com/launchpadsolo/literature/catalog
To get the most out of *Digging into Literature*, assign it with *LaunchPad Solo for Literature*, which can be packaged at a significant discount. With easy-to-use and easy-to-assign modules, reading comprehension quizzes, and engaging author videos, *LaunchPad Solo for Literature* guides students through three common assignment types: responding to a reading, drawing connections between and among texts, and instructor-led collaborative close reading. It also contains videos of students using the unique strategies from *Digging into Literature* to read poetry. Get all our great resources and activities in one fully customizable space online; then use our tools with your own content. Use ISBN 978-1-319-06237-8 to order *LaunchPad Solo for Literature* packaged with *Digging into Literature* for your students.

Discover instructor resources and teaching ideas you can use today

Are you looking for professional resources for teaching literature and writing? How about some help with planning classroom activities?

An instructor's manual, *Resources for Teaching* Digging into Literature is bound into the back of the instructor's edition. This comprehensive manual explains the research that underlies the book's pedagogy, and offers teaching support for every chapter, selection, and activity in the book. It also includes a detailed syllabus, suggested grading rubrics, and many recommendations for other literary works to assign in conjunction with *Digging into Literature*. If your copy of the book does not include these resources, order an instructor's edition using ISBN 978-1-4576-6489-2 or contact your Macmillan Learning/Bedford/St. Martin's sales representative at **macmillanhighered .com/myrep**.

Join our community! The Macmillan English Community is now home to Bedford/St.Martin's professional resources, featuring content to support the teaching of literature, including our popular blog site, *LitBits*. **Visit community .macmillan.com**. Community members can:

▸ **Share and discuss** Join the conversation about what makes literature important—and see the data that proves it! Find articles, research studies, and testimonials on the importance of literature in our classrooms and in our lives.

▸ **Connect with authors** *LitBits* is the place to see how literature teachers, scholars, and writers such as Heather Sellers, Joanne Diaz, David Eshelman, and Emily Isaacson are inspiring the next generation. Engage with them and share your ideas, too!

▸ **Review projects and ideas in the pipeline** We're hard at work on the educational books and media of the future, and we welcome your ideas to make them great.

Consider an e-book option

Digging into Literature is available in a variety of e-book formats. Visit **macmillanhighered.com/diggingintolit/catalog** for details.

Package one of our best-selling brief handbooks at a discount

Do you need a pocket-sized handbook for your course? Package *Easy Writer* by Andrea Lunsford or *A Pocket Style Manual* by Diana Hacker and Nancy Sommers with this text at a 20 percent discount. For more information, go to **macmillanhighered.com/easywriter/catalog** or **macmillanhighered.com /pocket/catalog**.

Teach longer works at a nice price

Volumes from our literary reprint series—the Case Studies in Contemporary Criticism series, Bedford Cultural Edition series, the Bedford Shakespeare series, and the Bedford College Editions—can be shrink-wrapped with *Digging into Literature* at a discount. For a complete list of available titles, visit **macmillanhighered.com/literature**.

Trade-Up and save 50%

Add more value and choice to your students' learning experiences by packaging their Bedford/St. Martin's textbook with one of a thousand titles from our sister publishers, including Farrar, Straus and Giroux and St. Martin's Press—at a discount of 50 percent off the regular price. Visit **macmillanhighered.com /tradeup** for details.

Contents

part 2
STRATEGIES FOR CLOSE READING 37

3 From Surface to Depth   39

4 Patterns   60

Digging into
Literature

part 1
INTRODUCING LITERARY ANALYSIS

part 1 » INTRODUCING LITERARY ANALYSIS

1 Why Join Critical Conversations about Literature?

The Harry Potter series of fantasy novels, by J. K. Rowling, is one of the best-selling series of all time. Imagine yourself attending a meeting where this series will be discussed. Now imagine how your discussion might differ if your group consisted of:

- twelve-year-olds
- middle-school teachers
- international college students
- religious leaders
- members of the "Mischief Managed" Harry Potter fan group

Each group would have different ideas about what in these novels is worth discussing. And each of these various conversations would be very different from the conversation about these novels that might take place in a college literature classroom or among academic literary critics.

In fact, you might wonder *what* exactly your college literature instructor or other literary critics might say about Harry Potter. After all, popular books and children's books are not what most people immediately think of when they hear the word *literature*. Yet literature professors and literary critics *do* have conversations about Harry Potter and many other popular books, films, and even television, and these differ markedly from the conversations other groups have about these subjects.

We can think of the different groups that have conversations about texts like Harry Potter as different **discourse communities**. A discourse community is a group of people who share basic values and ground rules about how communication should take place. For instance, a discourse community of twelve-year-old Harry Potter readers will use slang and share values different from those of a discourse community of teachers or an adult fan group.

Different discourse communities will use different vocabularies and different standards to judge the Harry Potter books. For instance, teachers will be interested in how they can use concepts from the books in their classroom lessons. Religious leaders will be concerned about the morals and religious references in the books. Members of the fan group will likely use vocabulary from the book in casual conversation, employing terms like *muggles, quidditch,* and *horcrux* as if they were ordinary English words.

So how does the discourse community of a college literature classroom discuss texts, even popular texts like the Harry Potter series? This textbook aims to answer this question by teaching you about the values literary critics share, the vocabulary they use, and—most importantly—the types of arguments they make. The study of literature in college often asks you implicitly to read, write, and argue as literary critics do. Like the members of other academic discourse communities, literary critics—and literature instructors—expect writers to make persuasive arguments. Your experience learning to write effectively for such a challenging audience will teach you important lessons about close, careful reading and thoughtful argumentation that you can apply when writing for other demanding audiences in your life and career. ∎

Exercise

Write a paragraph describing a discourse community to which you currently belong. This community might relate to your hobbies, your job, your religion, or your school life. It may consist of members who meet face-to-face or who communicate only online or through publications or correspondence. What brings these people together into a community you can identify? And very importantly, how does language use help define this community or help the community exist? What shared knowledge do members of this community have about language use that helps them communicate? How did members of the discourse community obtain this knowledge? And how aware do you think most members of the discourse community are about their possession of this knowledge? Prepare to share this paragraph with your classmates.

DISCOURSE COMMUNITIES AS PARLORS

The rhetorical scholar Kenneth Burke described the experience of learning to participate in an academic discourse community in this way:

> Imagine that you enter a parlor. You come late. When you arrive, others have long preceded you, and they are engaged in a heated discussion, a discussion too heated for them to pause and tell you exactly what it is about. In fact the discussion has already begun long before any of them got there, so that no one present is qualified to retrace for you all the steps that had gone before. You listen for a while, until you decide that you have caught the tenor of the argument; then you put in your oar. Someone answers; you answer him; another comes to your defense; another aligns himself against you, to either the embarrassment or gratification of your opponent, depending upon the quality of your ally's assistance. However, the discussion is interminable. The hour grows late, you must depart. And you do depart, with the discussion still vigorously in progress.[1]

In this passage Burke describes academic discourse communities as ongoing conversations, built on and informed by what other academics have already said. These conversations are at full steam before you arrive, and they will continue after you leave. The good news is that participating in such academic conversations, as college asks you to do, requires conversational skills you likely already possess. For instance, your ability to listen carefully to what has already

---

[1] Burke, Kenneth. *The Philosophy of Literary Form*. Berkeley: U of California P, 1968. 111. Print.

miakievy/iStock/Getty Images

been said and to politely agree or disagree with others will help you participate in the academic discourse communities that college exposes you to.

But your good conversation skills will need to be translated to a textual world of academic papers. While you will likely do a fair amount of conversing in your college classrooms, you will also do a great deal of paper writing, too. Your college instructors and other academics see the papers they share and publish as turns in a textual conversation. We invite you to see your papers as similar turns in a conversation that may begin with class discussions and continue as you and your classmates extend, refine, and argue with the ideas brought up during class.

Academic textual-conversation turns occur much more slowly than do face-to-face discussions. This has both advantages and disadvantages. While textual conversations may feel less immediate and exciting than spoken ones, they allow us to think more deeply, to gather research and evidence, and to turn it into thorough, well-reasoned and well-articulated arguments. Thus, textual conversations allow for a level of sophistication that is much harder to achieve with the quicker pace of face-to-face discussion.

Burke's metaphor of the parlor perfectly captures the way literary criticism works in college. This book aims to act as your "discussion ally," coming to your assistance to help you dip your oar into the conversation of literary criticism, so that other students, literary critics, and your instructor will take seriously what you have to say about the texts you study. We assist you by clarifying the strategies of argumentation that literary critics and literature instructors use—and expect others to use—in their discourse community.

For Discussion

What do you think of Burke's use of the term *parlor*? What are the connotations of this term? Does this setting suggest types of actions and stances that might be appropriate for the arguments that take place in it?

WHY JOIN THE CRITICAL CONVERSATION ON LITERATURE?

If you plan to major in English, then *Digging into Literature* will provide you with an introduction to reading and writing practices you can use throughout your college career. You may never see some of these practices described so explicitly again, but if you pay attention you will observe their use in lectures, class discussions, essays written by fellow students, and published criticism. You may recognize that you already use some of the strategies presented in the first part of this book, while some of those presented later may continue to challenge you even as you approach graduation. You may find yourself so drawn to these practices and the kinds of questions literary critics use them to pursue that you decide to further your studies in graduate school and deepen your commitment to membership in this discourse community.

If you are not planning on becoming an English major or a literary critic, you might wonder why you should bother trying to write like one. One answer is that, by understanding the conversations literary critics have in their discourse community, you will be better prepared to join conversations in other academic and professional discourse communities. Analyzing literature can prepare you for other types of analysis you will be asked to do in other areas of your life.

For instance, literary analysis teaches the art of interpreting patterns—a skill relevant to many professions, including those as far afield as economics, law, medicine, and engineering. Literary analysis also involves applying theoretical frames to understand literature. Other academic communities—such as sociology, psychology, nursing, and political science—similarly apply theoretical frames (though to understand people and their behaviors rather than literature). Thus, the foundational strategies of literary analysis—interpreting what something means, discovering patterns in seemingly unrelated phenomena, and using theories to understand a subject—have application in a wide variety of contexts.

Further, the skills of literary analysis are applicable to living a thoughtful, reflective, and even ethical life. Interpreting texts often involves exploring how we should live in complex circumstances or understanding how our culture came to shape our experiences and identities in the ways it did. The work of literary interpretation requires patient attention to details and respect for texts by other writers. To do this work you must be willing to dig beneath surfaces and consider possible layers of deeper meaning, each reflecting a different perspective or way of seeing the world. We won't say that writing literary analyses will make you a better person, but exploring such deeply meaningful questions may broaden your perspective and motivate you to participate in the discourse community of literary critics, even if only for a semester or two.

"TEXTS" AND THEIR "AUTHORS" AND "CRITICS"

We would like to explain the ways in which we will use a few key terms in this book in order to reduce potential confusion that can arise when we speak of texts and writers.

"Text" in literary and cultural analysis

Many people make severe distinctions between literary works and popular books and films, placing a sharp divide between the works of Shakespeare and Judd Apatow. However, in the past several decades, the field of English studies has been calling these distinctions between the literary and the popular into question. Newer literary theories have persuaded literary critics to broaden their notions of what they consider worth studying. In fact, what separates the discourse community of literary studies is not so much *what* texts literary critics study as it is the *kinds of questions* and *types of analysis* that they use to study those texts. Thus, the conversations that literary critics might have about a text such as Harry Potter differ dramatically from the types of conversations Harry Potter might generate in disciplines such as education or psychology.

This book uses the word ***text*** to refer to any literary or cultural work in whatever medium that a literary critic analyzes—whether a printed page, a television program, in a live performance, or a Web site. Most professional critics today agree that *any* text is worthy of study and analysis as long as the analysis shows the text to be complex and open to multiple layers of interpretation. Thus, literary critics have written about horror films such as *Dawn of the Dead*, television shows such as *The Office*, and children's books such as *Charlie and the Chocolate Factory*. The subject of a literary analysis is not necessarily limited to those texts that we might traditionally think of as "literature."

Thus, although we use the phrase ***literary analysis*** throughout this book, you should not take it to mean that we are just talking about analyzing classic works of literature such as Shakespeare's plays. Contemporary books, movies, television shows, stories, poems, and even television commercials can be analyzed using the strategies of literary analysis.

Author *vs.* literary critic

In this book, we use the word ***author*** to refer to the writer of the primary text (such as a story, film, or poem) being studied. The term ***literary critic*** or just ***critic*** refers to the person writing a literary analysis of that text.

The word *critic* here does not mean "critical" in the sense of finding fault but rather "critical" in the sense of important. A critic explains why certain features, themes, and images are important to understanding a text's meaning; analyzes a text in detail; and tells others what is important and meaningful.

Thus, in this book, William Shakespeare, Alice Walker, and Sylvia Plath are authors while you, your classmates, and your instructors are critics. (That said, some experience as an author can help you develop insights as a literary critic—and vice versa. For instance, trying to write a sonnet can provide insights on how authors use this form to make meaning. Therefore, we encourage you to try on the role of author as well as that of critic.)

LET'S GET STARTED: JOINING THE DISCOURSE COMMUNITY OF LITERARY CRITICS

Literary analyses, like all academic arguments, can be understood as turns in an ongoing conversation. As in any conversation, we often find the most thoughtful and useful participants have listened well before contributing. They have a sense of the nature of any disagreements occurring in the conversation and seek to respond to the other participants' concerns. Or they might have a keen sense of what issues have *not* been addressed yet but deserve attention.

Initially, your class conversations about texts will help you decide what counts as a valid contribution to the conversation. You should listen to your instructor and classmates not just to learn what they have to say but also to figure out how you can contribute something new to the conversation. You might, for instance, write a paper that uses as a jumping-off point a controversy left hanging in a previous discussion. It is then up to you to find something *new* to say about that controversy or the text itself—something that does not merely repeat arguments you have already heard.

As you progress in your ability to write effective arguments about literature, you will eventually begin to read published academic articles about the texts you are analyzing. These articles are further voices in the conversation that you are seeking to join. The later chapters in this book will help you learn to participate in the ever-unfolding published conversation about texts in order to clarify for yourself and communicate with others your own views on what you read.

Review

A **discourse community** is a group of individuals who share common rules, assumptions, and values about what "counts" as a valid contribution to a conversation. This book invites you to participate in the discourse community of literary scholars by teaching you to analyze the details of texts you read and to make arguments about what these details mean.

2 What Is Literary Analysis?

In the previous chapter you learned that there are different discourse communities that have their own unspoken rules about what kind of vocabulary, topics, and presentational styles are appropriate. Literary critics frequently write a type of text called a *literary analysis*, and they frequently publish these analytic essays in scholarly books and journals. The kinds of papers you may be asked to write in literature courses, while usually shorter, are very often related to this professional genre in terms of the issues you address and the ways you support your claims. Not every kind of discussion about literature, however, is a literary analysis. In this chapter, we will describe the basic criteria that distinguish literary analyses from other types of writing about literature.

A literary analysis does the following:

1. It makes interpretive claims

2. that are debatable,

3. that are supported with evidence from the text,

4. that together argue for a thesis about the text,

5. and that explore the complexity of the text.

A paper that meets all five of these criteria will be making the kind of argument—and demonstrating the critical thinking—that is valued by literary critics in their analyses. Meeting all five of these criteria does not, of course, guarantee that your essay will be perceived as persuasive or effective, but it will usually approximate the type of essay your instructor expects. A literary analysis that fails to meet these essential criteria will rarely receive a high evaluation, even if it is flawlessly organized with impeccable grammar and sentence structure. ■

A LITERARY ANALYSIS MAKES INTERPRETIVE CLAIMS

The ancient Greek and Roman rhetoricians recognized that before opponents in an argument could effectively plead their cases, they first needed to agree on the type of disagreement they were having. The rhetoricians classified arguments into five points of disagreement, which they called the argument's *stasis*—or the point at which the controversy rests. Identifying the point of disagreement helps people engaged in an argument understand the nature of their controversy.

The chart below provides examples of the five points of disagreement. While it is possible to argue about literature at any of these five points, literary scholars' arguments primarily hinge on issues of **interpretation**. We present all five points to help you distinguish arguments of interpretation from other types of arguments you might make about literature.

FIVE POINTS OF DISAGREEMENT, AS APPLIED TO LITERATURE

Argument type	Explanation	Questions
Existence or Fact	Seeks to establish what facts are depicted in a text	▸ What is the order of events depicted in the text?
Interpretation (most arguments hinge on this type of disagreement)	Characterizes how a text (or elements of a text working together) communicates a particular idea or meaning	▸ What does the text mean? ▸ What messages does the text communicate? ▸ What does a particular pattern or series of descriptions in the text indicate? ▸ How does seeing the text as a particular type or genre help us understand its meaning?

(continued)

(continued)

Evaluation	Makes a judgment about whether the text is good or bad, enjoyable or not, a masterpiece or not	▸ Is the text enjoyable? ▸ Is it pleasurable? ▸ Is it artistic?
Causal	Investigates how factors such as the author's life, time period, or social circumstances influenced the production of the text	▸ What circumstances or life events inspired the author to write this text?
Proposal	Argues that we take some sort of action regarding the text	▸ What should we do about this text? Should the text be banned? How should it be taught?

A literary analysis consists of a series of interpretive arguments that work together to explain what a text means. You can think of a literary analysis as an act of translating the "bigger picture" of a text for intelligent readers who are struggling to understand what they should get out of the text. It may address other argumentative questions as well, but its primary job is to explain what a text means and what messages readers should take away from it.

In this way, a literary analysis differs from other genres discussing literature. For instance, a literary analysis differs from **plot and character summaries** such as you might see in study guides like CliffsNotes or SparkNotes. Such summaries are focused on facts and are *not* what we mean when we talk about literary analysis.

Similarly, a literary analysis differs from **book** or **film reviews**, which *evaluate* a text by focusing on whether a critic finds it entertaining or artistic.

Here are some examples to help you distinguish literary analyses from literary reviews.

LITERARY ANALYSES *VS.* REVIEWS

Interpretive claim (literary analysis)	Evaluation claim (literary review)
George A. Romero's zombie film *Dawn of the Dead* is a satire of our consumer culture.	*Dawn of the Dead* is a great horror movie.
Alice's Adventures in Wonderland uses nonsense to show the conflict between the romance of childhood and the cynicism of adulthood.	The characters Lewis Carroll created in *Alice's Adventures in Wonderland* are some of the most unique and unforgettable in the world of literature.
Adventures of Huckleberry Finn parallels the unjust treatment of slaves like Jim to the treatment Huck receives at the hands of Pap to show that a society that owns slaves cannot be just, no matter how "civilized" that society believes and proclaims itself to be.	*Adventures of Huckleberry Finn* is a masterpiece that invites the reader to enter the story with all the shortcomings that human nature amply provides you with.
Hamlet's attitudes toward the women in the play reflect his psychological state. When Hamlet is indecisive, he sees the women in the play as treacherous and lustful. When Hamlet is at ease with his destiny, the women become worthy and true.	Hamlet is one of the most annoying characters in all of literature.

The examples in the left column all *interpret, explain, classify,* and/or *define.* All are possible arguments that could appear in a literary analysis. They tell us what these texts (or particular events, characters, or patterns in the texts) mean. By contrast, the examples in the right column all *judge, like, enjoy, appreciate, determine the worth of,* or *evaluate* a text. They are all possible statements that might appear in a book or film review but would rarely appear in a literary analysis, especially as a central or thesis claim.

Literary analyses also differ from **literary histories** and **biographies** that analyze an author's life or time period. Such literary histories focus on *causal*

George A. Romero's 1978 film Dawn of the Dead *can be interpreted as a satire of consumerism. The zombies press against the glass windows of the shopping mall, while the humans inside demonstrate their own brand of monstrosity.*

questions, such as, Why did the author write this text? While it is acceptable to use biographical details about an author or historical details about a time period to support an argument about a text's meaning, the text—and not the author—should be the focus of a literary analysis.

LITERARY ANALYSES *VS.* HISTORIES

Interpretive claim (literary analysis)	Causal claim (literary history)
George A. Romero's zombie film *Dawn of the Dead* is a satire of our consumer culture.	George A. Romero revolutionized horror films when he made *Night of the Living Dead* in 1968. Since then, countless zombie movies have saturated the marketplace, all stealing from Romero.

Alice's Adventures in Wonderland uses nonsense to show the conflict between the romance of childhood and the cynicism of adulthood.	Lewis Carroll is known to have been a drug user and many scenes in *Alice's Adventures in Wonderland* seem to be inspired by hallucinogenic drug use.
Adventures of Huckleberry Finn parallels the unjust treatment of slaves like Jim to the treatment Huck receives at the hands of Pap to show that a society that owns slaves cannot be just, no matter how "civilized" that society believes and proclaims itself to be.	*Adventures of Huckleberry Finn* is based upon Mark Twain's own boyhood adventures along the Mississippi River.

The Literary Analyses *vs.* Histories table illustrates the difference between interpretive and causal (or historical) claims about a text. The examples of literary analysis in the left column focus on what texts mean and show, whereas the literary history examples on the right discuss influences, inspirations, and backgrounds. Rather than focusing on meaning and interpretation, literary history focuses on causes and effects. While such literary history arguments are sometimes found in small amounts in literary analyses, they almost never are the central focus.

Proposal arguments about literature do exist, though they may be more common in public rather than scholarly debates. Example proposal argument claims include suggestions for an action, such as, "We should not teach *Huckleberry Finn* in the public schools because it contains racist language" or, "Literary scholars should pay more attention to Harriet Beecher Stowe because her work has been unfairly dismissed as popular fiction." Again, such claims are rarely the focus of a literary analysis.

These "rules" about literary analyses are all rules of thumb; it is possible to find published works of literary criticism that focus on proposal or cause/effect arguments. However, such exceptions are rare and generally require exceptional knowledge and expertise to pull off successfully. Until you are sure that you understand what makes a successful literary analysis, we recommend that you stick to making interpretive arguments—the main work of literary analysis.

To write in this genre successfully, you would be well advised to practice interpretive arguments and improve your skill at making them.

Exercise

For each passage below, decide whether it makes an interpretive claim (literary analysis), an evaluation claim (a review), or a causal claim (literary history or biography). Don't worry too much at this point if you have difficulty with this exercise.

1. Before Paul Laurence Dunbar began publishing his works, he was a member of the African Methodist Episcopal Church. However, in Dunbar's latter days he denounced his religion. The 1896 poem "We Wear the Mask" arises from Dunbar's despair over his lack of faith.

2. In the 1896 poem "We Wear the Mask," Dunbar uses an extended metaphor of a mask to reveal the African-American community's painful struggles for peace and equality.

3. In J. R. R. Tolkien's *The Fellowship of the Ring*, the Ring's ability to consume its bearer represents the dangers of individualism. The Ring thus represents a denial of the fellowship Tolkien's book celebrates.

4. The Lord of the Rings series may be fantasy novels, but they have a universal appeal. Tolkien has a way with words that can draw the reader deep into his work so that time flies past.

5. J. R. R. Tolkien and C. S. Lewis's all-night argument about God paved the way for both The Lord of the Rings and The Chronicles of Narnia. Were it not for that talk, it's possible that Tolkien's Middle-earth would have remained entirely a private obsession and quite likely that Lewis would never have found the gateway to Narnia.

6. George Bernard Shaw's *Pygmalion* uses mundane objects—such as napkins, neckties, and taxis—to ridicule the myth of artistic creation.

7. In *Mona in the Promised Land*, Gish Jen deftly whirls a large cast of characters into a crazy double helix of a plot, taking Mona through her first experiences of love, dignity, and trust. The reader, as well as Mona, gains a certain biting wisdom.

8. In the first acts of *Hamlet*, Ophelia's psyche is a blank slate that her father, brother, and lover control in order to support their own objectives. Ophelia's madness at the end can be read as an act of rebellion against these controlling male forces.

A LITERARY ANALYSIS MUST MAKE DEBATABLE CLAIMS

The main interpretive claims made in any literary analysis must be debatable. People who have read the text must be able to disagree with your key claims; otherwise, you do not have an argument. This is why summaries that describe what happened in a text are usually ineffective: anybody who has read the text should agree on the names of the characters and the order of the events and actions that occurred.

Assume that a reader is familiar with Lewis Carroll's novel *Alice's Adventures in Wonderland*. Which of the following statements will this reader find debatable?

1. *Alice* is about a young girl who follows a rabbit down a hole and discovers a strange, new world.

2. The absurd physical changes Alice experiences represent the changes that occur to an adolescent's body during puberty.

The first statement is simply a summary of the text's plot. It is hard to imagine anybody who has read the book disagreeing that Alice follows the rabbit down a hole. Any contradiction of this statement would be a deliberate denial of the book's basic plot.

By contrast, the second statement—that Alice's physical changes symbolize puberty—is debatable. Most people reading this statement would like to see evidence that could back up this argument. When readers want to see evidence after reading a statement—when there is some room for disagreement or other interpretations—we know we have an *arguable* or a *debatable thesis*.

It can sometimes be intimidating to argue something that others will disagree with. However, such arguments are essential. The fact that others have questions about your interpretation is a sign you are on the right track. Think about such questions as indicating readers' interest. By contrast, making statements that everyone already agrees with contributes nothing to the "parlor" of literary scholars trying to understand a text. Such safe statements run the risk of boring your readers.

John Tenniel, "Alice when she was tall."

Exercise

A debatable argument is one that raises questions or sparks disagreement. If all readers immediately agree with a statement you have made, then you do not have a debatable argument. The goal is to find a statement that will provoke some initial disagreement or raise questions and then persuade the reader to accept your argument.

To get some practice identifying debatable statements, first read the short story "The Man to Send Rain Clouds" on page 31. Once you have finished reading, examine the short passages below and rate each passage for how debatable you think it is.

1 = factual statement (not at all debatable)
2 = technically debatable, but no reasonable reader would disagree
3 = truly debatable: many readers will want to see this supported with evidence

1. "The Man to Send Rain Clouds" is about the clash of Native American and European Christian cultures.

2. "The Man to Send Rain Clouds" is set in New Mexico.

3. The Pueblo Indian rituals in "The Man to Send Rain Clouds" reflect the Indians' oneness with nature.

4. The Pueblo Indians in "The Man to Send Rain Clouds" scatter corn and sprinkle water to provide food and water for the spirit on its journey to the other world.

5. The ending of "The Man to Send Rain Clouds" shows how the Pueblo Indian viewpoint is able to absorb technological advances.

6. The priest in "The Man to Send Rain Clouds" resists seeing the similarities between his own religion and that of the Indians.

For Discussion

Share your rankings for the preceding exercise with other members of your class. How much consensus is there on your rankings? If there is disagreement, explore why. What characteristics do those passages you ranked as 3 have in common? What characteristics do those you ranked as 1 or 2 have in common?

A LITERARY ANALYSIS SUPPORTS ARGUMENTS WITH TEXTUAL EVIDENCE

Arguments that take risks—that point out the nonobvious, that make debatable claims—are valued in literary analysis. However, this does not mean that "anything goes" and any argument, no matter how outlandish, is valid. Just as a successful claim is one that a reader finds debatable, a successful essay is one that the reader finds persuasive. In order to persuade the reader, you must support your major claims with good reasons and evidence.

In general, what qualifies as evidence depends on your audience and purpose. For instance, an argument addressed to a business manager about the merits of purchasing a new company will most likely use statistical and quantitative evidence, while an argument addressed to an anthropologist will use detailed descriptions of actions, events, and people. For literary scholars, the most important source of evidence is the text itself, and literary analysis relies on direct quotations to support claims about literature. Although summaries and paraphrases can be used as evidence, most literary scholars value the careful interpretation and analysis of direct quotation. (In fact, direct quotation is so important to literary analysis that its citation conventions emphasize exact pages, scenes, or line numbers and use special indentation to make longer quotes stand out. By contrast, other disciplines place less emphasis on direct quotations in favor of other information, such as the year of publication.)

The following paragraph shows how an argument about *Alice's Adventures in Wonderland* is supported with both summaries and direct quotations from the text:

> In *Alice's Adventures in Wonderland,* Alice goes through a variety of absurd physical changes that symbolize the changes of an adolescent's body during puberty. In Chapter I, Alice is alternately too big and then too small to fit through the door leading to the garden. In Chapter IV, Alice becomes a giant, filling up an entire house and causing the animals outside to attack her. In Chapter V, her neck grows to an absurd length. These physical changes frustrate Alice and make her feel like an outcast. For instance, the dormouse tells Alice "you've got no right to grow here" and accuses her of growing "in a ridiculous fashion" (53). Similarly, when Alice is stuck in the house, she

sorrowfully reflects that she is all grown up, or "at least there's no room to grow up any more here" (15). These passages show how Alice's body marks her as a stranger who fits in neither the child nor the adult world. In fact, when she tells the Pigeon she is a little girl, she says so "rather doubtfully, as she remembered the number of changes she had gone through that day" and the Pigeon contradicts her "in a tone of deepest contempt" (222–23). Thus, Alice's fluctuating body makes both her and others question who she is and where she belongs. Her changes and her own and others' reactions to them illustrate the embarrassment and isolation that accompany the journey to adulthood.

This paragraph supports its argument first by briefly summarizing some of the major body changes Alice experiences and then by providing direct quotations to illustrate the embarrassment and isolation Alice experiences. The evidence here tries to persuade the reader to accept the critic's central argument that the text illustrates the isolation and embarrassment adolescents feel upon entering puberty.

Critics may also use direct quotations to support arguments. For instance, to support the argument that when Hamlet experiences indecisiveness, he sees the women in the play as monstrous and lustful, Linda Bamber uses specific lines from Hamlet's soliloquies and dialogue and a summary of the play's ending:

> Of all of Shakespeare's tragedies, *Hamlet* is the one in which the sex nausea is most pervasive. The other heroes all have to be brought by the action of the play to that low moment when their pain is translated into misogyny; Hamlet compares his mother to a beast in his very first scene:
>
>> O God, a beast that wants a discourse of reason
>> Would have mourned longer . . .
>> O, most wicked speed to post
>> With such dexterity to incestuous sheets! (I.ii.50–51, 156–57)
>
> And from the first his encounters with Ophelia are spattered with hostility and disgust:
>
>> I have heard of your paintings, well enough. God hath given you one face, and you make yourselves another. You jig and amble, and you lisp; you nickname God's creatures and make your wantonness your ignorance. (III.i.143–47)
>
> In the closet scene with Gertrude, Hamlet's loathing comes to its climax:

> . . . Nay, but to live
> In the rank sweat of an enseamed bed
> Stewed in corruption, honeying and making love
> Over the nasty sty. . . . (III.iv.92–95)
>
> Furthermore, there is no reconciliation with women at the end of the play. . . . Hamlet does throw himself into Ophelia's grave, but clearly this is more an act of aggression against Laertes than of reconciliation with the dead Ophelia.[1]

The quotes that Bamber provides in the above paragraph (which is just one short excerpt from a thirty-page argument on *Hamlet*) do a good job supporting her argument that Hamlet is repelled by female sexual desire. Words that appear in these quotes—such as "beast," "incestuous," "wantonness," "rank sweat," "corruption," "nasty sty"—provide ample and persuasive evidence that Hamlet is sexually nauseated by both Gertrude and Ophelia at these points in the play.

It is important to remember that because your argument must make debatable claims, the textual evidence you use to support your claims may very likely be interpreted differently by other readers. Or other readers may think of other sections of the text that contradict your argument. Above, Bamber considers the possibility that her readers will see Hamlet's act of jumping in Ophelia's grave as a contradiction of her argument that he is sexually nauseated by the women in the play. She counters or rebuts this possible contradiction by arguing that Hamlet's actions are intended to provoke her brother Laertes rather than symbolize his love of Ophelia. Thus, in supporting an argument, you must not only find textual evidence that supports your thesis but also respond to and interpret any evidence that might at first seem to contradict your argument.

The need to support an argument with textual evidence and to answer other possibly contradictory arguments with persuasive interpretations of textual evidence prevent literary analysis from being "anything goes." Thus, while it is possible to argue that *Dawn of the Dead* is a satire of our consumer culture because the film's central action takes place in a mall and features prominent

---

[1] Bamber, Linda. *Comic Women, Tragic Men.* Stanford: Stanford UP, 1982. 71. Print.

shots of zombies with hands and faces pressed against shop windows, there is not textual evidence to support a reading of *Hamlet* or "The Man to Send Rain Clouds" as statements on consumerism (although it should be noted that a 2000 film version of *Hamlet* that features the prince as a CEO has the famous "to be or not to be" soliloquy take place in a Blockbuster video store; this particular adaptation could be read as a statement on capitalism). In the next chapter, we will refer to arguments that "twist" details or events to fit a specific interpretation as *symbol-hunting*.

For Discussion

> Return to the passages that you ranked as debatable (as a 3) in the exercise on page 20. Try to find evidence from "The Man to Send Rain Clouds" to support these passages.

A LITERARY ANALYSIS ARGUES FOR A THESIS ABOUT THE TEXT

As we discussed earlier in this chapter, a literary analysis makes a series of interpretive claims about a text. These claims can be about rather different subjects, such as what a character description reveals, how the setting contributes to our understanding of the text, or what a particular object or action in the text indicates, among other things. However, it is important that the critic connect these different claims into a central argument, or **thesis**, about the text.

A thesis requires you to move from looking at the meaning of individual elements of a text to making a larger argument about what these individual elements taken together suggest about the text. Oftentimes, this central argument will provide the answer to one or more of the following questions about the text:

▸ What messages does this text communicate?

▸ What is the author trying to say with this text?

▸ What would different audiences (i.e., contemporary readers *vs.* readers of the author's own time period; white readers *vs.* African-American readers) have said about the text's meaning?

- What does this text reveal about the culture in which the author was working?
- What can be said about this text's meaning that other critics have overlooked?

The following table provides examples of some possible thesis statements, or overall arguments, answering these questions.

EXAMPLES OF THESIS STATEMENTS

Question	Example thesis
What messages does this text communicate?	*Adventures of Huckleberry Finn* parallels the unjust treatment of slaves like Jim to the treatment Huck receives at the hands of Pap to show that a society that owns slaves cannot be just, no matter how "civilized" that society believes and proclaims itself to be.
What is the author trying to say with this text?	George A. Romero uses the setting of a shopping mall to satirize American consumer culture. By placing his thoughtless and all-but-indistinguishable zombies in a commercial setting, Romero shows us how consumerism drains us of individual agency and makes us incapable of individual intellectual thought.
What would different audiences have said about the text's meaning?	At the time Lewis Carroll wrote *Alice's Adventures in Wonderland*, few books written specifically for children existed. In fact, children were considered to be small adults. Childhood was seen as a less capable and less advanced version of adulthood. With this novel, Carroll not only creates a story that children will find appealing but also communicates to adults that childhood is a unique place that operates by different rules than do adult versions of reality.
What does this text reveal about the culture in which the author was working?	The treatment of women in the play *Hamlet* shows both the limited roles women could play in the Renaissance and the fears men of that time had toward female sexuality.

Note that many of the thesis statements on page 25 contain multiple sentences. You may have been told in other classes, perhaps going as far back to high school, that a thesis statement should be contained in a single sentence. This single sentence rule of thumb may have been useful in writing relatively simple essays. However, this textbook tries to teach you how to make in-depth arguments for which a single-sentence thesis is often insufficient; in fact, it might even be a sign that you are onto something truly debatable and interesting if you cannot squeeze your entire thesis into a single sentence.

A LITERARY ANALYSIS EXPLORES THE COMPLEXITY OF THE TEXT

Literary analyses assume that literature is complex—that interesting texts present a web to be untangled and the work of untangling has some payoff for the reader. This makes sense. Would your professors and other literary scholars devote their professional lives to understanding texts that they believed really required no interpretation? Clearly not.

One goal of literary analysis, therefore, is to highlight how the texts under discussion offer us complex messages. This focus on complexity may feel strange if you are accustomed to discourse communities that prefer simple and straightforward explanations. For instance, many scientific communities value Occam's razor, or the principle that the simplest explanation is the best explanation. By contrast, for most literature scholars, complexity is a term of praise for both texts and interpretations.

Even when writing about texts that we would not normally think of as complex—a children's book or the latest 3-D action blockbuster, for example—literary critics try to show that the text contains complex messages. By contrast, claims that a text's meaning is simple or obvious imply it is not worth investigating.

The following table contrasts arguments that claim a text is simple with those that explore the text's complexity. Note that the complex examples do not directly use the word *complex*: instead they imply complexity by suggesting there is more to the text than just a simple story.

SIMPLE *VS.* COMPLEX VIEWS OF A TEXT

Emphasizing simplicity	Emphasizing complexity
Adventures of Huckleberry Finn is a book that tells the story of a young boy on a "vacation" from his reality: nothing less and nothing more.	The past's influence on character is a very important facet of *Adventures of Huckleberry Finn*.
Mark Twain did not write *Adventures of Huckleberry Finn* as an example of slavery; it is just a story. The dialects in the book are simply how people talked back then. There is no philosophical meaning deep down, just a story.	*Adventures of Huckleberry Finn* reveals that what individuals believe to be right or true is very much molded by their environment. Each character in the book comes from a different upbringing, creating tension between and within individuals.
Alice's Adventures in Wonderland clearly illustrates the wonders of childish imagination.	*Alice's Adventures in Wonderland* illustrates the isolation and embarrassment, as well as the sense of adventure, accompanying the journey from childhood to adolescence.

Because literary critics value complexity, we recommend you use with caution words and phrases such as *clearly, obviously, unquestionably, simply,* and *without a doubt* when writing literary analyses. Though these terms may seem to add emphasis to your claims, an audience of literary scholars may find them off-putting. If you argue that a text's meaning is *clear, obvious,* or *simple,* you may be implying your argument is not worth making. In a worst case scenario, your argument may truly be insightful, interesting, and complex, but by using the previous terms, you hide your insights and sell your ideas short.

In the following chapters, we discuss strategies literary scholars use to uncover multiple levels of meaning in a text. When you use these strategies in your writing, you will want to use them to argue for a work's complexity. If you want to argue that a work is simple or straightforward, you will also need to convince your audience that these characteristics are worth valuing because you will be starting from an assumption (that simplicity in a work is good) that a key member of your audience—your instructor—isn't likely to share.

Complexity of arguments *vs.* complexity of expression

When we say that a literary analysis needs to have a complex argument, we do not mean that the analysis has to use complicated words or that it needs to be difficult to follow or understand. In fact, some literary scholars have written vehement complaints against what they see as fellow critics trying to cover up a simple argument with the use of an inflated vocabulary or confusing organization. Instead, we mean that the *ideas* that you argue should be complex.

If an argument is well written, readers should be able to follow a complex idea with minimal difficulty. Critics use multiple coherence and organizational techniques to break down a complex argument into a series of steps that are easy to follow. Chapter 13 covers some of these techniques for making your entire essay coherent and easier for your readers to follow, techniques that prove especially useful the more complex your ideas and arguments become.

Review

This chapter explains that a literary analysis meets five criteria. A literary analysis:

1. makes interpretive claims
2. that are debatable,
3. that are supported with evidence from the text,
4. that together argue for a thesis about the text,
5. and that explore the complexity of the text.

Moreover, we have clarified that a complex interpretation of a text does not necessarily require complex wording or vocabulary. Ideally, your ideas should be complex, but how you state those ideas should be as clear and straightforward as possible.

∾ **NOW PRACTICE ON YOUR OWN: THE MAN TO SEND RAIN CLOUDS**

Below we reprint "The Man to Send Rain Clouds," a short story by Leslie Marmon Silko, a prominent Laguna Pueblo author. Read the story, and then examine the following sample paragraphs that respond to the story. For each paragraph, note which of the five criteria of literary analysis (listed above in the Review section) it meets and does not meet. Be prepared to defend your answers.

Leslie Marmon Silko
The Man to Send Rain Clouds   1981

THEY found him under a big cottonwood tree. His Levi jacket and pants were faded light blue so that he had been easy to find. The big cottonwood tree stood apart from a small grove of winterbare cottonwoods which grew in the wide, sandy arroyo. He had been dead for a day or more, and the sheep had wandered and scattered up and down the arroyo. Leon and his brother-in-law, Ken, gathered the sheep and left them in the pen at the sheep camp before they returned to the cottonwood tree. Leon waited under the tree while Ken drove the truck through the deep sand to the edge of the arroyo. He squinted up at the sun and unzipped his jacket—it sure was hot for this time of year. But high and northwest the blue mountains were still in snow. Ken came sliding down the low, crumbling bank about fifty yards down, and he was bringing the red blanket.

Before they wrapped the old man, Leon took a piece of string out of his pocket and tied a small gray feather in the old man's long white hair. Ken gave him the paint. Across the brown wrinkled forehead he drew a streak of white and along the high cheekbones he drew a strip of blue paint. He paused and watched Ken throw pinches of corn meal and pollen into the wind that fluttered the small gray feather. Then Leon painted with yellow under the old man's broad nose, and finally, when he had painted green across the chin, he smiled.

"Send us rain clouds, Grandfather." They laid the bundle in the back of the pickup and covered it with a heavy tarp before they started back to the pueblo.

They turned off the highway onto the sandy pueblo road. Not long after they passed the store and post office they saw Father Paul's car coming toward them. When he recognized their faces he slowed his car and waved for them to stop. The young priest rolled down the car window.

"Did you find old Teofilo?" he asked loudly.   5

Leon stopped the truck. "Good morning, Father. We were just out to the sheep camp. Everything is O.K. now."

"Thank God for that. Teofilo is a very old man. You really shouldn't allow him to stay at the sheep camp alone."

"No, he won't do that anymore now."

"Well, I'm glad you understand. I hope I'll be seeing you at Mass this week—we missed you last Sunday. See if you can get old Teofilo to come with you." The priest smiled and waved at them as they drove away.

Louise and Teresa were waiting. The table was set for lunch, and the coffee ₁₀ was boiling on the black iron stove. Leon looked at Louise and then at Teresa.

"We found him under a cottonwood tree in the big arroyo near sheep camp. I guess he sat down to rest in the shade and never got up again." Leon walked toward the old man's bed. The red plaid shawl had been shaken and spread carefully over the bed, and a new brown flannel shirt and pair of stiff new Levi's were arranged neatly beside the pillow. Louise held the screen door open while Leon and Ken carried in the red blanket. He looked small and shriveled, and after they dressed him in the new shirt and pants he seemed more shrunken.

It was noontime now because the church bells rang the Angelus. They ate the beans with hot bread, and nobody said anything until after Teresa poured the coffee.

Ken stood up and put on his jacket. "I'll see about the gravediggers. Only the top layer of soil is frozen. I think it can be ready before dark."

Leon nodded his head and finished his coffee. After Ken had been gone for a while, the neighbors and clanspeople came quietly to embrace Teofilo's family and to leave food on the table because the gravediggers would come to eat when they were finished.

The sky in the west was full of pale yellow light. Louise stood outside with ₁₅ her hands in the pockets of Leon's green army jacket that was too big for her. The funeral was over, and the old men had taken their candles and medicine bags and were gone. She waited until the body was laid into the pickup before she said anything to Leon. She touched his arm, and he noticed that her hands were still dusty from the corn meal that she had sprinkled around the old man. When she spoke, Leon could not hear her.

"What did you say? I didn't hear you."

"I said that I had been thinking about something."

"About what?"

"About the priest sprinkling holy water for Grandpa. So he won't be thirsty."

Leon stared at the new moccasins that Teofilo had made for the ceremonial   20
dances in the summer. They were nearly hidden by the red blanket. It was getting colder, and the wind pushed gray dust down the narrow pueblo road. The
sun was approaching the long mesa where it disappeared during the winter.
Louise stood there shivering and watching his face. Then he zipped up his
jacket and opened the truck door. "I'll see if he's there."

Ken stopped the pickup at the church, and Leon got out; and then Ken
drove down the hill to the graveyard where people were waiting. Leon knocked
at the old carved door with its symbols of the Lamb. While he waited he looked
up at the twin bells from the king of Spain with the last sunlight pouring
around them in their tower.

The priest opened the door and smiled when he saw who it was. "Come in!
What brings you here this evening?"

The priest walked toward the kitchen, and Leon stood with his cap in his
hand, playing with the earflaps and examining the living room—the brown sofa,
the green armchair, and the brass lamp that hung down from the ceiling by links
of chain. The priest dragged a chair out of the kitchen and offered it to Leon.

"No thank you, Father. I only came to ask you if you would bring your holy
water to the graveyard."

The priest turned away from Leon and looked out the window at the patio   25
full of shadows and the dining-room windows of the nuns' cloister across the
patio. The curtains were heavy, and the light from within faintly penetrated; it
was impossible to see the nuns inside eating supper. "Why didn't you tell me
he was dead? I could have brought the Last Rites anyway."

Leon smiled. "It wasn't necessary, Father."

The priest stared down at his scuffed brown loafers and the worn hem of his
cassock. "For a Christian burial it was necessary."

His voice was distant, and Leon thought that his blue eyes looked tired.

"It's O.K., Father, we just want him to have plenty of water."

The priest sank down into the green chair and picked up a glossy mission- 30
ary magazine. He turned the colored pages full of lepers and pagans without
looking at them.

"You know I can't do that, Leon. There should have been the Last Rites and
a funeral Mass at the very least."

Leon put on his green cap and pulled the flaps down over his ears. "It's getting late, Father. I've got to go."

When Leon opened the door Father Paul stood up and said, "Wait." He left
the room and came back wearing a long brown overcoat. He followed Leon
out the door and across the dim churchyard to the adobe steps in front of the
church. They stooped to fit through the low adobe entrance. And when they
started down the hill to the graveyard only half of the sun was visible above
the mesa.

The priest approached the grave slowly, wondering how they had managed
to dig into the frozen ground; and then he remembered that this was New
Mexico, and saw the pile of cold loose sand beside the hole. The people stood
close to each other with little clouds of steam puffing from their faces. The
priest looked at them and saw a pile of jackets, gloves, and scarves in the yellow, dry tumbleweeds that grew in the graveyard. He looked at the red blanket,
not sure that Teofilo was so small, wondering if it wasn't some perverse Indian
trick—something they did in March to ensure a good harvest—wondering if
maybe old Teofilo was actually at sheep camp corralling the sheep for the night.
But there he was, facing into a cold dry wind and squinting at the last sunlight,
ready to bury a red wool blanket while the faces of his parishioners were in
shadow with the last warmth of the sun on their backs.

His fingers were stiff, and it took him a long time to twist the lid off the holy 35
water. Drops of water fell on the red blanket and soaked into dark icy spots.
He sprinkled the grave and the water disappeared almost before it touched the

dim, cold sand; it reminded him of something—he tried to remember what it was, because he thought if he could remember he might understand this. He sprinkled more water; he shook the container until it was empty, and the water fell through the light from sundown like August rain that fell while the sun was still shining, almost evaporating before it touched the wilted squash flowers.

The wind pulled at the priest's brown Franciscan robe and swirled away the corn meal and pollen that had been sprinkled on the blanket. They lowered the bundle into the ground, and they didn't bother to untie the stiff pieces of new rope that were tied around the ends of the blanket. The sun was gone, and over on the highway the eastbound lane was full of headlights. The priest walked away slowly. Leon watched him climb the hill, and when he had disappeared within the tall, thick walls, Leon turned to look up at the high blue mountains in the deep snow that reflected a faint red light from the west. He felt good because it was finished, and he was happy about the sprinkling of the holy water; now the old man could send them big thunderclouds for sure.

Exercise

For each paragraph, note which of the five criteria of literary analysis (listed above) it meets and which it does not meet. Be prepared to defend your answers.

1. In "The Man to Send Rain Clouds," two Native American characters, Leon and Ken, prepare the body of an old man named Teofilo for burial. When the priest asks why Leon and Ken did not bring Teofilo to get his Last Rites, Leon replies, "It wasn't necessary, Father" (32). The priest tries to explain it was necessary for a Christian burial, but Teofilo's painted face and the feather tied to his head indicate that there was never an intention to bury him the Christian way. Eventually, the priest gives in to the Native Americans and allows his holy water to be used according to Native American traditions. As he sprinkles the water, he feels "it reminded him of something—he tried to remember what it was, because he thought if he could remember he might understand this" (34). However, the priest leaves the gravesite without ever achieving this moment of understanding. The story ends with Leon happy because the holy water means "the old man could send them big thunderclouds for sure" (34).

2. "The Man to Send Rain Clouds" illustrates how Native Americans are able to absorb other cultures into their own. For instance, Teofilo is buried in brand-new Levi's as well as traditional Native American moccasins, feathers, and face paint. This shows how Native Americans incorporate Western items into their own culture. We also see assimilation when Teresa asks for the priest's holy water— not so Teofilo can have a Christian burial, but as a way of extending Native American customs. When Father Paul eventually sprinkles the holy water over the grave, it immediately disappears into Teofilo's blanket, again suggesting the ability of Native Americans to absorb others' customs and traditions into their own. While Father Paul feels confused and defeated by this absorption, the text portrays it as a kind of miracle, "like August rain that fell while the sun was still shining" (34). This ability to hold incompatible elements (like sun and rain) together seems to be key to the survival of Native American culture.

3. The main theme of "The Man to Send Rain Clouds" is the essential role that culture plays in family life. Family traditions are passed down from one generation to the next. However, outside influences affect these traditions, making them richer and more complex as time moves on. Although the core beliefs remain, more ideas and traditions are added on. "The Man to Send Rain Clouds" shows how Catholic beliefs are continually incorporated into Laguna culture. However, Leon and his family still hold on to their Native American identities, which we see in their actions throughout the story. This story testifies to the essential role of storytelling in Laguna culture.

4. "The Man to Send Rain Clouds" shows us the limitations of assuming that Western worldviews are superior to those of other cultures. As a Catholic missionary priest with blue eyes, Father Paul represents a European perspective. The limitations of this perspective are first visible when he "loudly" tells Leon and Ken, "I'm glad you understand" (30). Father Paul seems to treat these men as children, but, ironically, he is the one who does not understand the meaning of their replies. The limitations of his perspective are reinforced when he arrives at the grave site and is unable to see the faces of his parishioners because their faces are in shadow while he stands "squinting at the last sunlight" (33). Again, Father Paul is unable to fully understand the Laguna people because he believes his Christian worldview is superior to theirs.

5. Originally published in *New Mexico Quarterly*, "The Man to Send Rain Clouds" is based on an incident Silko had heard about in her hometown of Laguna, New Mexico: an old man had been found dead in a sheep camp and had

been given a traditional Indian burial. The local Catholic priest resented the fact that he had not been called in to officiate at the service. The story is Silko's reimagining of this event. As someone who is of Laguna as well as Mexican and Anglo-American descent, Silko has firsthand experience with being an outsider. These experiences helped her craft this rich and evocative story.

6. Color plays an important role throughout "The Man to Send Rain Clouds." Ken and Leon bring a red blanket for Teofilo and paint his face: "[a]cross the brown wrinkled forehead he drew a streak of white and along the high cheekbones he drew a strip of blue paint" (30). The white and blue paint contrast strongly with the dull brown of Teofilo's forehead and the bareness of the New Mexico winter. This contrast is heightened as Leon continues to add yellow and green paint. At the end of the story, we see color in the landscape as Leon notes the "high blue mountains in the deep snow that reflected a faint red light from the west" (34). The color adds to the story's depth and richness.

For Discussion

Which of the passages in the previous exercise do you think does the best job showing that "The Man to Send Rain Clouds" offers a complex message? Why?

part 2

STRATEGIES FOR
CLOSE READING

part 2 » **STRATEGIES FOR CLOSE READING**

3 From Surface to Depth

Beginning with this chapter and through Chapter 10 we describe strategies for arguing about texts that literary critics use when writing analyses they hope other members of their discourse community will find persuasive. These strategies help critics make the kinds of claims we described in Chapter 2, claims that define what a text means and that are debatable, supported by textual evidence, and complex.

Literary critics use these strategies when reading and re-reading texts and coming up with ideas to write about. These strategies can help reveal multiple layers of meaning. They also provide a set of mental places that you can go to discover an argument that is likely to be persuasive to other critics. Ancient rhetoricians called such mental places for brainstorming *topoi*. The eight argumentative strategies or *topoi* introduced in this book can help you elucidate complexities in a text if you remind yourself of them while you read, re-read, take notes, and plan your analysis.

The strategies presented in this book are also persuasive strategies; they show other literary critics that you share many of their assumptions about what constitutes a good interpretative argument with good evidence and support for claims. As we discussed in Chapter 1, different disciplines and different discourse communities often share different assumptions about how to argue successfully. Your use of these strategies should make your arguments more persuasive to the literary scholars and students who read them.

The names we give these eight strategies are intended to provide you and your classmates with some common terms to describe the moves you see being made in the literary analyses you read and write. We also believe giving a name to these strategies will be useful to you as you brainstorm and plan for writing and revising your literary analyses.

Though for clarity's sake we will discuss each strategy separately, you should know in advance that it is quite common for literary scholars to use several of these strategies in one argument to make their case. In the sample essays included in this textbook, you should be able to see how critics use several sometimes overlapping strategies within one argument. Likewise, the more of these strategies you use in your papers, the more likely your literature instructors will be to find your arguments complex, sophisticated, and persuasive. So while practicing them, you may experiment with using each strategy separately, but in your papers you would be wise to use at least two or three, if not more, of these strategies together to support your arguments. ■

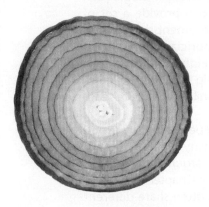

Using the surface/depth strategy is like peeling away the layers of an onion.
Robyn MacKenzie/Getty Images

WHAT IS THE SURFACE/ DEPTH STRATEGY?

This chapter introduces you to the most central strategy of literary analysis, one that we call **surface/depth**: finding deeper meanings beneath the surface interpretation of a text. This strategy is essential to writing a literary analysis, and it is hard to imagine being able to write a literary analysis without it.

To use the surface/depth strategy when writing an argument about literature, the critic points out the multiple layers of meaning. One layer is on the surface; it is the outermost, obvious meaning of the work that everyone who has read it likely sees and agrees on. The other layer (or layers) is the depth: a concept or thought not fully articulated in the text, something a first-time reader might not see because it does not lie on the surface. The critic's job is to link these layers—the surface and the depth—to argue for the full meaning of the text.

You might think of surface/depth as being like an onion. The surface is the outer skin of the onion: what you and other casual readers see when you first encounter a text—the obvious reading of a text. Your job as a critic is to argue about what lies below this surface reading, peeling away successive layers of the text.

To explore how surface/depth works, first read the Sylvia Plath poem below.

Sylvia Plath

Morning Song 1961

Love set you going like a fat gold watch.
The midwife slapped your footsoles, and your bald cry
Took its place among the elements.

Our voices echo, magnifying your arrival. New statue.
In a drafty museum, your nakedness 5
Shadows our safety. We stand round blankly as walls.

I'm no more your mother
Than the cloud that distills a mirror to reflect its own slow
Effacement at the wind's hand.

All night your moth-breath 10
Flickers among the flat pink roses. I wake to listen:
A far sea moves in my ear.

One cry, and I stumble from bed, cow-heavy and floral
In my Victorian nightgown.
Your mouth opens clean as a cat's. The window square 15

Whitens and swallows its dull stars. And now you try
Your handful of notes;
The clear vowels rise like balloons.

USING SURFACE/DEPTH TO BRAINSTORM

Step 1: Get a good grasp of the surface (literal) meaning

When you write a literary analysis, you should consider what your audience will perceive as the surface reading because your analysis ought to persuade these readers to see or understand still more in the text beyond this surface. This is another way of thinking about literary analysis as a debatable argument about a text's meaning.

Let's try this with "Morning Song." Make a list of everything you think readers would agree on after reading the poem just one time. This list of what a given group of readers will readily notice in a work can be understood as the *surface reading*. Once you have done this exercise a few times and compared your list with that of other members of your class, you will begin to get a sense of what a typical first-time reader will notice.

Here is a list of what a typical class might perceive as the surface reading of "Morning Song":

- The poem begins with a baby's birth.
- The third stanza compares the speaker to a cloud.
- The poem ends with the baby crying or cooing.
- "Morning Song" is about a new mother and her infant.

The actual text of the poem is also part of the surface reading. For instance, all readers will agree that line 7 reads "I'm no more your mother."

Getting a sense of a text's surface, literal meaning may prove more challenging with texts that are remote from your experience in terms of time, place, and culture than with texts that are written in your era and about experiences you are familiar with. There are many possible reasons for this, including significant changes to language over time. Thus, be prepared to work a little harder to determine the surface, literal meaning of texts from other cultures or from periods of history far from your own. For instance, you may need to consult a dictionary that charts the changing meaning and spelling of words, such as the *Oxford English Dictionary*, and the work of scholars who have studied a historical period or culture in order to fully understand the surface meaning of a Shakespeare play. Fortunately, many editions of such challenging texts are published with footnotes that literary scholars have prepared in order to assist new readers with grasping this surface meaning.

Similarly, the surface meaning of unconventional poetry or fiction can be particularly difficult to understand. Sometimes authors from your own time and culture may be working in literary traditions or experimental schools of thought with which you are unfamiliar. As a result, the style or syntax of these works may present challenges akin to those of works from equally unfamiliar cultures or time periods.

In order to illustrate how a literary scholar goes about understanding a text, we asked some literature professors to "think aloud" into a recording device while reading a literary text for the first time. This "thinking aloud" technique is a research method used to learn about thought processes that are otherwise very difficult to observe. We asked several literature professors to say aloud everything that was going through their heads as they read, no matter how seemingly trivial or insignificant. We then transcribed these "think-aloud" activities in order to pull back the curtain to expose thinking processes that are usually performed silently and alone.

On page 44–45 is part of a transcript of a professor "thinking aloud" while reading "Morning Song" and trying to understand its surface meaning. When reading it, bear in mind that these are the professor's tentative thoughts, normally only expressed silently to herself at her desk while reading the poem.

We see in this brief passage how even this expert needs to work to understand the surface meaning of the poem. The professor reads and re-reads, stopping to ask herself questions, and even looking up words to see if there are alternative meanings she has not considered. Note how this professor works particularly hard to understand a central comparison in the poem: "I'm no more your mother / Than the cloud."

TRANSCRIPT EXCERPT
Professor thinking aloud while reading "Morning Song"

Italicized words indicate the professor reading directly from the poem.

. . . New statue.
In a drafty museum, your nakedness
Shadows our safety.

A naked statue, drafty museum, where voices echo—oh, the voices magnify your, our voices echo and your bald cry takes its place among the elements. The elements being the other people in the room? Or the elements being something like gold, let's see, she called him *like a fat gold watch.* A watch isn't fat, is it?

New statue in a drafty museum, your nakedness shadows our, shadows our safety. So, it shadows, like cast a shadow over our safety. Doesn't sound like a good thing. *We stand round blankly as walls.* So, so is the baby the center of the museum and it makes everybody else walls?

I'm no more your mother
Than the cloud that distills a mirror to reflect its own slow
Effacement at the wind's hand.

Distills . . . *I'm no more your mother*—that doesn't sound so good. *Than the cloud that distills a mirror*—Distills? Like you distill whiskey? I need to look up "distills." OK [looking up word and reading from a dictionary]. *Distill, to let fall, exude, or precipitate in drops or in a wet mist.* OK. So to rain or mist. *To drip, to fall in drops.* OK, so drips. Than the cloud that drips a mirror? Ohhh, so clouds can drip water and create puddles that reflect them. *To reflect its own slow effacement at the wind's hand.* OK. So just like the mother kind of has a child come out of her, the cloud has a reflective puddle come out of it. OK. OK. I get it. *To reflect its own slow effacement at the wind's hand. Slow effacement . . .* Is that like "self-effacement"? Like a mother who gives so much of herself that there's nothing left for her to call her own? . . . So maybe this mother here has a baby in order to sort of see or reflect herself but then she also sees her own life passing, her own effacement, her own death. Like a cloud that disappears with rain. *To reflect its own slow effacement.* But at the same time the puddle the cloud creates is a mirror, reflecting it back. Then she's denying it. *I'm no more*

> *your mother,* ummm . . . So is she denying the baby, rejecting the baby? Or
> is she rejecting a kind of motherhood? Or both? Anyway, this isn't how new
> mothers are supposed to talk.

Step 2: Dig below the surface

As you read "Morning Song," or any other literary text, for the first time, you may
begin to get ideas about other possible layers of meaning in the text beyond the
surface, literal meaning. We can see the professor begin to do this in the preceding
"think-aloud" transcript segment when she begins to consider multiple possible
meanings for "elements" and begins to try to get at possible deeper meanings in
the comparison of a cloud to the speaker. To brainstorm potential ideas to develop
in your analysis, make note of your observations (many literary scholars annotate
the text by underlining, circling, and writing notes to themselves in the margins).
If you are stuck, or to develop even further hunches you developed on a first reading, re-read the text with pencil, pen, or other annotation device.

In the spirit of investigating multiple layers of meaning, consider many,
potentially conflicting ideas about possible deeper meanings to a text. As you
think further, you may rule out some of your initial ideas as being too implausible or dead ends. However, considering several layers of meaning may help
you better imagine possible counterarguments to the analysis you finally settle
on, or it may give you ideas for a truly complex interpretation that can account
for several layers of meaning in the text.

TRANSCRIPT EXCERPT
Professor making surface/depth interpretations while thinking aloud
Italicized words indicate the professor reading directly from the poem.

> *Our voices echo, our voices echo,* so something about the baby umm, uhh, and
> this is "Morning Song." There's morning sickness, morning song—that's also a
> good thing, like birth, morning, a new day.

> *. . . The window square*
> *Whitens and swallows . . .*
>
> OK, so the window outside, morning, oh, so this is a morning song for
> someone who's got up to deal with the baby? *Whitens and swallows*, OK,
> so *the window square whitens*—that's dawn? *And swallows its dull stars.* So
> there's this sense of morning but it also umm, is swallowing up the night.
> Both good and bad. Good because new day but bad because it's greedy,
> swallowing. I wonder why the stars are "dull"? Stars are usually described as
> bright . . . The day swallows the night, swallows the stars, and the window
> turns white, the baby swallows white milk . . . Is it the mother who's dull
> like the stars? She is stumbling out of bed at dawn.

In the preceding excerpt from the same transcript, we see the professor trying out ideas about deeper meanings below the surface of the text.

Here we see the professor attempting to plausibly link terms in the poem to meanings and concepts technically "outside" the text. In the first segment, she investigates multiple meanings of the title, connecting it to morning sickness as well as birth. She returns again to the title in the following segment, wondering if the morning song is for (or addressed to) the person who has to care for the baby. Further, she observes that the phrase "swallows its dull stars" shows the morning swallowing up the night and that the morning might be portrayed as "good" (hopeful) or as "greedy."

Note how the professor has worked to uncover at least three interpretations of *morning* in the poem: it can represent birth and a new day, morning sickness, and a greedy swallowing up of the night. In later segments, we'll see this professor testing these multiple interpretations to decide which will best fit her overall interpretation of the poem. Some of these interpretations she will keep and some she will drop.

Exercises

1. One of the keys to making surface/depth claims about poetry is looking at the **metaphors** in the poem. A metaphor involves carrying over the attributes of and associations with one subject to another unrelated subject. In the third

stanza of "Morning Song," we see Plath taking the subject of a cloud raining and producing a puddle or lake and carrying over the associations with this image to the idea of motherhood. Thus, concepts and associations that we normally have about clouds, such as the dreariness and grayness we associate with a rainy day or the temporariness we associate with clouds and weather in general, are transferred to the idea of motherhood.

What other metaphors do you see operating in this poem? See if you can find at least five. Be sure to state what concepts and ideas normally associated with subject A are being transferred to subject B. For example:

> A cloud (Subject A) is compared to motherhood (Subject B). Concepts normally associated with clouds, such as dreariness, temporariness, lack of substance, and grayness, are transferred to the idea of motherhood.

2. In the two transcript excerpts of a professor thinking aloud while reading (pages 44 and 45), we see the professor posing questions to herself about the meaning of the poem and then trying to answer them. For instance, she asks, "I wonder why the stars are 'dull'?" and then tries out various interpretations such as "Is it the mother who's dull like the stars?" This act of posing interpretive questions for oneself is the mark of an experienced reader. If a question is difficult to answer, your attempts to answer it could likely lead to a good thesis statement that will help you define the overall meaning of the text.

Review the two transcript excerpts and come up with your own set of questions and potential answers about the poem. Be prepared to share your questions with the class.

3. Is there anything about this professor's interpretation process that surprises you or strikes you as unusual? How are this professor's reading habits different from those you normally employ?

USING SURFACE/DEPTH TO WRITE PERSUASIVELY

As the transcripts on pages 44–45 and 46 excerpts illustrate, literary scholars use the surface/depth strategy as they read a text and begin to discover and develop possible interpretations of a text's meaning. The transcript excerpts also show that this process can appear "messy" to others. The professor whom we quote went on to produce several lists of words from the poem, producing separate lists for words that she associated with the infant in the poem and those she associated with the mother. She also read the poem a second time and began to flesh out and write down some of the claims she began to make about the poem's possible meanings. One of these claims eventually became the thesis statement (or central argument) for her essay on the poem.

Thus, the surface/depth strategy eventually moved from being a strategy the professor used to read and decipher the poem for herself to being a strategy she used to write a literary analysis of the poem to explain her interpretation to others.

When you begin writing your essay, you should consider which of the surface/depth claims you generated initially can be best supported. When you write these claims down, you will likely use one of two variations for presenting surface/depth claims in a literary analysis. The first variation uses a linking strategy to connect the literal meaning of the work to a deeper meaning; the second uses a contrasting strategy to show that a work has multiple levels of depth.

Using the surface/depth linking strategy

To use the surface/depth linking strategy in your literary analysis, try to link a surface reading (or a literal line from the text) to a concept, an idea, or a thought that is not explicitly stated in the text, that is, a layer of meaning beneath the surface reading. We call this concept, idea, or thought the **deeper interpretation** because it is not immediately obvious. Consider the following examples:

1.   The birth at the beginning of the poem *seems* **both happy and unpleasant.**

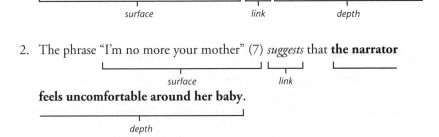

2.   The phrase "I'm no more your mother" (7) *suggests* that **the narrator feels uncomfortable around her baby.**

3. In "Morning Song," motherhood *is represented* through **images of emptiness**

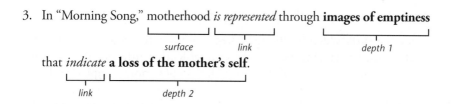

that *indicate* **a loss of the mother's self**.

4. The speaker **dehumanizes her role as mother** by *associating* it with

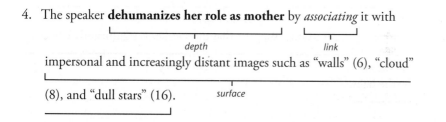

impersonal and increasingly distant images such as "walls" (6), "cloud"

(8), and "dull stars" (16).

Example 1 uses the verb *seems* to link the surface reading that the poem's beginning describes a birth with an interpretation of this event—that it's both happy and unpleasant. Because the concepts "happy" and "unpleasant" are not explicitly stated in the poem, they are part of the deeper interpretation. Many first-time readers will not notice (and possibly some will disagree) that the beginning of the poem contains both "happy" and "unpleasant" imagery.

COMMON VERBS USED TO LINK SURFACE TO DEPTH			
appears	is	reveals	stands for
connotes	masks	seems	suggests
figures	means	shows	symbolizes
illustrates	represents	signifies	underlies
indicates			

Using the surface/depth contrasting strategy

While the surface/depth linking strategy connects the literal meaning of a text to a concept outside the text, the surface/depth contrasting strategy contrasts a simplistic reading of the text with a deeper, more complex reading.

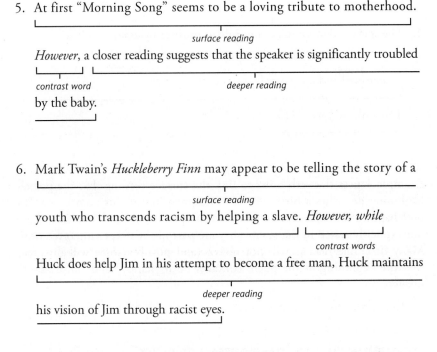

5. At first "Morning Song" seems to be a loving tribute to motherhood.

    surface reading

    However, a closer reading suggests that the speaker is significantly troubled

    contrast word   *deeper reading*

    by the baby.

6. Mark Twain's *Huckleberry Finn* may appear to be telling the story of a

    surface reading

    youth who transcends racism by helping a slave. *However, while*

    contrast words

    Huck does help Jim in his attempt to become a free man, Huck maintains

    deeper reading

    his vision of Jim through racist eyes.

Example 5 above opposes a common reading of "Morning Song" with a more complex, deeper reading. Phrases such as "at first" and "seems to be" are used to characterize the surface reading, and contrast words, such as "however," introduce a slightly more complex reading.

Similarly, example 6 contrasts a familiar reading of *Huckleberry Finn* as a story of overcoming racism with a much more negative interpretation of Huck's character. The phrase "appear to be" warns readers that the critic will be rejecting the familiar reading of *Huck*. Transitional words showing contrast— "however" and "while"—then introduce the more complex reading that will form the thesis of this essay.

Surface/depth contrasting strategies, like those in examples 5 and 6, are often used in the openings of literary analyses. The contrast move is a good way to start your turn in the conversation by showing a likely disagreement over the interpretation of the text. Such disagreement implies that you can make a complex argument about the text that will require explanation and support. Supporting complex yet plausible arguments is the goal of literary analysis.

Starting with a surface/depth contrasting argument may lead you to delay stating your thesis until the second or even third paragraph of a longer essay. You may choose to delay stating your thesis while you first describe in detail the surface reading your analysis will seek to dispel. However, be aware that there are varying preferences among literature instructors for the placement of a thesis statement: some may insist that you come forth with your thesis within the first paragraph, then work backward to describe more fully the surface interpretation before launching into your contrasting depth reading. You will find examples of both possible placements of thesis statements—initial and delayed—in the analytic essays presented in this book.

COMMON WORDS USED TO CONTRAST SURFACE AND DEEP READINGS

Words for characterizing a surface reading:	appears	may
	at first	seems
Words for introducing a deeper reading:	although	however
	but	now
	even though	while

PLAUSIBLE *VS.* IMPLAUSIBLE READINGS

The surface/depth strategy is central to all critical interpretations of a text, and you were likely already familiar with this strategy before you read this chapter. But as a strategy of argument, surface/depth can be used in more and less persuasive ways. Discerning how to use this strategy appropriately and persuasively presents the real challenge.

In general, the more surprising and nonobvious the interpretation, the better it is for a literary analysis. However, critics must also provide plausible reasons that can effectively persuade an open-minded reader to accept the interpretation. If a critic cannot persuade readers to accept his or her surface/depth interpretation, then that interpretation ultimately fails.

To persuade a reader to accept a surface/depth interpretation, critics provide good reasons and textual evidence in the form of quotations and paraphrases of the text. For instance, the surface/depth arguments in examples 1 or 5 might be supported with the following textual evidence:

> The birth at the beginning of the poem <u>seems</u> both happy and unpleasant. Words such as "love" (1), "gold" (1), and "new statue" (4) all <u>suggest</u> that the baby is loved and valuable. However, the first two stanzas also contain unpleasant images such as "slapped" (2), "bald" (2), "drafty" (5), and "blankly" (6). These words <u>suggest</u> something unpleasant about the baby's arrival.

Note that this example uses multiple quotations taken from several different lines and stanzas of the poem to support its argument. More complex arguments would require even more textual support. In general, showing several examples from multiple places in a text helps persuade readers to accept your interpretation. By contrast, surface/depth arguments that only quote a single line or section of a text are much less persuasive.

In addition to providing textual evidence as support, effective surface/depth arguments must be faithful to the surface meaning of the text. In other words, you need to clarify how your deeper meaning connects to and enhances the surface meaning that most readers will agree on. Let's illustrate by example: A student in one of our classes tried to interpret the "Morning Song" poem as a statement protesting the Vietnam War. This student argued that the "birth" at the beginning represents a fallen soldier taking his place in a graveyard in which the "statues" represented tombstones. This interpretation was supported with additional evidence of images that suggest death (such as "Effacement at the wind's hand" and "The window square / Whitens and swallows its dull stars"), and the essay concluded by suggesting that the "clear vowels [rising] like balloons" at the end was the funeral song played by a trumpeter.

This interpretation of "Morning Song" as a poem about war is certainly nonobvious but is ultimately not persuasive because this interpretation only works if we ignore the surface reading that the poem depicts a mother encountering her newborn baby. The student who argued that the poem was about the Vietnam War could not create a plausible connection between the war imagery he saw in the poem and the surface reading of motherhood that most readers agree on.

Moreover, such an interpretation ignores contextual information (which we will discuss more in the Chapter 7) about the author and time period: 1961, the year when the poem was written, is before the onset of the United States' involvement in the Vietnam War.

Such attempts to force a text to fit a given interpretation are sometimes referred to disparagingly as **symbol-hunting**. Symbol-hunting twists and forces the text into a series of symbols that are used to fit a preconceived interpretation. Such symbol-hunting is reductive (oversimplifying) rather than complex because it shuts down the multiple layers of meaning a text may have. Worse still, such symbol-hunting often disregards information that the community of readers of the text agree on, such as the surface meaning of the text or the historical context in which it was written.

Understanding the difference between obvious and complex and plausible and forced interpretations can be difficult. In this text, we give you a lot of practice exercises to help you understand these differences.

A NOTE ON PERSUASIVE INTERPRETATIONS

You may have heard someone in your literature classes say, "Well, that's my interpretation" or "It's a poem, so I can read into it whatever I want." Such comments indicate that the speaker does not understand the goal of a literary analysis, which is to persuade other readers to accept a complex interpretation. These comments suggest the speaker rejects the communal nature of literary analysis because he or she expresses no interest in retracing the steps of interpretive thinking so that others might be able to share in an understanding of the text. In other words, the interpretation remains closed to others and wholly personal and, as a result, has no obligation to the text or to other readers to be credible and persuasive.

In contrast, effective applications of the surface/depth strategy offer credible and persuasive reasons and evidence that allow thoughtful readers to better understand the text. Surface meanings that other readers would agree on are presented, and deeper interpretations—while perhaps surprising and not easily identified at first by all careful readers—are justified and supported with credible textual evidence and explanations.

Surface/depth readings that stretch logic, contradict textual evidence, or disregard historical and social context will be met with great skepticism—and will likely be dismissed altogether.

Exercise

The following passages all attempt to make surface/depth arguments. However, some of these arguments are much more plausible than others. For each passage, decide whether the surface/depth argument is (1) simple or obvious, (2) complex and plausible, or (3) implausible symbol-hunting.

1. The phrase "cow-heavy" (13) indicates a mother's breast filling with milk when her baby cries.

2. The phrase "cow-heavy" (13) suggests that the narrator no longer feels fully human in the baby's presence.

3. "Morning Song" illustrates a mother's mixed emotions toward her newborn. In the opening line, the child is described as a mechanical object, a "fat gold watch," that was jump-started not by its parents but by the midwife. This image implies that the mother sees the child as something alien that does not truly belong to her.

4. "Morning Song" illustrates Plath's psychological obsession with death. The reference to a watch in the first line suggests the ticking of Father Time, counting off the minutes to her child's death. The baby then, with a "bald cry" (2), takes its "place among the elements" (3), signifying its initiation into the cycle of life and death.

5. We know that the speaker is the infant's mother because she tells the baby in the first line that he is the result of love. She also tells him that a midwife was present and that he was naked. All the other descriptions of the event similarly indicate that she is indeed the mother.

6. At first "Morning Song" seems to be about child abuse, but a closer reading suggests that the narrator really does love her child.

For Discussion

Compare your responses to the previous exercise with those of other members of your class. As you discuss these passages more, do your responses change? Can you come to an agreement with your classmates on the most apt category for each passage?

Review

The surface/depth strategy helps show that texts are complex by revealing how they have multiple levels of meaning. Surface/depth is an essential brainstorming strategy as well as a strategy that you will use when writing your essays. When presenting surface/depth claims in your written essays, you may use one of the following variations:

Linking: the literal or surface meaning of the text is linked to a concept not explicitly mentioned in the text. The linking strategy shows that a text is more than it initially seems.

Contrasting: a comparatively simple or straightforward interpretation of the text is contrasted with a deeper, more complex interpretation. The contrasting strategy emphasizes that the text has multiple levels.

Unsuccessful uses of the surface/depth strategy occur when the critic fails to provide plausible reasons or evidence to support the interpretation or when the critic ignores the literal meaning of the text. Such implausible interpretations are sometimes referred to as symbol-hunting.

Exercise

Read the following short analysis of "Morning Song" and then answer the questions that follow it.

Loss In Sylvia Plath's "Morning Song"

While new motherhood is typically seen as a joyous occasion in which a mother celebrates her "new arrival," Sylvia Plath's poem "Morning Song" depicts motherhood in terms of loss and erasure. The first image of loss occurs in the second stanza when the speaker comments that the baby's presence "[s]hadows our safety" (6). This phrase indicates that the baby threatens the speaker and makes her feel insecure or inadequate to her new task. The phrase "[w]e stand round blankly as walls" (6) further reinforces the impression that the baby leaves the speaker feeling "blank," or empty and unsure of herself. The third stanza reveals the full extent of the speaker's fear of loss when she claims:

> I'm no more your mother
> Than the cloud that distills a mirror to reflect its own slow
> Effacement at the wind's hand. (7–9)

In this pivotal metaphor, the speaker compares motherhood to a cloud turning into rain and creating a rain puddle or lake. Both actions—rain and childbirth—create new entities, but we know that the cloud's act of creation will result in its eventual disappearance. In a similar way, the speaker of this poem seems to fear that her child will result in the erasure of herself.

Although the final stanza of the poem could be read as the speaker learning to take joy in her child, images of loss still dominate here. The stanza describes the rising sun, an image usually associated with hope and new life. However, here sunrise is described as swallowing the night (16). Like the baby, the new dawn is greedy and wipes out what existed before it. This interpretation can also be supported by the fact that the title of the poem, "Morning Song," sounds identical to "Mourning Song." This similarity suggests that the morning, or new life, in this poem is an occasion for sorrow rather than joy. Sylvia Plath thus uses this short poem to challenge traditional associations of childbirth and joy by showing us how motherhood also brings about a kind of loss for the mother.

Work Cited

Plath, Sylvia. "Morning Song." *Digging into Literature: Strategies for Analysis, Reading, and Writing.* Joanna Wolfe and Laura Wilder. Boston: Bedford/St. Martin's, 2016. 41. Print.

Questions

1. Note the various ways that surface/depth functions in this analysis. See if you can identify at least three different examples of the use of this strategy.

2. Do you agree with this interpretation? Why or why not? How could you support an alternative argument?

∾   **NOW PRACTICE ON YOUR OWN: GRETEL IN DARKNESS**

The following poem is by American poet Louise Glück. The poem references "Hansel and Gretel," a fairy tale popularized by brothers Jakob and Wilhelm Grimm in the nineteenth century. If you do not know the tale, you can find it easily on the Web. Using outside information to interpret a text is a strategy we cover in detail in Chapter 7, "Context" (p. 143), and if you are working with texts from unfamiliar time periods or cultures, the context strategy can be essential. For this exercise, though, it is enough simply to be familiar with the fairy tale Glück assumes her readers will know.

1. Read Louise Glück's "Gretel in Darkness." Try to come to an understanding of the surface meaning of the poem. Look up any words you aren't sure you fully understand. Identify any metaphors in the poem and try to rephrase them in simpler terms. Write a short paragraph explicating what you think most readers in your class will agree is the surface reading of the poem.

Louise Glück
Gretel in Darkness   1968

This is the world we wanted.
All who would have seen us dead
are dead. I hear the witch's cry
break in the moonlight through a sheet
of sugar: God rewards.   5
Her tongue shrivels into gas . . .

Now, far from women's arms
and memory of women, in our father's hut
we sleep, are never hungry.
Why do I not forget?   10
My father bars the door, bars harm
from this house, and it is years.

No one remembers. Even you, my brother,
summer afternoons you look at me as though
you meant to leave,   15
as though it never happened.
But I killed for you. I see armed firs,
the spires of that gleaming kiln—

Nights I turn to you to hold me
but you are not there.   20
Am I alone? Spies
hiss in the stillness, Hansel,
we are there still and it is real, real,
that black forest and the fire in earnest.

Exercises

1. Re-read the poem and pose questions for yourself about the meaning of various lines, words, metaphors, or images. Write your questions down, and then read the poem again and try to brainstorm some possible interpretations that might answer your questions.

2. Try to generate some surface/depth arguments linking images or words in the poem to concepts not explicitly mentioned, such as fear, trauma, or womanhood. Try to generate some surface/depth interpretations that you think your classmates will not immediately see but that you think you can persuade them to find plausible. Write at least three different surface/depth interpretations of the poem supported by textual evidence following the model of the passages in the exercise on page 56.

4 Patterns

Let's begin by reviewing our definition of a literary analysis. A literary analysis:

- ‣ makes interpretive claims
- ‣ that are debatable,
- ‣ that are supported with evidence from the text,
- ‣ that together argue for a thesis about the text,
- ‣ and that explore the complexity of the text.

Several of these criteria are met by good surface/depth arguments—essential strategies of a literary analysis. A surface/depth argument makes an interpretive claim about the text's meaning, should be debatable, and needs to be supported with evidence.

The **patterns strategy** involves pointing out multiple examples (both obvious and nonobvious) of an image, idea, linguistic feature, or other recurrent element in the text in order to support a surface/depth argument. It both provides the textual evidence for a surface/depth argument and is a strategy for discovering new surface/depth interpretations.

The patterns strategy illustrates a text's complexity by showing that evidence for a surface/depth argument can be found throughout a text—even in small details where it is unexpected. Patterns and surface/depth go hand in hand: by showing that evidence of an interpretation is present even in small, easily overlooked details in the text, the critic persuades the reader that an interpretation can be supported by the text.

As with other strategies discussed in this textbook, the patterns strategy is used both to brainstorm potential interpretations and to present arguments effectively in your writing. ■

USING PATTERNS TO BRAINSTORM

The patterns strategy can be used both before and after you have developed a surface/depth claim in your brainstorming. Using it beforehand helps you come up with plausible and complex surface/depth arguments. Using it afterward helps you improve these arguments and locate textual evidence to support them.

Using the patterns strategy before having clear surface/depth arguments in mind

A critic uses the patterns strategy to discover surface/depth arguments by noting repetitions and recurrences throughout a text and then working to make sense of possible deeper layers of meaning of these aspects of the text by considering the reasons they recur. For instance, in reading Silko's "The Man to Send Rain Clouds" (pp. 29–34) you might note repeated references to Father Paul's sight or vision. Trying to figure out why these references are repeated could lead to a surface/depth argument about his difficulties in truly seeing and understanding his Laguna parishioners.

In this way, the patterns strategy can be powerfully productive when you first set out to write a literary analysis. On a first reading of a text, especially a longer text such as a play or novel, you may begin to notice multiple instances of an image, an unusual word, or even a sound. On a second reading of a text, further instances and repetitions will likely become apparent to you that you missed the first time. On second and even third readings, you should aim to locate instances that are especially surprising to others who have not read as closely or with this pattern in mind. And bear in mind that for an image or a device to be recurrent, it need not reappear exactly the same way each time. Use plausible inferences and see if anything develops. For instance, you may begin to notice the color blue appear repeatedly throughout a text and then notice that both the title and the final image of the text refer to the sky. Though blue is not explicitly named in the title and in the final image, it seems plausible to connect the sky to this color.

Experienced literary scholars almost always mark the repetitions they start to see in the margins of texts. Then, they brainstorm to generate some ideas about what these patterns might mean. In other words, they move from noticing a pattern to making a surface/depth argument.

The following excerpts from the transcript of a literature professor thinking aloud while reading "Morning Song" (see Chapter 3, p. 41) illustrate how one experienced reader uses this strategy as she reads.[1] Notice her inclination to look for repeated images and ideas as a way to try to make sense of the poem, even if her perception of a possible repetition doesn't always turn out to be helpful to her. Before you continue, take a moment to review the poem.

TRANSCRIPT EXCERPT
Professor thinking aloud while noting a pattern of "mouth" imagery
Italicized words indicate the professor reading directly from the poem.

In my Victorian nightgown.
Your mouth opens clean as a cat's. The window square
Whitens and swallows its dull stars. And now you try
Your handful of notes;
The clear vowels rise like balloons.

Ahh, window, *window square whitens and swallows . . . handful of notes, the clear vowels rise*—OK, so clear vowels. All these images of the baby seem to have to do with its **mouth** . . . *moth-breath* and milk drinking, oh and all the crying—*bald cry* and *one cry* . . . So all this stuff about the baby and the whole cow-heavy thing have to do with . . . has to do with the **mouth**. The baby's hunger kind of reduces her to this animal, cow-heavy state? Umm, what was that I was puzzling over? *Window square whitens and swallows its dull stars. Whitens and swallows*, so it's kind of morning swallowing up night. That's another **mouth** image. Everything is hungry. This mother seems to feel like her identity has been swallowed up, her pre-motherhood identity . . . like the stars.

---

[1] For an explanation of the "thinking aloud" technique for observing a reader's and writer's thinking processes, see Chapter 3, p. 43.

In this transcript, we see the professor begin to note a pattern of mouth imagery in the poem. The professor connects mouths with both the baby's hunger and cry and with the rising sun (framed by her window), which is described as swallowing up the stars. By the end of the passage, the professor has suggested a possible surface/depth interpretation for the pattern she has noticed—that the mother's identity is being swallowed up or consumed.

In the next transcript excerpt, we see a slightly different tactic. Here, as the professor reaches the end of the poem, she remembers an earlier word—"elements"—that stood out to her. She then rereads from the beginning to see if she can make sense of this word by identifying a pattern in the poem.

TRANSCRIPT EXCERPT
Professor thinking aloud while noting a pattern of "science" imagery
Italicized words indicate the professor reading directly from the poem.

In the clear vowels rise like balloons.
The baby's vowels rise like balloons.
Clear vowels rise like balloons.

So . . . so that's an element—hydrogen. No. Helium. *Your bald cry took its place among the elements.* You kind of get that rising image. I'm going to keep going back through the beginning here . . .

Love set you going like a fat gold watch.
The midwife slapped your footsoles, and your bald cry
Took its place among the elements.
Our voices echo, magnifying your arrival.

So *magnifying, elements,* something **scientific**, maybe. Is "gold" an element?

And then *In a drafty museum* . . . could that be **science**? And then distillation, in the third stanza. That's like a **scientific process**, right? I mean, there's distilling booze, sure, but that sounds like a word I remember hearing in **science** fairs, too. Distilling . . . *magnifying* . . . There's, like, all these **science** terms here . . . words associated with **science**. Is it too much of a stretch to see **science** in other things, like *stars*? Astronomy. The sea? Moths? I'm not sure. Maybe the cloud? What's it called . . . meteorology? I dunno.

So why the **science** stuff? Let's see . . . *Elements . . . distills . . . magnifying*. Not sure about the others. So . . . **science** . . . objectivity . . . distance. Is this more about how this mother feels toward, or regards, this baby?

By the end of this excerpt, we see the professor identifying a pattern of science imagery. She tries to fit various images in the poem into this pattern, ultimately rejecting some as "too much of a stretch" to fit this pattern. By the end of this segment, she begins testing a surface/depth argument about what this pattern might signify (objectivity, distance, the mother's feelings).

In these transcripts, the professor identifies repeated instances of an image, which leads her to try out claims about the image's significance using the surface/depth strategy. The emphasis on the baby's mouth suggests to her that the speaker of the poem feels swallowed up by her new role, and the recurrence of scientific terms indicates that the speaker may feel a sort of clinical regard toward or objective, disinterested distance from the baby the way a scientist regards her specimen. Thus, the patterns strategy goes hand in hand with the surface/depth strategy.

There are no hard and steadfast rules about what kinds of patterns or repetitions you may find when analyzing a text. Instead, be curious about any type of repetition you encounter and see what you might be able to do with it in making sense of a text's deeper layers of meaning. (Chapter 5, "Digging Deeper," will examine specific aspects of a text that might recur and be worth exploring.)

Using the patterns strategy after having brainstormed some possible surface/depth arguments

Once you have developed a tentative surface/depth argument—whether about just one word, phrase, or aspect of a text or about an emerging pattern you are noticing—you can use the patterns strategy to discover evidence that will help you support this argument. The patterns strategy also can help you refine and improve the surface/depth arguments you develop.

To use the patterns strategy to locate textual evidence and develop your thinking about surface/depth arguments you have brainstormed, it is a good idea to think of your first surface/depth claims as provisional and rough. You should be open to revising and refining these claims in light of what further reading of the text you are analyzing reveals. Don't worry about whether your first surface/depth arguments are "right" or far-fetched: your use of the patterns strategy should help you determine whether these claims can be supported or need to be changed or abandoned. Once you have a provisional surface/depth interpretation in mind, you can use the patterns strategy to take notes listing all the places in the text that might support this interpretation.

For instance, the professor who thought aloud for us while reading "Morning Song" made an initial surface/depth argument that the poem had to do with the mother's feelings of *emptiness* upon her child's birth. *Emptiness* here is a surface/depth argument because it is a concept that is not immediately obvious and is not explicitly stated in the poem itself. To develop this interpretation, the professor re-read the poem and began underlining all the words she thought might possibly support her emptiness interpretation. Then she made a list of the images in the poem that she had underlined (see the figure below).

Empty Imagery	
<u>**Baby**</u>	**Her/others**
bald cry	blankly as walls
moth-breath	no more your mother
flickers	cloud
mouth open clean	mirror
clear vowels	effacement at wind
balloons	far sea
nakedness	window square whitens
	and swallows
	shadows

Professor's notes tracing an interpretative pattern of emptiness, or empty imagery, in "Morning Song."

The preceding figure shows that the professor organized these notes into two lists: one detailing all of the empty imagery associated with the baby and the other detailing empty imagery associated with the speaker or other people in the poem. After reviewing these notes, the professor came up with an argument that the poem uses empty imagery to equate motherhood with a loss of self. This surface/depth argument eventually went on to form part of the professor's thesis about the poem. Thus, by tracing in her notes a pattern related to one of her initial surface/depth arguments, then organizing these notes, and then reflecting on them, the professor was able to brainstorm an even deeper interpretation about the poem.

We highly recommend that you take notes tracing interpretative patterns on a separate sheet of paper, listing and organizing the evidence that might support various interpretative patterns. Looking at all of these images together can help you reflect on and deepen your original surface/depth arguments—a strategy that often leads to an arguable thesis illustrating the text's complexity.

Exercises

We have been observing a professor trace first a pattern of images of mouths and then a pattern of scientific images in Sylvia Plath's "Morning Song." Return to this poem in Chapter 3 (p. 41) and try using the patterns strategy to locate at least two additional possible patterns in this poem.

1. Make a list of words or other aspects of the poem that exemplify these two patterns. Title each list with a label that describes what brings these items together as a pattern.

2. Try to tie each pattern to a surface/depth claim about a possible layer of meaning to the poem. Write each claim down.

For Discussion

Compare your lists and two claims with those written by your classmates. Which claims make the most complex and persuasive arguments about the poem?

USING PATTERNS TO WRITE PERSUASIVELY

The patterns located during reading and brainstorming should next be used as textual evidence to persuade readers to accept your interpretive arguments. Here again patterns and surface/depth go hand in hand. A persuasive use of the patterns strategy not only presents multiple examples of a pattern, image, or theme but also connects them to a clear surface/depth interpretation. A strong analysis will move back and forth between these two strategies. The example below shows how one writer integrated these two strategies to analyze "Morning Song." (We have underlined key terms and phrases associated with using the patterns strategy and italicized phrases referring to the pattern the writer is tracing.)

> Many phrases and images throughout "Morning Song" equate motherhood with a *loss of identity*. Early in the poem, the mother tells the baby that "your nakedness / Shadows our safety" (5–6), suggesting that her former, secure *self feels threatened* by the vulnerable infant. The speaker goes on to compare herself to a "cloud that distills a mirror to reflect its own slow / Effacement at the wind's hand" (8–9). These lines compare a mother producing new life to a cloud raining to produce a puddle or lake. This image implies that just as rain means the *end of the cloud's life*, so a newborn means the *end of the mother's former life*. Near the end of the poem is another image suggesting that new life brings loss: "The window square / Whitens and swallows its dull stars" (15–16). These lines literally mean that it is dawn and the sun is rising, but morning here "swallows" and "whitens" out the stars that were previously shining. Thus, again, we see new life (morning) *erasing old life* (the stars). Even the title of the poem—"Morning Song"—could be heard as "Mourning Song," suggesting that the speaker is *mourning her old life*.

This paragraph begins with a surface/depth argument equating the images of motherhood in "Morning Song" to a loss of identity or self. The paragraph then cites four different examples of this image. The following figure breaks down how this paragraph works:

Patterns with *surface/depth claim*	Many phrases and images throughout "Morning Song" *equate motherhood with a loss of identity.*
Evidence 1 with *surface/depth claim*	Early in the poem, the mother tells the baby that "your nakedness / Shadows our safety" (5–6), *suggesting that her former, secure self feels threatened by the vulnerable infant.*
Evidence 2 with *surface/depth claim*	The speaker goes on to compare herself to a "cloud that distills a mirror to reflect its own slow / Effacement at the wind's hand" (8–9). *These lines compare a mother producing new life to a cloud raining to produce a puddle or lake. This image implies that just as rain means the end of the cloud's life, so a newborn means the end of the mother's former life.*
Evidence 3 with *surface/depth claim*	Near the end of the poem is another image suggesting that new life brings loss: "The window square / Whitens and swallows its dull stars" (15–16). *These lines literally mean that it is dawn and the sun is rising, but morning here "swallows" and "whitens" out the stars that were previously shining. Thus, again, we see new life (morning) erasing old life (the stars).*
Evidence 4 with *surface/depth claim*	Even the title of the poem—"Morning Song"—could be heard as "Mourning Song," *suggesting that the speaker is mourning her old life.*

Analysis of a paragraph making effective use of the patterns strategy. Bold emphasizes the textual evidence.

Note that this paragraph uses four pieces of evidence—in this case four quotations—to support its surface/depth argument that the poem illustrates a loss of identity. Each quotation is followed by a surface/depth claim. Thus, the passage moves back and forth between presenting evidence and making an argument. Such movement between evidence and argument is characteristic of a persuasive use of the patterns strategy.

Note also that the paragraph moves from the most obvious examples of loss of identity to the least obvious examples. The last example—the discussion of the title—is the most clever and helps illustrate the complexity of the text. If the title were the only example the critic had cited of loss of identity, we would not find it persuasive. However, given that it appears at the end of a list of other examples of loss of identity, we find this analysis persuasive.

To use the patterns strategy effectively, a critic:

- provides multiple pieces of evidence—quotations, paraphrases, or summaries—to illustrate a pattern
- connects the evidence illustrating the pattern to a surface/depth argument
- shuttles back and forth between evidence and argument
- usually begins with the most obvious example and moves to the least obvious

---

WORDS AND PHRASES ASSOCIATED WITH PATTERNS

Phrases used to introduce a patterns argument:

throughout, often, repeatedly, frequently, recurrently, many examples, many times, several instances

Phrases used to connect multiple examples in a patterns argument:

again, moreover, furthermore, additionally, also, another example, similarly, further, even, finally

---

Exercise

The following passages all use the patterns strategy; however, some are more successful than others. For each passage, indicate whether you think the passage is very successful, somewhat successful, or unsuccessful and explain why in a few sentences. For those you deem less successful, suggest what could be done to improve the passage.

1. Plath uses images of emptiness throughout "Morning Song" to illustrate a mother's unexpected sense of loss upon the birth of her child. The first image of emptiness is the drafty museum where the parents' voices echo (4–6). The

museum is thus empty and the parents seem lost inside it. This sense of loss is repeated in the following stanza when the speaker claims "I'm no more your mother" (7). This phrase suggests that the speaker feels troubled and lost within her new identity. Plath further emphasizes this sense of loss when she compares giving birth to a cloud raining to produce a puddle or lake. In this metaphor, rain empties a cloud just as a birth empties a mother. The use of the verb "distill"—which refers to a chemical process that removes impurities—further reinforces this sense of loss and emptiness since the cloud is being emptied of anything that is not perfect and pure, just like a mother is supposed to empty herself of anything negative and dark.

2. Plath refers to a newborn infant throughout "Morning Song." In the first stanza, the infant releases a "bald cry" (2) that takes its "place among the elements" (3). She describes the infant's breathing as "moth-breath" (10) and compares its mouth to a cat's mouth. Finally, at the end of the poem Plath describes the infant's cry as a "handful of notes" (17) that "rise like balloons" (18). These images all serve to reinforce the poem's central theme of mother/ child relationships.

3. There are several references to scientific imagery in "Morning Song." The poem refers to magnification (4) and reflection (8), both of which are scientific methods. The word "distills" (8) refers to a scientific, chemical process for removing impurities from a substance. The baby's cry is described as taking "its place among the elements" (3), which seems to refer to the periodic table of elements, the primordial matter of the universe. The watch in the first line is similarly a scientific tool and the gold the watch is made of is, of course, an element, like the baby's cry. Even the balloons in the last line have a scientific connotation since balloons are often used for measurements and experiments in science.

SAMPLE ESSAY USING PATTERNS AND SURFACE/DEPTH STRATEGIES

The short essay that follows is one we would evaluate highly in an introductory class asking students to write an essay of approximately 500–750 words (two to three double-spaced pages). We like this essay because it has a clear thesis, contains multiple surface/depth arguments, and persuasively interprets some patterns we did not see on the first reading of the poem. However, there are differences among instructors, and you should ask your instructor's opinion of this essay.

Note that this is a short analysis and some aspects may consequently feel abrupt or incomplete. Later chapters in this book will show you how to use other strategies to expand this interpretation into an even more complex argument.

Sylvia Plath's "Morning Song" and the Challenge of Motherly Identity

Sylvia Path's short poem "Morning Song" explores the conflicted emotions of a new mother. On the one hand, the mother recognizes that she is expected to treasure and celebrate her infant, but on the other hand, she feels strangely removed from the child. The poem uses a combination of scientific and natural imagery to illustrate the mother's feelings of alienation. By the end of the poem, however, we see a shift in this imagery as the mother begins to see the infant in more human terms.

There are several references to scientific imagery in "Morning Song" that suggest the mother is viewing the baby in clinical, scientific terms rather than as a new life. The poem refers to magnification (4) and reflection (8), both of which are scientific methods. The word "distills" (8) refers to a scientific, chemical process for removing impurities from a substance. The baby's cry is described as taking "its place among the elements" (3), which seems to refer to the periodic table of elements, the primordial matter of the universe. The watch in the first line is similarly a scientific tool and the gold the watch is made of is, of course, an element, like the baby's cry. Even the balloons in the last line have a scientific connotation since balloons are often used for measurements and experiments in science. These images all serve to show how the speaker feels distanced from the baby, who is like a scientific experiment she is conducting rather than a human being.

Natural imagery also seems to further dehumanize the baby, reducing it to nothing more than its mouth. The baby's breathing is compared to a moth in line 10, suggesting that the speaker feels the infant is fragile and is as likely to die as a moth dancing around candlelight. A few lines later, the baby's mouth is compared to another animal—a cat—who greedily opens its mouth for milk. Not only does the speaker seem to feel that the baby is like an animal, but she herself is turned into an animal, as she arises "cow-heavy" (13) to feed the infant. These images show how the speaker sees both the baby and herself as dumb animals who exist only to feed and be fed. Even the morning itself seems to be reduced to another mouth to feed as she describes how the dawn "swallows its dull stars" (16). These lines suggest that just as the sun swallows up the stars, so the baby will swallow up this mother.

However, in the last few lines the poem takes a hopeful turn as the speaker begins to view the baby as a human being. The baby's mouth, which has previously been greedy and animal-like, now becomes a source of music, producing a "handful of notes" (17) and "clear vowels" (18). Music is a distinctly human sound. No animals, and certainly not the cats, cows, or moths mentioned earlier in the poem, make music. This change in how the speaker perceives the baby's sounds—from animalistic cry to human song—suggests that she is beginning to relate to the baby as an individual. Even the word "handful" in the phrase "handful of notes" (17) seems hopeful in this context since this is the first time the mother has referred to the baby as having a distinctly human body part. When the baby's notes finally "rise like balloons" (18), the speaker seems to have arrived at a place where she can celebrate the infant. For the first time, the infant is giving something to the speaker rather than threatening to take something away. The mother seems to have finally accepted the child as an independent human being whose company she can celebrate.

Work Cited

Plath, Sylvia. "Morning Song." *The Collected Poems*. Ed. Ted Hughes. New York: Harper & Row, 1981. 156–57. Print.

Exercises

1. Pick one of the paragraphs in this essay and analyze how it combines patterns and surface/depth arguments. How is this paragraph similar to or different from the other paragraphs we have analyzed in this chapter?

2. Identify the thesis statement in this essay. How do the individual paragraphs in the body of the essay relate to this thesis?

3. Review the five criteria for a literary analysis discussed in Chapter 2 (p. 12). Does this essay meet all five of these criteria? Why or why not?

4. Do you agree with this interpretation? How does it compare with the interpretation offered at the end of Chapter 3? What about the poem does it successfully explain? What does it not explain as well?

Review

The goal of the **patterns strategy** is to point out multiple and unexpected examples of an image, a word, or even a sound that recur throughout a text. The patterns strategy may be used either before or after you have discovered a surface/depth argument; surface/depth and patterns strategies go hand in hand. Unsuccessful uses of the patterns strategy occur when a critic points out a repetition that is obvious with no unexpected examples or when a critic fails to link these examples to a deeper meaning of the text.

The patterns and surface/depth strategies are closely linked in practice and, like literary arguments in general, are most successful when they reveal complexities in a text—things that an average first-time reader will not notice. It is possible to write a complete and complex literary analysis using only the surface/depth and patterns strategies. You should practice recognizing how other critics integrate surface/depth and patterns into their writing and try to use successful examples of these strategies as models for your own writing.

∾ NOW PRACTICE ON YOUR OWN: THE CINNAMON PEELER

Below we reprint "The Cinnamon Peeler" by Michael Ondaatje, a Sri Lankan-born Canadian poet and novelist. Read the poem several times before attempting the questions that follow it; critical analysis of poetry depends on careful rereading.

Michael Ondaatje
The Cinnamon Peeler   1982

> If I were a cinnamon peeler
> I would ride your bed
> and leave the yellow bark dust
> on your pillow.

Your breasts and shoulders would reek 5
you could never walk through markets
without the profession of my fingers
floating over you. The blind would
stumble certain of whom they approached
though you might bathe 10
under rain gutters, monsoon.

Here on the upper thigh
at this smooth pasture
neighbour to your hair
or the crease 15
that cuts your back. This ankle.
You will be known among strangers
as the cinnamon peeler's wife.

I could hardly glance at you
before marriage 20
never touch you
—your keen nosed mother, your rough brothers.
I buried my hands
in saffron, disguised them
over smoking tar, 25
helped the honey gatherers . . .

        *

When we swam once
I touched you in water
and our bodies remained free,
you could hold me and be blind of smell. 30
You climbed the bank and said

this is how you touch other women
the grass cutter's wife, the lime burner's daughter.
And you searched your arms
for the missing perfume 35
and knew
what good is it
to be the lime burner's daughter

left with no trace
as if not spoken to in an act of love   40
as if wounded without the pleasure of a scar.

You touched
your belly to my hands
in the dry air and said
I am the cinnamon   45
peeler's wife. Smell me.

Questions

1. What is your surface interpretation of the poem? What is obvious about it? What will most readers notice upon a brief reading?

2. Using the patterns strategy, make a list of any recurring images, word choices, similar phrases, or any other pattern you see in the poem. Come up with as many patterns as you can discover.

3. Now, try to link these patterns to a concept or an idea not directly expressed in the text. In other words, try to think of what these recurring images or word choices or phrases might mean. Don't become frustrated if this is hard for you—it's supposed to be hard! Try to brainstorm for anything you can think of. In a class discussion, you can decide together which ones are plausible interpretations of the text. For now, take a stab at "freewriting" a paragraph in response to this prompt. Or if you prefer, make a list of possible interpretations your use of the patterns strategy enables you to make. At this stage don't be overly critical of your ideas—jot down whatever might seem plausible.

Exercises

1. After you have read and briefly reflected on "The Cinnamon Peeler," read the two response essays below. Note examples of the strategies (surface/depth and patterns) used in each of these essays. You can simply mark these strategies with abbreviations in the margins.

2. Indicate whether these essays meet the five criteria of a literary analysis as defined in Chapter 2. Which criteria does each essay meet?

3. Rank the two essays. Which makes the more complex argument? Why?

SAMPLE ESSAY A

"Smell Me": Eroticism in Michael Ondaatje's
"The Cinnamon Peeler"

Michael Ondaatje first published "The Cinnamon Peeler" in 1982 as part of his book, *Running in the Family*. "The Cinnamon Peeler" appeared later in Ondaatje's collection *Secular Love*. The poem may have been influenced by Ondaatje's separation from his wife in 1979 and his subsequent affair with another woman, Linda Spalding. In the poem, the speaker gives a very sensual description of his wife and their courtship, using the exotic qualities of cinnamon, especially its potent perfume, to underscore his irresistible lust.

The poem immediately captivates the reader with its erotic imagery as the speaker describes how he would like to "ride" (2) his lover's bed, suggesting sexual intercourse. The speaker goes on to state how he would leave yellow bark dust on his love's pillow, suggesting that their intercourse leaves an indelible mark on her.

The second stanza shows that this mark is not only visual but olfactory. The woman is totally and irrefutably saturated in the cinnamon peeler's scent. He writes, "Your breasts and shoulders would reek / you could never walk through markets / without the profession of my fingers / floating over you" (5–8). The use of the word "reek" in line 5 seems strange in the context of a love poem, but works in this instance.

The third stanza continues the erotic imagery as he lustfully imagines the sensual parts of her body, lingering in his descriptions of her "upper thigh" (12) and the "smooth pasture / neighbour to your hair" (13–14). The speaker even desires the non-erogenous parts of her body, such as the crease of her back and her ankle. He wants to claim every part of her body as his own. The use of sentence fragments such as "This ankle" (16) or "Here on the upper thigh / at this smooth pasture / neighbour to your hair" (12–14) in this section illustrates the speaker's desire for his beloved.

The fourth stanza jumps backward to the time before the couple was married and increases the erotic nature of the poem by showing how their physical love was prevented by the woman's "keen nosed mother, your rough brothers" (22). These family members are on guard to make sure that the couple stays chaste before marriage. The speaker tries to disguise his scent with other strong-smelling materials or spices, such as saffron, tar, and honey (24–26), but these scents do little to disguise the overpowering scent of cinnamon. The palpable use of scent in this section reinforces the primal sexual attraction that the couple feels for one another. The speaker writes how he could "hardly glance" (19) at his beloved for fear that her family might get the wrong message.

The poem then transitions and we encounter the enamored couple swimming in a river or pond. The woman is temporarily free of any trace of the cinnamon scent, which causes her to note the loss experienced by other women who are possessed by lesser men, "the grass cutter's wife, the lime burner's daughter" (33). She asserts that these women are in inferior relationships: "what good is it / to be the lime burner's daughter / left with no trace / as if not spoken to in an act of love" (37–40). Thus, the love between the cinnamon peeler and his wife is reaffirmed by her awareness of what other women are missing. While some women might find the cinnamon scent overpowering and a burden, the cinnamon peeler's wife takes pride in her scent, experiencing it as "the pleasure of a scar" (41). This unexpected imagery of a scar bringing pleasure illustrates the poem's central theme.

In the final stanza, the wife invites her husband to touch and smell her. The lilting and magical quality of the poem thus comes to a close with her final statement "I am the cinnamon / peeler's wife. Smell me" (45–46). These lines encapsulate the eroticism underlying the entire piece. These lines show that their love and erotic attraction is shared and she desires him as much as he desires her. Their primal attraction is masterfully concentrated in those two tiny yet commanding words: "Smell me."

Throughout the poem, the poet uses literal marks such as the bark dust and the unmistakable scent of cinnamon to talk about the metaphorical marks a man makes upon his beloved. The images in the poem rely primarily upon scent and smell rather than vision or sound. This unusual focus on smell accounts for the poem's effectiveness. Just as sex is primal, so are the effects of odor. Although the smell of cinnamon is not usually thought of as erotic, in this poem it becomes a powerful yet unusual metaphor for sexual desire.

"The Cinnamon Peeler" is a delicate and powerful narrative of erotic love. Ondaatje has woven a rich tapestry of images of longing and desire, a layered montage of profoundly beautiful language that displays all the richness of imagery and the piercing emotional truth. It is a perfect work of sensual longing, married love, and intimacy.

Work Cited

Ondaatje, Michael. "The Cinnamon Peeler." *Digging into Literature: Strategies for Reading, Analysis, and Writing*. Joanna Wolfe and Laura Wilder. Boston: Bedford/St. Martin's, 2016. 74–76. Print.

SAMPLE ESSAY B

Contradictory Desires in Michael Ondaatje's
"The Cinnamon Peeler"

Michael Ondaatje's "The Cinnamon Peeler" is a poem that provides contradictory images of lust. On one level, the poem shows a man who desires total ownership and possession of a woman, while at the same time it seems to suggest that this desire is an impossible fantasy. The poem implies that lust is neither as powerful nor all-encompassing as it might first seem.

The first half of the poem shows the speaker lusting after total domination of a woman. He imagines leaving a visible trace of himself on her pillow after he has been with her, suggesting that he wants to "mark" her as his own. He further imagines her body will "reek" (5) of his smell, even in a crowded marketplace, showing that he wants everyone to know, without doubt, that she belongs to him. This desire for total domination is perhaps best illustrated by the line "You will be known among strangers / as the cinnamon peeler's wife" (17–18). This line shows how the speaker wants this woman to be known only by her marital relationship to him. Moreover, this image reveals that he wants his domination of her to be so obvious that even strangers will recognize that she belongs to him.

The speaker's desire for total ownership of this woman is further illustrated in how he divides her body into pieces in the third stanza. He refers to her "breasts and shoulders" (5), her "upper thigh" (12), "the creases that cuts your back" (15–16), and "This ankle" (16), suggesting that he sees her as a series of body parts rather than as a whole person. Moreover, he talks about her body the way people often talk about land, describing her "pasture" and how her different parts act as "neighbours" to one another (13–14). These images show how the speaker wants to stake his claim to individual pieces of the woman's body much like a person might stake a claim to a plot of land or other physical piece of property.

However, even while "The Cinnamon Peeler" projects a male fantasy of domination there are many places in the poem that contradict this fantasy. The very first word of the poem is "if," which shows the reader that the speaker is in reality not a cinnamon peeler and that the domination and possession portrayed in the poem is a fantasy. The ellipses at the end of the first half (26) indicate that this fantasy cannot be maintained. Immediately afterward, the poem abruptly shifts tone and point of view, suggesting an alternate view of their relationship.

The second half of the poem contradicts the fantasy of total ownership depicted in the first half. In the first half of the poem, the speaker tells the woman that his smell completely defines her. The traces of his cinnamon perfume on her body provide guidance for the blind, who can "stumble certain of whom they approach" (9), suggesting that the most important, defining quality of this woman is not anything of her own but a smell she has acquired from her husband's profession. Moreover, his stamp on her is so strong that it cannot be erased even by a monsoon (8–11), showing that his control over her is stronger than the forces of nature. However, in the second half of the poem, the cinnamon scent is so weak that a short swim is enough to rid her of his perfume and make both of them "blind of smell" (30). This imagery suggests that the man's hold over this woman is temporary and easily washed away. Moreover, we find that the cinnamon peeler has touched other women whose smells overpower his own, further illustrating his inability to completely possess and define a woman. His lack of ownership is further emphasized by the fact that their bodies remain "free" (29) in the water, showing she is independent of him no matter how much he may want to possess her.

The second half of the poem thus illustrates that a single-minded, totalizing lust that marks lovers as belonging to one another is only a fantasy. Images of absence and loss are found in the second half of the poem: his perfume is "missing" (35), she imagines others "left with no trace" (39) and "not spoken to" (40) and, she is "blind of smell" (30). Even the opening line of this section emphasizes the temporary nature of their situation by stating "When we swam once" (27), suggesting that their contact was temporary and in the past. The poem thus seems to indicate that real love is marked by loss and the absence of totalizing and overpowering desire.

Yet, the second half of the poem is not all loss since it is only in this second half that the woman has a voice. Where the first half shows the speaker dominating a woman's obedient body with his lust, the second half shows two independent people cooperating in their desire. The last two lines of the poem are spoken by the woman and she is the one who initiates sexual action by pressing her belly to his hands and commanding him to smell her, thus illustrating her independence. Since we know that her swim has washed away the cinnamon smell, she seems to be commanding the speaker here to smell her as she really is, free of the cinnamon perfume. The ending of the poem suggests that the man does not simply "ride" her bed as in the first stanza but is invited there and implies that true possession requires the freedom and cooperation of a partner.

Work Cited

Ondaatje, Michael. "The Cinnamon Peeler." *Digging into Literature: Strategies for Reading, Analysis, and Writing.* Joanna Wolfe and Laura Wilder. Boston: Bedford/St. Martin's, 2016. 74–76. Print.

For Discussion

Compare your ranking of these two essays with your classmates' and your instructor's rankings.

5 Digging Deeper

By now you have learned that one of the main strategies of literary analysis is finding deeper meanings—what we are calling the *surface/depth strategy*—and that the overall goal of a literary analysis is to show how a work is *complex*. Moreover, you have learned that the *patterns strategy* is often used as a brainstorming tool that can help critics generate surface/depth interpretations and it is a way of supporting surface/depth arguments with repeated evidence.

This chapter gives an overview of aspects of texts we have seen literary critics pay special attention to when generating patterns and surface/depth arguments. Many students tell us that they learned about these aspects of literary texts in their high school language arts classes. However, these students generally find it helpful to review this material and to see it explicitly connected with the strategies we discuss here.

Because we hope this chapter can be used as a brainstorming tool to help you get started or "unstuck" when you prepare to write literary analyses, we keep explanations brief. If you would like greater detail, you can find more complete explanations and definitions in many literary handbooks, in glossaries, or on Web sites. The vocabulary and list of textual features we present are far from exhaustive, and your professors may introduce you to further useful terms—especially ones relevant to particular historical time periods and traditions you are studying.

Run through the textual aspects in this chapter when you feel short on ideas. Although not every textual aspect will be equally useful in every context, you can consider them to see if they help you generate new ideas or connections.

Before continuing with this chapter, re-read Leslie Marmon Silko's "The Man to Send Rain Clouds" on pages 29–34 and Louise Glück's "Gretel in Darkness" on pages 58–59. We will refer to these texts in a number of examples, so having them fresh in mind will be useful the first time you read this chapter. ∎

CHARACTER DESCRIPTIONS

While a character analysis should not be the end goal of an essay (your goal as a literary critic is to define what the text means), information presented about the people who appear in literary texts can be a good place to start your analysis. Below are potential questions you can use to begin to connect some of the surface features of the text to possible deeper meanings:

- How are characters physically described?

- What language does the author use to describe their actions? Are they active? Lazy? Deliberate? Careless? Happy? Angry? Confident? Defeated? Arrogant? Judgmental? Ignorant? Unaware?

- How do characters talk? What might the style of language—the use of things like slang or archaisms—reveal about the speakers, narrators, or characters who use the language?

- What actions do characters perform, particularly actions that seem contradictory or defy your expectations? Are there any contradictions in how the characters behave?

- Might the names the author gave to characters hold some significance?

- Traditionally, in fiction (whether a novel or short story) and in drama (whether a play or film) characters come into conflict. Can you identify the nature of a conflict or conflicts in the text? Is there a clear **protagonist** (or main character in a literary work) and **antagonist** (person with whom the protagonist struggles)? What does a focus on the nature of interpersonal (or internal) conflicts reveal about possible deeper meanings of the story?

A monk wearing a Franciscan robe.

OSTILL/Getty Images

Examples of character descriptions: There are several physical descriptions of Father Paul in the story "The Man to Send Rain Clouds," including the following passages:

1. When he recognized their faces he slowed his car and waved for them to stop. The young priest rolled down the car window.
   "Did you find old Teofilo?" he asked loudly. (30)

2. The priest stared down at his scuffed brown loafers and the worn hem of his cassock. "For a Christian burial it was necessary."
   His voice was distant, and Leon thought that his blue eyes looked tired.
   "It's O.K., Father, we just want him to have plenty of water."
   The priest sank down into the green chair and picked up a glossy missionary magazine. He turned the colored pages full of lepers and pagans without looking at them. (32–33)

3. The wind pulled at the priest's brown Franciscan robe and swirled away the corn meal and pollen that had been sprinkled on the blanket. . . . The priest walked away slowly. (34)

A critic might brainstorm about these passages to make the following arguments (bold text indicates surface/depth arguments):

The priest's loud voice **suggests that he fails to listen** to the Laguna people. He speaks as if he is going deaf, which **reflects his lack of understanding**.

The priest's blue eyes **emphasize his European heritage and his difference** from the Laguna people.

The priest's "scuffed brown loafers," "worn hem," and "tired" eyes **suggest he is being worn down by the passive resistance of the Laguna people**.

To discover complex arguments about a text, look carefully at elements such as character descriptions and brainstorm as many surface/depth arguments as possible. Don't censor yourself at this point. Once you have discovered some possible surface/depth arguments, use the patterns strategy to search the text for other passages, images, or words that might support these arguments. Talk through these arguments and your evidence with your peers and instructor.

Reject the interpretations that have limited support and keep the ones that you can persuasively support.

Exercise

> Return to the text of "The Man to Send Rain Clouds" (p. 29) and note at least three other passages in the story where the physical descriptions of Father Paul or the other characters seem significant. Try to generate surface/depth arguments about these descriptions.

SETTING

The setting of a text describes the time, place, and social environment of the world of the text. The physical and social environment in which a text is set differs from the environment in which the text was written (which we call **context**). For instance, many of Nathaniel Hawthorne's stories and novels are set in Puritan times around 1700, but were written circa 1850 in a culture that was still deeply influenced by its Puritan roots but also distanced from them. It is important to consider both when and where a story is set and the historical and cultural context in which the story was written.

To use the surface/depth strategy to brainstorm a text's setting, try examining closely the following details:

▸ Is there any significance to the time of year (or time of day) during which the events depicted take place?

▸ Does the location suggest anything potentially meaningful? Has the author described physical space in any revealing or suggestive ways? Does the place have any historical or cultural significance? (We will discuss how to bring in relevant historical information in Chapter 7, "Context.")

▸ Might the weather, climate, or atmosphere depicted be relevant to understanding deeper possible meanings?

▸ Look closely at how buildings are described. Do they suggest grandeur or squalor? Openness or claustrophobia? Loving upkeep or decay? Comfort or discomfort? Can you make any surface/depth arguments based on these observations?

▸ Is there anything revealing about the descriptions of furniture or decorations? Do they suggest that the owner takes pride in his/her possessions? Or do they evoke carelessness? Is any artwork described?

▸ Is the lighting significant? Is the setting illuminated in warm light, a harsh glare, partial shadow, or gloomy darkness?

▸ If the setting takes place outdoors, is nature portrayed as welcoming or foreboding? Is the landscape wild or cultivated by humans? Is it thriving or rotten? Are there open expanses or lush growth? Is it gentle or dangerous?

Symbol of the Lamb.
Marc Salvatore/
iStock/Getty Images

Example of setting: "The Man to Send Rain Clouds" contains the following description of the church:

> Leon knocked at the old carved door with its symbols of the Lamb. While he waited he looked up at the twin bells from the king of Spain with the last sunlight pouring around them in their tower. (32)

A critic can use these observations about the setting to brainstorm potential surface/depth arguments such as (bold text indicates surface/depth arguments):

The symbol of the Lamb on the church door **suggests similarities** between the Laguna way of life and Christianity. Just as Teofilo is a shepherd whose death will save his people by bringing them rain clouds, so is Father Paul a Christian shepherd who believes in saving the souls of the Laguna people. However, these similarities are obscured by the signs of colonial power, which **emphasize distance and hierarchy**. The "twin bells from the king of Spain" (32) are high above the heads of the Laguna people where they block the sunlight. These bells symbolize the Spaniards' perspective, which is at such an elevated distance it cannot see the Laguna people clearly.

Exercise

Note at least three other passages in "The Man to Send Rain Clouds" where descriptions of the setting seem significant. Try to generate surface/depth arguments about these descriptions.

PERSPECTIVE

To get below the surface of the text, you can also try looking at the perspective, or viewpoint, from which it is told. For instance, some of "A Man to Send Rain Clouds" is told from Leon's perspective, or viewpoint, and some is told from Father Paul's perspective. In other words, sometimes the text describes events as if we were seeing them through Leon's eyes and at other times we seem to be seeing the story through Father Paul's eyes. Paying particular attention to when the perspective of a story shifts from one character to another can help you find surface/depth arguments.

Other aspects of perspective you might consider include:

▸ What biases does the narrator or speaker have? This aspect is particularly important to consider if a text is written in **first-person narrative**, a story told from the perspective of one of the characters using the pronoun *I*. (In **third-person narrative** as opposed to first-person narrative, the narrator is not a character in the story.) Since a first-person narrator is a character in the story, we might ask whether she or he is a **reliable narrator**—a narrator whose accounts and perspective we trust—or an **unreliable narrator** we do not trust. For instance, if a story is told from a child's perspective, we might question how reliable the narrator is since a child can describe events without understanding them. Likewise, we would consider a psychologically disturbed person to be an unreliable narrator.

▸ How broad or limited is the narrator's perspective? Is the narrator **omniscient**, or all knowing? Or is the narrator **limited**, only able to see events through the eyes of a particular character? How do these limitations affect our understanding of events?

▸ Are there any shifts in the narrator's perspective? This is particularly important in third-person narrative where the viewpoint may shift among characters. Look at when these shifts occur and note what sorts of issues, themes, and images seem to reoccur when we see the story from one person's perspective versus another's. What might such differences reveal about the possible meanings of the text?

▸ If analyzing a film, what perspective does the camera seem to inhabit? Do we see the events of the film as if we are one of the characters? Does the camera angle seem to be looking down on characters, making them seem small and insignificant? Or is the camera up close and personal, creating intimacy between the viewer and the characters? Does the camera perspective shift or remain fixed?

Example of perspective: Although "The Man to Send Rain Clouds" is entirely written in the third-person point of view, the narrative perspective shifts among the characters. In the following passage from page 33 of the story, we see the point of view shift from Leon to Father Paul.

> When Leon opened the door Father Paul stood up and said, "Wait." He left the room and came back wearing a long brown overcoat. He followed Leon out the door and across the dim churchyard to the adobe steps in front of the church. They stooped to fit through the low adobe entrance. And when they started down the hill to the graveyard only half of the sun was visible above the mesa.

Leon's perspective

> The priest approached the grave slowly, wondering how they had managed to dig into the frozen ground; and then he remembered that this was New Mexico, and saw the pile of cold loose sand beside the hole. The people stood close to each other with little clouds of steam puffing from their faces. The priest looked at them and saw a pile of jackets, gloves, and scarves in the yellow, dry tumbleweeds that grew in the graveyard. He looked at the red blanket, not sure that Teofilo was so small, wondering if it wasn't some perverse Indian trick—something they did in March to ensure a good harvest—wondering if maybe old Teofilo was actually at sheep camp corralling the sheep for the night.

Father Paul's perspective

The first half of the story appears to be narrated from Leon's perspective. Although the story is in third person, we experience events filtered through Leon's viewpoint as he interacts with the environment, his wife, and Father Paul:

> He squinted up at the sun and unzipped his jacket—it sure was hot for this time of year. (30)

> She touched his arm, and he noticed that her hands were still dusty. . . . When she spoke, Leon could not hear her. (31)

> Leon thought that his [Father Paul's] blue eyes looked tired. (32)

These passages all record thoughts and observations specific to Leon. We do not get similar information from the other characters in the story, until the perspective switches to the priest's viewpoint in the passage above. At this point, we start to obtain information about the priest's thoughts, fears, and biases. We see the clanspeople as the priest would see them—and not as they would describe one another.

We can use these observations about perspective to make arguments such as (bold text indicates surface/depth arguments):

> Once the priest approaches the grave, the perspective shifts to his point of view and we see how limited his understanding of his parishioners really is. He does not refer to them by name, and when he looks out on "the people," he sees not individual faces, but "a pile of jackets, gloves, and scarves" (33). This **suggests that Father Paul cannot usefully distinguish among his parishioners**. Moreover, the Laguna people are standing so that their faces are in shadow, **suggesting that Father Paul may never really be able to know them**. From Father Paul's perspective, the Laguna people **appear unknowable and indistinguishable**.

Exercise

In the final paragraph of "The Man to Send Rain Clouds," the perspective switches back to Leon's viewpoint. Identify the point where this shift occurs and then try to make some surface/depth arguments about the importance of this shift.

COMPARISONS

Often, authors use comparisons to describe events, objects, or people. Such comparisons transfer the set of ideas associated with one object or phenomenon to something else. Consequently, comparisons make for very rich and deep descriptions that critics can closely examine to find arguments about a text.

Comparisons always have two parts: a subject that is being described and a set of concepts or attributes that are being transferred back to the original subject. A **metaphor** is one type of comparison in which a person, a place, or an object is described as being something else. For instance, in the metaphor *All the world's a stage*, "the world" is the main subject being described and "a stage" is the comparison subject. All the concepts and qualities we associated with "a stage"—including actors, lines, exits and entrances, audiences, a playwright—are transferred back to "the world." Thus, this metaphor works by associating "the world" with the qualities of "a stage."

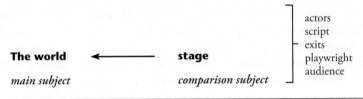

Analysis of the metaphor "All the world's a stage."

Comparisons do not need to be explicitly stated. For instance, in Glück's poem "Gretel in Darkness," consider line 6: *Her tongue shrivels into gas.* There is an implied comparison here between "her tongue" and "gas."

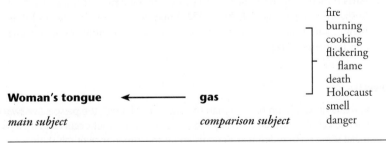

Analysis of the metaphor "Her tongue shrivels into gas."

Thus, in this comparison, the dangers and deadliness we associate with gas are being transferred to a woman's tongue. This comparison might be used to make a surface/depth argument that the poem associates women's speech with death and danger or, perhaps more specifically, that the poem treats female speech as something that burns and consumes.

When analyzing comparisons in texts, first identify what subjects are being compared. Then brainstorm about what concepts from the comparison subject are being transferred back to the main subject. Finally, try to imagine what surface/depth arguments this comparison suggests. How does the comparison help us understand the text's meaning or significance?

Specific questions to consider about comparisons include:

▸ What metaphors or **similes** (explicit comparisons that use the words *like*, *as*; unlike metaphors, similes call attention to the act of comparing) does the text use? What qualities and attributes are being transferred to the main subject? What does the text gain by bringing these associations together? What surface/depth arguments could you make about the significance of these comparisons?

▸ Is the text an allegory for something else? An **allegory** is an extended comparison in which people and events in a text represent specific ideas or concepts. The purpose of an allegory is usually to teach an idea or a principle. What qualities from the characters and events in the text are being transferred to the original subject? What is the author trying to say with this allegory? What surface/depth arguments might you make by comparing the events, actions, and characters in the text with those they represent?

▸ Do any of the comparisons in the text seem to reverse typical, standard meanings? What arguments could be made about such reversals?

Examples of comparisons: In Silko's, "The Man to Send Rain Clouds," we see a simile as Father Paul pours the holy water over Teofilo's grave:

> He sprinkled more water; he shook the container until it was empty, and the water fell through the light from sundown like August rain that fell while the sun was still shining, almost evaporating before it touched the wilted squash flowers. (34)

The holy water sprinkling out of the container is compared to August rain that falls while the sun is shining. Thus, the qualities we might associate with rain falling on a sunny day—including disbelief and a sense of impossibility or the miraculous—are transferred to the holy water falling over the grave.

At the same time, the rain in this simile is specifically described as "August rain" falling over "wilted squash flowers," images that bring up associations of thirst, drought, and insufficiency. Thus, at the same time the holy water is associated with the miraculous, it is also associated with death, need, and insufficiency.

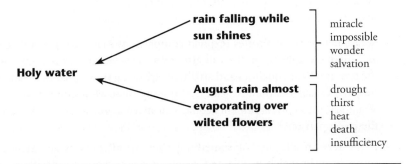

Analysis of complex simile: "[T]he water fell through the light from sundown like August rain that fell while the sun was still shining, almost evaporating before it touched the wilted squash flowers."

A critic might use this analysis of the complex way this simile functions to make the following surface/depth arguments (bold text indicates surface/depth arguments):

Father Paul's act of sprinkling holy water over Teofilo's grave is compared to the wonder of rain falling on a sunny day, **indicating that this ceremony truly has a miraculous character**. At the same time, however, this miraculous rain "almost evaporates" before it reaches the thirsting landscape, which **suggests that this miracle will, at best, be barely sufficient to sustain the needs of Father Paul's Laguna parishioners.**

Exercise

Try to find and analyze at least three comparisons in "The Man to Send Rain Clouds" (or another text that your instructor suggests). For each comparison, note:

1. the subjects being compared
2. the concepts or qualities being transferred back to the original subject
3. any surface/depth arguments you can make about these comparisons

IRONIES

We can also find surface/depth arguments in a text by looking closely at ironies. **Irony** is a difficult concept to understand because it refers to a diverse range of events and statements; however, all ironies involve a tension between an expected or apparent state of things and the real or underlying state.

For instance, a firehouse burning down is ironic because there is a tension between what we expect (that places for preventing fires should be safe from fire) and what actually occurred. Such tensions between expected and actual situations are called **situational irony**.

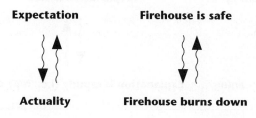

Expectation   **Firehouse is safe**

Actuality   **Firehouse burns down**

Situational irony

Irony also occurs when there is an incongruity between what the audience knows and what a character believes. For instance, if the audience knows a character in a play is about to die and the character innocently says, "I'll see you tomorrow," the resulting tension between the character's expectations and the audience's knowledge provides **dramatic irony**.

Dramatic irony

We also see irony when the literal meaning of a word or phrase conflicts with an implied, or underlying, meaning. For instance, if a person says, "That explanation was as clear as mud," on the literal, or surface, level, she is saying that the explanation is clear but on the implied, or underlying, level she is saying the opposite: that the explanation is muddy and confusing. Such conflicts between literal and underlying meanings are called **verbal irony**. Unlike situational and dramatic irony, verbal irony is often intended by the speaker.

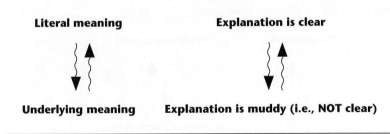

Verbal irony

Although we have identified three types of irony here, we believe it is less important that you identify the particular type of irony than that you use irony as a strategy to identify multiple states or meanings that are in tension. Ironies are powerful places to look for surface/depth arguments in texts because they point to multiple levels of reality, meaning, or interpretation.

Specific questions to ask about irony include:

▸ Does the text suggest a tension between our expectations and what actually occurs in the text? Or between different ways of looking at the world? Or between literal and underlying meanings?

▸ How do these tensions help us understand central meanings, themes, ideas, or patterns in the text?

▸ What surface/depth arguments could be made about these tensions?

Examples of irony: In "Gretel in Darkness" we can see irony in the lines

My father bars the door, bars harm
from this house, and it is years. (11–12)

These lines are ironic because, on a literal level, Gretel's father is locking the door to protect her. However, the repetition of the word "bars" and the phrase "it is years" also seem to suggest the bars of a prison, or the bars of the witch's cage. Thus, an action meant to protect Gretel, ironically, also seems to threaten her with imprisonment.

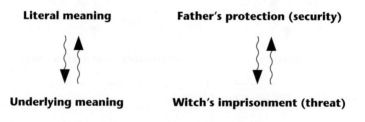

Irony in the line "My father bars the door, bars harm."

A critic might use this analysis of irony in the poem to make the following interpretation (bold text indicates surface/depth arguments):

In Gretel's posttraumatic state, the actions her father takes to protect her ironically take on a threatening tone. Although on a literal level these lines indicate that Gretel's father is trying to protect her, the repetition of the word "bars" and the word "years" also **suggest the image of a prison cell—or perhaps the bars of the witch's hut**. This tension between security and threat **implies that, for Gretel, no physical action can protect her from the psychological threat posed by her memories**.

We can similarly see irony in "The Man to Send Rain Clouds" when Leon visits Father Paul to ask for holy water:

> The priest sank down into the green chair and picked up a glossy missionary magazine. He turned the colored pages full of lepers and pagans without looking at them. (33)

There is a tension here between what we expect of a missionary and the actuality of Father Paul's situation where he is consulted only after other rituals have been performed and where he fails to truly look at the people he is called to lead.

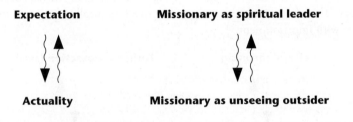

Irony of Father Paul's missionary calling

A critic might interpret this passage as follows (bold text indicates surface/depth arguments):

> As a missionary, Father Paul should be the spiritual leader of his parish. His missionary magazine, with its colorful, glossy pages "full of lepers and pagans" (33) **suggests that this should be a glamorous job full of miraculous acts of salvation**. The reality of Father's Paul's life, however, is quite different. Instead of leading his parish, he finds himself on the outside, informed of Teofilo's death only after the primary burial ceremony has been completed. Rather

than shepherding his parish toward the light of God, he ironically finds himself kept in the dark by his more-knowing flock. However, the way Father Paul flips through the missionary magazine "without looking" **indicates that he is at least partially responsible for his outsider status**, for he fails to truly look at his parishioners and see them for who they are. **Father Paul's desire to save seems to prevent him from understanding those he wishes to help**.

Exercises

Analyze the ironies in the follow passages from Silko's "The Man to Send Rain Clouds" (29) and Glück's "Gretel in Darkness" (58). For each passage, do the following:

▸ Draw a diagram, such as the figures on pages 93–96, illustrating the tension between two states.
▸ Write a short paragraph making surface/depth arguments about these tensions.

1. "Did you find old Teofilo?" he asked loudly.
   Leon stopped the truck. "Good morning, Father. We were just out to the sheep camp. Everything is O.K. now."
   "Thank God for that. Teofilo is a very old man. You really shouldn't allow him to stay at the sheep camp alone."
   "No, he won't do that anymore now."
   "Well, I'm glad you understand. I hope I'll be seeing you at Mass this week—we missed you last Sunday. See if you can get old Teofilo to come with you." The priest smiled and waved at them as they drove away. (Silko 30)

2. But there he was, facing into a cold dry wind and squinting at the last sunlight, ready to bury a red wool blanket while the faces of his parishioners were in shadow with the last warmth of the sun on their backs. (Silko 33)

3. This is the world we wanted. (Glück line 1)

TIME AND SEQUENCE

Looking at the way a text plays with time or the sequence of events may trigger some fruitful ideas about a text's possible deeper meanings. If we consider how the events in a text would proceed in real time as a baseline, we can examine whether the text speeds time up or slows time down. In addition, we can look at whether the text presents events in the order that they would have occurred in real time—or if the text changes the order through the use of flashbacks, flash-forwards, or other devices.

Questions to ask about time and sequence include:

▸ Does the text do anything to call our attention to the passage of time?

▸ Does the text seem to speed time up? Or slow time down? What might such changes to time indicate?

▸ Does the order in which events are presented differ from the actual chronological order of events? Why might the author have changed this order? Can you make any surface/depth arguments about the order in which events are presented?

▸ What verb tense is used? Do verb tenses shift at any point? What might such shifts in verb tense indicate about the text?

Example of time: In much of "The Man to Send Rain Clouds," time proceeds at a steady pace, much as we might expect in real time. However, when Father Paul pours the holy water on Teofilo's grave, we witness an extended reflection that seems to slow time down:

> Drops of water fell on the red blanket and soaked into dark icy spots. He sprinkled the grave and the water disappeared almost before it touched the dim, cold sand; it reminded him of something—he tried to remember what it was, because he thought if he could remember he might understand this. He sprinkled more water; he shook the container until it was empty, and the water fell through the light from sundown like August rain that fell while the sun was still shining, almost evaporating before it touched the wilted squash flowers. (33–34)

The thoughts Father Paul has during this moment seem to last far longer than the physical act of pouring water over a grave would take. A critic might interpret the elongated time in this passage as follows (bold text indicates surface/depth arguments):

> When Father Paul pours the holy water over Teofilo's grave, time seems to slow down as he tries to remember what this action reminds him of. Father Paul's thoughts here seem to stretch far beyond the time it would take to complete his physical actions. This slowness stresses the importance of the moment and **suggests that something eternal or timeless may be occurring here**. This sense of timelessness is further reinforced by the fact that even though it is winter, Father Paul is reminded of August rain. By collapsing winter and summer, **the text seems to suggest that the significance of the holy water transcends earthly concerns**.

Example of text sequence: The order of events presented in "Gretel in Darkness" differs from the chronological order of events as Gretel experiences a series of flashbacks to her time with the witch. If we break the poem down into a series of events or thoughts, we see the following order of presentation:

1. Hansel, Gretel, and their father are living happily ever after. (lines 1–3)
2. Gretel relives the moment of killing the witch. (lines 3–6)
3. Hansel, Gretel, and their father are living happily ever after. (lines 7–9)
4. Gretel remembers killing the witch. (line 10)
5. Hansel, Gretel, and their father are living happily ever after. (lines 11–13)
6. Hansel thinks of leaving. (lines 13–16)
7. Gretel relives killing the witch. (lines 17–18)
8. Gretel fears Hansel has left her alone. (lines 19–22)
9. Gretel relives killing the witch. (lines 23–24)

One possible argument a critic might make about the text sequence is (bold text indicates surface/depth arguments):

> "Gretel in Darkness" **shows the difficulty of moving beyond traumatic events**. Every few lines, Gretel returns to the scene of killing the witch. This

event is mentioned in lines 3–6, 10, 17–18, and 23–24. Every time Gretel tries to take comfort in her present happy situation, her memory interrupts her and she relives the past. This continual refrain **shows how Gretel is stuck in the past and unable to move into the future**.

Exercise

What other surface/depth arguments might you make about the text sequence of "Gretel in Darkness"?

TITLES AND EPIGRAPHS

Literary scholars often see titles and **epigraphs** (brief quotations from another text that are used as a preface) as potentially key clues to interpreting a text's deeper meanings.

- ▸ What might a text's title suggest about the text's possible further layers of meaning?
- ▸ Did the author attach an epigraph to preface the text with? What might this selection reveal about the text's possible deeper layers of meaning?
- ▸ Is there any research or further reading you could do in order to more fully understand a text's title or epigraph?

Example of a title analysis: The poem "Morning Song" (from Chapter 3, p. 41) has a provocative title. On the surface level, this title suggests a mother getting up at dawn to feed her infant—an action that we see in the last two stanzas of the poem. However, there are at least two other meanings that can be associated with this title.

First, a "morning song" is a traditional genre of poem originating in the Middle Ages (when it was referred to as an *aubade*) that describes two lovers separating at daybreak. This information could be used to suggest that the infant's arrival is similarly a kind of separation for the mother. Just as lovers separating at dawn experience love and loss simultaneously, so does the arrival of the newborn cause the mother to feel both love and loss. (We will provide additional examples of how genre can be used to make an interpretation in Chapter 8.)

Second, the word *morning* in the title is a homophone for *mourning*. (A homophone is a pair of words that are pronounced identically but have different meanings.) Thus, the title "Morning Song" can simultaneously refer to the joy associated with a new day and to the bereavement associated with death. A critic might therefore argue that the title suggests both the dawn of a new life (the infant's arrival) and the passing of an old life (the mother's loss of self).

SPECIFIC WORDS

Of course, literary scholars pay close attention to language. In preparing to write a literary analysis, these readers often explore the meanings of individual words and phrases. Words that stand out as unusual or unexpected, or that are repeated and emphasized are often probed further in these ways:

- ▸ Consider the **denotative** (or literal) **meanings** of a word. Many words have multiple denotations. For instance, the word *spirit* can denote a human soul, a ghost, or an emotional attribute (as in *She sang with spirit*). An author might have chosen a particular word because it has multiple denotative meanings. Consider looking up the meaning of words you are curious about or stumped by; even words whose denotations you are familiar with may have secondary meanings of which you are unaware. Do these secondary meanings connect with any patterns you see in the text? Can you make surface/depth arguments about them?

- ▸ Consider the **connotative** (or emotional or cultural) **meanings** of a word. For instance, the word *spirit* tends to have positive religious connotations while the word *ghost* has more physical connotations in that ghosts are typically associated with a particular place and have a recognizable form. What emotional or cultural associations does a word bring up? What unique associations does this word have that we do not find with other synonyms that have the same denotative meaning? Do these connotative meanings help you support or discover any patterns in the text? Can you use these connotative meanings to make surface/depth arguments about the author's selection of this particular word?

▸ Does the author make up any words? Or play with conventional grammar? Why do you think he or she does this? What might these decisions contribute to the deeper meanings of the text?

▸ What do descriptive words—adjectives and adverbs—as well as vividly described sensory images reveal about a text's possible meaning?

▸ Beginnings and endings of texts are particularly useful places to find surface/depth arguments. What special significance might there be to specific words at the beginning or the ending of the text?

▸ Are any words repeated, forming unusual patterns? What might this repetition suggest?

Looking closely at individual words is important to the analysis of any text; however, it is absolutely essential to the study and analysis of poetry. Because poems have comparatively small numbers of words, the analysis of each individual word in a poem is particularly relevant. Chapter 7, "Context," contains more information on how to look up words using the *Oxford English Dictionary* (*OED*).

To some students, such an in-depth analysis of tiny details, such as individual words, may feel like symbol-hunting. However, one of the key values of literary analysis consists of finding larger meanings in small details. Literary critics consequently use the patterns strategy to analyze how multiple details and individual interpretations fit together as a whole. If a particular interpretation can be found in small as well as large details in a text, it becomes all the more persuasive to a literary critic.

Examples of specific words being analyzed: In "Gretel in Darkness" (58), the word "armed" in line 17 has multiple meanings.

> But I killed for you. I see armed firs,
> the spires of that gleaming kiln—

We see multiple denotative meanings to the word *armed*. When applied to plants (such as fir trees), the word *armed* means that the plants have bristles or thorns for protection. Thus, at this level the image "armed firs" simply means that the pine trees in the forest have needles. However, *armed* also refers to having weapons, suggesting that the trees are ready to fight.

The connotative associations of *armed* bring to mind warfare and armies as well as *armed robbery*. There is something menacing about the word *armed* that we might not associate with synonyms such as *fortified, equipped*, or *girded*. Compared to these other similar words, *armed* suggests a readiness to attack and go on the offensive.

A critic might make the following argument based on this observation (bold text indicate surface depth argument):

> Gretel's description of the trees **illustrates how she is unable to take solace in nature.** Instead of peaceful "summer afternoons" (14), Gretel sees "armed firs" (17) that remind her of "spires" and a "gleaming kiln" (18), presumably her memory of the witch's oven. The word "armed" suggests that the trees are humanlike and ready to take weapons against her—an interpretation reinforced by the words "spires" (which are symbols of martial power) and "gleaming" (an adjective often used to describe swords and shields). Taken together these lines **suggest that Gretel sees nature as turning against her.**

Exercise

The word "arms" also appears in line 7 of the poem. What surface/depth arguments can you make about the line "far from women's arms"?

SOUND

Reading a text aloud may cause you to hear repetitions or aural aspects that may be useful in digging below its surface meaning. Hence reading aloud can play an important role in your brainstorming activity, especially for poems that the author may intend to have delivered orally. Reading aloud sections of dialogue or narration in fiction or drama can also help you hear qualities of a character's or a narrator's "voice" you might otherwise miss. Further, some texts, such as films and experimental multimodal texts, are composed with sounds such as actors' voices, sound effects, and music soundtracks.

Here are just a few issues related to sound you must train your ears to hear:

- **Alliteration** is the repetition of an initial consonant sound in a series of words or phrases. **Assonance** is the repetition of vowel sounds, and **consonance** is the repetition of ending consonants. In this text we refer to all the above simply as **repetitions**.

- **Meter** is the basic rhythmic structure of a poem. Meter can depend on the number of syllables in a line and on the arrangement of stressed and unstressed syllables. You can find more about meter in the Resources section (Learning Lab > Glossary of Poetic Terms) at the Poetry Foundation's Web site.

- Are the sounds of words suggestive? Are there noteworthy repetitions of vowel or consonant sounds that suggest different emotions or emphasize different connotative meanings of the words involved?

- When lines rhyme or words repeat sounds, they are often thematically linked. Are there patterns of rhymes or repeated consonant and vowel sounds that cause you to group particular words, lines, or ideas together, treating them as a unit? What surface/depth arguments can you make about these groupings?

- Do you detect a meter, or rhythm, to a poem? Different metrical patterns can sometimes be interpreted as producing particular emotional effects, such as suggesting happiness, dread, chaos, or innocence.

- Are there places where the meter or rhyme pattern is suddenly broken? For instance, if each line in a poem has twelve syllables and one suddenly has thirteen, we would describe the metrical pattern as broken. What might this shift suggest?

- In film, sound effects may be used to heighten some sounds, such as the slamming of a door. Can you detect any of the ways sounds in a film have been heightened or altered? What effects on the meaning of the film do these manipulations of sound have?

▸ In film and some multimodal texts, music may accompany images and words. What relationships do you see between the music and other aspects of the text? If the music has lyrics, those words, too, can be probed for further meaning.

Exercises

1. Note the repeated "w" sounds in lines 1–8 and the repeated "s" sounds in lines 21–23 of "Gretel in Darkness." What surface/depth arguments can you make about either of these sound patterns?

2. What other specific sounds or rhythms do you note in "Gretel in Darkness"? What surface/depth arguments can you make about these sounds?

BREAKS AND GROUPINGS

Just as the sounds in a text can suggest particular groupings of lines, words, or images, so can line, chapter, stanza, or scene breaks provide groupings and separations that you can analyze. A **stanza** is a unit in poetry formed by two or more lines set off by spaces. For instance, "Gretel in Darkness" has four stanzas. A **stanza break** refers to where the stanza ends.

▸ Does punctuation, or a lack of punctuation, call attention to itself in the text? Why do you think the author made these punctuation choices?

▸ In prose, might the author's choices to divide the text into paragraphs, whether long or short, illuminate something about the text's meaning?

▸ In drama, is there any significance to where a playwright ends particular scenes?

▸ In poetry, grouping lines into stanzas suggests that they are thematically linked. Are there any interpretations you might make about how stanzas operate as units of meaning? Comparably, do stanza breaks suggest anything meaningful?

▸ Is there an **enjambment** or a breaking of a line of poetry midstream in the middle of a sentence, phrase, or clause? Does this enjambment cause you to see two possible meanings in a line: a linguistic unit that ends with the line and another, different meaning that ends with the punctuation on the following line? Can you make surface/depth arguments about these multiple readings of the line? Do these enjambments contribute to the mood or feeling of the poem?

Exercises

1. Note the enjambment in lines 11–12 of "Gretel in Darkness":

   My father bars the door, bars harm
   from this house, and it is years.

   How is the meaning of the poem affected by Glück's choice to end line 11 with the word "harm" rather than the phrase "from this house" in line 12? How different might the line read or feel if Glück had continued the phrase?

2. What other enjambments do you note in "Gretel in Darkness"? What arguments can you make about Glück's choices about where to end her lines?

VISUAL APPEARANCE

Just as the sounds in a text can suggest deeper meanings, the appearance of texts on the page—or the stage or screen—can also provide material that allows you to dig beneath the surface.

▸ Poems are sometimes designed to use white space, indentation, and other visual design elements. Is there anything unusual about the shape and appearance of the printed words themselves on the page? What might these elements signify?

▸ Films, graphic novels, and other multimodal texts combine visual images with words. What is the nature of this combination in the text you are analyzing? Do the visuals support the words or contradict them? The visual elements of film may require learning a new way of "reading" them. Pay attention to where and when different camera angles are used. Looking upward or face on at a character may produce different effects on viewers' understandings of a character. Close-ups, wide shots, and intercutting of scenes are also useful to examine for the meaning they convey.

▸ When reading a play, the stage directions a playwright includes are important to consider, as they indicate how the play should appear on the stage. Thus, it is important to visualize them in your imagination when you read and to consider how these visuals relate to the words characters speak. How are characters dressed, settings staged, and props used?

Review

This chapter lists a number of features of texts that literary critics pay attention to when reading a text closely and critically. Critics use the **patterns strategy** to note when some of these features appear repeatedly in a text, and they use the **surface/depth strategy** to first explore and later compose claims about what deeper layers of meaning these features reveal in a text.

While you are learning to read closely and critically in a similar fashion, it may help to be prompted to consider some of these aspects of texts that you might not pay attention to otherwise. For this reason, we provide the following list of all the aspects of texts that this chapter covered. When brainstorming to write a literary analysis, you may want to keep this list nearby and consult it when you are stuck or want to find textual evidence that goes well beyond the obvious. As you continue to study literature, you may learn of further textual features to add to this list.

WHEN READING AND BRAINSTORMING, CONSIDER AS MANY OF THESE ASPECTS AS POSSIBLE:

Character Descriptions	▸ How are characters' appearances and actions described? ▸ How do they talk? ▸ Are their names significant? ▸ How do they come into conflict?
Setting	▸ How is the setting described? ▸ Is there any significance to the time of day or time of year? ▸ Is there any significance to the weather or atmosphere depicted?
Perspective	▸ Who is the narrator? Or who is the speaker of the poem? Is there a persona you can describe? ▸ What is the relationship between the narrator or speaker and the other characters or events? Is the narrator a first-person narrator, omniscient, or of limited omniscience?

	‣ How reliable is the narrator or speaker? ‣ Are there any shifts in perspective that might be significant?
Comparisons	‣ What does the text gain by transferring the images and concepts associated with one subject to another? What do these metaphors and similes suggest about its meaning? ‣ Is the text an allegory for something else? ‣ Do any of the comparisons in the text seem to reverse typical, standard meanings?
Ironies	‣ Does the text suggest a tension between our expectations and what actually occurs in the text? Or between different ways of looking at the world? Or between literal and underlying meanings? ‣ How do these tensions help us understand central themes, ideas, or patterns in the text?
Time and Text Sequence	‣ Does the text do anything to call our attention to the passage of time, such as speeding time up or slowing it down? ‣ Does the order of presentation in the text differ from the chronological order of events? ‣ What verb tense is used? Are there shifts in tense?
Titles and Epigraphs	‣ What is the relationship between the title and the text? ‣ How do any epigraphs relate to the text's meaning?
Specific Words	‣ Are there words with multiple possible denotations? ‣ What are these words' connotations? ‣ What images do highly descriptive adjectives and adverbs paint? What might these images mean? ‣ Are any words repeated? What might these repetitions suggest?
Sound	‣ Do rhymes, rhythms, or meters suggest a mood that contributes to the text's meaning? ‣ Do rhymes or repeated sounds create any unusual groupings of words or phrases that you could analyze? ‣ Do sound effects and music soundtracks influence the meaning of the text?

(continued)

Breaks and Groupings	▸ Is there any significance to where an author decided to break chapters, scenes, or paragraphs? ▸ Are there any interpretations you might make about how poetic stanzas operate as units of meaning? ▸ Do stanza breaks or line enjambments suggest anything meaningful?
Visual Appearance	▸ Does the appearance of the text on the page (or screen or stage) relate to the text's meaning? ▸ How is the text punctuated? Where do new paragraphs or line breaks and stanzas appear? ▸ What is the relationship between the images on the screen or stage and the text's meaning?

∾ NOW PRACTICE ON YOUR OWN: ANTLERS

Below we reprint "Antlers," a short story by Rick Bass, an American writer and environmental activist. Read the story, then answer the questions we ask about character, setting, and point of view.

Rick Bass

Antlers   1997

HALLOWEEN brings us closer. The Halloween party at the saloon is when we—all three dozen or so of us—recollect again why we live in this cold, blue valley. Sometimes tourists come when the summer grass is high, and the valley opens up a little. People slip in and out of it; in summer it's almost a regular place. But in October the less hardy of heart leave as the snow begins to fall. It becomes our valley again, and there's a feeling like a sigh, a sigh after the great full meal of summer.

We don't bother with masks at the party because we know one another so well, if not through direct contact, then through word of mouth—what Dick said Becky said about Don, and so on. Instead, we strap horns on our heads, moose antlers, deer antlers, or even the high throwback of elk antlers. We have a big potluck supper and get drunk as hell, even those of us who do not generally drink. We put the tables and chairs outside in the gust-driven snow and put nickels in the juke box and dance until early morning to Elvis, The Doors, or Marty Robbins. Mock battles occur when the men and women bang their antlers against each other. We clomp and sway in the barn.

Around two or three in the morning we drive or ski or snowshoe home, or we ride back on horses—however we got to the party is how we'll return. It usually snows big on Halloween—a foot, a foot and a half. Whoever drove down to the saloon will give the skiers a lift by fastening a long rope to the rear bumper of his truck, and the skiers hold on to that rope, still wearing antlers, too drunk or tired to take them off. Pulled up the hill, gliding silently on the road's hard ice, we keep our heads tucked against the wind and snow. Like children dropped off at a bus stop, we let go of the rope when the truck reaches our dark cabin. It would be nice to be greeted by a glowing lantern in the window, but you don't ever go to sleep or leave with a lantern burning like that—it can burn your cabin down in the night. We return to dark houses, all of us.

The antlers feel natural after having them lashed to our heads for so long. Sometimes we bump them against the door frame going in, and knock them off.

There is a woman up here, Suzie, who has moved through the valley with 5 a rhythm that is all her own. Over the years Suzie has been with all the able-bodied men of the valley. All, that is, except for Randy. He still wishes for his chance, but because he is a bowhunter—he uses a strong compound bow and wicked, heart-gleaming aluminum arrows with a whole spindle of razor blades at one end—she will have nothing to do with him.

At times I wanted to defend him, even though I strongly objected to bowhunting. Bowhunting, it seemed to me, was brutal. But Randy was just Randy, no better or worse than any of the rest of us who had dated Suzie. Wolves eviscerate their prey; it's a hard life. Dead's dead, right? And isn't pain the same everywhere?

Suzie has sandy red hair, high cold cheeks, and fury-blue eyes. She is short, no taller than even a short man's shoulders. Suzie's boyfriends have lasted, on average, for three months. No man has ever left her—even the sworn bachelors among us have enjoyed her company. It is always Suzie who goes away from the men first.

When she settled for me, I'm proud to say that we stayed together for five months, longer than she'd ever been with anyone—long enough for people to talk, and to kid her about it.

Our dates were simple. We'd drive up into the snowy mountains, on those mountains that had roads, as far as we could go before the snow stopped us, and gaze at the valley. Or we'd drive into town, sixty miles away on a one-lane, rutted, cliff-hanging road, for dinner and a movie. I could see how there might not have been enough heat and wild romance in it for some of the other men— there'd been talk—but for me it was warm and right while it lasted.

When she left, I did not think I would ever eat or drink again. It felt as if my heart had been torn from my chest, as if my lungs were on fire; every breath burned. I didn't understand why she had to leave. I'd known it would come someday, but still, it caught me by surprise.

Besides being a bowhunter, Randy is a carpenter. He does odd jobs for people in the valley, usually of the sort that requires fixing up old cabins. He keeps his own schedule, and stops work entirely in the fall so he can hunt to his heart's content. He'll roam the valley for days, exploring the wildest places. We all hunt in the fall—grouse, deer, elk, though we leave the moose and bear alone because they are not as common—but none of us is clever or stealthy enough to bowhunt. With a bow, you have to get close to the animal.

Suzie doesn't approve of hunting in any form. "That's what cattle are for," she said one day in the saloon. "Cattle are like city people. Cattle expect, even deserve, what they've got coming. But wild animals are different. Wild animals enjoy life. They live in the woods on purpose. It's cruel to go in after them and kill them. It's cruel."

We all hoo-rahed her and ordered more beers.

She doesn't get angry, exactly. She understands that everyone hunts here, men and women alike. She knows we love animals, but for one or two months out of the year we also love to hunt them.

Randy is so good at what he does it makes us jealous. He can crawl to within   15 thirty yards of an animal when it is feeding, or he can sit so still that it walks right past him. Once shot, the animal runs but a short way—it bleeds to death or dies from trauma. The blood trail is easy to follow, especially in the snow. No one wants it to happen this way, but there's nothing to be done about it; bowhunting is like that. The others of us look at it as being much fairer than hunting with a rifle, because you have to get so close to the animal to get a good shot. Thirty, thirty-five yards, max. Close enough to hear water sloshing in the elk's belly, from where he's just taken a drink from the creek. Close enough to hear the intakes of breath. Close enough to be fair. But Suzie doesn't see it that way. She'll serve Randy his drinks and chat with him, be polite, but her face is blank, her smiles stiff.

Last summer Randy tried to gain Suzie's favor by building her things. Davey, the bartender—the man she was with at the time—didn't really mind. It wasn't as if there were any threat of Randy stealing her away, and besides, Davey liked the objects Randy built her. And, too, it might have added a small bit of white heat to Davey and Suzie's relationship, though I cannot say for sure.

Randy made her a porch swing out of bright larch wood and stained it with tung oil. He gave it to her at the saloon one night after spending a week on it, sanding it and getting it just right. We gathered around and admired it, running our hands over its smoothness. Suzie smiled a little—a polite smile, which was, in a way, worse than if she had looked angry—and said nothing, not even thank you, and she and Davey took it home in the back of Davey's truck.

Randy built her other things too, small things she could fit on her dresser—a little mahogany box for her earrings, of which she had several pairs—and a walking stick with a deer antler for the grip. She said she didn't want the walking stick but would take the earring box.

That summer I lay awake in my cabin some nights and thought about how Suzie was with Davey. I felt vaguely sorry for him, because I knew she would leave him too. I'd lie on my side and look out my bedroom window at the northern lights flashing. The river runs by my cabin, and the strange flashing reflected on the river in a way that made it seem that the light was coming from beneath the water as well. On nights like those, it felt as if my heart would never heal—in fact, I was certain of it. By then I didn't love Suzie anymore—at least I didn't think I did—but I wanted to love someone, and to be loved.

In the evenings, back when we'd been together, Suzie and I would sit on the porch after she got in from work. There was still plenty of daylight left, and we'd watch large herds of deer, their antlers still covered with summer velvet, wade into the cool shadows of the river to bathe, like ladies. They made delicate splashing sounds as they stepped into the current. Water fell from their muzzles when they lifted their heads from drinking. As the sun moved lower, their bodies grew increasingly indistinct, blurring into shadows. Later, Suzie and I would wrap a single blanket about ourselves and nap. When we opened our eyes we would watch for falling stars, and wait until we saw one go ripping across the sky, shot through all the other stars, and once in a great while they came close enough for us to hear the crackle and hiss as they burned. 20

In early July, Randy, whose house sits in a field up at the base of the mountains, began practicing with his bow. Standing in the field at various marked distances—ten, twenty, thirty, forty yards—he shot arrow after arrow at a bull's-eye stapled to bales of hay. It was unusual to drive past then and not see him outside, shirtless, perspiring, his cheeks flushed. He lived by himself and there was probably nothing else to do. The bowhunting season began in late August, months before the shooting season.

It made Suzie furious to see Randy practicing with his bow and arrows. She circulated a petition in the valley to ban bowhunting.

But we would have been out doing the same thing if we'd had the skill, hunting giant elk with bows for the thrill of it, luring them with calls and rattles to our hiding places in the dark woods. Provoked, the bulls would rush in, heads down, their great antlers ripping through the underbrush and knocking against the overhanging limbs of trees.

If only we could have brought them in close. But we weren't good enough to do that.

We couldn't sign the petition. Not even Davey could sign it. 25

"But it's wrong," Suzie said.

"It's personal choice," Davey said. "If you use the meat, and apologize to the spirit right before you do it and right after, if you give thanks, it's all right. It's a man's choice, honey."

If there was one thing Suzie hated, it was that man/woman stuff. She shut her eyes and held them shut as if she were trying to be in some other place. "He's trying to prove something," she said.

"Randy's just doing something he cares about, dear," Davey said.

"He's trying to prove his manhood—to me, to all of us," she said. "He's 30 dangerous."

"No," Davey said, "that's not right. He likes it and hates it both. It fascinates him, is all."

"It's sick," she said. "He's dangerous."

I could see that Suzie and Davey did not have that long to go.

I went bowhunting with Randy once to see how it was done. I saw him shoot an elk, saw the arrow go in behind the bull's shoulder where the heart and lungs are hidden. I saw, too, the way the bull looked around in wild-eyed surprise before galloping off through the timber, seemingly uninjured, running hard. We listened for a long time to the clack-clack of the aluminum arrow banging against the trees.

Randy was wearing camouflage fatigues. He'd painted his face in stripes, like a tiger's. "Now we sit and wait." Randy seemed confident, not shaky at all, though I was. It had looked like a record bull, massive and dark. I had smelled anger from the bull—fury—when the arrow first snapped into his ribs, and when he lunged away. I didn't believe we'd ever see him again. 35

After two hours we got up and began to follow the blood trail. There wasn't much of it at first, just a drop or two in the dry leaves, already turning brown and cracking, drops that I would never have seen had Randy not pointed them out. A quarter of a mile down the hill we began to see more of it, a widening stream of blood, until it seemed that surely all of the bull's blood had drained out. We passed two places where the bull had lain down beneath a tree to die, but had then gotten up and moved on. We found him by the creek a half mile away, down in the shadows, his huge antlers rising into a patch of sun and gleaming. The arrow did not seem large enough to have killed him. The creek made a gentle trickling sound.

We sat down beside the elk and admired him, studied him. Randy, who because of the scent did not smoke during the hunting season, at least not until he had his elk, pulled out a pack of cigarettes, shook one out, and lit it.

"I'm not sure why I do it," he said, reading my mind. "I feel kind of bad about it each time I see one like this, but I keep doing it." He shrugged. I listened to the sound of the creek. "I know it's cruel, but I can't help it, I have to do it," he said.

"What do you think it feels like?" Suzie once asked me at the saloon. "What do you think it feels like to run with an arrow in your heart, knowing you're going to die for it?" She was red-faced, self-righteous.

I told her I didn't know, it was just the way it was. I paid for my drink and left. 40

Late in July, Suzie left Davey, as I'd predicted. It was an amicable separation, and we all had a party down at the saloon to celebrate. An entire deer was roasted in honor of the occasion: Bud Jennings had hit the deer with his truck the night before, coming back from town with supplies. We sat outside in the early evening and ate the steaming meat off paper plates with barbecue sauce and crisp apples from Idaho. The river that dovetailed with the road glinted in the fading light. This was back when Old Terjaney was still alive, and he played his accordion, a sad, sweet sound. We drank beer and told stories.

All this time I'd been uncertain about whether it was right or wrong to hunt if you used the meat and said those prayers. And I'm still not entirely convinced one way or the other. But I have a better picture of what it's like to be the elk or deer. And I understand Suzie a little better too. She was frightened. Fright—sometimes plain fright, even more than terror—is every bit as bad as pain, and maybe worse.

Suzie went home with me that night, after the party.

She had made her rounds of the men in the valley, and now she was choosing to come back to me.

"I've got to go somewhere," she said. "I hate being alone. I can't stand to be 45 alone." She slipped her hand into mine as we walked home. Randy and Davey were still sitting at the picnic table, eating slices of venison. The sun hadn't quite set. Ducks flew down the river.

"I guess that's as close to 'I love you' as I'll get," I said.

"I'm serious," she said, twisting my hand. "You don't understand. It's horrible. I can't stand it. It's not like other people's loneliness. It's worse."

"Why?" I asked.

"No reason," Suzie said. "I'm just scared, jumpy. I can't help it."

"It's okay," I said.   50

We walked down the road like that, holding hands in the dusk. It was about three miles down the gravel road to my cabin. Suzie knew the way. We heard owls as we walked along the river, and saw lots of deer. Once, I thought I heard some wild sound and turned to look back, but I saw nothing, saw no one.

If Randy can have such white-hot passion for bowhunting, he surely can have just as much heat in his hate. It spooks me the way he doesn't bring Suzie presents anymore in the old hopeful way. The flat looks he gives me could mean anything: they unnerve me.

Sometimes I'm afraid to go in the woods, but I go anyway. I hunt, working along a ridge, moving in and out of the shadows between the forest and the meadow, walking this line at dusk and thinking about Suzie, sometimes, instead of hunting. I'll think about how comfortable I am with her—how gratified—if not actually in love. I move slowly through the woods, trying to be as quiet as I can. There are times now when I feel someone or something is just behind me, following at a distance, and I'll turn around, frightened and angry both, and I won't see anything.

The day before Halloween it began to snow, and it didn't stop for our party the following night. The roof over the saloon groaned under its heavy load. But we all managed to get together for the dance anyway, swirling around the room, pausing to drink or arm wrestle, the antlers tied securely on our heads. We pretended to be deer or elk, as we always do on Halloween, and pawed at the wideboard floor with our boots. Davey and Suzie waltzed in widening circles; she seemed so light and free that I couldn't help but grin. Randy sat drinking beer off in a corner. At one point he smiled. It was a polite smile.

The beer ran out at three in the morning, and we started to gather our   55 things. Those of us who had skied down to the saloon tried to find someone to tow us home. Because Randy and I lived up the same road, Davey offered us both a ride, and Suzie took hold of the tow rope with us.

Davey drove slowly through the storm. The snowflakes were as large as goose feathers. We kept our eyes on the brake lights in front of us, with the snow spiraling into our faces, and concentrated on gripping the rope.

Suzie had had a lot to drink, we all had, and she held the rope with both hands, her deer antlers slightly askew. She began asking Randy about his hunting—not razzing him, as I thought she would, but simply questioning him—things she'd been wondering for a long time, I supposed, but had been too angry to ask.

"What's it like?" Suzie kept wanting to know. "I mean, what's it really like?"

We were sliding through the night, holding on to the rope. The snow struck our faces, caking our eyebrows, and it was so cold that it was hard to speak without shivering. "You're too cold-blooded for me," she said when Randy wouldn't answer. "You scare me, mister."

Randy stared straight ahead, his face hard and flat and blank.   60

"Suzie, honey," I started to say. I had no idea what I was going to say after that—something to defend Randy, perhaps—but I stopped, because Randy turned and looked at me, for just a second, with a fury I could feel as well as see, even in my drunkenness. But then the mask, the polite mask, came back down over him, and we continued down the road in silence, the antlers on our heads bobbing and weaving, a fine target for anyone who might not have understood that we weren't wild animals.

Questions about Character

1. There are three main characters in the story: Suzie, Randy, and the narrator. Make a list of the adjectives you might associate with each character. Be prepared to defend your adjective choices by referring to specific examples in the text. Are there any ironies or contradictions in the characters' personalities or behaviors that might help you make a surface/depth argument?

2. What places, or physical settings, do you associate with each of the characters? What objects do you associate with them? How might you make surface/depth arguments out of these associations?

3. Although physical descriptions of the characters are rare, the few that exist have potential insights into the characters' personalities. Can you make any surface/depth arguments based on these descriptions?

Questions about Setting

4. The story begins and ends on Halloween. Think about what Halloween normally represents and then compare and contrast the actions of the valley residents. What arguments can you make about the day on which this story takes place?

5. Although some of the story takes place indoors, indoor settings are rarely described. Re-read the story, paying careful attention to descriptions of both inside and outside settings. Do you see any patterns in these descriptions?

Questions about Point of View

6. The voice in "Antlers" shifts between "I" and "we/us." Why do you think the narrator makes these shifts? Why do you think we never learn the narrator's name?

6

Opposites

As we explained in Chapter 2, literary critics value interpretations that show how a text is complex. One particularly productive strategy for discovering complex interpretations is to look for apparent opposites in a text and show how they share unanticipated characteristics. We see such a use of opposites in the following interpretation of hunting in Rick Bass's short story "Antlers" (which appears at the end of Chapter 5). This interpretation shows us how two opposites—hunter and hunted—are not as neatly opposed as we might first assume:

> Although we typically perceive the hunter as the one in control of the hunt, it is also true that the hunted shapes the hunter. For instance, in Bass's "Antlers," Randy (the bowhunter) is shaped by the elk he hunts. He learns how to be silent and still for hours at a time; he stops smoking during the hunting season; he wears camouflage and paints his face; he spends days training shirtless in the summer sun. These actions all show how the elk direct Randy's movements and behavior. Overall, the elk seem to have a profound influence on Randy's actions over time, while Randy only influences whether a single elk lives or dies. Moreover, because the other people in the valley seem to relate to Randy primarily as a bowhunter, Randy's hunting overshadows his entire life. Thus, rather than illustrating a hunter's mastery over his prey, hunting in "Antlers" also demonstrates how a hunter's identity and actions are shaped by the prey he pursues.

This example passage takes two concepts we usually consider to be opposite of one another—hunter and hunted—and reverses how we think about them. Thus, our example shows a special application of the surface/depth-contrasting strategy: a normal, or standard, way of looking at the hunter/hunted relationship is contrasted with a more complex one that shows how the prey controls the hunter as much as (if not more than) the hunter controls the prey.

Interpretations that break down opposites are particularly valued in literary studies because they make us not only see the text differently—but they can also influence how we see the world. For instance, the figure below challenges our typical understanding of the words *true* and *false* by suggesting that truth can be contained within falsehood. While it is not always possible to make an argument about opposites in a text, searching for such arguments is usually productive because this search almost inevitably leads to other insights that can help you find a complex argument about a text. In this chapter, we discuss how looking for opposites is a productive way to discover previously unnoticed patterns in a text and to brainstorm surface/depth arguments. ■

Reproduced with the permission of Scott Kim.

OPPOSITES *VS.* IRONY

You may have noticed that the opposites strategy bears some similarities to the discussion of irony in Chapter 5. Irony occurs when two states (e.g., ideal/actual;

expectation/reality) or two meanings (literal/underlying) are in tension. In this sense, the tension between predator and prey in the previous example is ironic because we *expect* the predator to be in control, but *in actuality*, we see the prey shaping the predator. This tension between expected and actual states is ironic.

However, this example moves beyond exposing and analyzing an ironic tension to reversing, or subverting, how we see concepts. It suggests that the prey dominates the predator. Thus, where irony exposes tensions, the opposites strategy breaks these tensions down and changes how we see the concepts involved. While many opposites arguments will begin by noting an ironic tension, the opposites strategy goes further, producing a more complex argument that changes how we perceive the world.

USING OPPOSITES TO BRAINSTORM

To use the opposites strategy, look for concepts, ideas, patterns, characters, or settings that appear to be in tension. Common opposites, or tensions, you might look for include:

life/death	inside/outside
natural/unnatural or human-made	youth/age
male/female	love/hate
strong/weak	truth/deception
self/other	West/East

This list is by no means exhaustive. Any **binary opposition**—or pair of related terms or concepts that are opposite in meaning—can provide a productive starting place for looking for complex arguments about a text.

In Western culture, most binary oppositions have a hierarchy, or order, where one of the two terms is perceived as superior to the other. Thus, natural is perceived as superior to unnatural; truth is superior to deception; youth is superior to age. Most arguments with the opposites strategy complicate these hierarchies—for instance, by showing that the idea of "natural" is a human-made (and thus unnatural) concept or that apparent weakness is sometimes a sign of true strength.

Because we tend to organize our world and value systems by oppositions, things we identify as opposite often have more similarities than they have differences. Noting the similarities that persist or prevail in the face of difference often helps us discover complex arguments. Moreover, looking at what something *is not* is often a good way to define more precisely what it *is*. Thus, examining opposites often leads us to fresh observations that can be used to develop new patterns and surface/depth arguments.

To see how this works, consider again Rick Bass's short story "Antlers," which seems to highlight the tension between opposites. We see one such set of oppositions in the characters of Suzie and Randy. Most readers will immediately identify these two characters as having different value systems and different ways of approaching the world.

To better explore the tensions between Suzie and Randy—and to discover what these tensions might mean—it is helpful to make a list of their similarities and differences like the one below:

COMPARISON AND CONTRAST OF SUZIE AND RANDY

Suzie	Randy
Female	Male
Protects animals	*Hunts animals*
Inside (works in bar)	Outside (*hunting elk*—but also makes household items for Suzie)
Compassionate (*except toward Randy*)	*Cruel* (but has sympathy for elk)
Rejects Randy	Tries to woo Suzie; makes things for her
Talks (most talkative character)	Usually silent
Fearful	Dangerous
Acts out of principle?	Acts on instinct?
Hurts Randy; hurts narrator (hurts other men?)	*Hurts elk*

Underlined items suggest compassion and italicized items suggest cruelty.

This list catalogs some of the major differences between Suzie and Randy. However, there are also some interesting similarities. Both Suzie and Randy have characteristics that suggest both cruelty and compassion. To highlight these traits, we have underlined items on the list that suggest compassion and italicized items that suggest cruelty.

We can see from this list that Suzie seems to be compassionate and protective toward animals, but her behavior toward the men in the valley, especially toward Randy, could be described as coldhearted. Similarly, at first glance, Randy seems to be cruel and predatory, but his sympathy for the elk that he kills and his attempts to win Suzie's affection suggest a softer side. At the very least, Randy seems to incite the sympathy of most readers, even if Suzie remains unmoved by his desires. The interconnected relationship between compassion and cruelty in this story suggests a tension that requires additional interpretation.

To dig further into this relationship, we might explore additional tensions within these characters. For instance, we can interpret some aspects of Randy's character as animalistic and others as human. Such a list of the different sides of Randy's nature might look like this:

Animal trait	Human trait
Hunts deer	Uses bow
Explores "wildest" places	Fixes up cabins
Pursues Suzie?	Pursues Suzie?
Goes shirtless in summer	Wears "polite mask," "polite smile"
Wears tiger paint and camouflage	Makes swing, earring box, walking stick
Stops smoking during hunting season	
Doesn't know why he does it (instinct)	Feels guilt; feels "bad about it"
Primitive anger & fury (like elk's anger)	Wears antlers (celebrates Halloween)
Wears antlers	

Comparison and contrast of Randy's animal and human characteristics.

We might notice from this list how many of Randy's human characteristics seem to be inspired by Suzie. He makes gifts he thinks she will appreciate; he mimics Suzie's "polite smile" and "flat looks"; he seems to internalize her compassion for the deer. This further reinforces the argument that Randy and Suzie, although at first seeming to be opposites, share many characteristics. Critics will dig into this apparent contradiction in order to reveal increasingly complex interpretations of this text.

The opposites strategy will not always lead you to a complex argument, but it is almost always a good strategy for getting yourself to look more closely at a text and notice patterns and surface/depth interpretations you may have missed on an initial reading.

Exercises

1. Are there other opposites you might explore in "Antlers"? Try to make a list like the ones above comparing and contrasting these opposites. Do your lists help you note any new surface/depth interpretations of the text that are not discussed above?

2. Revisit "The Man to Send Rain Clouds" (p. 29) and make a list noting similarities and differences between Teofilo and Father Paul. See if you can use your list to generate new interpretations of the story.

USING OPPOSITES TO WRITE PERSUASIVELY

When critics use the opposites strategy, their arguments usually have several steps:

1. They note opposites at tension in a text—often through a surface/depth-contrasting argument.

2. They provide textual evidence that elaborates on these tensions.

3. They explain how the text subverts, or overthrows, our normal way of looking at these opposites.

See if you can identify these three moves in the following example:

> Although Suzie feels intense compassion for wild animals, her compassion contains elements of cruelty. We see this cruelty when Suzie argues for a petition to ban bowhunting by saying, "Cattle are like city people. Cattle expect, even deserve, what they've got coming. But wild animals are different. Wild animals enjoy life. They live in the woods on purpose. It's cruel to go in after them and kill them" (113). Although Suzie is sympathizing with, and trying to protect, wild animals, her statements about cattle and city people are anything but compassionate. Suzie implies that cattle (and city people) are less valuable than wild animals and deserve death. We also see Suzie's cruelty in her treatment of Randy. Again, because she has such strong sympathy for hunted animals, Suzie rejects Randy, even refusing to thank him for the beautiful, handmade gifts he brings her. This treatment shows contempt for Randy's feelings and desires. Suzie seems to want to cause Randy an emotional pain that hurts as much as the physical pain he inflicts on the elk. Thus, Suzie's compassion paradoxically makes her cruel.

This example begins by noting a contradiction in the text—that Suzie is both compassionate and cruel. This tension is then supported by both a quotation and a paraphrase that show how Suzie's words and actions cause cruelty even as she attempts to demonstrate compassion. The paragraph then ends by suggesting that, for Suzie, compassion causes cruelty, which is clearly different from our normal way of looking at these opposites.

Note that this example ends by calling Suzie's actions paradoxical. A **paradoxical statement** is an assertion that seems to be self-contradictory, yet on closer inspection, also appears to contain a truth. Such statements often startle us because they appear to defy logic (how can two things that are opposite really be the same?) while also revealing some profound truth.

An example of a paradoxical statement can be seen in the following quote attributed to Mother Teresa:

> I have found the paradox, that if you love until it hurts, there can be no more hurt, only more love.

Mother Teresa's assertion initially seems contradictory since she describes love as both causing and conquering pain. However, most people recognize a truth to this statement. It is possible to see love as both a cause of pain and a resource for overcoming pain. Thus, love makes us vulnerable and strong at the same time. Likewise, our previous example points out a paradox: Suzie's compassion is both protective and aggressive. Although this observation seems contradictory, we can also see how the impulse to protect the weak can lead us to hurt those we perceive as strong.

Paradoxes call our attention to competing value systems, showing us how neither set of values is absolute. For instance, Mother Teresa's assertion calls into question our tendency to see self-sacrifice and self-preservation as at odds. Our example likewise shows us how a value we perceive as positive (protecting the weak) can be a negative.

Paradoxes are particularly valued in literary analysis because they can help us move from analyzing a text to analyzing our culture or society. They make us challenge how we see the world and cause us to reflect more deeply on our values. Another way of saying this is that paradoxes enable us to argue for the **social relevance** of our analyses. Social relevance is the assumption that life and literature are connected and that, regardless of when it was written, literature can help us understand our contemporary social situation. We will talk about social relevance as its own strategy of literary analysis in Chapter 9. For the time being, it is sufficient that you see how paradoxes can make us reflect on our world.

COMMON WORDS AND PHRASES ASSOCIATED WITH CONTEXT		
although	contrasting	rooted in the same ___
appears opposed	ironically	two facets of the same ___
at first seems opposed	paradoxically	while

Exercise

Read the passage on page 129 and identify the three steps of an opposites argument: (1) note opposites at tension; (2) provide textual evidence elaborating on these tensions; (3) explain how the text subverts our normal way of looking at these opposites.

Throughout "Antlers" Suzie draws sharp distinctions between ideals such as wild/tame, cruel/compassionate, and predator/prey. Ironically, however, many of Suzie's actions seem bent on erasing the distinctions she fights so hard to maintain. As a case in point, the primary difference between cattle and the wild animals Suzie admires is that cattle are protected, domestic animals while deer and other wild animals live independently of humans. Yet, by trying to pass a law that would protect deer from their natural predators (humans), Suzie is erasing one of the primary distinctions between wild animals that she believes "live in the woods on purpose" and domestic ones that "expect, even deserve, what they've got coming" (113). Like cattle, Suzie's petition would make deer dependent on human institutions for life and death. Thus, her desire to protect wild animals paradoxically risks turning them into the human-dependent, domestic animals she despises.

Review

The opposites strategy involves noting opposites, or apparent contradictions, in a text and upending our normal way of seeing those contradictions. As with the surface/depth-contrasting strategy, a surface interpretation is replaced with a deeper, more complex one.

Opposites may be a difficult strategy to use effectively, but it can lead to some very interesting and nonobvious interpretations. If you notice two opposites in a text that appear connected in some way, you should brainstorm possible ways this observation could be relevant to understanding the meaning of the text. Discussing your insight with your instructor and classmates can be a good way to develop this observation into a complex interpretation.

∾ NOW PRACTICE ON YOUR OWN: EVERYDAY USE

On page 131 we reprint "Everyday Use," a short story by Alice Walker, an African American author and activist. After you have read the story, respond to our questions focusing on the opposites strategy.

1. What values does "Everyday Use" challenge, question, or affirm? You may want to list the values under the appropriate categories of "challenge," "question," and "affirm."

2. Next, identify some opposites that seem to be in tension in the story. Make a list, such as the one on page 124, comparing and contrasting these opposites. Some good options include:

   ‣ Mama *vs*. Dee
   ‣ cultural heritage *vs*. familial heritage
   ‣ lived heritage *vs*. learned heritage
   ‣ oppressor *vs*. oppressed

   Make detailed lists for at least two sets of opposites (you can select from the options above or use opposites that you noted on your own). A good list will note *similarities* as well as *differences*. Be prepared to share your lists with your classmates.

3. Review your lists, noting any surprising similarities in things that at first glance appear to be opposed—or surprising differences in things you assumed were similar. Use your observations to write a paragraph about "Everyday Use" using the opposites strategy.

Alice Walker

Everyday Use   1973

For your Grandmama

I WILL wait for her in the yard that Maggie and I made so clean and wavy yesterday afternoon. A yard like this is more comfortable than most people know. It is not just a yard. It is like an extended living room. When the hard clay is swept clean as a floor and the fine sand around the edges lined with tiny, irregular grooves, anyone can come and sit and look up into the elm tree and wait for the breezes that never come inside the house.

Maggie will be nervous until after her sister goes: she will stand hopelessly in corners, homely and ashamed of the burn scars down her arms and legs, eying her sister with a mixture of envy and awe. She thinks her sister has held life always in the palm of one hand, that "no" is a word the world never learned to say to her.

You've no doubt seen those TV shows where the child who has "made it" is confronted, as a surprise, by her own mother and father, tottering in weakly from backstage. (A pleasant surprise, of course: What would they do if parent and child came on the show only to curse out and insult each other?) On TV mother and child embrace and smile into each other's faces. Sometimes the mother and father weep, the child wraps them in her arms and leans across the table to tell how she would not have made it without their help. I have seen these programs.

Sometimes I dream a dream in which Dee and I are suddenly brought together on a TV program of this sort. Out of a dark and soft-seated limousine

I am ushered into a bright room filled with many people. There I meet a smiling, gray, sporty man like Johnny Carson who shakes my hand and tells me what a fine girl I have. Then we are on the stage and Dee is embracing me with tears in her eyes. She pins on my dress a large orchid, even though she has told me once that she thinks orchids are tacky flowers.

In real life I am a large, big-boned woman with rough, man-working hands. 5 In the winter I wear flannel nightgowns to bed and overalls during the day. I can kill and clean a hog as mercilessly as a man. My fat keeps me hot in zero weather. I can work outside all day, breaking ice to get water for washing; I can eat pork liver cooked over the open fire minutes after it comes steaming from the hog. One winter I knocked a bull calf straight in the brain between the eyes with a sledge hammer and had the meat hung up to chill before nightfall. But of course all this does not show on television. I am the way my daughter would want me to be: a hundred pounds lighter, my skin like an uncooked barley pancake. My hair glistens in the hot bright lights. Johnny Carson has much to do to keep up with my quick and witty tongue.

But that is a mistake. I know even before I wake up. Who ever knew a Johnson with a quick tongue? Who can even imagine me looking a strange white man in the eye? It seems to me I have talked to them always with one foot raised in flight, with my head turned in whichever way is farthest from them. Dee, though. She would always look anyone in the eye. Hesitation was no part of her nature.

"How do I look, Mama?" Maggie says, showing just enough of her thin body enveloped in a pink skirt and red blouse for me to know she's there, almost hidden by the door.

"Come out into the yard," I say.

Have you ever seen a lame animal, perhaps a dog run over by some careless person rich enough to own a car, sidle up to someone who is ignorant enough to be kind to him? That is the way my Maggie walks. She has been like this, chin on chest, eyes on ground, feet in shuffle, ever since the fire that burned the other house to the ground.

Dee is lighter than Maggie, with nicer hair and a fuller figure. She's a wom- 10 an now, though sometimes I forget. How long ago was it that the other house burned? Ten, twelve years? Sometimes I can still hear the flames and feel Maggie's arms sticking to me, her hair smoking and her dress falling off her in little black papery flakes. Her eyes seemed stretched open, blazed open by the flames reflected in them. And Dee. I see her standing off under the sweet gum tree she used to dig gum out of; a look of concentration on her face as she watched the last dingy gray board of the house fall in toward the red-hot brick chimney. Why don't you do a dance around the ashes? I'd wanted to ask her. She had hated the house that much.

I used to think she hated Maggie, too. But that was before we raised money, the church and me, to send her to Augusta to school. She used to read to us without pity; forcing words, lies, other folks' habits, whole lives upon us two, sitting trapped and ignorant underneath her voice. She washed us in a river of make-believe, burned us with a lot of knowledge we didn't necessarily need to know. Pressed us to her with the serious way she read, to shove us away at just the moment, like dimwits, we seemed about to understand.

Dee wanted nice things. A yellow organdy dress to wear to her graduation from high school; black pumps to match a green suit she'd made from an old suit somebody gave me. She was determined to stare down any disaster in her efforts. Her eyelids would not flicker for minutes at a time. Often I fought off the temptation to shake her. At sixteen she had a style of her own: and knew what style was.

I never had an education myself. After second grade the school was closed down. Don't ask me why: in 1927 colored asked fewer questions than they do now. Sometimes Maggie reads to me. She stumbles along good-naturedly but can't see well. She knows she is not bright. Like good looks and money, quickness passed her by. She will marry John Thomas (who has mossy teeth in an earnest face) and then I'll be free to sit here and I guess just sing church songs to myself. Although I never was a good singer. Never could carry a tune. I was always better at a man's job. I used to love to milk till I was hooked in the side in '49. Cows are soothing and slow and don't bother you, unless you try to milk them the wrong way.

I have deliberately turned my back on the house. It is three rooms, just like the one that burned, except the roof is tin; they don't make shingle roofs any more. There are no real windows, just some holes cut in the sides, like the portholes in a ship, but not round and not square, with rawhide holding the shutters up on the outside. This house is in a pasture, too, like the other one. No doubt when Dee sees it she will want to tear it down. She wrote me once that no matter where we "choose" to live, she will manage to come see us. But she will never bring her friends. Maggie and I thought about this and Maggie asked me, "Mama, when did Dee ever *have* any friends?"

She had a few. Furtive boys in pink shirts hanging about on washday after   15 school. Nervous girls who never laughed. Impressed with her they worshiped the well-turned phrase, the cute shape, the scalding humor that erupted like bubbles in lye. She read to them.

When she was courting Jimmy T she didn't have much time to pay to us, but turned all her faultfinding power on him. He *flew* to marry a cheap city girl from a family of ignorant flashy people. She hardly had time to recompose herself.

When she comes I will meet—but there they are!

Maggie attempts to make a dash for the house, in her shuffling way, but I stay her with my hand. "Come back here," I say. And she stops and tries to dig a well in the sand with her toe.

It is hard to see them clearly through the strong sun. But even the first glimpse of leg out of the car tells me it is Dee. Her feet were always neat-looking, as if God himself had shaped them with a certain style. From the other side of the car comes a short, stocky man. Hair is all over his head a foot long and hanging from his chin like a kinky mule tail. I hear Maggie suck in her breath. "Uhnnnh," is what it sounds like. Like when you see the wriggling end of a snake just in front of your foot on the road. "Uhnnnh."

Dee next. A dress down to the ground, in this hot weather. A dress so 20 loud it hurts my eyes. There are yellows and oranges enough to throw back the light of the sun. I feel my whole face warming from the heat waves it throws out. Earrings gold, too, and hanging down to her shoulders. Bracelets dangling and making noises when she moves her arm up to shake the folds of the dress out of her armpits. The dress is loose and flows, and as she walks closer, I like it. I hear Maggie go "Uhnnnh" again. It is her sister's hair. It stands straight up like the wool on a sheep. It is black as night and around the edges are two long pigtails that rope about like small lizards disappearing behind her ears.

"Wa-su-zo-Tean-o!" she says, coming on in that gliding way the dress makes her move. The short stocky fellow with the hair to his navel is all grinning and he follows up with "Asalamalakim, my mother and sister!" He moves to hug Maggie but she falls back, right up against the back of my chair. I feel her trembling there and when I look up I see the perspiration falling off her chin.

"Don't get up," says Dee. Since I am stout it takes something of a push. You can see me trying to move a second or two before I make it. She turns, showing white heels through her sandals, and goes back to the car. Out she peeks next with a Polaroid. She stoops down quickly and lines up picture after picture of me sitting there in front of the house with Maggie cowering behind me. She never takes a shot without making sure the house is included. When a cow comes nibbling around the edge of the yard she snaps it and me and Maggie and the house. Then she puts the Polaroid in the back seat of the car, and comes up and kisses me on the forehead.

Meanwhile Asalamalakim is going through motions with Maggie's hand. Maggie's hand is as limp as a fish, and probably as cold, despite the sweat, and she keeps trying to pull it back. It looks like Asalamalakim wants to shake hands but wants to do it fancy. Or maybe he don't know how people shake hands. Anyhow, he soon gives up on Maggie.

"Well," I say. "Dee."

"No, Mama," she says. "Not 'Dee,' Wangero Leewanika Kemanjo!"   25

"What happened to 'Dee'?" I wanted to know.

"She's dead," Wangero said. "I couldn't bear it any longer, being named after the people who oppress me."

"You know as well as me you was named after your aunt Dicie," I said. Dicie is my sister. She named Dee. We called her "Big Dee" after Dee was born.

"But who was she named after?" asked Wangero.

"I guess after Grandma Dee," I said.   30

"And who was she named after?" asked Wangero.

"Her mother," I said, and saw Wangero was getting tired. "That's about as far back as I can trace it," I said. Though, in fact, I probably could have carried it back beyond the Civil War through the branches.

"Well," said Asalamalakim, "there you are."

"Uhnnnh," I heard Maggie say.

"There I was not," I said, "before 'Dicie' cropped up in our family, so why   35 should I try to trace it that far back?"

He just stood there grinning, looking down on me like somebody inspecting a Model A car. Every once in a while he and Wangero sent eye signals over my head.

"How do you pronounce this name?" I asked.

"You don't have to call me by it if you don't want to," said Wangero.

"Why shouldn't I?" I asked. "If that's what you want us to call you, we'll call you."

"I know it might sound awkward at first," said Wangero.   40

"I'll get used to it," I said. "Ream it out again."

Well, soon we got the name out of the way. Asalamalakim had a name twice as long and three times as hard. After I tripped over it two or three times he told me to just call him Hakim-a-barber. I wanted to ask him was he a barber, but I didn't really think he was, so I didn't ask.

"You must belong to those beef-cattle peoples down the road," I said. They said "Asalamalakim" when they met you, too, but they didn't shake hands. Always too busy: feeding the cattle, fixing the fences, putting up salt-lick shelters, throwing down hay. When the white folks poisoned some of the herd the men stayed up all night with rifles in their hands. I walked a mile and a half just to see the sight.

Hakim-a-barber said, "I accept some of their doctrines, but farming and raising cattle is not my style." (They didn't tell me, and I didn't ask, whether Wangero [Dee] had really gone and married him.)

We sat down to eat and right away he said he didn't eat collards and pork was unclean. Wangero, though, went on through the chitlins and corn bread, the greens and everything else. She talked a blue streak over the sweet potatoes. Everything delighted her. Even the fact that we still used the benches her daddy made for the table when we couldn't afford to buy chairs. 45

"Oh, Mama!" she cried. Then turned to Hakim-a-barber. "I never knew how lovely these benches are. You can feel the rump prints," she said, running her hands underneath her and along the bench. Then she gave a sigh and her hand closed over Grandma Dee's butter dish. "That's it!" she said. "I knew there was something I wanted to ask you if I could have." She jumped up from the table and went over in the corner where the churn stood, the milk in it clabber by now. She looked at the churn and looked at it.

"This churn top is what I need," she said. "Didn't Uncle Buddy whittle it out of a tree you all used to have?"

"Yes," I said.

"Un huh," she said happily. "And I want the dasher, too."

"Uncle Buddy whittle that, too?" asked the barber. 50

Dee (Wangero) looked up at me.

"Aunt Dee's first husband whittled the dash," said Maggie so low you almost couldn't hear her. "His name was Henry, but they called him Stash."

"Maggie's brain is like an elephant's," Wangero said, laughing. "I can use the churn top as a centerpiece for the alcove table," she said, sliding a plate over the churn, "and I'll think of something artistic to do with the dasher."

When she finished wrapping the dasher the handle stuck out. I took it for a moment in my hands. You didn't even have to look close to see where hands pushing the dasher up and down to make butter had left a kind of sink in the wood. In fact, there were a lot of small sinks; you could see where thumbs and fingers had sunk into the wood. It was beautiful light yellow wood, from a tree that grew in the yard where Big Dee and Stash had lived.

After dinner Dee (Wangero) went to the trunk at the foot of my bed and   55
started rifling through it. Maggie hung back in the kitchen over the dishpan. Out came Wangero with two quilts. They had been pieced by Grandma Dee and then Big Dee and me had hung them on the quilt frames on the front porch and quilted them. One was in the Lone Star pattern. The other was Walk Around the Mountain. In both of them were scraps of dresses Grandma Dee had worn fifty and more years ago. Bits and pieces of Grandpa Jarrell's Paisley shirts. And one teeny faded blue piece, about the size of a penny matchbox, that was from Great Grandpa Ezra's uniform that he wore in the Civil War.

"Mama," Wangero said sweet as a bird. "Can I have these old quilts?"

I heard something fall in the kitchen, and a minute later the kitchen door slammed.

"Why don't you take one or two of the others?" I asked. "These old things was just done by me and Big Dee from some tops your grandma pieced before she died."

"No," said Wangero. "I don't want those. They are stitched around the borders by machine."

"That'll make them last better," I said.   60

"That's not the point," said Wangero. "These are all pieces of dresses Grandma used to wear. She did all this stitching by hand. Imagine!" She held the quilts securely in her arms, stroking them.

"Some of the pieces, like those lavender ones, come from old clothes her mother handed down to her," I said, moving up to touch the quilts. Dee (Wangero) moved back just enough so that I couldn't reach the quilts. They already belonged to her.

"Imagine!" she breathed again, clutching them closely to her bosom.

"The truth is," I said, "I promised to give them quilts to Maggie, for when she marries John Thomas."

She gasped like a bee had stung her.   65

"Maggie can't appreciate these quilts!" she said. "She'd probably be backward enough to put them to everyday use."

"I reckon she would," I said. "God knows I been saving 'em for long enough with nobody using 'em. I hope she will!" I didn't want to bring up how I had offered Dee (Wangero) a quilt when she went away to college. Then she had told me they were old-fashioned, out of style.

"But they're *priceless*!" she was saying now, furiously; for she has a temper. "Maggie would put them on the bed and in five years they'd be in rags. Less than that!"

"She can always make some more," I said. "Maggie knows how to quilt."

Dee (Wangero) looked at me with hatred. "You just will not understand. 70 The point is these quilts, *these* quilts!"

"Well," I said, stumped. "What would *you* do with them?"

"Hang them," she said. As if that was the only thing you *could* do with quilts.

Maggie by now was standing in the door. I could almost hear the sound her feet made as they scraped over each other.

"She can have them, Mama," she said, like somebody used to never winning anything, or having anything reserved for her. "I can 'member Grandma Dee without the quilts."

I looked at her hard. She had filled her bottom lip with checkerberry snuff 75 and it gave her face a kind of dopey, hangdog look. It was Grandma Dee and Big Dee who taught her how to quilt herself. She stood there with her scarred hands hidden in the folds of her skirt. She looked at her sister with something like fear but she wasn't mad at her. This was Maggie's portion. This was the way she knew God to work.

When I looked at her like that something hit me in the top of my head and ran down to the soles of my feet. Just like when I'm in church and the spirit of God touches me and I get happy and shout. I did something I never done before: hugged Maggie to me, then dragged her on into the room, snatched the quilts out of Miss Wangero's hands and dumped them into Maggie's lap. Maggie just sat there on my bed with her mouth open.

"Take one or two of the others," I said to Dee.

But she turned without a word and went out to Hakim-a-barber.

"You just don't understand," she said. as Maggie and I came out to the car.

"What don't I understand?" I wanted to know. 80

"Your heritage," she said. And then she turned to Maggie, kissed her, and said, "You ought to try to make something of yourself, too, Maggie. It's really a new day for us. But from the way you and Mama still live you'd never know it."

She put on some sunglasses that hid everything above the tip of her nose and chin.

Maggie smiled; maybe at the sunglasses. But a real smile, not scared. After we watched the car dust settle I asked Maggie to bring me a dip of snuff. And then the two of us sat there just enjoying, until it was time to go in the house and go to bed.

part 3 »

STRATEGIES FOR GOING BEYOND THE TEXT

part 3 » **STRATEGIES FOR GOING BEYOND THE TEXT**

7 Context

So far, this textbook has focused on interpretive strategies that are sometimes referred to as close reading strategies. A close reading interprets a text through careful, close attention to the text's details—each word on the page and aspect of a text such as those reviewed in Chapter 5. In the next several chapters, we will focus on strategies that take literary critics' and their readers' attention beyond the text at hand while still contributing to the ultimate goal of interpreting that text.

Context goes beyond close reading by bringing in cultural and historical information external to the text to support, deepen, or discover a new interpretation of the text. The context strategy may involve looking up references to events, people, or other works mentioned in a text to create surface/depth arguments about their meaning. The context strategy may also involve researching the social and cultural context in which a text was written to learn how its original audience may have understood it.

Texts that were written further away from us both in terms of history and geography may understandably benefit from use of the context strategy to understand their layers of meaning. Because language and culture change over time, meanings potent to a text's original audience or to its author may become obscure and difficult for us to see readily in the text. For instance, we know cultural norms of dress have changed greatly over human history; as a result, a reference to a character's clothing that would have carried significant information to a contemporary audience may today simply present an unfamiliar word.

However, interpretations of texts written closer to us can still benefit from application of this strategy. Though written in your own country and time, a text may refer to the customs or slang of a subculture you are an outsider to, and you could find yourself just as estranged or confused as you are with a text from centuries ago.

Thus, the context strategy requires using external help. In order to use context effectively, you need to bring in information about a particular time period, culture, or reference in the text. You can get this information from class discussion or from doing your own research, but in either case you should seek to bring in information that can help you deepen your interpretations and support more complex surface/depth arguments.

The example below illustrates use of the context strategy.

> Alice Walker uses her short story "Everyday Use" to criticize African-Americans who shed their unique heritage in favor of a misguided Africanism. This is most clearly seen in the character of Dee who has changed her name to Wangero Leewanika Kemanjo, a name that at first seems to be authentically African. However, as Helga Hoel shows, all three names are misspellings of traditional African names. Moreover, the middle name derives from a completely different African ethnic tribe than the first and last name's. It seems that Walker is trying to portray Dee as confused and as having only a superficial knowledge of African culture in order to ridicule African-Americans who reject their slave heritage in favor of some sort of romantically idealized African legacy.

The previous example brings in outside contextual information about the name of a central character in the short story "Everyday Use." This contextual information helps support the writer's argument that Alice Walker is criticizing African-Americans who have rejected their unique culture by

---

[1] The Works Cited page from which this example is drawn includes the following entries: Hoel, Helga. "Personal Names and Heritages: Alice Walker's 'Everyday Use.'" *American Studies in Scandinavia* 31.1 (1999): n. pag. Web. 28 Feb. 2010; Walker, Alice. "Everyday Use." *Digging into Literature: Strategies for Reading, Analysis, and Writing.* Joanna Wolfe and Laura Wilder. Boston: Bedford/St. Martin's, 2016. 131–40. Print.

showing how the central character is misguided and superficial in her choice to adopt an African name. The contextual information in this passage is clearly linked to a surface/depth argument that shows how the text is complex because even the names of the characters are related to the story's meaning. ■

COMMON TYPES OF CONTEXTUAL INFORMATION

Persuasive uses of context bring in external information to support a surface/depth claim. Common types of contextual information that might be brought in for this purpose include information about:

- **the historical period or culture in which the text was written:** information about the civil rights movement might be used to help us interpret Walker's "Everyday Use," while information about the Laguna in New Mexico and their cultural traditions might help us make more complex arguments about the cultural tensions underlying Leslie Marmon Silko's "The Man to Send Rain Clouds."

- **cultural references within a text:** the example on page 144 uses information about African cultures to make an argument about Dee's character in "Everyday Use." Information about a famous event, person, or place mentioned in a text (even if only briefly) might help us elaborate on a surface/depth argument. For instance, a critic studying "The Man to Send Rain Clouds" might want to research the Symbol of the Lamb carved on the monastery door.

- **the historical meaning of particular words used in a text:** words change meanings over time. For instance, most people today if asked to define the word *nice* would respond with something like "kind," "agreeable," "pleasant," or "good-natured." However, this positive association with the word *nice* only began to appear in the later eighteenth century, even though the word has been around far longer than that. Prior to the eighteenth century, one of the most common meanings of the word was "foolish, silly, simple; ignorant," a meaning that is now obsolete (has fallen out of usage). Thus, a critic analyzing a Shakespearean play might look up information about what the word *nice* meant in Shakespeare's time (in addition to foolish, it could also mean wanton, or lustful) and use this information to make an argument about the text. We provide more information later in the chapter about how to look up words in the *Oxford English Dictionary* (*OED*) to discover their histories and etymologies and to identify what these words meant to authors and readers from a particular historical time period.

▸ **other texts mentioned or alluded to in the work:** whenever an author shows a character reading a particular book or seeing a specific movie or play, casually mentions what is on a character's bookshelf, refers to a particular piece of music, or describes events in such a way that a reference (or **allusion**) to another text becomes apparent, this information may be useful in unlocking further meaning in the text. Thus, information from *Grimm's Fairy Tales* might be brought in to help us better understand Louise Glück's "Gretel in Darkness." In the film *Fatal Attraction*, a character repeatedly plays a recording of *Madame Butterfly* in her apartment; researching the plot of this opera can help us interpret events in the film.

▸ **other writings by the same author or his/her contemporaries— including other literary works, philosophical writings, and/or personal correspondence:** for instance, information from Rick Bass's other short stories, also set in the Rocky Mountains, might be used as contextual evidence to support the argument that "Antlers" is concerned with a uniquely American way of understanding the frontier. Quotes and insights from Alice Walker's famous essay "In Search of Our Mothers' Gardens," which describes the role of the black female artist in the American South, can be used as evidence for interpreting "Everyday Use."

Occasionally, critics will also bring in biographical information about an author to help support an argument. For instance, the example above might be strengthened with information that Alice Walker did indeed visit Africa on many occasions and made it a point to study the cultures she encountered there. This biographical information lends support to the claim that Wangero's name is deliberately misspelled and that the various parts of her name come from different tribal traditions.

However, we recommend you use biographical information sparingly in your analyses. Overly relying on biographical information can lead you to make causal arguments (see Chapter 2) about how events in an author's life caused him or her to write a particular text, distracting you from your goal of arguing for an interpretation of the text's meaning. Moreover, by focusing on biographical information you run the risk of producing overly reductive inter-pretations that see only one level of meaning in a text: the autobiographical. We call this potentially reductive because interpreting a text as being simply and only a thin mask for the author's life denies the possibility of other layers of meaning coexisting in the text, which runs counter to the usual goals of literary analysis.

USING CONTEXT TO BRAINSTORM

Because using the context strategy involves making connections to knowledge drawn from history, anthropology, or biography, it often appears in literary scholars' reading and brainstorming practices as notes to themselves to look something up or research something later. An unusual word or a familiar word used in an unexpected way may prompt a literary critic to consult the *Oxford English Dictionary*, a dictionary unique in the way it traces the development of the meanings of words over time, or a critic may make a note in the mar-gin of a text to re-read another text to which she thinks she spots an allusion. Obviously not all these things can be done at once, so the "behind-the-scenes" work of using this strategy may actually involve several hours of research and reading of other texts.

In the excerpt that follows from the transcript of a professor thinking aloud while reading "The Man to Send Rain Clouds," we see the professor using the context strategy to ask questions about the story.[2] As she reads, she wonders

---

[2] For an explanation of the "think-aloud" technique for observing a reader's and writer's thinking pro-cesses, see Chapter 3, p. 43.

about the significance of items such as cottonwood trees and Levi's clothing and makes plans to research this information. She also wonders about the significance of ritual in Laguna culture, something else she plans to research.

TRANSCRIPT EXCERPT
Professor thinking aloud while reading "The Man to Send Rain Clouds"
Italicized words indicate the professor reading directly from the text.

> OK. So let's go back to the story. *They found him under a big cottonwood tree.* I'm thinking, is there significance to cottonwood in Laguna culture? I don't know. I'd have to look that up. *His Levi jacket and pants were faded light blue so that he had been easy to find.* So this suggests an incorporation into a greater American system, although that's going to be tinged with the ethnic resonance of the name of Levi's. Which I've also never looked into, and that might be interesting. Anyway. [. . .]
>
> *"Send us rain clouds, Grandfather." They laid the bundle in the back of the pickup and covered it with a heavy tarp before they started back to the pueblo.* Again, I would be tempted to go look up some ethnographic research, to see if the Laguna often appeal to the dead to send rain, and the significance of doing so.

Note that this professor is not looking up information just for the sake of including factual details: she is doing so in order to create surface/depth arguments. For instance, she already has some surface/depth arguments in mind about the significance of Levi's in American culture. In other cases, her research might lead her to discover that cottonwood trees are a sign of water (because they grow near permanent sources of water) in New Mexican deserts and that the word *laguna* means "lake" or "pond" in Spanish. This information could then lead the professor to use the patterns strategy to look more carefully at other references to water in the text (and in the context of Laguna culture) and create a surface/depth argument about the significance of water in the story.

FINDING CONTEXTUAL INFORMATION

Researching to find potentially useful contextual information requires some imagination and curiosity and a willingness to play detective by following up on hunches and leads—as well as a willingness to abandon those that don't pan out. Your first instinct when researching the context of a literary text may be to use the title and author's name as search terms in Internet search engines and your library's online catalog. However, using the title and author's name will not likely lead you to contextual information that has not already been used to analyze the text. To make new connections to context, you need to "think outside the box" and brainstorm other search terms that will lead you to what you need.

For instance, in the preceding transcript the professor wonders if Teofilo's Levi's jeans have any significance in "The Man to Send Rain Clouds." To locate this information, she is not going to use "Silko" or "The Man to Send Rain Clouds" as search terms. Instead, she needs to use search terms that will lead her to information about the ethnic origins of the name "Levi" and, in a separate search, possible terms that will yield information about Laguna culture.

Finding contextual information using general Web searches

In Chapter 11, we will explore good reasons to use the author and title as search terms in online scholarly databases to locate published, peer-reviewed literary criticism about the text you are writing on. But to locate useful contextual information, you can often turn to everyday search engines, such as Google, to find information. Beware, however, that such engines can turn up a hodgepodge of information, and getting useful results from them will require you to patiently sift through many links, critique the reliability of Web sites, and be alert to possibly incorrect information. Look for an "About" link on Web sites you are unfamiliar with or skeptical of to learn more about who put up the site and their motivations for posting it.

For instance, in searching for information about the name "Levi," the professor who thought aloud while reading for us was reminded that the creator of Levi's jeans was named Levi Strauss. She examined *Wikipedia*'s biography of him and found referenced a book available online by Frances Dinkelspiel with a promising title and a reputable publisher (see the figure below). Clicking the link for this book took the professor to an e-book, which she searched for the term "Levi Strauss," discovering on page 145 that Levi Strauss had been one of a number of German Jews who had migrated to northern California during the latter part of the gold rush, became successful businessmen, and formed a Jewish social circle.

At this point, the professor had information that confirmed her hunch that while Levi's jeans are an American icon, their founder was an immigrant and a member of a religious and an ethnic minority. This gave her thoughts about a possible surface/depth argument about American identity that should help her interpret and reveal complexities in "The Man to Send Rain Clouds." Hence, contextual information helped her dig deeper below a surface detail about an article of clothing referenced in the story and see how the inclusion of this detail may contribute to a larger pattern of tension between the American dominant culture and ethnic minorities in the story.

In her final paper, the professor will cite the book by Dinkelspiel as an e-book (see the following figure), since that is the version of the book she used. She will not cite *Wikipedia*, since she used that site only as a means to locate a reliable source on Strauss's life. Generally speaking, encyclopedias, whether online

References [edit]

1. ^ Downey, Lynn (2008). "Levi Strauss: a short biography" . Levi Strauss & Co.. Retrieved 1 January 2011.
2. ^ Dinkelspiel, Frances (2010). *Towers of Gold: How One Jewish Immigrant Named Isaias Hellman Created California* . St. Martin's Press. p. 145. ISBN 9780312355272. Retrieved 2011-09-08.
3. ^ Carey, Charles W. (2002). *American inventors, entrepreneurs and business visionaries* . Facts on File. pp. 331–332. ISBN 9780816045594. Retrieved 2011-09-08.
4. ^ Transcript, Levi Strauss vs. H.B. Elfelt, District of California Circuit Court of the United States Ninth Judicial Circuit, 1874. National Archives, Pacific Sierra Region
5. ^ US 139121 , Davis, Jacob & Levi Strauss, "Improvement in fastening pocket-openings" published 9 August 1902, issued 20 May 1873

Wikipedia can be a useful tool for finding credible resources on contextual information.

or in print, are not considered scholarly sources since their function is to summarize other primary and secondary sources. However, they can serve as very helpful introductions that point you to more authoritative and reliable sources.

Dinkelspiel, Frances. *Towers of Gold: How One Jewish Immigrant Named Isaias Hellman Created California.* St. Martin's Press, 2010. Web. 27 Dec. 2011. <http://books.google.com>.

Works Cited entry for an e-book. See Chapter 14 for more information about citing sources.

Finding contextual information using library databases

Your campus library and library Web site can serve as important portals to excellent contextual information not available through everyday Web searches. Libraries purchase subscriptions to resources that, while often available with an Internet connection, are not reachable through Google or other popular search engines. Instead, to access these resources you need to log on, often using a password that recognizes the user as a student, faculty member, or campus guest. For instance, one of our campus library's Web pages links us to databases that contain U.S. newspaper articles from the nineteenth century that might be useful in contextualizing the concerns of readers and writers of American literature from that time period.

The professor who thought aloud for us while reading "The Man to Send Rain Clouds" expressed a desire to learn more about Laguna culture and Laguna rituals, and she anticipated that many Web resources on this topic would be unreliable. Many groups and individuals are fascinated by Native American culture but generally do not perform the scholarly research necessary to distinguish reliable from unreliable information. Often, individuals writing on popular topics are more interested in discussing information that supports preexisting beliefs or that they personally find fascinating—whether or not this information is factually true.

Thus, this professor turned to her campus library to find credible information on Laguna culture. She was particularly interested in information written by anthropologists, since anthropology is the scholarly study of cultures. Her library, like many other college libraries, pays for a subscription to a database called *JSTOR*, which contains scholarly articles from a number of disciplines, including anthropology. Articles in most library databases, like *JSTOR*, are **peer-reviewed**, meaning that other experts on a topic have reviewed the article and believe it is worthy of publication. (See Chapter 15 for more information on the peer-review process.)

Using search terms, such as "Laguna culture death ritual" and "Laguna pueblo culture" in *JSTOR*, this professor turned up a large number of potentially relevant (and many irrelevant) articles. She found an article that surveyed anthropological literature on the Pueblo Indians of the Southwest that, while dated, contained useful information about cultural change among the Pueblo peoples (see the figure below). Another article on the symbolic importance of Pueblo mission churches, written in 2000, also caught her eye because it appeared to explain a key aspect of an important setting in "The Man to Send Rain Clouds."

Search Results

laguna pueblo culture anthropology `SEARCH`

Search within these results

SHOWING 11–20 OF 1121

Sort by Relevance `GO`   Display 10 per page `GO`   MODIFY SEARCH

Show:
All results | Only results with images
All content | Only content I can access

Save Citation   Email Citation   Export Citation   Track Citation

Select/unselect all

- You have access to this content
- You have access to part of this content
- Full text on external site
- Citation access – see access options

11. The Archaeology of the Pueblo Revolt and the Formation of the Modern Pueblo World
Matthew Liebmann, Robert W. Preucel
The Kiva, Vol. 73, No. 2, The Rio Arriba (Winter, 2007), pp. 195-217
Page Scan   PDF   Summary

12. Astronomy, Architecture, and Adaptation at Pueblo Bonito
Jonathan E. Reyman
Science, New Series, Vol. 193, No. 4257 (Sep. 10, 1976), pp. 957-962
Page Scan   PDF   Summary

13. The Pueblo Indians of the Southwest: A Survey of the Anthropological Literature and a Review of Theory, Method, and Results
Edward P. Dozier
Current Anthropology, Vol. 5, No. 2 (Apr., 1964), pp. 79-97
Page Scan   PDF   Summary

Results of a **JSTOR** *search on Laguna pueblo culture.*

Although neither article was exactly on the topic the professor started her search with, they both offered useful information that she will likely quote or paraphrase in her interpretation of the story and include in her list of works cited.

Finding contextual information using the *Oxford English Dictionary* (OED)

An important resource for learning about the meaning of particular words in different time periods is the *Oxford English Dictionary*, or the *OED*. The *OED* goes far beyond the mission of other dictionaries in that it not only defines what words mean but also provides the evolving history of the meaning of words over time and illustrates these different meanings with copious examples. The information it provides goes so beyond other dictionaries that in its print form the *OED* takes up a whole library shelf with its many volumes. Many college libraries provide access to the *OED* online. If you aren't sure of what a word in a text means, or you are curious if a word may have had a different denotation in another time period, the *OED* is the resource to consult.

Examine Phillis Wheatley's short poem, "On Being Brought from Africa to America."

Phillis Wheatley
On Being Brought from Africa to America   1773

'Twas mercy brought me from my Pagan land,
Taught my benighted soul to understand
That there's a God, that there's a Saviour too:
Once I redemption neither sought nor knew.
Some view our sable race with scornful eye,   5
"Their colour is a diabolic die."
Remember, Christians, Negros, black as Cain,
May be refin'd and join th' angelic train.

A critic setting out to write about this short poem is first struck by how grateful the speaker of the poem sounds for being enslaved. But something about the fourth line, "Once I redemption neither sought nor knew," complicates this sense of gratitude because it seems to indicate that there was a time, perhaps a peaceful time prior to being enslaved, when the speaker had no need for redemption, or being saved by Christ. To better understand this line, a critic might search the word *redemption* in the *OED* to see how Wheatley, writing in the eighteenth century, understood this term.

The first definition the critic finds is the one he took the poem to mean: "deliverance from sin and damnation, esp. by the atonement of Christ; salvation." Indeed, the *OED* indicates that this definition has a history in print that takes it back at least to 1384. But the second definition of the term with

redemption, *n.*

1.

a. *Theol.* Deliverance from sin and damnation, esp. by the atonement of Christ; salvation.

c1384–2007

b. *the year of (our) redemption:* (preceding a date and usu. with *in*) Anno Domini, in the year (now rare).

1513–1920

2.

a. The action of freeing a prisoner, captive, or slave by payment; the fact of being freed in this way. Also occas.: the payment itself.

Also in extended use with reference to the bodies of those killed in battle and held by the enemy.

1387–2008

b. *Judaism.* The symbolic redeeming of one's firstborn son from a priest; the ceremony at which this occurs. See Pidyon Haben *n.*

Definition of the word redemption *in the* OED.

redemption

n.

1. The act of redeeming or the condition of having been redeemed.
2. Recovery of something pawned or mortgaged.
3. The payment of an obligation, as a government's payment of the value of its bonds.
4. Deliverance upon payment of ransom; rescue.
5. *Christianity* Salvation from sin through Jesus's sacrifice.

Definition of the word **redemption** *at thefreedictionary.com.*

Copyright © 2014 by Houghton Mifflin Harcourt Publishing Company. Reproduced by permission from the online edition of **The American Heritage Dictionary of the English Language**, *Fifth Edition at ahdictionary.com.*

a history equally as long is "the action of freeing a prisoner, captive, or slave by payment; the fact of being freed in this way." Wheatley was likely aware of both meanings.

The critic uses this information about the history of *redemption* to craft a surface/depth argument claiming Wheatley's poem is more subversive than it first appears. While on one level Wheatley tells her white, American readers that she is grateful for her enslavement because it led to her spiritual salvation, on another level her words may also indicate resentment because in Africa she had no need to seek release from captivity: there she was free.

For Discussion

1. What do you look for when determining whether a Web site is trustworthy or not?
2. What differences do you note between the *OED* entry and the Free Dictionary entry?
3. What other words from Wheatley's poem do you think would be useful to look up in the *OED*?

∾ NOW PRACTICE ON YOUR OWN: THE WORLD IS TOO MUCH WITH US

Below we reprint "The World Is Too Much with Us," by William Wordsworth, one of the major poets of the English Romantic movement of the late eighteenth and early nineteenth centuries. Do not be surprised if the poem initially proves difficult to interpret.

1. Read the poem carefully and write a short paragraph on what it appears to be about. What is your most obvious, or surface, understanding of the poem?

2. Next, brainstorm what contextual information in the poem might help you make a deeper interpretation of the poem's significance. What references does the poem make that you would like to understand? What would you like to know about the cultural context in which the poem was written or the genre of the poem?

3. Finally, try researching some of this information. Begin with basic Web searches for now. Which of your searches led to information that might help you make a stronger surface/depth argument about the poem? Which resulted in dead ends?

William Wordsworth
The World Is Too Much with Us   1802

The world is too much with us; late and soon,
Getting and spending, we lay waste our powers;—
Little we see in Nature that is ours;
We have given our hearts away, a sordid boon!
This Sea that bares her bosom to the moon;   5
The winds that will be howling at all hours,
And are up-gathered now like sleeping flowers;
For this, for everything, we are out of tune;
It moves us not. Great God! I'd rather be
A Pagan suckled in a creed outworn;   10
So might I, standing on this pleasant lea,
Have glimpses that would make me less forlorn;
Have sight of Proteus rising from the sea;
Or hear old Triton blow his wreathèd horn.

USING CONTEXT TO WRITE PERSUASIVELY

Context is used most effectively when it:

▸ supports a surface/depth argument;

▸ contains only as much information as is needed to support this argument;

▸ correctly cites information that is not common knowledge;

▸ illustrates the complexity of a text.

The following passages both use contextual information to discuss the significance of the Black Power movement to "Everyday Use," but one does so much more effectively than the other.

"Everyday Use" was originally published in Alice Walker's 1973 collection of short stories, *In Love and Trouble*. The story is set during the heyday of the Black Power movement, which was a political movement popularized by Stokley Carmichael, who defined the phrase "Black Power" as "black people coming together to form a political force" ("Black"). Unlike earlier African-American leaders, such as W. E. B. Du Bois or Martin Luther King Jr., who advocated a peaceful struggle for equality, many leaders of the Black Power movement were more confrontational and argued for Black separatism. One arm of the Black Power movement was the Black Panthers, founded by Huey P. Newton and Bobby Seale, which advocated outright violence ("In Search"). Not all members of the Black Power movement supported the Black Panthers, however. Many leaders advocated slogans such as "Black is beautiful" and encouraged the study of black history and culture. These included the poet Amiri Baraka, who founded the Black Arts Movement ("Black"). These artists adopted African customs, dress, and styles, such as Afros, and ate traditionally African-American "soul food" such as yams and collard greens ("Black"). The character of Dee in "Everyday Use" is clearly a member of the Black Power movement. She adopts an African name, has a natural Afro hairstyle, and wears a brightly colored African dress.[3]

---

[3] The Works Cited page for this paper contains the following two entries: "Black Power." *Wikipedia*. Wikimedia Foundation, 11 Dec. 2012. Web. 14 Dec. 2012; "In Search of African America: The Black Power Movement 1968–1980." *The Herbert Hoover Presidential Library and Museum*. Web. 14 Dec. 2012.

The following passage is excerpted from David White's "'Everyday Use': Defining African-American Heritage."[4]

> Walker uses Dee to symbolize the Black Power movement, which was characterized by bright and beautiful blacks who were vocal and aggressive in their demands. Many of them spoke disparagingly about their "Uncle Tom" ancestors and adopted certain aspects of African culture in their speech and dress. Mama's descriptions of Dee portray her as this type of individual: "Dee, though. She would always look anyone in the eye. Hesitation was no part of her nature. . . . She was determined to stare down any disaster in her efforts. Her eyelids would not flicker for minutes at a time. . . . At sixteen she had a style of her own: and knew what style was" (409). These personality traits, along with her style of dress and speech, establish her identity as a symbol of the Black Power movement.
>
> It is important to recognize that Walker is not condemning the Black Power movement as a whole. Rather, she is challenging that part of the movement that does not acknowledge and properly respect the many African-Americans who endured incredible hardships in their efforts to survive in a hostile environment. She uses the character of Dee to demonstrate this misguided black pride.

Both analyses use contextual information to argue that Dee represents the Black Power movement. However, the second example makes a much more complex argument since it not only claims that Dee symbolizes Black Power, but that her character illustrates the lack of respect and "misguided black pride" of some Black Power activists.

Moreover, the second analysis is much more strategic in what contextual information it includes. Whereas in the first extract it is hard to see how the names of the various Black Power leaders or the discussion of the various arms

---

[4] White, David. "'Everyday Use': Defining African-American Heritage." 2001. *Anniina's Alice Walker Page*. 19 Sept. 2002. Web. 27 Dec. 2011.

of the movement could be relevant to our understanding of "Everyday Use," the text written by David White makes every contextual detail seem relevant and necessary. The material in the first text is used largely as filler (it takes up space but doesn't make a complex interpretive argument). While this historical information may "warm up" readers to the story, it does not help us appreciate new complexities in the text.

Using the context strategy effectively can be challenging because it is easy to get carried away by the outside information and let the context, rather than an argument about the text's meaning, become your focus. Weak uses of the context strategy simply add contextual information without making us see anything new about the text at hand. Avoid turning your analysis over to the contextual findings, making the paper a report on the life or time period of the author rather than an interpretation of the meaning of the author's text or texts.

COMMON WORDS AND PHRASES ASSOCIATED WITH CONTEXT

anachronistic	contextualize	historical	political
contemporary	cultural	historicize	situate
context	genealogy	intertextual	social

Exercise

Rank each of the following passages on a scale from 1 to 3, with 1 being "ineffective use" of context and 3 being "very effective use." Be prepared to justify your ranking by explaining which of the criteria in the following list it does or does not meet. Then for each passage, determine what type of contextual information it supplies (see Common Types of Contextual Information on pp. 145–46).

▸ support a surface/depth argument
▸ contain only as much information as is needed to support this argument
▸ correctly cite information that is not common knowledge
▸ illustrate the complexity of a text

PASSAGE 1

In his well-known poem "Ode: Intimations of Immortality from Recollections of Early Childhood," written around the same time as "The World Is Too Much with Us," Wordsworth articulates his theory that we are born with souls capable of seeing the divine, but this ability fades as we age. According to Wordsworth, children are still connected to the spiritual world, but adults have lost this connection. "The World Is Too Much with Us" draws on a similar theme, showing how humans' ability to see the majesty in nature has declined as our cultures have grown more civilized. While more primitive "Pagan" (10) cultures see the gods in Nature, Wordsworth feels that contemporary humans can only obtain "glimpses" (12) of this tremendous spiritual force. Because our spiritual memories have faded, there is "[l]ittle we see in Nature that is ours" (3).

Works Cited

Wordsworth, William. "Ode: Intimations of Immortality from Recollections of Early Childhood." *The Collected Poems of William Wordsworth*. Hertfordshire: Wordsworth Editions, 1998. 701–04. Print.

---. "The World Is Too Much with Us." *The Collected Poems of William Wordsworth*. Hertfordshire: Wordsworth Editions, 1998. 307. Print.

PASSAGE 2

William Wordsworth was born in 1770 in the mountains of Cumberland, England. Wordsworth grew up in the country and spent a great deal of his time playing outdoors, in what he would later remember as "a pure communion with nature" ("Wordsworth's"). "The World Is Too Much with Us," written in 1802, reflects Wordsworth's childhood connection to nature.

Work Cited

"Wordsworth's Poetry." *SparkNotes.com*. SparkNotes LLC. 2002. Web. 2 Aug. 2011.

PASSAGE 3

Sylvia Plath was a twentieth-century feminist poet who wrote about the crucial issues of her life. Her most famous work was published after her death. These late poems were written over a short period of intense productivity and are generally considered to be her best work. "Morning Song" was written around the time of the birth of Plath's first daughter, Frieda, and is one of Plath's most popular poems. Less than two years after the birth of her daughter, Plath's marriage to the poet Ted Hughes ended in separation, and in 1963 Plath committed suicide by gas (Beckmann). "Morning Song" shows a mother's ambivalence to her newborn child.

Work Cited

Beckmann, Anja. "Sylvia Plath (1932–1963): Short Biography." www .sylviaplath.de 16 Apr. 2007. Web. 19 July 2008.

PASSAGE 4

Historically, Anglo-Americans sought to eradicate and replace Pueblo Indian customs and rituals. Dozier describes how mid-nineteenth-century Anglo-Americans judged Indian ceremonies as "obscene" and "immoral" and took steps to stop them (91). While some Indian groups responded by rejecting Anglo-American religion and customs, the Pueblo living in New Mexico took a more indirect approach by fusing new ceremonies and customs with their own.

We see such indirect resistance in "The Man to Send Rain Clouds" as the Laguna Indians fuse the holy water from the Catholic last rites into their own funeral ceremony. Like the Indian groups Dozier describes, the Laguna in this story borrow Christian rituals and ceremonies but reject the social organization associated with them. Thus, Leon and Teresa ask Father Paul to bring his holy water, but they reject the social hierarchy that has the priest presiding over the last rites. Perhaps more significantly, the Indians reject the priest's right to interpret the significance of the ceremony and of Teofilo's death. Where Father Paul sees Teofilo as a (lost) soul crossing over to another world, Leon and

Teresa see him as an ongoing force in their world. Thus, "The Man to Send Rain Clouds" shows us how acceptance can be a form of resistance that is ultimately more powerful than more direct forms of Anglo-American domination.

Work Cited

Dozier, Edward P. "The Pueblo Indians of the Southwest: A Survey of the Anthropological Literature and a Review of Theory, Method, and Results." *Current Anthropology* 5.2 (1964): 79–97. Print.

PASSAGE 5

In his essay "The Pueblo Indians of the Southwest: A Survey of the Anthropological Literature and a Review of Theory, Method, and Results," the anthropologist Edward P. Dozier describes how in the mid-nineteenth century, Anglo-Americans judged Indian ceremonies as "obscene" and "immoral" and took steps to stop them, removing Indian children from their homes, cutting their long hair, placing children in schools where the use of Indian languages was forbidden, and clothing them "in attire which befitted American standards of decency and morality" (91). The priest in Leslie Marmon Silko's "The Man to Send Rain Clouds" represents this Anglo-American heritage. He wants the Indians to give up their own customs and instead adopt his Catholic rituals and ceremonies.

Work Cited

Dozier, Edward P. "The Pueblo Indians of the Southwest: A Survey of the Anthropological Literature and a Review of Theory, Method, and Results." *Current Anthropology* 5.2 (1964): 79–97. Print.

OPTIONS FOR THE SCOPE OF THE CONTEXT STRATEGY

Most of the examples that have been used so far illustrate small uses of context to elaborate on a specific symbol or reference in the text. These are described as small uses of context because they bolster larger arguments about the text. They can also help support the patterns strategy by showing yet another way that the details of the text reveal a particular pattern or recurring meaning.

For instance, the example on page 144 uses contextual information about a character's name to make a surface/depth argument about Walker's criticism of individuals who reject African-American culture in favor of recovering an unrecoverable "African" past. The contextual information is just one small example of the larger surface/depth thesis of this essay which claims that the story shows the errors of rejecting slavery's legacy. The contextual information helps support a point and then the critic goes on to the next argument.

However, it is also possible to use the context strategy in a larger sense—as the central focus of your entire essay. For instance, the following opening from an essay on "Morning Song" uses the context strategy as the central focus of its interpretation in order to situate the poem in the 1960s debate on parenting practices. (The poem appears on p. 41 of this text.)

The context strategy can also be used to completely reframe an argument about a text.

Maria Maarbes/Shutterstock

Competing Parental Philosophies in Sylvia Plath's "Morning Song"

At the time when "Morning Song" was written in 1961, conflicting conceptions of parenting were making motherhood a difficult if not impossible enterprise. Sociologist Rebecca Bach, who studied parenting magazines from the 1950s through 1990s, states that in the 1950s a scientific approach to parenting dominated. Births were expected to take place in hospitals and the mother needed to follow the directions of scientific authorities, such as doctors, in making decisions about the baby's care.

The birth in "Morning Song" contains numerous references to scientific tools, methods, and processes that seem to criticize this scientific approach to parenthood. Thus, the parents are described as "magnifying" (4) the baby's arrival, as if the parents were scientists peering through lenses to appreciate the newborn. The gold watch in the opening line similarly suggests that the primary function of birth is to start a clock—a very scientific metaphor for the beginning of life. The baby's cry is described as taking "its place among the elements" (3), which may refer to the periodic table of elements and also has a scientific connotation. Finally, the word "distills" (8) refers to a chemical process for removing impurities and seems to associate the mother with an impure, unvalued substance and the child with a pure precious metal (the gold of line 1) that is methodically and precisely removed from its mother. All of these scientific images and word choices in the poem make the mother/child relationship seem cold and distant.

At the same time, the more natural "earth mother" image of motherhood that Bach describes as slowly starting to take hold by the early 1960s also seems inadequate to Plath. The earth mother stereotype glorified the naturalness associated with childbirth and encouraged naturalistic practices such as breast-feeding. However, rather than turn the mother into a goddess, the more naturalistic imagery that we see in lines such as "[a] far sea moves in my ear" (12) or "cow-heavy and floral" (13) seems to dehumanize the mother. She is not an earth goddess but an animal acting out of instinct. She has been turned into nothing more than a milk source for the child.

Works Cited

Bach, Rebecca. "Familial Changes: Recent Thinking on Motherhood and Families." Duke University, Durham. 26 Sept. 2000. Lecture. Reported in Hines, Karen. "Role of Motherhood Takes Center Stage." 29 Sept. 2000. *Duke University News and Communications*. Web. 1 Mar. 2010.

Plath, Sylvia. "Morning Song." *The Collected Poems*. Ed. Ted Hughes. New York: Harper & Row, 1981. 156–57. Print.

This use of context illustrates to the reader what childbirth and motherhood meant in the 1960s. This essay could go on to cite other information about parenting at the time and could perhaps quote some parenting handbooks from this time period that Plath might have had an opportunity to read. Thus, 1960s medical and psychological advice about parenting becomes a framework for this essay, helping explain the different images and conflicting emotions in the poem.

It is possible that using the context strategy in this large-scale scope can lead to a choice to delay stating the thesis. A delayed thesis, which does not appear at the end of the first paragraph (where conventionally readers of literary analysis expect a thesis to appear), may be useful in order to establish sufficient background information at the beginning of the essay.

CONTEXT AND AUTHORIAL INTENTION: PRODUCTIVE TENSIONS

The emergence of the context strategy in contemporary literary analysis points to a debate in literary studies: what role should an author's intentions play in a critic's analysis of a work? In their famous 1946 essay, "The Intentional Fallacy," W. K. Wimsatt and Monroe Beardsley argue that an author's stated intentions, background, and biography have no bearing on critical interpretations of a work. However, recent critics have argued that an author's intentions should play an important, illuminating role in the act of interpretation and should not be outright dismissed.

These more recent critics argue that one has to understand history in order to join the author's intended audience. In other words, interpretations of a work should be informed by what people at the time the author was writing would have known or understood. Similarly, many critics argue that deeper meaning beneath a text's surface meaning can often only be seen and understood in light of literary, cultural, and political history.

Contextual details thus often ensure that a critic does not completely ignore an author's intentions when making an interpretation. However, because an author never has complete control over a text—interpretation is always an act shared between speakers and listeners, authors and readers—the author's professed intentions in writing are not the "final answer" in literary studies.

The context strategy can also be used to help us understand how culture may profoundly shape authors and texts, regardless of an author's stated intentions. For instance, an essay that shows how Ernest Hemingway often used black characters in his works to undermine a white protagonist's confidence in his own powers might acknowledge that Hemingway may not consciously have been trying to make a statement about race but that nonetheless his writing reveals a fear of blackness. Such an analysis shows us how Hemingway's work often illustrates racial tensions and fears found in the dominant culture of his time.

Interestingly, a critic's use of the context strategy seems intimately related to her much larger theoretical allegiances (which we will discuss in the Chapter 10). Wimsatt and Beardsley's argument that use of an author's stated intentions is fallacious is very much related to their theoretical approach to literature known as New Criticism. Because of his interest in seeing the text on its own terms, a New Critic might not use the context strategy at all. More recent approaches to literature such as New Historicism and cultural studies have a very different appreciation for the use of contextual information when interpreting texts. Further, reader-response theories highlight for us the importance of what readers bring to understanding and decoding a text, while psychoanalytic theories stress the consideration of unconscious intent.

CITING CONTEXTUAL INFORMATION

Effective uses of the context strategy will usually contain citations to appropriate scholarly or informational works. Most of the time, it is sufficient to paraphrase these works. However, if the source you are citing phrases something in an unusual or unique way (such as the quotation from the seventeenth-century Dutch governor in the exercise on page 169), you may use a direct quotation. Direct quotations always require a citation.

If the contextual information you are using is common knowledge, on the other hand, you do not need a citation. Common knowledge includes standard definitions that you state in your own words, historical dates, and facts that appear in multiple sources, such as well-known encyclopedias, as well as information that can be presumed to be shared by members of a specific community. This last category is tricky since it depends on your assessment of what a specific community knows. If you are writing for a professional, academic journal in a specific field, then you can assume that anything that would be known to most readers of the journal is common knowledge. If you are writing an essay as a class assignment, you should assume that this specific community is members of your class unless told otherwise. Thus, information that should be known to most members of the class does not need to be cited. If you are not sure whether something is common knowledge, it is always best to include a citation even if it may not be necessary.

When you cite contextual information, you need to include both an in-text citation and an entry in a list of works cited. (See Chapter 14 on MLA guidelines for citing sources: how to format quotations, in-text citations, and the list of works cited.)

Review

The context strategy involves bringing in information external to the text to support, deepen, or discover a new interpretation of the text. This may include information about the historical time period in which the text was written, cultural references in the text, the historical meaning of particular words, other texts alluded to in the work, or other writings by the author or his/her contemporaries.

Finding contextual information will require research. You can begin your research with basic Web searches and encyclopedias, such as *Wikipedia* but generally only as a resource for locating more credible sources you can cite. You can also find credible information using library databases that link to peer-reviewed journals. The *Oxford English Dictionary* (or *OED*) is an excellent resource for finding the historical meanings of particular words.

Arguments using context are most persuasive when they support a clear surface/depth interpretation, do not contain unnecessary "filler," follow proper citation practices, and help reveal the text's complexity.

Context is most frequently used in a small sense, to illustrate a particular reference or support another argument. However, contextual information can also be used to reframe an entire argument. In these cases, essays usually start off with contextual information and use this information to inform the thesis for the entire essay. Such a large-scale use of context will often result in an essay with a delayed thesis that does not come at the end of the first paragraph.

Exercise

In Chapter 4 on the patterns strategy you read an analysis of Michael Ondaatje's poem "The Cinnamon Peeler" that argued the poem shows contradictory images of lust. The thesis of this essay read:

> On one level, the poem shows a man who desires total ownership and possession of a woman, while at the same time it seems to suggest that this desire is an impossible fantasy. The poem implies that lust is neither as powerful nor as all-encompassing as it might first seem.

This thesis was supported by examining the poem as two halves. The writer used the patterns strategy to show us multiple images of ownership and domination in the first half of the poem. But then the writer traced patterns of absence and loss and female self-assertion in the second half of the poem that contradicted the images from the first half. The essay ultimately argues that this contradiction between the two halves of the poem shows us that the desire to totally own and possess someone is a fantasy that cannot be maintained.

The essay makes a quite different argument about "The Cinnamon Peeler," using contextual evidence to argue that the poem makes a statement about Sri Lankan culture and history. Take a moment to first review the poem (see p. 74). Then read this new essay and answer these questions.

1. Identify the different types of contextual information used in this essay. Is this contextual information used effectively? How would you characterize the scope of the context strategy here: Is context used extensively or is it used in a small sense to help support the patterns strategy?

2. Identify the thesis and its placement in the essay. Is this an effective placement of the thesis? Why or why not?

3. Compare this short analysis to the essays on "The Cinnamon Peeler" at the end of Chapter 4 (p. 79). How does the contextual information in the essay below expand our understanding of the poem?

4. What are the strengths and weaknesses of this essay?

Smelling Sri Lanka in Michael Ondaatje's "The Cinnamon Peeler"

"The Cinnamon Peeler" originally appeared in Michael Ondaatje's 1982 memoir, *Running in the Family*, which describes his childhood in Sri Lanka. Sri Lankan history and culture have been profoundly shaped by the cinnamon trade. Beginning in the sixteenth century, European countries began invading Sri Lanka in order to exploit its cinnamon crops, and long wars were fought in order to control Sri Lanka. Cinnamon is so closely associated with Sri Lanka that its very name *Cinnamomum zeylanicum* is derived from the word *Ceylon*, as

Sri Lanka was formerly known (Ratwatte). The early Dutch governor Rijckloff van Goens Jr. (1675–1680) described cinnamon as "the bride around whom they dance in Ceylon" (Paranavitana), and Ondaatje himself in *Running in the Family* describes how when Dutch ships approached the island "captains would spill cinnamon onto the deck and invite passengers on board to smell Ceylon before the island even came into view. . . . This island was a paradise to be sacked " (80–81).

Ondaatje plays with this tradition of cinnamon as a seductive woman to be conquered in "The Cinnamon Peeler." The speaker in the first half of this poem wants to replicate the actions of the colonial powers that came to Sri Lanka to exploit its cinnamon crops. He desires total possession over the woman/country and sees her as an object to be divided up into individual parts. Thus, lines 12–16, which list a series of body parts ("the upper thigh," "smooth pasture / neighbour to your hair," "This ankle") can be seen both as a man treating a woman as a sexual object and as a colonial power dividing up a submissive country. As a Sri Lankan native, the speaker of this poem wants to possess his country in the same way that the greedy colonial powers possessed her. However, the "[i]f" (1) that begins the poem indicates that this desire may only be a fantasy.

In the second half of the poem, the speaker realizes that he has to form a new relationship with his native country. In 1948 Sri Lanka gained independence and beginning in the 1970s the country was torn by internal conflict between two native communities. Thus, it seems that the colonial strategy of objectifying, dividing, and claiming ownership over the land that we saw in the first half has proved ineffective and destructive. In the second half of the poem, we learn that no one can truly possess Sri Lanka. Thus, whereas the cinnamon smell totally dominates the woman in the first half of the poem, in the second half, she floats in the water and their "bodies remained free, / you could hold me and be blind of smell" (29–30). This image suggests a vision of Sri Lanka that is not defined purely by natural resources such as cinnamon. If the woman represents Sri Lanka, then the second stanza shows her acquiring an identity that is not completely defined by someone else's lust.

The changed relationship that the speaker imagines with his native country is illustrated in the poem by a transition from a blindly monogamous relationship in the first half to a possibly "open" relationship with multiple partners in the second half. This transition is surprising since we are accustomed to thinking of monogamy as an ideal in marriage. However, the monogamous relationship in the first half of the poem is described in fierce, lustful, and colonizing terms: the cinnamon peeler wants to "ride" his wife's bed as if she were an animal to be mounted and tamed, emphasizing her animalistic qualities. Similarly, she is described as bathing in rain gutters or monsoons, showing her close relationship to nature rather than a colonizing, Western civilization. Her family, moreover, is described as "keen nosed" and "rough," suggesting that they operate more on physical instinct than civilized principles. Even the association of the woman's body with terms we typically use to describe land, such as "smooth pasture" (13), "neighbour" (14), or "crease / that cuts your back" (15–16), which is perhaps reminiscent of a field being plowed or a land being parceled out and divided, emphasizes both her close relationship to nature and his sense of ownership over her. Thus, the relationship described in the first half of the poem seems to be monogamous, but this monogamy is associated with possessiveness. The woman is fiercely, possessively owned by either the speaker or her mother and brothers.

The ending of the poem replaces this fiercely possessive monogamous relationship with a relationship that seems to give the woman much more independence. At first, this open relationship is associated with a sense of loss as the wife searches her arms for the "missing perfume" (35) and imagines her husband with other women. However, the water that they swim in and that washes away the cinnamon smell can also be seen as a rebirth, a chance to start over again. When the wife commands her partner to "[s]mell me" (46), she seems to be insisting that he recognize her desires. Moreover, the use of the word "belly" (43) refers to a part of the woman's body that is more often associated with pregnancy or fertility than sex, possibly suggesting that this new relationship might breed new life.

Ondaatje seems to be suggesting that if Sri Lanka is to survive as an independent country, its citizens must give up desires implanted by colonial authorities to completely control her and instead see her natural resources as just one part of her total culture. Ondaatje's poem implies it is time for Sri Lanka to find her own voice. This voice will be one that manages to acknowledge Sri Lanka's seductive, sensuous nature without becoming totally consumed by it.

Works Cited

Ondaatje, Michael. "The Cinnamon Peeler." *Digging into Literature: Strategies for Reading, Analysis, and Writing.* Joanna Wolfe and Laura Wilder. Boston: Bedford/St. Martin's, 2016. 74–76. Print.

---. *Running in the Family.* New York: Penguin Books, 1982. Print.

Paranavitana, K. D. "Cinnamon Gardens & Cinnamon Trade in Sri Lanka." July 2006. *The Virtual Library of Sri Lanka.* Web. 18 Dec. 2006.

Ratwatte, Florence. *The Spice of Life: Cinnamon and Ceylon.* May 1991. Web. 18 Dec. 2006.

8 Genre and Form

....

Considering a text's genre is a special application of the context strategy that is so important we have given it its own chapter. **Genre** is an imprecise term that refers to the categories used to group similar texts. Texts grouped together in a particular genre share similar *purposes, audiences,* and *conventions* (including conventions of form, subject matter, tone, and style). Genres differ in how important these three elements are. For instance, a romantic comedy has a purpose of celebrating love and an audience that typically includes young women. While a romantic comedy follows particular genre conventions—for instance, we typically expect the characters to encounter and overcome obstacles and for the overall tone to be lighthearted—these conventions are flexible and not very constraining.

By contrast, a poetic elegy has the very specific purpose of lamenting loss or death and can have a very specific convention requiring couplets written with an exact meter of six stressed syllables (paired with unstressed beats) followed by a line of five stressed syllables. However, the audience of an elegy is loosely defined and varies according to circumstances.

Genre can refer to broad categories of texts, such as:

poetry   fiction   drama   nonfiction

or

comedy   tragedy   history

Or it can refer to more specific groupings, such as the following poetic genres:

elegy   sonnet   ballad   ode   dramatic monologue

or the following popular genres:

romance   mystery   horror   western   courtroom drama

We could name hundreds of textual genres—far more than we could possibly cover in this text. Because of this impossibility, instead of teaching you to recognize specific genres, this chapter teaches you to use information about genres to make surface/depth arguments. We start by showing how to use your knowledge of familiar popular genres and then move to a likely unfamiliar poetic genre—the sonnet. Our hope is that you will be able to apply the strategies in this chapter to information your instructor shares with you (or information you research) on other genres you will encounter in your literature classes. Strictly speaking, some of what we call genres here are actually verse forms. A **verse form** is a recognized poetic structure consisting of specific patterns of rhyme, meter, or lines. However, since so many verse forms have conventions and histories that go beyond their structure or form, we find it useful to discuss these verse forms as we do genres. ■

MAKING ARGUMENTS ABOUT GENRE

Considering genre is an important strategy because genres are not only collections of recurrent forms, subject matter, and style—but they also contain particular historical and cultural associations. For instance, when we watch a science fiction film, we recall other famous texts in this genre. The themes, characters, and plot elements from these earlier texts resonate as we experience the new text. A contemporary novelist writing in a science fiction setting is choosing to invoke a tradition associated with technology, exploration, and questions about what it means to be human.

Likewise, when we read a sonnet, we it in the context of our memory of other sonnets. A **sonnet** is a fourteen-line poem arranged in one of a number of rhyme schemes. English sonnets typically have ten syllables per line. A contemporary poet choosing to write a sonnet is deliberately associating his poem in a very old, classical tradition.

Arguments about genre are most persuasive when they support a clear surface/depth interpretation, do not contain extraneous information, follow proper citation practices, and illustrate the complexity of the text. To see how we might make an argument about genre, consider the western: a genre typically associated with themes such as independence, freedom, personal honor, and conquering the wide-open frontier. Western films and stories are filled with images of sprawling, forbidding landscapes and independent, rugged heroes; the stereotypical western ends with a cowboy riding off alone into the sunset. Most westerns are set in the latter half of the nineteenth century—after the Civil War and during the great American westward expansion—and populated by clear heroes and villains. The genre is associated with popular culture—including mass-produced "dime" novels and early television shows—and is a masculine genre, written and consumed primarily by men.

However, the contemporary novelist Cormac McCarthy writes serious literature in the western genre. Most of McCarthy's westerns are set in the 1940s and later—well after the typical time period associated with this genre. In fact, many of McCarthy's westerns are set during the period when westerns were most popular, and television shows such as *Gunsmoke*, *The Lone Ranger*, and *Bonanza* dominated the airwaves. A critic might use this information to argue that McCarthy's decision to set his novels in the time when westerns were popular, rather than the time of the gold rush and western expansion, calls into question our nostalgia for the past.

Confronting the western landscape in a relatively modern era, McCarthy's characters in *All the Pretty Horses* find not wide-open landscapes untouched by human hand but a terrain dotted by fences, oil wells, abandoned towns, and highways:

> They came up out of the river breaks riding slowly side by side along the dusty road and onto a high plateau where they could see out over the country

to the south, rolling country covered with grass and wild daisies. To the west a mile away ran a wire fence strung from pole to pole like a bad suture across the gray grasslands and beyond that a small band of antelope all of whom were watching them. . . .

By noon they'd left the road and were riding southwest through the open grassland. They watered their horses at a steel stocktank under an old F. W. Axtell windmill that creaked slowly in the wind. . . .

That evening they crossed the Southern Pacific tracks just east of Pumpville, Texas, and made camp a half mile on the far side of the right of way. By the time they had the horses brushed and staked and a fire built it was dark. John Grady stood his saddle upright to the fire and walked out on the prairie and stood listening. He could see the Pumpville watertank against the purple sky. Beside it was the horned moon. (38–42)[1]

Still from the opening of the 2007 film adaptation of Cormac McCarthy's No Country for Old Men. *In the background is a typical western horizon stretching out into the distance, but a fence cuts across the foreground.*

---

[1] McCarthy, Cormac. *All the Pretty Horses*. 1992. Republished in *The Border Trilogy*. New York: Alfred A. Knopf, 1999. Print.

Here is how a critic might make an argument about genre based on these descriptions in *All the Pretty Horses*:

> The landscape John Grady and Rawlins ride across in *All the Pretty Horses* bears many conventional descriptions we come to expect from westerns. There is a "high plateau" (38), "rolling country" (38), "open grassland" (41), a "band of antelope" (42), "purple sky" (42), and a "horned moon" (42). This is the romantic landscape of the West, promising freedom and escape from civilization and its pressures. But we also see signs that this landscape and the independence it seems to offer are off limits to the young protagonists. Across the open grassland and rolling country lies a "wire fence strung from pole to pole like a bad suture" (38). A suture is stitching used to close a wound and McCarthy's use of this comparison suggests that the pristine open country is wounded. Moreover, the two boys are camped near Pumpville, Texas, a former railroad town that lost most of its population when trains switched from steam to diesel power (Troesser). Thus, the open countryside of the West has already been inhabited and abandoned. Signs of civilization and technology, like the Pumpville watertank, scar the wide-open vistas. Even the name, Pumpville, suggests a land that has been used and pumped dry of its resources and glory.
>
> The contrast between the land John Grady and Rawlins encounter and the idealized landscape we associate with the western genre suggest that the American ideals of independence, honor, and true grit that the western represents have passed from contemporary culture. One can no longer "Go West" to prove one's manhood and escape civilization because the West has already been conquered. Significantly, the two protagonists move South, toward Mexico, rather than West. . . .[2]

---

[2] The Works Cited page from which this example is drawn includes the following entries: McCarthy, Cormac. *All the Pretty Horses*. 1992. Republished in *The Border Trilogy*. New York: Alfred A. Knopf, 1999. Print; Troesser, John. "Pumpville, Texas." Web. 27 Dec. 2011. <http://www.texasescapes.com/TOWNS/Texas_ghost_towns/Pumpville_Texas/Pumpville_Texas.htm>

Exercises

1. What strategies of literary analysis, in addition to genre, can you identify in the previous literary analysis?
2. What arguments can you make about the still from *No Country for Old Men*, knowing that this image is from a contemporary film set in the 1980s in the western genre?

USING GENRE TO BRAINSTORM

To use genre as a strategy, begin by first identifying the genre or genres of the text you are analyzing. You are almost certainly already familiar with many common fictional and dramatic genres including westerns, science fiction, mystery, legal dramas, romantic comedies, and many others. Later in this chapter, we provide additional examples of genres, especially poetic ones, you may have less familiarity with.

Arguments about genre are often most significant when an author breaks or disrupts the conventions of the genre, thereby defying the audience's expectations. Thus, it is useful to begin by thinking about what we expect from the genre. Questions to ask yourself about a genre include those regarding:

- ▸ *Cultural associations*: Who usually reads and writes this genre? Is this genre associated with a particular ethnic or social group? Is it generally considered a highbrow or a lowbrow genre?
- ▸ *Subject matter*: What kinds of subjects or content matter do we expect to find in this genre? What sorts of conflicts does the genre tend to include? Are there particular themes or motifs that are common?
- ▸ *Purpose*: Does this genre have a particular purpose, such as to celebrate or mourn? Does it aim to teach readers a lesson or convey a particular moral?
- ▸ *Style and tone*: Does the genre tend to be dark and serious or light and humorous? Does it tend to use elevated diction (big words) or plain speech? Is there a certain set of vocabulary that you associate with this genre?
- ▸ *Characters or speakers*: How would you describe the typical protagonist or speaker in this genre? Are there any "stock" characters typically found in this genre? What kinds of personality traits are common?

> *Settings (for fiction, drama, and film)*: In what kinds of settings does this genre usually take place? Does the action tend to occur indoors or outdoors? In what time period is this genre usually set? What are some typical descriptions you would expect to see in this genre?

> *Music and camera shots (for drama and film)*: What types of background music usually accompany this genre? Are there particular establishing camera shots you associate with this genre?

> *Rhythm, meter, and rhyme (for poetry)*: Is this genre associated with a particular rhyme scheme or meter (such as iambic pentameter)? Is there a specific order or pattern that the genre is supposed to follow? What kinds of variations are common in this poetic genre? (See below for more information on poetic genres.)

Once you have identified the defining features of a text's genre, look for places where the text breaks from the elements or conventions commonly associated with that genre. Focus on elements that are missing or changed or that seem out of place. Common ways that texts break from genres include:

> **omitting or changing a feature commonly associated with the genre.** This can include omitting expected actions or plot elements, changing character types, changing the setting, or breaking from an expected rhyme scheme or meter.

> **using the genre to raise subjects or themes or address readers not usually associated with it**

> **combining elements of multiple genres in surprising ways**

For instance, the analysis on page 176 argues that *All the Pretty Horses* departs from the western genre by portraying a setting filled with fences and other signs of civilization rather than a wide-open landscape. It then argues for the significance of this departure by claiming that the fences show that the West has already been conquered. These changes to the traditional western setting also call into question the themes of freedom and independence typically associated with the genre.

Exercise

To help you see how you can make arguments about genres, we will begin with a genre you are probably familiar with: horror. In the television premiere of *Buffy the Vampire Slayer*, a series whose title suggests the horror genre, a teenage boy breaks into a high school and brings along a reluctant girl, promising her mischief. There are long shots of empty corridors, the camera lingers over dissection experiments in the biology lab, and ominous music plays in the background. The boy and girl begin kissing in one of the hallways while the camera looms above them. After a few seconds, the girl hears a noise and turns in alarm (see still at left below).

The boy mocks the girl, telling her there is nothing to fear. However, a moment later, the tables are turned when the girl's face morphs into that of a vampire. She becomes the attacker and the rebellious boy her victim (see still at right below).

To use the genre strategy to make an argument about "Welcome to the Hellmouth," follow these steps:

1. Brainstorm what you know about the horror genre. What kinds of cultural associations does this genre have? Who watches it? What kinds of characters are common? What sort of setting, music, lighting, and tone does the genre have? What kinds of themes or subject matters does horror usually address? Do horror texts typically convey particular morals or lessons?

**Stills from "Welcome to the Hellmouth," the first episode of
Buffy the Vampire Slayer.**

The girl hears a noise and turns in alarm.   *The girl turns into a vampire and attacks the boy.*

2. Examine the two stills on page 179 and the accompanying summary of this scene. In what ways does this scene conform to the genre? In what ways does it break from horror genre conventions? What arguments can you make about what these deviations from horror genre conventions might mean? What significance might these deviations hold? See if you can make a surface/depth argument about why the text breaks from these conventions of the horror genre.

USING UNFAMILIAR VERSE GENRES: THE SONNET

Your literature classes will challenge you not only to make arguments about genres you know but also to learn to make arguments about genres you don't know. To give you practice with unfamiliar genres, we provide some background on the sonnet, one of the most well-known poetic verse forms.

What is a sonnet?

The term *sonnet* originates from the Italian language and means "little sound or song." A sonnet is characterized by the following features:

- It has fourteen lines.
- It follows a defined rhyme scheme.
- It is typically written in **iambic pentameter**, with five pairs of stressed and unstressed syllables per line.
- It expresses a single theme or sentiment.
- It typically has a "turn" or shift in its sentiment. For instance, the poem may begin by describing a problem and then turn or shift to a resolution or an answer. Or the poem may begin with an optimistic tone and then turn to sadness or even despair.

A given poem does not have to have all of these features for us to recognize it as a sonnet—just as a film doesn't necessarily have to show corpses for us to recognize it as belonging to the horror genre. If sufficient other features are found, we will recognize it as belonging to a genre even as it violates some of our expectations of that genre.

Of the various features of the sonnet, students struggle most with identifying iambic pentameter, a form of meter consisting of five pairs of stressed and unstressed syllables, producing a total of ten syllables per line. The figure below illustrates a line of iambic pentameter from Shakespeare's "Sonnet 129."

```
 ˘  ´   ˘   ´    ˘     ´    ˘  ´  ˘   ´
Is per | jur'd, mur | derous, blood | y, full | of blame
  1        2            3              4         5
```

Iambic pentameter consists of five pairs of unstressed and stressed syllables.

The line in the preceding figure contains ten syllables: five are unstressed (marked with a ˘) and five are stressed (marked with a ´). The iambic pentameter of a sonnet does not have to be exact—some flexibility is acceptable. For instance, some lines may have an extra syllable or contain words that vary the stress patterns. The line above the figure shows this flexibility in the word *murderous*, which would normally be pronounced with three syllables, here needs to be slurred into a two-syllable word for the rhythm to work. Such breaks from ideal iambic pentameter may sometimes provide evidence for surface/depth arguments.

Many newcomers to formal poetry struggle trying to identify which syllables are stressed and which are unstressed. This ability improves with practice. You should remember that sometimes even experts disagree over which syllables should be stressed. In fact, these different readings of a poem (where the reader stresses different syllables) can sometimes give way to different interpretations of the poem's tone and meaning.

Petrarchan and Shakespearean sonnets

There are two main variations of the sonnet form: the Petrarchan (or Italian) sonnet and the Shakespearean (or English) sonnet.

The **Petrarchan sonnet** is the older of the two forms. It is named after the fourteenth-century Italian writer Francesco Petrarca, who wrote numerous poems in this form about his unrequited love for a woman called Laura. You can recognize a Petrarchan sonnet because it has two parts: an eight-line

octave and a six-line **sestet**. The octave has a rhyme scheme of ABBA ABBA, while the sestet is more flexible, most commonly rhymed CDECDE or CDCDCD—although other sestet variations are not rare.

Together the two parts of a Petrarchan sonnet form an "argument." The octave describes a problem while the sestet proposes a resolution. Typically, the ninth line creates what is called the **turn**, which signals the move from proposition to resolution. Even in sonnets that don't strictly follow the problem/resolution structure, the ninth line still often marks a turn by signaling a change in the tone, mood, or stance of the poem.

The typical subject matter of the Petrarchan sonnet is unattainable love. The sonnet typically describes a lady as a model of perfection and inspiration. Wordsworth's "The World Is Too Much with Us" is an example of a Petrarchan sonnet in which Nature (rather than a lady) is addressed as the object of unattainable love.

William Wordsworth
The World Is Too Much with Us   1802

	a	The world is too much with us; late and soon,	1
	b	Getting and spending, we lay waste our powers;—	2
	b	Little we see in Nature that is ours;	3
octave	a	We have given our hearts away, a sordid boon!	4
	a	This Sea that bares her bosom to the moon;	5
	b	The winds that will be howling at all hours,	6
	b	And are up-gathered now like sleeping flowers;	7
	a	For this, for everything, we are out of tune;	8
	c	It moves us not. Great God! I'd rather be	9
	d	A Pagan suckled in a creed outworn;	10
sestet	c	So might I, standing on this pleasant lea,	11
	d	Have glimpses that would make me less forlorn;	12
	c	Have sight of Proteus rising from the sea;	13
	d	Or hear old Triton blow his wreathèd horn.	14

The **Shakespearean sonnet** is named after William Shakespeare, not because he was the first to write in this form but because he became its most famous practitioner.

The form of a Shakespearean sonnet consists of three groups of four lines (called **quatrains**) and a pair of lines called a **couplet**. The usual rhyme scheme is end-rhymed ABAB CDCD EFEF GG. In some sonnets, the third quatrain generally introduces an unexpected sharp turn. In Shakespeare's sonnets, however, the turn usually comes in the couplet and usually summarizes the theme of the poem or introduces a fresh new look at the theme.

Shakespeare's sonnets focused on subjects such as love and its torments, time, and the immortality of poetry compared to the fleeting beauty of youth. In the seventeenth century, John Donne extended the sonnet's scope to religion, while Milton extended it to politics.

Shakespeare's "Sonnet 129" is an example of the Shakespearean sonnet.

William Shakespeare
Sonnet 129   1609

quatrain 1	a	The expense of spirit in a waste of shame	1
	b	Is lust in action; and till action, lust	2
	a	Is perjured, murderous, bloody, full of blame,	3
	b	Savage, extreme, rude, cruel, not to trust,	4
quatrain 2	c	Enjoy'd no sooner but despised straight,	5
	d	Past reason hunted, and no sooner had	6
	c	Past reason hated, as a swallow'd bait	7
	d	On purpose laid to make the taker mad;	8
quatrain 3	e	Mad in pursuit and in possession so;	9
	f	Had, having, and in quest to have, extreme;	10
	e	A bliss in proof, and proved, a very woe;	11
	f	Before, a joy proposed; behind, a dream.	12
couplet	g	All this the world well knows; yet none knows well	13
	g	To shun the heaven that leads men to this hell.	14

USING GENRE TO WRITE PERSUASIVELY

Genre, like context, is used most effectively when it:

- supports a surface/depth argument
- contains only as much information about the genre as is needed to support this argument
- illustrates the complexity of a text

The following passages both use information about the Petrarchan sonnet to make a surface/depth argument about Wordsworth's "The World Is Too Much with Us," but one does so much more effectively than the other:

PASSAGE 1

Wordsworth's poem "The World Is Too Much with Us" is written in the form of a Petrarchan sonnet. It has eight lines that follow the rhyme scheme ABBAABBA and six lines that follow the rhyme scheme CDCDCD. In most Petrarchan sonnets, the first eight lines (the octave) propose a question or an idea that the next six lines (the sestet) answer. In "The World Is Too Much with Us," the speaker asks in the first eight lines why we have given away our connection to nature. The question is answered in the next six lines with a plea to turn back to the primitive spirituality of pagan times, which were connected to nature.

PASSAGE 2

In his poem "The World Is Too Much with Us," Wordsworth makes ironic use of the sonnet form. While the poem's basic message is a plea to turn back from the materialism of civilized life, which is filled with "[g]etting and spending" (2), it is written in one of the most civilized and complex genres in our culture. The sonnet was first created by the Italians in the thirteenth century and then popularized by Shakespeare and other English poets in the sixteenth century. Thus, the sonnet is hardly a pagan form of poetry. By choosing to write his poem in this genre, Wordsworth may be showing that he is conflicted about the benefits of civilization. On the one hand, civilization takes us away from the raw spirituality of earlier times, but on the other hand, it brings its own unique forms of beauty to replace what we may have lost.

Where the first example primarily uses information about the sonnet form to identify the genre of Wordsworth's poem, the second uses information about the history and cultural associations of the sonnet to interpret the poem by arguing that it is ironic and conflicted. The second example makes a surface/depth–contrasting argument to show that the poem is not just an indictment of civilized society but is also more conflicted than we might first realize; thus, it uses arguments about genre to illustrate the complexity of the text.

COMMON WORDS AND PHRASES ASSOCIATED WITH GENRE

breaks from	plays with	surprises
contradicts	subverts	unexpected
overturns		

Text A subverts the conventions of the genre . . .

Text A plays with the genre conventions . . .

The genre enhances/contradicts text A's theme . . .

Exercise

The paragraphs on page 186 use information about poetic genre or form to make arguments. For each paragraph, first determine *how* the critic is arguing that genre is *being broken*:

▸ by changing or omitting a feature usually associated with this genre

▸ by using the genre to raise subjects or themes (or address readers) not usually associated with it

▸ by combining elements of multiple genres in surprising ways

Then rank each paragraph as making (1) very effective, (2) somewhat effective, or (3) not effective use of genre to illustrate the complexity of the poem they are analyzing.

Finally, for each paragraph, indicate how the argument might be improved. Is there additional information the critic might use? Additional arguments that might be made? Material that should be deleted?

1. Typically, a Petrarchan sonnet is addressed to an unattainable lady from whom the speaker takes inspiration. In "The World Is Too Much with Us," Wordsworth casts Mother Nature in the role of the beloved. However, unlike the typical Petrarchan poet, the speaker in "The World Is Too Much with Us" finds himself unable to properly worship and take inspiration from his beloved. Thus, Wordsworth's choice of a genre so closely associated with idealized love emphasizes how much humanity has fallen from the ideal relationship with Nature.

2. Shakespeare's "Sonnet 129" largely follows iambic pentameter, as one would expect in a Shakespearean sonnet. However, some lines have additional stressed syllables. For instance, line 4 begins with a stressed syllable that interrupts the line later on and makes us read the word "cruel" as two syllables:

   Savage, | extreme, | rude, cru | el, not | to trust,

   Line 10 similarly disrupts the even, soothing sound of iambic pentameter by beginning with two stressed syllables:

   Had, hav | ing, and | in quest | to have, | extreme;

   The predominance of heavy stresses and short words in the poem underscores the speaker's agitated state of mind.

3. Most Shakespearean sonnets experience a turn (sometimes referred to by the Italian word *volta*) in the final couplet. This turn often summarizes the main theme of the poem, as in "Sonnet 129" where the turn emphasizes the poem's lesson that lust should be avoided. In the final couplet, the speaker warns the reader that no matter how good lust may feel in the moment, it ultimately leads one to hell. By ending the poem with the word "hell," Shakespeare sums up all that is wrong with lust.

4. An *aubade* is a poem or song about lovers separating at dawn. The aubade is often a dialogue between the two lovers with one saying that since dawn is near they must part and the other lover saying no. As Marjorie Perloff suggests, Sylvia Plath's "Morning Song" turns the aubade convention inside out. Instead of a sweet farewell, "Morning Song" is an anxious and fraught welcoming. Here the infant speaks the part of one of the lovers with its cries, mentioned in lines 2, 13, and 17, acting as lines of dialogue. The mother who attends to the child is the other lover who feels anxiety rather than tenderness. Plath plays

with this love poem genre to emphasize her basic theme that motherhood inspires anxiety and fear as well as love and tenderness.[3]

5. A heroic couplet consists of rhyming pairs of lines written in iambic pentameter. The heroic couplet was first used by Chaucer in the thirteenth century, but the form was most popularized by Alexander Pope, who used it in the eighteenth century to translate Greek and Roman classics, such as Homer's *Iliad*, into English verse. Thus, it is associated with lofty subjects. Phyllis Wheatley's poem "On Being Brought from Africa to America" uses heroic couplets to discuss slavery.

LEARNING MORE ABOUT GENRES

This chapter has illustrated how you can use information you already possess about popular genres—such as westerns and horror shows—to make surface/depth arguments about texts. We provided background information on one formal poetic genre—the sonnet—to show how to use information about genres centered on verse forms to make surface/depth arguments. The sonnet, of course, is not the only verse form with a long history and set of conventions. To find out more about the conventions and traditions associated with other verse forms, as well as unfamiliar narrative and dramatic genres, you can reference a handbook of literary terms, such as *The Bedford Glossary of Critical and Literary Terms*, by Ross Murfin and Supryia M. Ray, or look at a credible Web site, such as that of the Poetry Foundation, which includes a glossary section (http://www.poetryfoundation.org/learning/glossary-terms).

---

[3] Citation from Perloff, Marjorie. "Angst and Animism in the Poetry of Sylvia Plath." *Critical Essays on Sylvia Plath*. Ed. Linda Wagner. Boston: G.K. Hall & Company, 1984. Print.

Review

This chapter explains that genres have their own conventions, histories, and cultural associations. When texts break from our expectations for a particular genre, critics can make arguments about what these deviations mean. Common ways that texts break from genres include:

▸ omitting or changing a feature expected in the genre
▸ using the genre to raise subjects or themes or address readers not usually associated with it
▸ combining elements of multiple genres in surprising ways

Arguments about genre are most persuasive when they support a clear surface/depth interpretation, do not contain extraneous information, follow proper citation practices, and illustrate the complexity of the text.

You will probably find it easiest to make arguments about popular genres—such as those found in contemporary film—since you are immersed in the conventions of these genres. By contrast, formal, poetic, and historical genres will require more work on your part to discover the conventions and traditions associated with them.

∾ NOW PRACTICE ON YOUR OWN: DESIRE

Below we reprint "Desire" by Molly Peacock, an American-Canadian poet, essayist, and creative nonfiction writer. Read the poem then answer our questions about it to develop an argument using the genre strategy.

Molly Peacock
Desire   1984

It doesn't speak and it isn't schooled,
like a small foetal animal with wettened fur.
It is the blind instinct for life unruled,

visceral frankincense and animal myrrh.
It is what babies bring to kings,   5
an eyes-shut, ears-shut medicine of the heart
that smells and touches endings and beginnings
without the details of time's experienced *part-*
fit-into-part-fit-into-part. Like a paw,
it is blunt; like a pet who knows you   10
and nudges your knee with its snout—but more raw
and blinder and younger and more divine, too,
than the tamed wild—it's the drive for what is real,
deeper than the brain's detail: the drive to feel.

Questions

1. Determine the rhyme scheme of "Desire." Which type of sonnet is it?

2. In what ways does "Desire" follow sonnet conventions? How does it break from them?

3. One convention "Desire" violates is the iambic pentameter rhythm. Lines range from eight syllables to thirteen, far exceeding the small breaks from rhythm we sometimes expect in this genre. What might be the significance of Peacock's choice to use a sonnet rhyme scheme but not a sonnet rhythm? Try to make a surface/depth argument about Peacock's unconventional rhythm in this sonnet.

4. Because "Desire" has the same verse form and subject matter as Shakespeare's famous "Sonnet 129," we can think of "Sonnet 129" as part of the context of "Desire." How might Peacock be responding to, or revising, the theme of lust in "Sonnet 129"?

9

Social Relevance

In Chapter 2, we described complexity as the core value of literary analysis. All literary and cultural analyses work to draw out multiple levels of meaning in a text to show it as complex. Complexity is not the only value of literary analysis, though.

A secondary value of literary analysis is **social relevance**: the assumption that life and literature are connected and that literature, regardless of when it was written, can speak in some way to our contemporary situation. Unlike complexity, social relevance is not essential to a literary analysis: you can write a good literary analysis without indicating a text's social relevance. But many critics examine literature because they see it as relevant to understanding our social relationships and obligations likely underpins and motivates many critics' work. This value is widespread enough among critics to deserve your attention.

The social relevance strategy assumes that a first step toward social change lies in bringing hidden social problems and power relations to light and analyzing how these problems operate. When you make an argument invoking the value of social relevance, you move outward from the text to a statement about the relevance of this problem beyond the text itself. This move can give an **exigency**, or motivation, for literary analysis that goes beyond understanding the text itself to helping us understand larger social problems, forces, and issues.

The essay "Smelling Sri Lanka in Michael Ondaatje's 'The Cinnamon Peeler'" on page 168 in Chapter 7 invokes the value of social relevance at the end when the essay moves from an analysis of the poem to a statement about Sri Lankan identity and independence:

Ondaatje seems to be suggesting that if Sri Lanka is to survive as an independent country, its citizens must give up desires implanted by colonial authorities to completely control her and instead see her natural resources as just one part of her total culture. Ondaatje's poem implies it is time for Sri Lanka to find her own voice. This voice will be one that manages to acknowledge Sri Lanka's seductive, sensuous nature without becoming totally consumed by it.

While the body of this essay is concerned with understanding the poem, the final paragraph suggests a political statement implied by the poem. Because it moves outward, away from the text, *social relevance often appears most clearly in the final paragraphs of an essay*. But social relevance can also inform an entire essay, starting with topic selection. Social relevance arguments can be suggested in an essay's thesis statement, even though such arguments are generally not fully developed until the essay's conclusion.

Social relevance works in two ways when you are writing literary analyses. First, it may inform topic choice or what you choose to look for. Second, social relevance may be a strategy that you draw out in your essay—particularly in the concluding paragraph—by showing how a work is socially relevant for our society and culture. ■

USING SOCIAL RELEVANCE TO BRAINSTORM

It is worth noting what topics contemporary scholars tend to see as socially relevant since essays on these topics will be perceived as particularly interesting and insightful to many of your professors. What literature scholars see as socially relevant changes over time: what's considered socially relevant today might not be the same as what was seen as relevant twenty or thirty years ago—and it will likely differ from what is considered relevant twenty or thirty years from now.

Since at least 1990, the following topics have been particularly prominent concerns in literary scholarship:

▸ gender, race, ethnicity, sexual orientation, or social class and the complex and often hidden ways in which discrimination against certain groups functions, the often subversive ways oppressed or marginalized groups resist or fight back against their oppression, or the ways in which oppressed or marginalized groups paradoxically participate in their own oppression

- nationalism or national identity, particularly in postcolonial works (texts written after a former colony, such as India, Jamaica, Sri Lanka, Nigeria, or Mexico to name a few, has gained independence from a colonial power or influence)
- power and power struggles
- interpretation and how we make meaning or how we understand ourselves in a culture in which there are a range of competing perspectives, viewpoints, and realities
- boundaries between self and other
- relationships between the past and present
- relationships between "human" and "natural" worlds

You may find it helpful as a brainstorming activity to think of connections between the text you are analyzing and one or more of these topics. For instance, in the transcript excerpt below of a professor thinking aloud while reading "The Man to Send Rain Clouds" the professor uses the topics of nationalism and power struggles to help her generate surface/depth arguments.[1]

TRANSCRIPT EXCERPT
Professor using social relevance to interpret Silko's "The Man to Send Rain Clouds" while thinking aloud
Italicized words indicate the professor reading directly from the text.

While he waited he looked up at the twin bells from the king of Spain. Invocation of the colonial power . . . *with the last sunlight pouring around them in their tower.* Up above, away from the people, which is opposed to all these other earthy things that they ritually evoke: cornmeal; paint, presumably made out of clay and natural dyes. Things that come from the earth are associated with the Laguna people. Things up in the sky, ensconced in towers, are associated with the Spanish colonial influence.

---

[1] For an explanation of the "think-aloud" technique for observing a reader's and writer's thinking processes, see Chapter 3, p. 43.

USING SOCIAL RELEVANCE TO WRITE PERSUASIVELY

Critics are often most explicit about the contemporary social relevance of their arguments in their concluding paragraphs. After persuading their readers to see new layers of meaning in the text, they "step back" and discuss any larger ramifications of their argument for readers' understandings of our social world. The following example shows a concluding paragraph to an essay that clearly relates the analysis of the text to a socially relevant message:

> By having Mama embrace her heritage and her daughter Maggie, rather than accepting Dee's ideals, Walker's "Everyday Use" suggests that African-Americans should remember and accept their American heritage. They should not deny their past; rather, they should embrace it and use it every day, like the quilts. Through Mama, "Everyday Use" argues that movements to reject American heritage and embrace only one's African heritage are superficial and do not do justice to the past.

This paragraph clearly touches on several of the topics in the list above. Most obviously, it deals with issues of race and ethnicity. This paragraph also deals with issues of the boundary between past and present by arguing how the text puts forward a proposal for how African-Americans should relate to their painful and complicated backgrounds. We see how social relevance intersects with the need for a literary analysis to define the text's meaning as a whole, moving from specific details about the characters to the text's socially relevant overall message.

The next paragraph, also taken from the end of an essay, similarly invokes issues and themes that literary scholars find socially relevant:

> As Peter states, "They're us." Romero's zombies are us, Western culture, in all of our rotten, ludicrous glory. Like *Dawn*'s ravenous mall-walking ghouls, we are a culture obsessed with consuming. More tellingly, like Romero's zombies, we seek out those not like us in an attempt to change them, to *zombify* them into behaving as we do. Similarly, the zombies of *Dawn of the Dead* reflect the dehumanizing and destructive effects of our drive to seek fulfillment through individualistic consumption—an individualism that paradoxically causes us

to become mindless mirrors of one another. Romero's metaphor, although not subtle, remains sadly relevant today.

This critic invokes issues of the relationship between self and other by claiming that *Dawn of the Dead* shows how our consumer culture destroys individuality by turning individuals into "mindless mirrors of one another." The topic of the boundary between self and other is one that has long appealed to literary scholars. By combining this argument about self and other with a statement on today's consumer culture, this analysis makes itself socially relevant. It moves from a discussion of the details of the text to a larger argument about how the text is commenting on society.

HOW SOCIAL RELEVANCE WORKS WITH OTHER STRATEGIES OF LITERARY ANALYSIS

Social relevance is not just something that you "tack on" to the end of your essay. Instead, when used, it often will inform your entire argument. As such, it works hand in hand with the other strategies of literary analysis we have discussed thus far.

▸ **Surface/depth and social relevance work together to reveal the hidden details of how this systematic problem functions.** As with all strategies of literary analysis, social relevance needs to work to uncover nonobvious complexities in a text. For instance, a female character looking at herself in a mirror can on the surface be simply preparing for a party, but on a deeper level this action can take on social significance when we consider the role that mirrors often play in stories about women. This act of glancing in the mirror can show the woman as concerned with the male gaze and making herself pleasing to men, or it could show her as falling into the trap of female vanity. In either case, we can make an argument claiming that on a deeper level this seemingly insignificant act is representative of a larger social problem that ties a woman's worth to her beauty.

▸ **Patterns and social relevance work together to uncover systematic social problems embedded in a text.** These problems can be intended by the author, as in the case of "The Cinnamon Peeler" where Ondaatje may have intended the poem to be read (at least by his fellow Sri Lankans) as a statement of his newly independent country's relationship to its most significant natural resource, cinnamon. These problems can also be unintended by the author: for instance, many critics have examined seemingly unintended racism in the works of authors such as Ernest Hemingway or Herman Melville—authors who may not have had such a concern on their minds. Social relevance works with the patterns strategy to show how the effects of power and privilege can be so pervasive that they are embedded in common everyday occurrences or seemingly insignificant textual details. Thus, the literary critic works to find evidence of a particular problem or issue in both obvious and surprising areas of a text.

▸ **Context and social relevance work together to show how a text can reveal something about culture or society.** We see many of the essays in Chapter 7, "Context," deal with socially relevant themes. For instance, David White's argument in "'Everyday Use': Defining African-American Heritage" (excerpted on p. 158) is that through this story Alice Walker challenges the Black Power social movement to show greater respect for the complicated and uniquely American cultural legacies of African-Americans living in the rural South. In the passage below he uses contextual information about the Black Power movement to make this socially relevant point about the continued complex legacies of slavery.

> Walker uses Dee to symbolize the Black Power movement, which was characterized by bright and beautiful blacks who were vocal and aggressive in their demands. Many of them spoke disparagingly about their "Uncle Tom" ancestors and adopted certain aspects of African culture in their speech and dress. Mama's descriptions of Dee portray her as this type of individual: "Dee, though. She would always look anyone in the eye. Hesitation was no part of her nature, . . . She was determined to stare down any disaster in her efforts. Her eyelids would

not flicker for minutes at a time. . . . At sixteen she had a style of her own: and she knew what style was" (409). These personality traits, along with her style of dress and speech, establish her identity as a symbol of the Black Power movement.

It is important to recognize that Walker is not condemning the Black Power movement as a whole. Rather, she is challenging that part of the movement that does not acknowledge and properly respect the many African-Americans who endured incredible hardships in their efforts to survive in a hostile environment. She uses the character of Dee to demonstrate this misguided black pride.

Social relevance also informs the theoretical lens strategy, as we will see in the following chapter. In all these cases, social relevance moves outward from the text to help us understand the relevance of this problem beyond the text itself.

CRITICISM CHANGES OVER TIME

The strategies described in this textbook have changed in their use and acceptability over time. Prior to the twentieth century, much literary criticism was focused on author biography or linguistics. However, in the early twentieth century, a new movement in literary criticism, known as New Criticism, began to advocate for interpretations that strictly focused on the text and its meaning, with little reference to material outside the primary text. The close reading strategies described in Part 2 of this book are primarily inherited from the era of New Criticism.

Beginning in the late 1960s, the membership of the field of English studies began to diversify. The perspectives brought by women and minorities entering this discipline forever changed how English studies understands its own work. As women and minorities became literary critics, they challenged the field not only to consider new works but also to adopt new methods of interpretation. The social relevance strategy discussed in this chapter and the theoretical lens strategy discussed in the next chapter are two such relatively recent methods of interpretation that have changed how we think of literary criticism. Literary criticism no longer treats texts as isolated objects but rather as parts of a network of social forces.

Our point here is that criticism has changed over time and will continue to change. The critics who successfully challenged previous modes of criticism did so by using interpretive and argumentative strategies that were well established at the time. Thus, using established argumentative strategies does not prevent new strategies and arguments from developing. The discourse community (see Chapter 1) of literary criticism will continue to evolve as new voices enter the conversation and influence the way we interpret and think about texts.

Review

This chapter describes a value that underpins many critics' motivations for interpreting literary texts: the belief that digging beneath the surface of such texts can yield insights useful for improving our present-day lives. We give this value the name "social relevance" and suggest ways awareness of this discourse community's preference for it can inform your brainstorming, writing, and revising. We also note that social relevance is a relatively new value in the field of literary criticism; its prominence today shows us that criticism changes over time and, as new members enter the conversation about textual interpretation, the field's values and methods of interpretation will continue to evolve.

Exercise

Re-read either "Sylvia Plath's 'Morning Song' and the Challenge of Motherly Identity" (p. 71) or "Contradictory Desires in Michael Ondaatje's 'The Cinnamon Peeler'" (p. 79). Use the social relevance strategy to write a new thesis statement and concluding paragraph to the essay you have chosen.

For Discussion

Share your paragraphs from the preceding exercise with your classmates. Do your classmates' uses of social relevance seem to expand and add depth to the essays, or do they feel tacked on? How might the writers make additional use of social relevance in revising and expanding these essays?

10 Theoretical Lens

This chapter introduces you to a strategy that, like the context strategy, uses material from outside the text to help with interpretation. With the **theoretical lens strategy**, a critic makes explicit use another argument or theory—sometimes from a discipline outside literary studies—to explain a possible layer of meaning in a text. Theoretical lens is a powerful strategy because it helps us dig deeper into a text and reveal its complexities while also arguing for the text's social relevance.

Although the theoretical lens strategy might initially seem unfamiliar, the truth is you already interpret literature through a lens. For instance, most of the interpretations we have provided of "Morning Song" thus far look at this poem through the lens of twentieth-century ideas of motherhood or American values of identity and individualism. Likewise, our discussions of Silko's "The Man to Send Rain Clouds" use religion and colonialism as lenses for looking at the text. The difference between these readings and the theoretical lens strategy is that with the latter you explicitly name, and reflect on, a particular theory.

What do we mean by a theory? One simple definition is that a **theory** is an argument that attempts to explain something. Literary critics often draw on theories of language, society, and individuality (to name a few) to help them understand texts. The theoretical lens strategy explicitly cites an author or a text associated with a particular theory and uses it to dig beneath the surface of a literary text.

We can see a short example of this strategy in an excerpt on page 200, which provides a potential thesis for an essay using the theoretical lens strategy.

In her book *The Second Sex*, the feminist philosopher Simone de Beauvoir describes how many mothers initially feel indifferent toward and estranged from their new infants, asserting that though "the woman would like to feel that the new baby is surely hers as is her own hand, . . . she does not recognize him because . . . she has experienced her pregnancy without him: she has no past in common with this little stranger" (507). Sylvia Plath's "Morning Song" exemplifies the indifference and estrangement that de Beauvoir describes. However, where de Beauvoir asserts that "a whole complex of economical and sentimental considerations makes the baby seem either a hindrance or a jewel" (510), Plath's poem illustrates how a child can simultaneously be both hindrance and jewel. Ultimately, "Morning Song" shows us how new mothers can overcome the conflicting emotions de Beauvoir describes.[1]

In this analysis, de Beauvoir's *The Second Sex* is the **theoretical text** that acts as a lens for reading the **primary text**, Plath's "Morning Song." The analysis begins by briefly summarizing the theoretical text. The second sentence then describes how concepts from the theoretical text (such as estrangement and alienation) are found in the primary text (i.e., "Morning Song"). Finally, the critic reverses the direction of the analysis by reflecting back on the theoretical text. Thus, the last sentence suggests that a reading of "Morning Song" can help us better understand issues described in *The Second Sex*.

You might notice that this analysis provides a similar reading of "Morning Song" to the one in Chapter 4 (see p. 71). Both analyses argue that the mother feels alienated from her infant but appears to be overcoming this feeling by the end of the poem. One key difference between these two analyses is that the one above explicitly names a

---

[1] The Works Cited page for this paper contains two entries: De Beauvoir, Simone. *The Second Sex*. New York: McClelland and Stewart, 1953. Print; Plath, Sylvia. "Morning Song." *The Collected Poems*. Ed. Ted Hughes. New York: Harper & Row, 1981. 156–57. Print. This passage is by Daniel DiGiacomo (*From Mourning Song to "Morning Song": The Maturation of a Maternal Bond*. Web. 22 Dec. 2006).

theoretical text and uses it to structure the analysis. By describing de Beauvoir's philosophy, it makes explicit the ideas about motherhood that will be used to look at Plath's poem, rather than leaving those ideas as unstated assumptions. As a result, analyses that use the theoretical lens strategy place their explanatory assumptions, as well as their interpretations, on the table for readers to inspect and debate.

The figure below illustrates this relationship between theoretical and primary text. There are two parts to the theoretical lens strategy. In part 1, the theoretical text acts as a lens for discovering arguments in the primary text. Some aspects of the primary text become magnified while others recede to the background. Part 2 is a feature of more sophisticated analyses, which use the primary text to reflect back on the theoretical text by challenging or extending some aspect of the theory. As you are a beginning literary critic, completing part 1 may be sufficient, but as you become more experienced and confident in your analyses, you should try to implement part 2 of this strategy.

This image presents the theoretical text in capital letters because this text often provides an organizing structure for the analysis, which begins and ends with a discussion of the theoretical lens. The thesis in

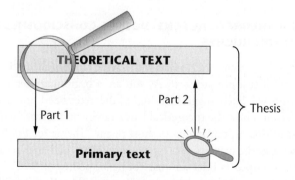

Relationship between theoretical and primary texts. *Part 1 uses the theoretical text as a lens for interpretation, while part 2 uses the primary text to reflect on the theory.*

a theoretical lens essay attempts to capture this relationship between theoretical and primary text. ■

THEORETICAL LENS *VS.* CONTEXT

Many students are initially confused about the difference between the theoretical lens and the context strategy. Both strategies make use of material from outside the text to deepen an interpretation and both involve citing other work. The difference has to do with the type of text cited and the extent to which that text is used as a framework for analysis and interpretation.

Whereas the context strategy often uses factual information to inform an interpretation, the theoretical lens strategy uses complex explanatory arguments as an interpretive tool. These theoretical arguments are generally referred to throughout the analysis and often become a focus in and of themselves as the critic uses the primary text to challenge or extend the theoretical text.

Don't worry if you are confused at the moment—this is a challenging analytic strategy! We believe as you begin to read theoretical texts and look at examples of the theoretical lens strategy in action, you will start to see how it may be used in your own writing.

APPLYING A THEORETICAL LENS: DOUBLE-CONSCIOUSNESS AND LANGSTON HUGHES

Experienced literary critics are familiar with a wide range of theoretical texts they can use to interpret a primary text. As you are a beginning literature student, your instructors will likely suggest pairings of theoretical and primary texts.

To understand how the theoretical lens strategy might work with one such pairing, first read Langston Hughes's short poem "Theme for English B." This poem will serve as the primary text for the discussions and analyses that follow. Then read the **synopsis** (a brief summary of major points) of W. E. B. Du Bois's essay "Of Our Spiritual Strivings," originally printed in *The Souls of Black Folk*. This synopsis, which explains key concepts in "Of Our Spiritual Strivings," will be the theoretical text used to analyze Hughes's poem. The complete text of Du Bois's essay appears in the appendix of theoretical lenses on page 327. If your instructor assigns the complete essay, you may find it useful first to read the full essay and then use the synopsis on page 204 to double-check your understanding of the key concepts. (The page references in the synopsis refer to the appendix in this book.)

Langston Hughes

Theme for English B   1951

The instructor said,
> *Go home and write*
> *a page tonight.*
> *And let that page come out of you—*
> *Then, it will be true.*   5
I wonder if it's that simple?
I am twenty-two, colored, born in Winston-Salem.
I went to school there, then Durham, then here
to this college on the hill above Harlem.
I am the only colored student in my class.   10
The steps from the hill lead down into Harlem,
through a park, then I cross St. Nicholas,
Eighth Avenue, Seventh, and I come to the Y,
the Harlem Branch Y, where I take the elevator
up to my room, sit down, and write this page: 15

It's not easy to know what is true for you or me
at twenty-two, my age. But I guess I'm what
I feel and see and hear, Harlem, I hear you:
hear you, hear me—we two—you, me, talk on this page.
(I hear New York, too.) Me—who?   20
Well, I like to eat, sleep, drink, and be in love.
I like to work, read, learn, and understand life.
I like a pipe for a Christmas present,
or records—Bessie, bop, or Bach.
I guess being colored doesn't make me *not* like   25
the same things other folks like who are other races.

So will my page be colored that I write?
Being me, it will not be white.
But it will be
a part of you, instructor.   30
You are white—
yet a part of me, as I am a part of you.
That's American.
Sometimes perhaps you don't want to be a part of me.
Nor do I often want to be a part of you.   35
But we are, that's true!
As I learn from you,
I guess you learn from me—
although you're older—and white—
and somewhat more free.   40

This is my page for English B.

Exercise

What is the surface meaning of Hughes's "Theme for English B"? What are
some surface interpretations that you think most of your classmates will
immediately agree on?

SYNOPSIS
The Veil and Double-consciousness in Du Bois's "Of Our Spiritual Strivings"

In his 1903 text *The Souls of Black Folk* W. E. B. Du Bois introduces two related
concepts to describe the Black[2] experience in America: "the veil" and "double-
consciousness." The first mention of the veil occurs when Du Bois reflects on his
childhood relationships with White classmates:

Then it dawned upon me with a certain suddenness that I was different
from the others; or like [them perhaps] in heart and life and longing, but
shut out from their world by a vast veil. (326)

---

[2] We use the word *Black* rather than *African-American* deliberately since the term African-American
suggests a level of acceptance of African-Americans into mainstream White culture that did not exist
at the time Du Bois was writing.

He goes on to generalize his experience, describing all Black Americans as "born with a veil, and gifted with second-sight in this American world"— a world which yields him no true self-consciousness, but only lets him see himself through the revelation of the other world (326).

Du Bois's use of the veil to describe Black consciousness works at least three ways. First, and most obviously, the veil (like skin color) is an external marker of difference that separates Blacks from Whites. This veil allows Blacks to see the opportunities available to Whites, and its transparency may even lead them to believe these opportunities are within reach. However, the veil is also a barrier, preventing Blacks from fulfilling their ambitions.

Secondly, the veil prevents Whites from perceiving Blacks' individuality. Someone wearing a veil presents not a face, but a veil to the world. This veil is indistinguishable from other veils. Thus, Whites looking at Blacks see their own racist assumptions (symbolized by the veil) rather than the individual humans that reside underneath.

Finally, and most insidiously, the veil prevents Blacks from fully knowing themselves. Someone looking into a mirror while wearing a veil sees not a face, but a veil. They have no opportunity to study their own uniqueness. When Blacks try to understand themselves or their cultures, what they see are the racist assumptions that define how others see them.

This experience of always seeing oneself through a veil produces what Du Bois calls "double-consciousness." In perhaps his most quoted passage, Du Bois writes:

> It is a peculiar sensation, this double-consciousness, this sense of always looking at one's self through the eyes of others, of measuring one's soul by the tape of a world that looks on in amused contempt and pity. One ever feels his two-ness,—an American, a Negro; two souls, two thoughts, two unreconciled strivings; two warring ideals in one dark body, whose dogged strength alone keeps it from being torn asunder. (327)

Double-consciousness involves two identities: a true identity hidden from the world and an identity others see. But the constant awareness that the perception of White Americans is more powerful than one's self-perception creates great inner turmoil, a struggle between self-loathing and self-respect.

At the same time, double-consciousness represents Blacks' desire to fully join American culture without giving up the customs and values that White America judge as ignorant and inferior. This dilemma is particularly strong for Black intellectuals: to be accepted by Whites, they need to shed the beliefs and customs of their Black upbringing. But to be leaders of their Black communities, they need to align themselves with qualities that Whites scorn. Du Bois explains:

> The history of the American Negro is the history of this strife,—this longing to attain self-conscious manhood, to merge his double self into a better and truer self. In this merging he wishes neither of the older selves to be lost. He would not Africanize America, for America has too much to teach the world and Africa. He would not bleach his Negro soul in a flood of white Americanism, for he knows that Negro blood has a message for the world. He simply wishes to make it possible for a man to be both a Negro and an American, without being cursed and spit upon by his fellows, without having the doors of Opportunity closed roughly in his face. (327)

Du Bois argues that Blacks should be allowed to take what is best from both their African and their American heritages and merge them. Only then will the veil that prevents African Americans from realizing their potential be removed.

Exercises

1. In your own words, define the concepts "the veil" and "double-consciousness."

2. How would you describe the relationship between these two concepts? Are they identical? Different aspects of the same phenomena? Can one exist without the other?

3. Du Bois states that double-consciousness was central to Black life in the early 1900s, but this does not mean that only African-Americans experience double-consciousness. Provide an example of a situation in which someone other than an African-American might experience double-consciousness.

4. If you are visually oriented, try drawing a picture that illustrates the concept of double-consciousness.

USING THE THEORETICAL LENS STRATEGY TO BRAINSTORM

Step 1. Choose a theoretical lens

We have suggested using W. E. B. Du Bois's theory of the veil and double-consciousness as a lens for "Theme for English B." However, as you become more experienced at reading theoretical texts, you will be able to pick your own lenses. You might read a primary text and be reminded of a theoretical text that can help explain it. Other times, you may read a theoretical text and recall a primary text that illustrates the theory. As literary critics become more advanced, they often develop commitments to particular theoretical lenses through which they interpret a wide range of primary texts.

Step 2. Work to understand the surface meaning of both primary and theoretical texts

To use the theoretical lens strategy effectively, first make sure you understand the surface meaning of both the primary and the theoretical texts. The preceding exercises should help you test your understanding of both Hughes and Du Bois.

Step 3. Re-read the primary text using the surface/depth strategy

Now look for passages with deeper meanings that can be explained by arguments in the theoretical text. For instance, once you feel you understand Du Bois's essay, try re-reading "Theme for English B" with the concepts of the veil and double-consciousness in mind. Can you now see these concepts beneath the surface of parts of the poem? Do these concepts help you understand possible deeper layers of meaning in parts of the poem? Try to make surface/depth arguments that explain passages in the primary text using concepts drawn from the theoretical text. Remember to use the patterns strategy to locate other related surface/depth interpretations. Try out different connections between the primary text and the theoretical text and decide later which ones you can best support.

Step 4. Reflect on how the primary text differs from the theoretical text

Finally, brainstorm for ways you see the primary text differing from or extending the theoretical text. Do Hughes and Du Bois have similar or different interpretations of the African-American experience (especially that of the African-American intellectual)? Had the African-American experience changed in the fifty years between when the two were writing? Does the primary literary text offer any solutions or different ways of looking at a problem or issue from the theoretical text?

You may find that ideas for this step occur as you are drafting your analysis. Rather than ignore what cannot be explained by the lens text, keep track of these observations because they may help you craft a sophisticated development of the ideas in the theoretical text. As with literal lenses (in microscopes, corrective eyewear, cameras, etc.), each theoretical lens obscures some aspects of what it surveys just as it brings into greater clarity other aspects. While the bulk of the work of a critic using the theoretical lens strategy is to argue for what the lens text helps us see, considering what it cannot explain may lead to insights for contributing to the discourse community's theoretical discussions.

The following excerpt from a transcript of a professor thinking aloud while reading illustrates how this professor used Du Bois's *The Souls of Black Folk* to interpret "Theme for English B."[3] Note how the professor refers repeatedly to the "veil" and "double-consciousness" in testing out different interpretations.

TRANSCRIPT EXCERPT
Professor using theoretical lens to interpret "Theme for English B" while thinking aloud
Italicized words indicate the professor reading directly from the poem.

So will my page be colored that I write?

I guess here he's worried that the instructor is going to judge him by the color of his skin rather than what he writes. He's maybe worried his instructor will just see the veil.

---

[3] For an explanation of the "think-aloud" technique for observing a reader's and writer's thinking processes, see Chapter 3, p. 43.

So will my page be colored that I write?
Being me, it will not be white.

Huh. So he's agreeing that his color does affect what he writes. I guess this is him agreeing with Du Bois? Du Bois says the veil's unique to African-Americans and Hughes seems to say that his skin color will make his paper different than everyone else's.

But it will be
a part of you, instructor.
You are white—
yet a part of me, as I am a part of you.
That's American.

Now the first time I read this it seemed really pat . . . like we're all happy here, everything's good. But I wonder . . . he's saying his paper is going to be part White, part not White. This could be good but maybe it also means he can't see himself like Du Bois says. All he sees is the "not white" parts of himself—the veil. Or is that too strong? I'm not sure.

But it will be
a part of you, instructor.

Instructor . . . The way that comes out it's like he's acknowledging the instructor's authority, but he's also calling him out. Maybe accusing him? The instructor is the one who assigned the essay. Is that why it's part of the instructor?

You are white—
yet a part of me, as I am a part of you.
That's American.

The instructor is White here. Is Hughes reversing things, suggesting that the veil prevents him from seeing the instructor? Du Bois says White culture, White education, defines Blackness. But Hughes seems to be reversing things . . . part of White culture is African-American culture.

You are white—
yet a part of me, as I am a part of you.
That's American.

So American is both Black and White. Like the page he's writing on. Black ink on white paper. Yet he is worried the instructor won't be able to see this. He's instructing the instructor on what it means to be African-American. Or maybe he's saying the instructor's Whiteness couldn't exist without some Blackness to contrast it to. Huh. Or maybe this is an attempt to make the White instructor feel double-consciousness by showing what a Black student thinks of him? That's interesting. I still don't know whether to read this as hopeful or resigned.

In this transcript excerpt, the professor looks for what she thinks may be examples of "veils" and "double-consciousness" in Hughes's poem. This strategy allows her to delve beneath the surface of the poem and suggest some interpretations. At the same time, the professor is using her reading of the poem to question how double-consciousness might affect Whites as well as African-Americans—something Du Bois does not explore in his original essay defining double-consciousness.

Exercises

1. The professor in the preceding think-aloud transcript uses the concepts of the veil and double-consciousness to interpret lines 27–33 of the poem. Find at least three other passages in the poem (see p. 203) that you can analyze using these concepts. For each passage, make a surface/depth argument indicating how these lines can help us reflect on either the veil or double-consciousness.

2. The professor in the think-aloud suggests Hughes "seems to be reversing" Du Bois's description of double-consciousness. What do you think she means by this? Do you see Hughes as agreeing with Du Bois's theory of double-consciousness—or is there something different in how Hughes is describing African-American consciousness?

USING A THEORETICAL LENS TO WRITE PERSUASIVELY

Much like the "smaller" application of the context strategy, it is possible to use the theoretical lens strategy on the small scale by "name-dropping" a theorist or theoretical argument as support for a specific interpretation. This smaller application of the theoretical lens strategy would be done briefly by summarizing the theoretical concept, explaining how this concept illuminates some aspect of the primary text, and properly citing the theoretical text.

However, it is more common to use a theoretical lens as an overarching frame for an entire essay. If your brainstorming found several interesting points of connection between the theoretical text and the primary text, you may benefit from using an extended application of the theoretical lens strategy. To make such an extended argument, you should:

▸ **name and cite the theoretical text and accurately summarize this text's argument.** Usually this short summary appears in one to two paragraphs at the beginning of the essay. You will want to be sure your summary includes the key concepts you use in your paper to analyze the primary literary text.

▸ **use the surface/depth strategy to show how deeper meanings in the primary text can be explained by concepts from the theoretical text.** You might think about this as creating a "match argument" between the literary and theoretical texts. Take important points made in the theoretical argument and match them to particular events or descriptions in the literary text. For instance, you could argue Hughes's line *So will my page be colored that I write?* (27) matches Du Bois's argument that the veil prevents Whites from seeing Blacks' individuality. Such a match argument can form an organizing structure for the essay as you develop whole paragraphs to support different points of connection between the theoretical and primary texts. You may be able to devote an entire paragraph to the claim that Du Bois's concept of "the veil" can help us understand Hughes's depiction of the challenges his speaker faces in asking his instructor to see him on his own terms.

▸ **support your surface/depth claims linking the primary and theoretical texts with textual evidence from the primary text.** If you claim that a particular passage exemplifies a particular theory, you need to provide evidence in the form of quotations or paraphrases to support this interpretation. This evidence will most certainly need to be provided from the primary literary text you are analyzing but perhaps also occasionally from the theoretical text, too, especially if you connect the literary text to a small detail in the theoretical text or if the wording of the theoretical text helps you explain something in the primary text. Use the patterns strategy (see Chapter 4) to provide multiple examples from the primary text supporting your claims that it matches elements of the theoretical text.

▸ **reveal something complex and unexpected about the primary text.** The goal of the theoretical lens strategy—like all strategies of literary analysis—should be to show that the text you are analyzing is complex and can be understood on multiple levels.

▸ **challenge, extend, or reevaluate the theoretical text (for more sophisticated analyses).** The most sophisticated uses of the theoretical lens strategy not only help you better understand the primary text but also help you better understand—and reveal complexities in—the theoretical text. When you first start applying this strategy, it may be sufficient to argue how the theoretical text helps us understand the primary text, but as you advance, you should attempt the second part of this strategy and use the primary text to extend or challenge the theoretical argument. Such arguments may serve as starting points for you to contribute to literary theory as a theorist yourself. These arguments are often made in the concluding paragraphs of literary analyses using the theoretical lens strategy.

Because the theoretical lens strategy requires briefly summarizing a theoretical argument before focusing on the analysis, it often results in a **delayed thesis**—a thesis that appears after the first or second paragraph. Often, complex arguments require a critic to spend time elaborating on the background for an argument before stating an explicit thesis. However, some professors have strong preferences for an early thesis. Therefore, while the delayed thesis is a valid organizational strategy, you may wish to check your instructor's preferences before using it.

COMMON WORDS AND PHRASES ASSOCIATED WITH THEORETICAL LENS		
concept	helps us understand	is an example of
exemplifies	illuminates	structure
framework	illustrates	testifies to

The following short essay uses W. E. B. Du Bois's *The Souls of Black Folk* as a theoretical lens for analyzing Langston Hughes's "Theme for English B."
Read the essay then try the exercise that follows it.

> ### Double-consciousness in "Theme for English B"
>
> The post-slavery history of African-Americans in the United States has been one of struggle for recognition. This struggle continued through the civil rights movement in the 1970s and '80s. W. E. B. Du Bois, one of the most influential African-American leaders of the early twentieth century, described the complicated effects racism had on African-American selfhood. In his treatise *The Souls of Black Folk*, Du Bois introduces the term "double-consciousness" to describe African-Americans' struggle for self-recognition. Double-consciousness is the sense of "always looking at one's self through the eyes of others" (8). It means that an African-American "[e]ver feels his two-ness—an American, a Negro; two souls, two thoughts, two unreconciled strivings; two warring ideals in one dark body" (8). According to Du Bois, double-consciousness means that African-Americans are always judging themselves through a veil of racism, experiencing how others judge and define them rather than how they might define and express themselves.

Langston Hughes's poem "Theme for English B," written nearly fifty years after Du Bois's essay, depicts one African-American's continued struggle with double-consciousness. However, where Du Bois sees double-consciousness as a painful condition he hopes will one day disappear, Hughes seems to have a more positive view, suggesting that mainstream Americans should also have an opportunity to experience this condition. Instead of eradicating double-consciousness, Hughes seeks to universalize it. His poem suggests that true equality will be possible when all cultures are able to experience and appreciate double-consciousness.

We see the poem's speaker struggling with double-consciousness when he expresses difficulty articulating what is "true" for himself. Hughes writes:

> It's not easy to know what is true for you or me
> at twenty-two, my age. But I guess I'm what
> I feel and see and hear, Harlem, I hear you:
> hear you, hear me—we two—you, me, talk on this page.
> (I hear New York, too.) Me—who? (16–20)

In this passage, which concludes with a question about who he is, the speaker expresses a divided self. At first, he seems to identify with Harlem, an African-American neighborhood in New York, where he is currently sitting and writing. However, this identification becomes troubled by his acknowledgment that Harlem does not completely define him. When the speaker writes "hear you, hear me—we two" (19), he suggests that "you" (referring to Harlem) and "me" (referring to himself) are intimately related but not identical. They are two voices that, while both present in his poem, still "talk" (19) to one another. The fact that these voices converse, rather than speak as one, indicates they are not completely merged.

This sense of a divided self is further reinforced by the claim "(I hear New York, too.)" (20). This aside is interesting because it establishes Harlem (a neighborhood in New York) as both separate from and connected to the larger city. This division reflects what Du Bois calls the "two-ness [of being] an American [and] a Negro" (8). By placing

New York in parentheses, the speaker may be suggesting that the American part of himself represented by New York plays a weaker role in his identity than the African-American self represented by Harlem. Like Du Bois, the speaker in "Theme for English B" experiences inner conflict when he tries to reconcile the different parts of himself.

We further see evidence of the speaker's conflict when he writes that he likes "Bessie, bop, or Bach" (24). "Bessie" refers to the popular blues singer Bessie Smith, an African-American woman who sang a very African-American style of music. At the other end of the spectrum is "Bach," which refers to the classical European composer J. S. Bach and represents a traditionally White form of music. In the middle is "bop," which refers to "bebop," a form of jazz made popular in the 1940s that inspired a particular form of dance mostly practiced by White teenagers at the time. In saying that he likes all of these forms of music, the speaker indicates that he is a mix of both African and European identities—like Du Bois, he feels both traditional White and traditional African-American culture calling him.

The "page" that the poem's speaker has been asked to write likewise reflects the two-ness of being African-American. An essay can be thought of as black ink on white paper, which in the context of this poem represents Black identity articulated against a White background. The speaker refers to this conflict of identities when he writes, "So will my page be colored that I write? / Being me, it will not be white" (27–28). These lines suggest that the speaker is worried that his instructor will only see him as a representative Black student. It shows how the speaker is caught in a double bind: when the teacher asks the class to write something "true" (5), he will expect this particular student (who in the first stanza tells us he is the only colored student in the class) to write in a way consistent with his obvious Black heritage. But the student is aware that his White teacher doesn't really know what it means to be Black. Thus, if he writes in a way that fulfills his instructor's expectations, he will write a page that seems to a White teacher to be an authentic depiction of what it means to be Black—in other words, a White representation of Blackness. This dilemma illustrates what Du Bois refers to as "always looking at one's self through the eyes of others" (8). Because the speaker in the poem is so aware of what his instructor (and possibly the other students in the class) already thinks of him, he is having difficulty articulating just whom he really is.

At the end of the poem, however, instead of calling for the eradication of double-consciousness as Du Bois does when he longs for the day that African-Americans will be able to "merge his double-self into a better and truer self" (9), Hughes seems to suggest that instead his instructor needs to feel the double-identity that he feels so strongly. Thus, he writes "You are white— / yet a part of me, as I am a part of you" (31–32) and "As I learn from you, / I guess you learn from me—" (36–37). These lines indicate that the White instructor needs to accept African-American identity as part of his own culture, just as the speaker has needed to see both parts of his identity calling him. This ability to feel and be multiple perspectives, cultures, and backgrounds at once is labeled "American" in the second stanza. Hughes seems to be suggesting that even though the "two-ness" he feels is often difficult and painful, it needs to be seen as central to American—and not just African-American—identity. When he states at the end of the poem, "I guess you learn from me" (38), he is turning the tables on the teacher, and on Whites in general, by suggesting that they have as much to learn from exploring Black culture as Blacks have to learn by studying classic White culture.

Works Cited

Du Bois, W. E. B. *The Souls of Black Folk*. 1903. New York: Penguin Books, 1989. Print.

Hughes, Langston. "Theme for English B." *Digging into Literature: Strategies for Reading, Analysis, and Writing.* Joanna Wolfe and Laura Wilder. Boston: Bedford/St. Martin's, 2016. 203. Print.

Exercises

1. This analysis uses the theoretical lens strategy. What does it do well? In other words, which of the criteria for an effective use of theoretical lens (see p. 211) does it meet?

2. What other strategies of literary analysis do you see used in this essay? Mark all the strategies you see. How effectively does this writer use these strategies? Which of the arguments made in the analysis do you think a literature professor would identify as most complex? Which are least complex or least persuasive? Why?

3. Identify the essay's thesis. Is this a good placement of the thesis? How is this thesis developed in each of the paragraphs in the essay's body? Is this organization effective?

4. Although this essay is over one thousand words, there are still parts of the poem it has not mentioned at all. Write another paragraph that analyses a section of the poem not discussed in this essay, arguing how it supports or expands Du Bois's idea of double-consciousness.

ADDITIONAL THEORETICAL TEXTS

As you become more familiar with academic writing, you will discover texts and theories from your classes that may make effective theoretical lenses. Literary analyses have successfully used texts from anthropology, history, psychology, philosophy, science, and literary theory as theoretical paradigms that can reveal complexities in a literary text. These theoretical texts are often then reinterpreted and reevaluated by close examination of their workings in the primary text under discussion.

There are literally thousands of texts that can be used as theoretical lenses to interpret literature. However, not surprisingly, certain types of theoretical texts are more useful than others. Critics tend to group similar theoretical texts into various schools of thought. Some of the more common of these schools are included in the following table.

New Criticism	Marxist criticism
Structuralism	New Historicism
Deconstruction	Postcolonial criticism
Feminist criticism	Reader response criticism
Psychoanalytic criticism	

Reviewing these different schools of criticism is beyond the scope of this book, but you can find out more about them in a number of guides and anthologies, including Ross Murfin and Supryia M. Ray's *The Bedford Glossary of Critical and Literary Terms* and David H. Richter's *The Critical Tradition: Classic Texts and Contemporary Trends.*

To give you more practice applying the theoretical lens strategy, we have included three additional theoretical texts in the appendix that can provide productive theoretical lenses for the literary texts included in this textbook. These theoretical texts represent different schools of criticism and, with some effort, should be accessible to you. The appendix provides a summary of each text, which you can use to gauge your understanding of its theoretical concepts, as well as prompts for applying the text to the stories and poems in this book.

Review

This chapter focuses on the theoretical lens strategy, which explicitly names, cites, and uses a theoretical text as a lens for interpreting a primary text. There are two parts to a theoretical lens argument. In the first part, key details in the primary text are matched to the theoretical text in order to reveal complexities beneath the surface. The second part, found in more sophisticated analyses, uses the primary text to challenge or reinterpret the theoretical text.

This chapter also introduces and summarizes Du Bois's theory of double-consciousness, which is the sense of always seeing oneself through others' eyes. Du Bois argues that double-consciousness defined African-American existence at the turn of the twentieth century and limited what African-Americans could achieve.

∾ NOW PRACTICE ON YOUR OWN: DOUBLE-CONSCIOUSNESS

1. We have read two other texts by African-Americans in this book: Phillis Wheatley's short poem "On Being Brought from Africa to America" (p. 153) and Alice Walker's short story "Everyday Use," (p. 131). How might you use the concept of double-consciousness or the veil to interpret either of these primary texts?

2. Leslie Marmon Silko's "The Man to Send Rain Clouds" (p. 29) is a story about another minority group, Native Americans, in the United States. Try rereading this short story while looking for passages that suggest either the veil or double-consciousness. Do these concepts help us understand this story or its characters? Does the story help us understand other ways that the veil or double-consciousness might function when dominant and minority groups interact? How might Du Bois's theories help us understand the similarities and differences between Native American and African-American experiences?

11 Joining the Critical Conversation

There are good reasons, beyond merely citing authorities, to draw on published literary criticism in your literary analyses. Rather than see published criticism as providing the definitive (and dead-end) solutions to your interpretive puzzles, we invite you to treat these publications as further, extended turns in the conversations about texts that you and your classmates have been having. This chapter will assist you in signaling to your readers that you have something new to add not only to your classroom conversations about a literary text but also to the discourse community of published (and actively publishing) literary critics. ■

REPEATING THE CONVERSATION *VS.* CONTRIBUTING SOMETHING NEW TO THE CONVERSATION

You may already be familiar with one method of using published literary criticism in your literary analyses: repeating what a published critic has said because it bolsters your own argument. Repeating what a critic has said serves a legitimate, but limited, function. There are times when you will want to repeat a good idea that you have read (for example, if you learned something new about a text from reading a critic, or if a critic makes an unusually strong argument you want to cite). But there are other times when student writers repeat what other critics have said without adding anything new. The following passage is an example of simply repeating a critic's argument.

In "On Being Brought from Africa to America," Phillis Wheatley strategically uses ambiguity to criticize slaveholders in ways that would make it difficult to accuse her of insubordination. As James Levernier writes, "Ambiguities . . . indicate that Wheatley was far from comfortable with the racist attitudes of her white contemporaries, and that while propriety kept a black female slave from openly criticizing an institution like slavery, Wheatley used her considerable linguistic talent to embed in the poem, at a very sophisticated level, a far different message than that which the poem superficially conveys" (25). In particular, Levernier points to "a deliberate ambiguity" at the end of the poem "over who is being addressed by the verb 'Remember'" (26). Levernier claims that on a literal level Wheatley is asking white Christians to remember that "Negros" (Wheatley 7) have "souls which can be saved" (Levernier 26). But on a deeper level she is reminding her readers that "both Christians and Negroes, like Cain, are sons of Adam and that as sons of Adam they both inherit equally the fruits of original sin, of which slavery and economic greed are a part" (Levernier 26).

Works Cited

Levernier, James. "Wheatley's 'On Being Brought from Africa to America.'" *Explicator* 40.1 (1981): 25–26. *EBSCO*. Web. 20 Dec. 2011.

Wheatley, Phillis. "On Being Brought from Africa to America." *Digging into Literature: Strategies for Reading, Analysis, and Writing*. Joanna Wolfe and Laura Wilder. Boston: Bedford/St. Martin's, 2016. 153. Print.

This analysis repeats James Levernier's published observations about Wheatley's "On Being Brought from Africa to America." What might appear to be the student's own claim in the first sentence is simply a paraphrase of Levernier's quotation in the second sentence. The other citations of Levernier in this passage merely restate his ideas, too. While this student writer cannot be accused of plagiarism—he fairly attributes the ideas to Levernier—he brings nothing new to the discussion.

If repeating what has already been said about a text to support your argument is the only reason you cite published critics, you, like the author of the previous analysis, will never add anything new to the critical conversation. The same would be true if your papers only repeated what your instructor or classmates said during class discussion of a text. You wouldn't be telling your audience anything they do not already know. Instead, we encourage you to move beyond citing published criticism only in this "because the experts say so" fashion and join the conversation as a participant who has something original to add.

MOVING BEYOND "BECAUSE THE EXPERTS SAY SO"

A trip to the library or a perusal of an online database of published criticism of a text will quickly reveal that the "experts" disagree with one another on matters of interpretation. So while we stand to learn a good deal from published literary critics, their disagreements make clear that we should not take any one interpretation to be definitive. In fact, recognizing the nature of disagreement among literary scholars can provide an important starting point for your own turn in the conversation.

One of the most famous, most often anthologized, and most written about short stories of the last century is "A Rose for Emily," by William Faulkner. Published in 1930, its complex narrative and understated but chilling ending have prompted many critical essays and countless student papers. Let's examine how two literary critics use unresolved or overlooked areas (marked in boldface) in published scholarship as a starting point for their discussions of the story. The first passage is from a scholarly article by Milinda Schwab titled "A Watch for Emily".[1]

> The critical attention given to the subject of time in Faulkner most certainly fills as many pages as the longest novel of Yoknapatawpha County. A goodly number of those pages of criticism deal with the well-known short story, "A Rose for Emily." Several scholars, most notably Paul McGlynn, have worked to untangle the confusing chronology of this work (461–62).

---

[1] Schwab, Milinda. "A Watch for Emily." *Studies in Short Fiction* 28.2 (1991): 215–17. Web. 5 Aug. 2011.

Others have given a variety of symbolic and psychological reasons for Emily Grierson's inability (or refusal) to acknowledge the passage of time. **Yet in all of this careful literary analysis, no one has discussed one troubling and therefore highly significant detail. When we first meet Miss Emily, she carries in a pocket somewhere within her clothing an "invisible watch ticking at the end of [a] gold chain" (Faulkner 121).** What would a woman like Emily Grierson, who seems to us fixed in the past and oblivious to any passing of time, need with a watch? An awareness of the significance of this watch, however, is crucial for a clear understanding of Miss Emily herself. The watch's placement in her pocket, its unusually loud ticking, and the chain to which it is attached illustrate both her attempts to control the passage of the years and the consequences of such an ultimately futile effort (215).

The second is from a scholarly article by Thomas Fick and Eva Gold titled "'He Liked Men': Homer, Homosexuality, and the Culture of Manhood in Faulkner's 'A Rose for Emily.'"[2]

Over the last few years critics have discussed homosexuality in Faulkner's "A Rose for Emily," one of Faulkner's most frequently anthologized works and a mainstay of literature classes at all levels. Hal Blythe, for example, asserts outright that Homer Barron is gay, while in a more nuanced reading James Wallace argues that the narrator merely wishes to suggest that Barron is homosexual in order to implicate the reader in a culture of gossip (Blythe 49–50; Wallace 105–07). Both readings rest on this comment by the narrator: "Then we said, 'She will persuade him yet,' because Homer himself had remarked—he liked men, and it was known that he drank with the younger men at the Elks' Club—that he was not a marrying man" (Faulkner 126). . . . **While we agree that the narrator's comment suggests something important about Homer's sexual orientation, in contrast with Blythe we believe that it says Homer is combatively heterosexual.**

---

[2] Fick, Thomas, and Eva Gold. "'He Liked Men': Homer, Homosexuality, and the Culture of Manhood in Faulkner's 'A Rose for Emily.'" *Eureka Studies in Teaching Short Fiction* 8.1 (2007): 99–107. Web. 5 Aug. 2011.

In the first example above, Milinda Schwab describes how other critics have dealt with the subject of time in Faulkner's work but then she notes a detail these critics have overlooked: Miss Emily's watch. Schwab uses both surface/depth and patterns strategies to argue for the importance of this overlooked detail. In the next example, Thomas Fick and Eva Gold take issue with how other critics have interpreted Homer Barron's character in "A Rose for Emily." They use a surface/depth–contrasting argument to suggest an alternative interpretation: that rather than being homosexual, Homer is "combatively heterosexual."

In both example passages, the writers recognize they are not the first critics to write on "A Rose for Emily." They carefully summarize what other critics have said and phrase their own arguments to "speak back" to these other critics. Schwab speaks back by offering a new observation that contributes to a debate about time in the story. Fick and Gold speak back by disagreeing with previous interpretations. Both examples show that the authors have listened to others, and each offers new arguments to ongoing conversations about the text. As one professor we interviewed stated, "[W]e don't just come up with these analyses and publish them without looking at what else has been done." When we cite other critics, we listen carefully to what they have said—and then try to say something new.

When engaging with other critics, a typical move is either to summarize or paraphrase what other critics have said. A **summary** distills others' arguments or describes the situation to which you are responding. For example, Schwab focuses on the situation (McGlynn has tried to untangle the chronology; other critics have looked at reasons why Emily does not acknowledge the passage of time) while Fick and Gold summarize in a few words the arguments of Hal Blythe and James Wallace. Depending on the needs of your own argument, you may summarize in a sentence or so, or at some length. In any case, the summary will be far briefer than the arguments you are representing. By contrast, a **paraphrase** restates a text in your own words, often acting as a kind of translation of a complex passage. A paraphrase can run longer than the original passage, and it sometimes makes use of language (indicated by quotation marks) directly from the original passage with which you are engaging. Most often, you will find yourself summarizing or quoting critics when you enter a critical conversation. We say more about the uses of quotation and paraphrase in Chapter 14, starting on page 296.

ENTERING THE DISCOURSE COMMUNITY OF PUBLISHED CRITICISM

When you enter a conversation, it is important both to connect to what other people have said and to say something different from what has come before. Imagine you have walked in on a group of people discussing time in "A Rose for Emily." It would be strange immediately to switch the conversation to a different topic without at least acknowledging that others were discussing time. Likewise, it would be just as strange for you to repeat the exact same point that someone else just made. Good conversationalists know how to signal that they have listened to what others have said while at the same time steering the conversation to the topics that most interest them.

Here are three ways to join a critical conversation that connect to previous discussions and signal that you have something new to say.

Add new evidence

The first way to contribute to a conversation is to support a claim already made with evidence that others have not mentioned and may not have noticed. In the previous passage from "A Watch for Emily," critic Milinda Schwab recounts an ongoing conversation about time in "A Rose for Emily" and then points to an aspect of the text that has been overlooked in this conversation—Miss Emily's watch—that she claims is pertinent to understanding time in the story. She then goes on to explain how it is pertinent.

Add new interpretations

Even if other critics have already interpreted passages in a text you are writing about you can interpret those same passages in new ways. Doing so demonstrates that a complex text can yield multiple possible layers of meaning beneath its surface. For instance, the student writer of the excerpt on page 221 could, after reviewing Chapter 5 and consulting the *OED*, add a new interpretation to the word *remember* in Wheatley's "On Being Brought from Africa to America" that critic James Levernier does not mention.

In addition to the ambiguity Levernier describes, "Remember" can also call to mind the homonym "re-member," which the *OED* defines as the act of putting together again or the reverse of dismembering. This homonym can further support Levernier's claim that Wheatley is reminding her readers that both Blacks and Whites are "sons of Adam" (Levernier 26). By asking Christians to "re-member," Wheatley is calling for the reunification of White and Black Christians within their shared religion, in which all are fallen members of one human race.

Disagree with previous interpretations

During class discussions of texts you have doubtlessly found yourself at times nodding in agreement as others speak and at other times shaking your head as you question the validity of a classmate's interpretation. As you read published criticism, you may similarly find yourself at times nodding and at other times shaking your head. Your disagreement with a critic could serve as a starting point for your own argument in which you explain what is wrong with the other viewpoint and defend your own. Critics often treat these rebuttals as correcting the misperceptions or flawed readings of others. You might also contribute to a conversation by correcting a misinterpretation.

We see a good example of this disagreement in Fick and Gold's analysis. They discuss interpretations other critics have made about a passage describing Homer Barron's sexuality and offer a corrective. While other critics have claimed Barron is homosexual, Fick and Gold argue he most definitely is not.

Exercise

Read the following four excerpts of published criticism on Alice Walker's "Everyday Use." (See Chapter 6, p. 131, for the full text of this short story.)

▸ For each excerpt, note whether it repeats something that has already been said in the critical conversation or adds something new to the critical conversation.

▸ If the excerpt adds something new, which of the three approaches to joining the conversation (adding new evidence, adding new interpretations, or disagreeing with previous interpretations) do you see the critic using?

EXCERPT ONE[3]

Most readers of Alice Walker's short story "Everyday Use" agree that the point of the story is to show, as Nancy Tuten argues, a mother's "awakening to one daughter's superficiality and to the other's deep-seated understanding of heritage" (Tuten 125). [See also Baker and Pierce-Baker; Bauer; and Winchell.] These readers praise the "simplicity" of Maggie and her mother, along with their allegiance to their specific family identity and folk heritage. . . . Such a reading condemns the older, more worldly sister, Dee, as "shallow," "condescending," and "manipulative," as overly concerned with style, fashion, and aesthetics, and thus as lacking a "true" understanding of her heritage. In this essay, conversely, I will argue that this popular view is far too simple a reading of the story. While Dee is certainly insensitive and selfish to a certain degree, she nevertheless offers a view of heritage and a strategy for contemporary African-Americans to cope with an oppressive society that is, in some ways, more valid than that offered by Mama and Maggie.

[3] Farrell, Susan. "Fight vs. Flight: A Re-evaluation of Dee in Alice Walker's 'Everyday Use.'" *Studies in Short Fiction* 35.2 (1998): 179–86. Web. 1 Sept. 2011.

EXCERPT TWO[4]

[Wangero] wants the photographs—and presently the churn lid, the dasher, and the quilts—for purposes of display, reminders that she no longer has to live in such a house, care for such a cow, have daily intercourse with such a mother and sister. She "makes the mistake," says Donna Haisty Winchell, "of believing that one's heritage is something that one puts on display if and when such a display is fashionable" (81). Wangero seems to think the African-American past can be rescued only by being commodified.

4 Cowart, David. "Heritage and Deracination in Walker's 'Everyday Use.'" *Studies in Short Fiction* 33.2 (1996): 171–84. Web. 1 Sept. 2011.

EXCERPT THREE[5]

Particularly revealing is the second paragraph of the story, in which Mama pictures to herself how Maggie will act when Dee arrives. She believes that "Maggie will be nervous until after her sister goes: she will stand hopelessly in corners, homely and ashamed of the burn scars down her arms and legs, eyeing her sister with a mixture of envy and awe" (47). Most critics adopt Mama's view of Maggie, assuming her assessment to be accurate. Hirsch, for example, refers to Maggie's "resigned acquiescence" and "angerless fear" and describes her as "powerless" and "pathetic" (205).

The subsequent action of the story, however, in no way supports Mama's reading of her younger daughter. Instead, Maggie's behavior—even her limited use of language—conveys disgust with her sister rather than envy and awe.

5 Tuten, Nancy. "Alice Walker's 'Everyday Use'." *Explicator* 51.2 (1993): 125–28. *MLA International Bibliography*. Web. 24 May 2013.

EXCERPT FOUR[6]

I agree with Hirsch when she mentions Mama's "ability to take pleasure in her daughter's difference without conceding any of her own choices and values" and her ability to maintain a distance from Dee "without visibly rejecting her" (203). While critics often point to Dee's aggressiveness, which intrudes into the pastoral calm of Mama's home, by quoting Mama's comment that the dress Dee wears is "so loud it hurts my eyes," they fail to note that Mama says shortly after, "I like it" (28). Mama has held a place for "Dee," and if "Dee" is no longer there, she will try to accommodate "Wangero."

[6] Whitsitt, Sam. "In Spite of It All: A Reading of Alice Walker's 'Everyday Use.'" *African American Review* 34.3 (2000): 443–59. Web. 1 Sept. 2011.

USING THE CRITICAL CONVERSATION TO BRAINSTORM

Reading arguments by other critics can be a great way to generate ideas about issues, patterns, or problems worth noticing in a text. Sometimes, however reading published criticism before you have formulated your own ideas about a text can cause you to accept what other critics have said and shut your mind to your own, possibly original, interpretations.

In general, we recommend that you wait until you have developed a series of questions about the text before you begin reading the published criticism about it. These questions should be about sections of the text that puzzle you and that could possibly lead to some complex arguments. Then use your reading of the published criticism to evaluate how persuasively other critics seem to be answering your questions.

Example questions might include:

- I have noted some moments in the text that seem significant but I'm not sure how to interpret them. Have other critics made arguments about these same moments? Have they created plausible interpretations? Am I satisfied with their interpretations?
- I have noticed a pattern in the text. Have other critics noticed this pattern? Have they made persuasive surface/depth interpretations about this pattern?

▶ I have done some initial research on some contextual references in the text and have some ideas about how to interpret them. Have other critics noticed these contextual details? Have they made similar interpretations? Are there any contextual details that critics seem to be misinterpreting?

▶ I am interested in the socially relevant issues that this text seems to raise. What have other critics said about race or gender or other socially relevant issues in this text?

▶ I am thinking about using a particular theoretical lens to interpret the text. What other theoretical lenses have critics used? Have they used the lens I am thinking of, or might my use of it yield interpretations others have not already made?

Having particular questions in mind as you read others' interpretations allows you to maintain your own perspective as you prepare to converse with published critics. One professor describes how he begins his investigation of published criticism by noting a problem in a text that he is trying to interpret:

> In my case, sometimes there's a problem in a text, or an aspect of the text that seems ill understood, and I come up with some way of understanding it. You get struck by something, and sometimes it turns out everybody else has been, too, and they've written about it quite well. Sometimes it turns out people haven't seen it that way. You have solved a problem, which it turns out everyone else has talked around.[7]

As this professor indicates, sometimes the search of published criticism will mean abandoning a particular topic because others have already persuasively solved the problem. However, at other times, he realizes that he has a new way of looking at a problem that others have just "talked around." Having particular questions or "problems" in mind before you begin your search of published criticism can help you realize what you have to contribute to the critical conversation.

---

[7] Warren, J. E. Literary Scholars Processing Poetry and Constructing Arguments. *Written Communication* 23.2 (2006): 202–26. Print.

Once your search has yielded some published criticism, read as much of it as you can. Initially, it is okay to skim and consider several articles before settling on those you will actually use in your writing. Make note of where your tentative ideas about the text add new evidence or interpretations. You will then need to read the critics carefully for *what they say* as well as *what they do not say*. When you have an idea about evidence or meaning that they do not address, you may have located a gap in the discourse community's knowledge that you can seek to fill in your paper. Likewise, you will want to note interpretations that do not seem plausible to you and figure out whether you could develop a full rebuttal that explains why you disagree and offers your counterinterpretation.

FINDING PUBLISHED CRITICISM

Most professional criticism is published in journals that can only be accessed with a paid subscription. Your institution's library will have paid this subscription fee for many, if not most, of these journals. However, this means you need to access these journals through your library—and not through regular Web searches. Your library will also have paid subscription fees to specialized databases that can help you access these journals.

Good databases for accessing literary criticism include:

- *Literature Online (LION)*
- *JSTOR*
- *Project Muse*
- *MLA International Bibliography*

Begin your search of these databases using as your search term the title of the literary text you are analyzing. Doing this should lead you to published criticism on the text you are writing about and help you determine if you have new evidence, new interpretations, or disagreements to bring to this conversation.

Sometimes you will not be able to access full text articles online, but your library will have a print copy of the journal where an article that interests you appears. In this case, write down the title of the journal and the volume, year, and page numbers for your article. Then look the journal up in your library's catalog database where you will obtain a call number. The bookshelves in your library are ordered by these call numbers. Use this information to locate the journal.

If you are unsure of how to find articles online or on the shelves of your library, your campus librarians should be able to help you. Librarians tend to be helpful people with expertise in finding specialized information, so don't be afraid to ask them for assistance.

WHAT IF THERE IS LITTLE OR NO CONVERSATION ABOUT A TEXT?

Occasionally you may find that using the title as a search term yields too few useful published articles or perhaps no hits at all. You may be working with a recently published text or an overlooked or neglected text about which no one has published criticism. But even when a text has not yet been written about, critics still try to find ways to start or join a conversation because they want their readers to see how their interpretation of this text can be useful to this discourse community.

One way to start such a conversation is to join one about other literary texts by the same author. For instance, if you were the first critic to write on "Everyday Use," you might note the types of claims critics have made about Walker's other texts and see if those claims apply to "Everyday Use." Hence, "Everyday Use" could provide new evidence to support the claims made about Walker's entire literary career, rather than just one text. To locate such conversations on an author's other texts, use the author's full name as a search term in the databases described on page 231.

Another option for starting or joining a conversation when you cannot find published criticism on a text is to look at criticism on the genre of the text (e.g., nature writing, westerns, courtship narratives) and extend these critics' insights to the text that interests you. To locate these conversations, you may need to try several search terms. Once you identify the genre or genres the literary text you are analyzing belongs to, you can use these labels as search terms.

Still another option may be to contribute to a conversation about literary texts written in the same time period and geographic region as the text you are analyzing. There are thousands of conversations ongoing about literary texts; with creativity and research, you can find one that you can contribute to.

Lastly, sometimes when critics work with new texts, they cite book reviews as examples of conversations that have already been occurring about an author or a text. If your library subscribes, you can find book reviews in *Book Review Digest Plus*, an online database dedicated solely to book reviews. (Search for the name of your author using the "author, personal" field.)

For instance, Rick Bass, the author of "Antlers," has received relatively little attention in published literary criticism. When we searched for criticism on Bass, we found fewer than twenty critical works published in English, many of which were not available in our library, and no criticism that dealt directly with the story "Antlers."

However, newspaper reviews of Bass's work often indicate that readers comment on Bass's environmental activism and consider him a nature writer. Such insights might lead us to look for more general criticism on the topic of nature writing or environmental fiction. From this research, we may find insights about nature writing or environmental writing that we could extend to an analysis of "Antlers."

When we look up newspaper reviews of *In the Loyal Mountains*, the fiction collection in which "Antlers" first appeared, we find claims we might support with evidence from "Antlers." For instance, one reviewer, Tobin Harshaw of the *New York Times*, describes Bass as creating a "revisionist masculinity."[8] In other words, this review claims that Bass is revising what it means to be masculine in contemporary culture by creating characters who seem relatively passive and peaceful or who are conflicted about traditional masculine activities. Thus, we might extend Harshaw's insight by exploring masculinity in "Antlers."

---

[8] Harshaw, Tobin. "Book Review Desk." *New York Times* 16 July 1995, sec. 7: 20. Print.

In a review from *Booklist*, reviewer Donna Seaman describes the characters in *In the Loyal Mountains* as:

> . . . held fast in the grip of a loneliness deeper than memory, of anger without certain cause, and driven by a need for solitude and a fierce desire for something that "will last, and will not leave."[9]

We might extend this insight by looking carefully at the role loneliness plays in "Antlers." Alternatively, if we disagree with part of Seaman's quote, we could offer a corrective to her reading.

Although book reviews are not peer reviewed (see Chapter 15), they can be useful for generating ideas and finding ways to join a conversation about a text on which little has been published. However, you should generally avoid using book reviews if peer-reviewed literary criticism on a text is available.

PEER-REVIEWED CRITICISM *VS.* SPARKNOTES, ᴇNOTES, AND OTHER STUDY GUIDES

In your research and Web searches, you may have come across Web sites such as SparkNotes or eNotes that offer critical interpretations of texts. While such Web sites can occasionally be useful for generating ideas about a text, they are not what most professors have in mind when they ask you to find published criticism on a text.

In general, we recommend that you avoid "study guide" sources such as SparkNotes or CliffsNotes. These study guides offer single, definitive interpretations that can shut down your ability to critically interact with a text. Moreover, such study guides do not necessarily offer good interpretations of texts. We have both read interpretations in study guides that we do not find persuasive—we have even discovered information in these guides that is factually incorrect!

---

[9] Seaman, Donna. Review of *In the Loyal Mountains* by Rick Bass. *Booklist* 91. 1 June 1995: 1726. Print.

Study guides, such as SparkNotes, are not peer reviewed. Thus, unlike articles in published journals of literary criticism, the authors of these study guides have not had to persuade other literary scholars that they have interesting, well-supported analyses.

Such study guides seem to offer a simple shortcut to the definitive, "symbol-hunting" solution to an interpretive puzzle rather than acknowledge the complexity of several plausible layers of meaning. Consequently, many professors will react negatively to your using these sources, and citing them in your paper may hurt your credibility.

Exercise

Using one of the databases listed on page 231, locate two articles that you could use to join a critical conversation related to one of the literary texts you have read. What search terms did you use to locate them?

USING THE CRITICAL CONVERSATION TO WRITE PERSUASIVELY

Your essay's introduction is often a good place to explain to your readers how you will be adding something new to a critical conversation. This is especially true when your paper's thesis adds something new to previously published criticism. Clarifying right away how your essay contributes something new to the conversation will anticipate skeptical questions readers typically ask, like "So what?" or "Why bother?" If you promise something new, readers will be motivated to keep reading.

However, you need not limit your introduction to explanations of how you have something to add to the conversation. You may find it useful to respond to critics throughout your essay, wherever you see a clear way in which your argument is building on the work of others. Professional literary critics seem to show no standard preference for where in their essays this strategy should be used, so you have a lot of freedom to decide where, for the purposes of your argument, it would be most persuasive to employ the strategy.

To signal to your readers that you have something new to add to a critical conversation, you must first remind them of what has already been said, then distinguish your views from those of others, and ultimately fully support your views and any claims you make.

1. Remind readers what has been said in the conversation you are joining

Conversations that occur in the pages of written literary analyses differ from classroom and face-to-face conversations in one crucial way: they unfold much more slowly over time. While this allows critics time for reflection and revision, it also means that critics have some work to do to help readers understand the conversation they are joining.

Hence, the first step is to restate briefly what has been said before. You may respond to a single aspect of what one critic has said, or you may respond to what several critics have said. Summarize or directly quote the relevant claims these other critics made. When doing this, be sure you:

> ‣ **understand the critics you are citing.** Published criticism can sometimes be difficult to understand, but this does not mean that you should include quotations or arguments you don't comprehend. Use the strategies of literary analysis we have described in this book to help you locate the main arguments and interpretations in other critics' work. A good technique for helping you understand is to freewrite immediately after reading an article, summarizing its main arguments as best you can. You can ask your instructor for help with arguments you still do not understand.

> ‣ **use proper conventions for quotations and documentation.** Chapter 14 provides advice on how to quote and document sources effectively. Be sure to follow the "quotation sandwich" advice from that chapter by introducing quotations or paraphrases appropriately and concluding them with a statement explaining how they fit into your argument.

2. Distinguish your views from those of the critics you cite

Here a professor describes the shortcomings of a student essay that she otherwise thought was strong:

> The one problem, and it's a fairly big one, is that the thesis in the opening paragraph is not [the writer's] own. It's a quotation from someone else, so again, there's the understanding that you can build off other people's ideas, but to me, this read as the presentation of someone else's thesis. However, I did see what I thought was an original thesis on page four . . . maybe not until page four. As I read it, I thought . . . now that expands upon that article that is quoted.

Although this student writer did, in fact, provide original evidence that supported and extended a previous critic's argument, readers of the essay had a hard time distinguishing what was original in the essay and what was a paraphrase of another critic's views.

Literary critics seek to clearly distinguish their own views from those of others. To do this, critics sometimes use the first-person pronoun *I* to distinguish their arguments from what others have said. They may use phrases such as "While Critic A has argued *X*, I argue *Y* instead" or "While Critic A's interpretation of *X* is valid, I see another layer of meaning in this passage." Below are some specific ways critics distinguish their views from previously published views when adding new evidence, when adding new interpretations, or when disagreeing with other critics.

Distinguishing your views when adding new evidence: You can further support a published critic's claim interpreting one part of a text with new evidence drawn from other parts of the same text—or from another relevant text. For instance, Antonio T. Bly's claim that Phillis Wheatley's poem "To the University of Cambridge, in New England" denounces the hypocrisy of white Christians and expresses a strong sense of black pride (205–06) could be extended to apply to Wheatley's "On Being Brought from Africa to America."[10] To write this analysis, you would need to show how textual evidence from "On Being Brought" can support Bly's claims about hypocrisy and black pride. The claim may not be new, but the evidence is, and it helps us get a fuller understanding of Wheatley's artistic career.

---

[10] Bly, Antonio T. "Wheatley's 'To the University of Cambridge, in New England.'" *Explicator* 55.4 (1997): 205–08. *EBSCO*. Web. 22 Dec. 2011.

Critic's Claim	Critic's Claim
Passage or Text A	**New Passage or Text B**

Claims made about one text can be extended to interpret a new text.

Critics can also point out new contextual evidence and argue that this new information affects our understanding of the primary text. For instance, critic Gene Moore points out how the original, unrevised draft of "A Rose for Emily" might help us understand the chronology of the story:

> Over the past thirty years, no fewer than *eight* different chronologies have been proposed to account for the events occurring in William Faulkner's celebrated short story "A Rose for Emily." [*Moore goes on to discuss the different chronologies various critics have proposed.*] . . . Given the amount of interest generated by this question and the range of evidence employed in the various arguments, **it is remarkable that no one seems ever to have regarded the original manuscript as a possible source of chronological information; in fact, evidence from the manuscript makes it possible to solve some of the problems of Miss Emily's chronology by fixing the date of her father's death.**[11]

Moore, in the boldface passage, thus suggests that by looking at Faulkner's original draft we can shed new light on an issue that has been occupying critics for decades. Clearly such evidence has the potential to make a valuable contribution to an ongoing conversation about "A Rose for Emily."

Distinguishing your views when adding new interpretations: When you have a new interpretation of passages that other critics have persuasively but not fully explained, you can signal to your readers that these previous interpretations are valid but that you have discovered still another layer of meaning. For example, Mary McAleer Balkun adds a new layer to the previous

---

[11] Moore, Gene M. "Of Time and Its Mathematical Progression: Problems of Chronology in Faulkner's 'A Rose for Emily.'" *Studies in Short Fiction* 29.2 (1992): 195–204. *EBSCO*. Web. 5 Aug. 2011.

published interpretations of Phillis Wheatley's "On Being Brought from Africa to America" and "To the University of Cambridge, in New England":

> As previous critics have pointed out, Wheatley's poetry is not devoid of racial awareness, as had long been suggested. Antonio T. Bly asserts that Wheatley used her poems not simply to "denounce the hypocrisy practiced by white Christians, but also [to] express a strong sense of black pride to her fellow slaves, who were often read her poetry by slave masters who thought that her writings were harmless" (205–06). A number of the poems can be seen as direct appeals to her black counterparts to accept the Christian God as a means of salvation, if not in this world then certainly in the next. **However, critics have yet to consider fully the possibility that Wheatley might have crafted her poems to work specifically upon the white audience that would have constituted her main readership, aside from overt pleas to accept the possibility of black Christians.**[12]

In the boldface sentence, Balkan's words "critics have yet to consider fully" signal that she is about to add another valid interpretation.

Distinguishing your views when disagreeing with a critic: Using disagreement as an entryway through which to join a critical conversation often relies on a surface/depth–contrast strategy. We can see this technique clearly in Helen Nebeker's analysis of "A Rose for Emily":

> The general view of critics regarding the anonymous, ubiquitous narrator is that he is a kind of innocuous, naïve, passive citizen of Jefferson, who relates for the reader the story of Miss Emily's life and death. [*Nebeker goes on to cite several specific critics.*] . . . From these more or less similar views of the narrator, the critics proceed to develop their interpretations of Miss Emily as the proud, unbending monument of the Old South who somehow triumphs over time and change, thereby evoking admiration conjoined with pity.
>
> **On the surface, such explanation of both narrator and theme may suffice. But if one looks sharply and critically at the point of view chosen by**

---

[12] Balkun, Mary McAleer. "Phillis Wheatley's Construction of Otherness and the Rhetoric of Performed Ideology." *African American Review* 36.1 (2002): 121–35. *EBSCO*. Web. 22 Dec. 2011.

Faulkner, remembering that the basic structural resource of a writer is point of view . . . and if one acknowledges the mastery of Faulkner in merging person, time, place, and events, **the importance of his chosen point of view should not be so lightly dismissed**. However, in just such a dismissal, readers and critics alike have permitted themselves to be fooled by a master storyteller who lays out point by point the details of a horror far more monstrous than that of a poor demented woman who kills her lover.[13]

Here Nebeker uses an explicit surface/depth–contrast strategy to characterize other critics' interpretations of the narrator as "surface" reading. She then offers a corrective to these simple readings, showing how the narrator's use of pronouns (*they/them vs. we/our/us*) illustrates the way older generations in the South have conspired to hide their crimes and decaying moral values from younger generations. Nebeker's use of surface/depth–contrasting strategy tells us that she offers her interpretation as a corrective to previous critics' more simplistic reading of the text.

3. Support your views

Once you have clearly distinguished your interpretive claims from the claims made by other critics, it is time to support your claims. The rest of your paper can focus on using the other strategies of literary analysis to make your case for your thesis, just like the other analytic papers you have written about before. Occasionally you may want to respond to a specific claim from another critic's argument, in which case you would follow steps 1 and 2 again, briefly summarizing the critic's specific claim and distinguishing your new claim from it. You may especially need to return repeatedly to the ideas of another critic when your thesis claim expresses disagreement. For such an argument, you may need to not only support your own claims but also persuasively explain the shortcomings of the other critic's interpretive claims.

---

[13] Nebeker, Helen E. "Emily's Rose of Love: Thematic Implications of Point of View in Faulkner's 'A Rose for Emily.'" *Bulletin of the Rocky Mountain Modern Language Association* 24.1 (1970): 3–13. *MLA International Bibliography*. Web. 31 Dec. 2012.

PHRASES ASSOCIATED WITH JOINING THE CRITICAL CONVERSATION

There are a seemingly endless number of ways to join a critical conversation. Here are just a few examples illustrating how you might signal that your analysis has something new to add to a critical conversation. You should feel free to vary these templates to fit your own needs.

PHRASES ASSOCIATED WITH ADDING NEW EVIDENCE

- Critics have had a lot to say about X, but what they have not noted is Y.
- Critics have discussed X, but no one has mentioned Y.
- Critics have debated X. However, if we note Y, many of these issues are resolved.
- Critics have discussed X but have generally shown little interest in Y.
- Critic A has said X about text Y. A similar argument can be made about text Z.

PHRASES ASSOCIATED WITH ADDING NEW INTERPRETATIONS

- Critics have discussed X, but they have yet to consider this understanding of X.
- Critics have interpreted X in several ways, but they have not seen this meaning in X.

PHRASES ASSOCIATED WITH DISAGREEING WITH PREVIOUS INTERPRETATIONS

- Critics have said X. In this essay, conversely, I will argue Y.
- Critic A has said X. On the surface, this interpretation seems plausible. However, if we look at Y, Critic A's interpretation cannot hold.
- Critics have interpreted X as Y. While I agree with X, I disagree that it means Y. Instead, I argue Z.

Exercise

Re-read the sample paragraphs in the exercise on page 226 and the sample analyses in this chapter. Underline words and phrases that seem to be associated with signaling to readers that a critic is saying something new or joining a critical conversation. Make a list of these words and phrases designating which of the three approaches to joining a critical conversation eash belongs to: adding new evidence, adding new interpretations, and disagreeing with previous interpretations. Compare your list with those your classmates have generated.

For Discussion

1. Sometimes critics use the first-person *I* when writing about texts. Review the examples of published criticism in this chapter and note uses of the first person. Are these effective?

2. Examine the examples of published criticism in this chapter and note when critics mention the titles of the works they cite in the text of their essays. When do published critics spell out the entire title of the works they cite and when do they just state the critic's name? What rules can you infer about when to include titles of the works you are citing in the body of your essay?

Review

In this chapter, we distinguish between two different ways of using published literary criticism in your essays. The first, a likely familiar way, is to repeat what critics say because their authority bolsters a similar (if not the same) claim you wish to make. A more advanced way to use published criticism is to see each article as an extended turn in a critical conversation and to join that conversation by contributing something new.

We describe three approaches to contributing something new to a critical conversation:

1. Adding new evidence
2. Adding new interpretations
3. Disagreeing with a critic

We discuss methods for locating published criticism and understanding these sometimes difficult texts. Lastly, we examine the ways critics signal to their readers how they are contributing something new to the critical conversation.

Exercise

Find a literary analysis from a peer-reviewed journal that makes an argument about a text your class has studied.

1. Begin by looking at the list of works cited. What kinds of texts are cited? How many appear to be from peer-reviewed journals? How many appear to be theoretical texts? How many are texts used to provide contextual information?

2. Look at the essay itself. Where do most of the citations to secondary criticism occur? To the literary text being interpreted? Do you see any patterns in how the essay uses citations?

3. Look for places in the essay itself where the author seems to be joining the critical conversation. How does the critic signal to readers that he/she has something new to say? What key words does the critic use in joining the conversation?

4. Lastly, do you see the critic using any of the strategies for literary analysis that we have been studying? Where and how? Use quotations from the article to support your claims.

12

Using All the Strategies on a Single Work

Throughout this book, we have provided a variety of strategies that can help you dig into texts, including texts that at first seem difficult to understand even on the surface level. By patiently using the strategies for reading and writing literary analysis—and returning to different strategies each time you make progress—you can begin to uncover interpretations of even the most seemingly difficult texts.

In this chapter we present an experimental play that many students and professors find confusing on a first reading. The play is *As the Crow Flies* by David Henry Hwang, an American playwright, librettist, screenwriter, and theater professor. With the play as our text, we model how the strategies of literary analysis we have presented chapter by chapter can uncover multiple levels of meaning that at first escaped our understanding. Be aware that not all the suggestions and questions we include here will be equally useful: literary analysis involves learning to abandon dead ends as well as follow productive, if unexpected, avenues. However, it is also the case that ideas one critic rejects as irrelevant to a particular argument will emerge as central to another critic's interpretation. This is part of the surprise and delight of literary analysis. ■

David Henry Hwang

As the Crow Flies

1983

A living room in an upper-middle-class home, owned by Mrs. Chan, a Chinese woman in her seventies, and her husband, P. K. Up right, a door leads out to the front driveway.

Stage left is a door leading to the rest of the house. Mrs. Chan sits in a large chair, centerstage, looking downstage out into a garden. Around her, Hannah, a black woman in her late sixties, cleans. She has been their cleaning woman for over a decade.

HANNAH: I guess I never told you this before, Mrs. Chan, but I think the time is right now. See, I'm really two different folks. You've been knowin' me as Hannah Carter, 'cuz when I'm over here cleanin', that's who I am. But at night, or when I'm outside and stuff, I turn into Sandra Smith. (*Beat.*) Is that all clear?

CHAN: Um. Yeah.   5

HANNAH: You got all that?

CHAN: When you are here, you are Hannah Carter—

HANNAH: Right.

CHAN: And, then, you go outside, and you are . . . someone . . . someone . . .

HANNAH: Sandra Smith.   10

CHAN: Um. Okay.

Pause.

HANNAH: You don't have any questions 'bout that?

CHAN: Hannah Carter, Sandra Smith—I understand.

HANNAH: Well, you know how you can tell the two apart?

CHAN: No. Because I have not seen Sandra—Sandra . . .   15

HANNAH: Smith. Well, when I'm Sandra Smith, see, I look different. First of all, I'm a lot younger.

CHAN: Good.

HANNAH: And, you know, since I'm younger, well, guess I'm looser, too. What I mean by that, is, when I talk, well, I use different words. Young words. And,   20 Mrs. Chan, since I'm younger, my hair color's a lot different too. And I don't clean floors. 'Cuz young people nowadays, they don't clean floors. They stay up around the clock, and make themselves into lazy good-for-nothings, and drink a lot, and dance themselves into a state. Young people—I just don't know what's got into them. But whatever it is, the same thing's gotten into Sandra Smith.   25 (*Pause.*) You don't think this is all a little strange?

CHAN: No.

HANNAH: Well, that's the first time . . . I remember when I told Mrs. Washburn about Sandra Smith—she just fell right over.

CHAN: So what? So you have two different people.   30

HANNAH: That's right. Living inside me.

CHAN: So what? My uncle had six!

HANNAH: Six people?

CHAN: Maybe even seven. Who can keep count?

HANNAH: Seven? All in one guy? 35

CHAN: Way back in China—my second uncle—he had seven, maybe even eight people—inside here. I don't . . . is hard to remember all their name.

HANNAH: I can believe that.

CHAN: Chan Yup Lee—he was, uh, I think, the businessman. He runs Uncle's import-export association. Good man. Very stingy. I like him. Then, I think there was 40 another: ah, C. Y. Sing—he is the family man. Then, one man, Fat-Fingers Lew. Introduce this sport—what is the name? Ball goes through big hoop.

HANNAH: Basketball?

CHAN: Yes, yes—introduce that to our village. Then, there is Big Ear Tong—collects debt for C. Y.'s company. Never talks, only fight. Then, also, one who has been to 45 America—Morty Fong. He all the time warns us about Communists. And, then, oh, maybe two or three others that I hardly ever meet.

HANNAH: This is all one guy?

CHAN: Mmmmm.

HANNAH: Isn't that somethin'? 50

CHAN: No.

HANNAH: Huh?

CHAN: Whatever you can tell me—man with six persons inside, man with three heads, man who sees a flying ghost, a sitting ghost, a ghost disguise to look like his dead wife—none of these are so unusual. 55

HANNAH: No?

CHAN: I have lived a long time.

HANNAH: Well, so have I, Mrs. Chan, so have I. And I'm still scared of Sandra Smith.

CHAN: Scare? Why scare? Happens all the time.

HANNAH: I don't want Sandra comin' round to any of my houses that I clean. 60

CHAN: Aaah—do not worry.

HANNAH: Whaddya mean? Sandra's got no respect for authority.

CHAN: Do not worry. She will not come into any house.

HANNAH: What makes you so sure?

CHAN: You have to know how ghosts think. You say, Sandra appears outdoors. 65 Therefore, she is the outside ghost. She cannot come inside.

HANNAH: Yeah? They got rules like that? In ghost-land?

CHAN: Yes—there are rules everyplace! Have you ever been someplace where there were none?

HANNAH: Well, no, but— 70

CHAN: You see? Ghosts cannot kill a man if there is a goldfish in the room. They will think the fish is gold, and take it instead. They cannot enter a house if there is a raised step in the doorway. Ghosts do not look, so they trip over it instead.

HANNAH: These ghosts don't sound like they got a lot on the ball.

CHAN: Some ghosts, they are smart. But most ghosts, they are like most people. 75 When alive, they were stupid. After death, they remain the same.

HANNAH: Well, I don't think Sandra's got much respect for those rules. That's probably why she showed up at Mrs. Washburn's.

CHAN: Inside the house?

HANNAH: 'Fraid so.

CHAN: Oh. Mrs. Washburn—does she have a goldfish? 80

HANNAH: No, no—I don't think so.

CHAN: There—you see?

HANNAH: Anyway, Mrs. Chan, I just thought I oughta tell you about her, on account of what happened to Mrs. Washburn. I been working for all you people ten, 85 sometimes twenty years. All my clients—they're gettin' up there. We're all startin' to show our age. Can't compete with the young girls no more.

CHAN: I never try—even when I was one.

HANNAH: Well, the older I get, the more I see of Sandra, so I just thought I oughta be warnin' you. 90

CHAN: I am not afraid of Sandra Smith.

HANNAH: Well, good then. Good for you.

CHAN: She comes here, I will fight her. Not like these Americans. So stupid. Never think of these things. Never think of ghost. Never think of death. Never prepare for anything. Always think, life goes on and on, forever. And so, always, it ends. 95

HANNAH: Okay. Glad to hear it. Guess I'll go take the slime off the shower walls.

Hannah exits, into the house. Chan just stares downstage, from her chair. Silence. P. K. enters from the driveway, golf clubs slung over his shoulder.

P. K.: Hi, Popo!

CHAN: Hello.

P. K.: Do you have a beer?

CHAN: Look in 'frigerator.

P. K.: Just return from a good game of golf! 100

CHAN: Ah! What are you talking about?

P. K.: Eighteen holes, Popo!

CHAN: Ai! You cannot remember anything anymore!

P. K.: So? I remember that I go to golf!

CHAN: How can this be? You do not drive! 105

P. K.: What do you mean? I drive the Eldorado.

CHAN: You cannot drive the Eldorado.

P. K.: I do!

CHAN: Hanh! We sell it many years ago!

P. K.: What? 110

CHAN: Yes! Remember? We sell it! To John, your nephew.

P. K.: Huh? How much did he pay?

CHAN: Who cares?

P. K.: I want to know!

CHAN: I always tell you, John buys the car; you always ask me, how much does he pay? 115

P. K.: It is important! It is worth—lots of money!

CHAN: Ah, not so much money.

P. K.: No! Lots!

CHAN: Not after Humphrey breaks the back window by trying to lower top while driving. 120

P. K.: Yes! I tell Humphrey—cannot lower while driving. He says, "Of course! Can! This is a luxury car!" How come we sell the car?

CHAN: Ah! You cannot remember anything!

P. K.: No. Gung Gung cannot remember anything anymore.

CHAN: We sell, because you can no longer drive. 125

P. K.: I can! I can!

CHAN: You cannot pass the test.

P. K.: Can Humphrey pass the test?

CHAN: Of course! Of course, he passes it.

P. K.: How can? He is the one who lowers top while driving! 130

CHAN: Gung Gung! Because he is young, so he can pass the test!

P. K.: Young, but not so smart.

CHAN: Stupid.

P. K.: Sometimes, stupid.

CHAN: Stupid does not matter. Many stupid people drive. 135

Pause.

P. K.: So I did not go to golf?

CHAN: No! How can you go to golf? You cannot go anyplace.

P. K. (*points to clubs*)**:** Then, what are these?

CHAN: You just put them on your shoulder, then walk outside. Two hour later, you
    return. 140

P. K.: Where did I go?

CHAN: I don't know! You tell me!

P. K.: I cannot remember anything, anymore. I thought that I go to play eighteen-
    hole golf. But there is no golf course. So perhaps I walk into those hills. Maybe I
    shoot a few balls in the hills. Maybe I sink a putt into a gopher hole. 145

Pause.

CHAN: Gung Gung.

P. K.: Yes, Popo?

CHAN: I saw a ghost today.

P. K.: Popo! A ghost?

CHAN: Yes—a warning ghost. 150

P. K.: Which is this?

CHAN: They warn that another ghost will soon come. Bigger. More dangerous. Fatter.

P. K.: Oh! Popo! Why do they send this warning ghost?

CHAN: Because, they are stupid! This is how, they become dead to begin with. Because
    when they were living, they were too stupid to listen to the warning ghost! 155

P. K.: Popo! Will you die? (*He starts to cry.*) What will Gung Gung do without you?

CHAN: No.

P. K.: Without Popo, I will be completely all lost.

CHAN: No, Gung Gung.

P. K.: I will walk around all day, not know where I am going, not know where I come 160
    from, only saying, "Popo? Where is Popo? Where is—?"

CHAN: No! Will you listen to me? You ask the question, then you will not listen to
    the answer! Talk, talk, talk! If I die, leave you alone, I would be lucky!

P. K.: You mean, you will not die?

CHAN: No, I will not die. 165

P. K.: How can this be?

CHAN: They are stupid enough to send the warning ghost. This is how I know, they will not defeat me.

P. K.: But, when the ghost come, no one can resist.

CHAN: Who says this?   170

P. K.: Ummm . . .

CHAN: See? Maybe, Gung Gung, you cannot resist.

P. K.: No. I cannot resist.

CHAN: But you have no responsibilities. I have. I have responsibility. I cannot leave you alone, Gung Gung. And also, I must watch the grandchildren grow to adults.   175

P. K.: Yes—this would be good.

CHAN: So, you see, I cannot die.

P. K.: This makes me so happy.

CHAN: I will defeat the ghost.

P. K.: Yes! Popo! You can do it! Popo is very smart!   180

CHAN: Yeah, yeah, yeah, we all know this already.

P. K.: I am fortunate to marry such a smart wife.

CHAN: Not smart. Smart is not enough.

P. K.: More than smart.

CHAN: Fight. Fight is more important. l am willing to fight. I like to fight.   185

Pause.

P. K.: Why do l carry these golf clubs?

CHAN: I do not know! You ask so many times already!

P. K.: Oh—I suppose—l must go to golf.

Pause.

CHAN: Yes—you must go to golf.

P. K.: Okay. I will leave now. Take the Eldorado. Bye, Popo.   190

CHAN: Bye, Gung Gung.

P. K.: You will have a cold can of beer in the 'frigerator, for when I return?

CHAN: I will, Gung Gung. I will.

P. K. starts to exit out the upstage door.

CHAN: Gung Gung!

P. K.: Yes, Popo?   195

CHAN: Have a good game, okay, Gung Gung?

P. K.: I will have a good game, okay, Popo. (*He exits.*)

CHAN: l arrive in America one day, June 16, 1976. Many times, I have come here before, to visit children, but on this day, I arrive to stay. All my friends, all the Chinese in the Philippine, they tell me, "We thought you are stupid when you send all your children to America. We even feel sorry for you, that you will grow old all alone—no family around you." This is what they tell me. 200

The day I arrive in America, I do not feel sorry. I do not miss the Philippine, I do not look forward live in America. Just like, I do not miss China, when I leave it many years ago—go live in Philippine. Just like, I do not miss Manila, when Japanese take our home during wartime, and we are all have to move to Baguio, and live in haunted house. It is all same to me. Go, one home to the next, one city to another, nation to nation, across ocean big and small. 205

We are born traveling. We travel—all our lives. I am not looking for a home. I know there is none. The day I was marry, my mother put many gold bracelets on my arm, and so many necklaces that the back of my head grows sore. "These," she tells me. "These are for the times when you will have to run." 210

The upstage door opens. Hannah is standing there, dressed as Sandra Smith. Sandra wears a bright orange fright wig and a tight dress, sports huge sunglasses, and swings a small purse.

SANDRA: Well, hello there! Howdy, howdy, howdy!

CHAN: Hi.

SANDRA: Say, you seen Hannah? Hannah Carter? I understand she works here on Wednesdays. 215

CHAN: I think, she just leave.

SANDRA: Oh, well, that's a shame. I usually don't get to visit where she works. We were supposed to go for dinner at Chicken on Fire, but, looks like we're just not connecting. Damn! Always happens, whenever I try to meet her at one of these houses. 220

CHAN: So, would you like to go home, now?

SANDRA: Mmmm. Guess I could, but I wouldn't mind enjoying some of your hospitality.

CHAN: What is this, hospitality? 225

SANDRA: You know. What you show your guests.

CHAN: We do not have guests here! Only relatives, and, ah, servants.

SANDRA: Well, what do you do when someone comes over?

CHAN: They tell me what they want. Then, they leave.

SANDRA: No time to socialize?   230

CHAN: What is, socialize?

SANDRA: You know. You're not gonna offer me a tea, coffee, cake, Sanka?

CHAN: No.

SANDRA: I can't hardly believe this house.

CHAN: People—they are like cats. If you feed them, they will always return.   235

SANDRA: What ever happened to old fashioned manners?

CHAN: My manners—they are very old. We act like this for centuries.

SANDRA: My name's Sandra. Sandra Smith.

CHAN: This is no surprise. Are you finish, now? Hannah is not here.

SANDRA: No—I can see that. (*Pause.*) You know, I've known Hannah—well, ever   240
since she was a little girl. She wasn't very pretty. No one in Louisville paid much
attention to her. Yeah, she's had five husbands and all, okay, that's true, but my
personal guess is that most of 'em married her because she was a hard-working
woman who could bring home the bacon week after week. Certain men will
hold their noses for a free lunch. Hannah thinks the same thing, though she   245
hardly ever talks about it. How can she think anything else when all five of
them left her as soon as they got a whiff of some girl with pipe cleaners for legs?
Hard for her to think she's much more than some mule, placed on this earth to
work her back. She spends most of her life wanderin' from one beautiful house
to the next, knowing intimately every detail, but never layin' down her head in   250
any of 'em. She's what they call a good woman. Men know it, rich folks know
it. Everyplace is beautiful, 'cept the place where she lives. Home is a dark room,
she knows it well, knows its limits. She knows she can't travel nowhere without
returnin' to that room once the sun goes down. Home is fixed, it does not move,
even as the rest of the world circles 'round and 'round, picking up speed.   255

CHAN: You are a ghost.

SANDRA: I have a good time, if that's what you mean.

CHAN: I was warned that you would come.

SANDRA: By Hannah? She's always tellin' people about me. Like I was some kinda
celebrity or somethin'.   260

CHAN: I fight ghosts. I chase them.

SANDRA: Can't chase anything, unless you get it runnin' from ya first.
CHAN: In Baguio, we live in a haunted house.
SANDRA: In where?
CHAN: Baguio. In the Philippine. 265
SANDRA: I never been there.
CHAN: During the war, we live in a haunted house. I chase the ghost out, with pots
and pan. So, I know I can defeat them.
SANDRA: Hannah—she lives in a haunted house right now.
CHAN: Yes—haunted with you. 270
SANDRA: I show her how to make her life a little easier. Someone's gotta do it, after all
her sixty-some-odd years. How 'bout you? Anything I can help you with?
CHAN: Ha! I do not need a thing!
SANDRA: I'm not sure if I believe that, Mrs. . . . Mrs. . . . whatever. Hannah sees you
sittin' here, day after day— 275
CHAN: I am old! Of course I sit!
SANDRA: —starin' out into that garden—
CHAN: So?
SANDRA: First off, it's mostly dirt.
CHAN: This way, easier to take care of. 280
SANDRA: But you stare like there's somethin' out there.
CHAN: Yes! The sun is out there!
SANDRA: Lookin' at the sun, Mrs.—ma'am? Gotta be careful you don't burn your
eyeballs out.
CHAN: I only look outside because—sky, clouds, sun—they are all there—interesting 285
to watch.
SANDRA: Real pretty, huh?
CHAN: Yes. Sometimes pretty.
SANDRA: Looks like home.
CHAN: What is this? All the time, you talk about home, home, home? 290
SANDRA: Just like you do.
CHAN: I never talk about home. Barely talk at all.
SANDRA: You think you keep your lips buttoned, that means all your secrets are safe
inside? If they're strong enough, things make themselves known, one way or
another. Hannah knows, she's not stupid. She'd never tell anyone but me. But 295
me, I'd tell anybody. (*Pause.*) Want me to tell you?

CHAN: Tell me what?

SANDRA: What you're lookin' at out there?

Pause.

CHAN: I can defeat you. I defeat ghost before.

SANDRA: Honey, it's not a fight no more. I've been around fifteen years. I already   300
know you. You know me. We see the same thing. Out there. (*Pause.*) There's a
crow sitting on a window sill. And two kids who chase it down a steep ravine.
Their path grows darker and darker, but the crow continues, and the kids don't
tire, even when the blisters start to show on their feet. Mud, sleet, rain, and
snow, all try to make the kids give up the chase. The crow caws—mountains   305
fall in its wake, but still the children continue. And then it becomes dark, so
dark, and the crow throws disasters at their feet. Floods, droughts, wars. The
children see nothing, now. They follow the crow only by the catastrophes it
leaves in its path. Where there is famine, the crow must have been. Where
there are earthquakes, it has rested. They run on faith now, passing through   310
territories uncharted, following the sound of their suffering. And it is in this
way that they pass through their lives. Hardly noticing that they've entered.
Without stopping to note its passing. Just following a crow, with single
dedication, forgetting how they started, or why they're chasing, or even what
may happen if they catch it. Running without pause or pleasure, past the point   315
of their beginning.

*Over the next Section, Mrs. Chan's dress slowly rises into the air. She wears a white slip
beneath. She stands up from the chair, for the first time in the play, and walks over to
Sandra.*

SANDRA: I see it in the distance.

CHAN: It is waiting for me.

SANDRA: I cannot stop my running.

CHAN: I cannot rest, even for a second.   320

SANDRA: There's a field out in the distance.

CHAN: There's a wooden gate in that field.

SANDRA: There is a crow sitting on that gate.

CHAN: It caws.

SANDRA: It caws.   325

CHAN: And disaster comes.

SANDRA: Once again.
CHAN: Nothing new.
SANDRA: Nothing blue.
CHAN: Only the scent of home. 330
SANDRA: I don't know why I follow it.
CHAN: I don't care to know.
SANDRA: Not now.
CHAN: Not here.
SANDRA: Not ever. Perhaps someday. 335
CHAN: Maybe to remember.
SANDRA: Why I run.
CHAN: Why I chase.
SANDRA: Until I am so—
CHAN: So tired. 340
SANDRA: Another disaster.
CHAN: Another lonely child.
SANDRA: We follow the scent of home.

Sandra removes her wig, glasses, tight dress. She too wears a white slip. She is Hannah again. Mrs. Chan moves towards the door. Hannah ever so slowly lowers herself into Mrs. Chan's chair. Hannah sits in it, beams.

HANNAH: Ooooh. Nice home, Mrs. Chan.
CHAN: I see it. 345
HANNAH: So do I, so do I.
CHAN: I see all the way past those mountains.
HANNAH: Welcome home, Mrs. Chan.
CHAN: Welcome home, Hannah.

Mrs. Chan exits through the garden. Hannah looks around her like a kid with a new toy. Upstage, P. K. enters with golf clubs. He cannot see Hannah in the chair.

P. K.: Hi, Popo! (*Pause.*) Where is my beer? 350

Hannah closes her eyes, a smile on her face.

P. K.: You leave a beer in the 'frigerator? (*Pause.*) Popo? Popo?

P. K. is walking towards the chair as lights fade to black.

∾ NOW PRACTICE ON YOUR OWN: AS THE CROW FLIES

Patterns

When confronted with a difficult text, you will usually find it productive to begin with the patterns strategy. Look for a concept, an image, a word, or an idea that seems to be repeated throughout the text—or, alternatively, start with something in the text that seems to stand out and then try to find other examples of this same phenomenon and see if a pattern starts to emerge.

1. In *As the Crow Flies*, we noted that the concept of **home** seems to recur throughout the play. Start with this concept and make a list of the different occurrences of home. Look not just for dialogue using the word *home* but also at stage descriptions. How is Mrs. Chan's home portrayed onstage? What surface/depth arguments might you make about the concept of home in this play?

2. As you looked for examples of the concept of home in the play, you might also have noted a pattern of references to its opposite—**travel**, or movement. Make a list of travel references. Look not just at the dialogue but also at the stage movements of the characters. Who moves and travels in this play and who stays at rest? Do any of the movements in this play support or contradict the dialogue? Can you make any surface/depth arguments about travel or movement in this play?

3. There seems to be a tension between **age** and **youth** in the play. Make a list of places where this tension seems to occur—or where you see references to one or the other concept.

4. What other patterns do you see in *As the Crow Flies*? Make lists of these patterns and see if you can begin to propose surface/depth arguments about some of them.

Digging Deeper

5. Review the list of aspects to consider about texts in Chapter 5 (pp. 108–10) and on the inside front cover of this book. Can you use these to expand any of your lists? For instance, the names of the characters—Chan, Carter, Smith—are very typical (perhaps even stereotypical) names for people of Chinese or African-American ancestry. Can you make a surface/depth argument about why Hwang used such common names? What other elements of the text help you extend or deepen your interpretations?

Opposites

The opposites and patterns strategies often overlap one another as critics begin to note relationships among the different patterns and interpretations that they uncover. *As the Crow Flies* lends itself well to an analysis of opposites. Recall that the goal of using the opposites strategy is generally to break down binaries: we look for similarities in things that on the surface appear different, and we look for differences in what at first seem to be similar phenomena.

6. **Hannah** and **Mrs. Chan**—the African-American maid and her Chinese employer—seem to share differences as well as similarities. Make a list of the ways their characters differ from and resemble one another. Analyze their physical descriptions and their stage movements as well as the dialogue they exchange. Start first by analyzing Hannah when she is herself and then analyze Hannah when she is Sandra Smith. Are there any surprising similarities between Hannah and Mrs. Chan? Any particularly notable differences? Can you make surface/depth arguments from any of these observations?

7. **Home** and **travel** seem to be opposites in this play; yet, there are many ways in which these two concepts seem to overlap. Use the lists you prepared with the patterns strategy to make a new list identifying ways that home and travel are similar as well as different in this play. Try to brainstorm any surface/depth arguments you might make about these similarities.

8. Mrs. Chan several times seems dismissive of Americans and American culture. Analyze the similarities and differences between **Chinese** and **American** cultures in the play. Can you make any surface/depth arguments about the relationships between these two cultures?

9. **Age** and **youth** also seem to be opposites, but Hannah contains both a young and an old self. Are there any ways in which this binary seems to break down and we see age and youth sharing traits in common? Can you make any surface/depth arguments about what this play seems to be saying about age?

Context

As the Crow Flies obviously makes many references to Chinese culture and the Chinese immigrant experience. You may find it useful to research some of this history, but be careful about including too much context in your interpretation. Your analysis needs to focus on the text and not on explaining the context surrounding it. We suggest a few contextual elements in the play that may be worth additional research and reflection.

10. The idiom "as the crow flies" typically refers to the shortest distance between two points. However, the **crow** is a common symbol in many cultures. Research common meanings of the crow in the various cultures depicted in this play and see if you can make a surface/depth argument about what the phrase "as the crow flies" may mean in the context of this play.

11. Mrs. Chan states that **June 16, 1976**, is the day she came to America. This is the date of the South African Soweto uprising and is also several weeks before the bicentennial celebration of the Declaration of Independence. Hwang may or may not have intended this date to be significant, and interpretations that place too much emphasis on this date may easily verge into symbol-hunting. Do you see any ways that the events on or near this date might support patterns or interpretations you have already noted? Brainstorm for connections and surface/depth arguments, but be prepared to drop these arguments if you later decide they are not persuasive and seem to veer into symbol-hunting.

12. Hwang included a preface to his play when it was first published. In this preface, Hwang writes[1]:

> One theme I trace through all my work is this kind of fluidity of identity. In a lot of my plays, from *FOB* to *M. Butterfly*, people become other people. It has a lot to do with the nature *vs.* nurture question. To what degree do you have an inherited identity, and to what degree is your personality shaped by the influences and environment around you?
>
> This question is intimately related to my desire to know myself. I happened to be born Chinese-American in the United States. Would I be different if I was born in China? Or if I had a different skin color in this country? I also think it's interesting to explore racism and stereotyping between different minority groups in this culture, because that's really where the future lies. If we're becoming a culture of many different ethnicities, then the way these ethnic groups relate to one another will be increasingly important—at least as important as the way these ethnicities combined relate to white America.

---

[1] Hwang, David Henry. *Between the Worlds: Contemporary Asian-American Plays.* Ed. Misha Berson. New York: Theatre Communications Group, 1990. 91–95. Print.

I find it fascinating that the term "Asian" only exists in the West. People who live in Asian countries see themselves as Chinese or Japanese or Korean—just as people in France or Germany see themselves as French or German first, not European.

Asian is really our term, and I like it—first because I think the experiences of Asians in this country are rather similar. Secondly, because I don't see the point of being nationalistic, and the concept of "Asian" stops nationalism dead. A person in Japan and a person in China would most likely not have the same close friendship as Philip Gotanda and I. (Hwang 94)

Do any of Hwang's comments lend support to interpretations you have already developed—or help you refine or elaborate on these interpretations? Does Hwang's discussion of his own motivations for writing give you a new idea for analyzing the play?

13. Are there other **cultural references** in the play? Is there anything in Chinese-American history that might deepen and enrich our interpretation of the play? Be aware that many aspects of a text that you might research will often be dead ends. Take care not to symbol-hunt as you look for ways to deepen existing arguments.

Genre and Form

14. **Theater of the Absurd** (or **absurdist drama**) is a form of theatrical drama that uses irrational dialogue and confusing plots to illustrate how humans respond to a world seemingly without meaning or purpose. Common characteristics of Theater of the Absurd include broad comedy mixed with tragic events; characters forced into repetitive, meaningless actions; plots without realistic or logical development; and dialogue full of clichés, wordplay, or nonsense. Realism and logical thought in these plays break down into irrational speech and silence. Well-known absurdist plays include Samuel Beckett's *Waiting for Godot* and *Endgame*, Eugène Ionesco's *Rhinoceros,* and Tom Stoppard's *Rosencrantz and Guildenstern Are Dead.*

As the Crow Flies clearly shares many characteristics of Theater of the Absurd. Conduct additional research on this genre and look for ways in which *As the Crow Flies* might differ or break from the conventions of absurdist drama. For instance, could the ending of the play be read as more hopeful or as containing more of a resolution than the endings of similar absurdist plays?

15. Mrs. Chan delivers a **soliloquy** midway through the play. The speaker of a soliloquy is typically alone and delivers a speech to him- or herself. Soliloquies were widely used by Shakespeare and other playwrights of his era but are comparatively rare in contemporary drama, particularly in realist dramas. Mrs. Chan's soliloquy also stands out in that it includes others' dialogue. What surface/depth arguments can you make about the inclusion of this soliloquy in a contemporary play? What might this choice of device reveal about Mrs. Chan's character?

16. Mrs. Chan's soliloquy is paralleled by Sandra Smith's **monologue** a few moments later. Like a soliloquy, a monologue is a long speech that interrupts the action of a play; however, unlike a soliloquy, a monologue is delivered in the presence of other characters. Compare and contrast these two speeches and see if you can use your comparisons to elaborate on or deepen any of your earlier observations of these characters.

17. As Mrs. Chan and Hannah discuss the crow, they begin to share lines of dialogue, echoing and repeating one another in an almost musical fashion. This back-and-forth, musical dialogue resembles **call-and-response**, a form of verbal interaction in which the statements of one speaker (calls) are answered by expressions (responses) from others. Call-and-response is common in African-American sermons, speeches, and music. What surface/ depth arguments might you make about the incorporation of call-and-response dialogue in this play?

18. The call-and-response interaction about the crow is characterized by **repetitions** and **doublings**, as is common in call-and-response. What other repetitions or doublings do you see in the play? Return to the patterns strategy to make a list of doublings. Can you make a surface/depth argument about any of these repetitions?

Social Relevance

19. Any surface interpretation of *As the Crow Flies*—with its Chinese immigrant family and their African-American housekeeper—is likely to note that the play is making an argument about race. You may, however, be able to deepen this interpretation by reflecting on the histories and oppressions faced by these two races.

Theoretical Lens

20. Of the various theoretical lenses we describe in the appendix of in this book, Jerome Bruner's "Self-Making Narratives" and W. E. B. Du Bois's theory of

double-consciousness in *The Souls of Black Folk* seem most relevant to the analysis of *As the Crow Flies*. Can you use these lenses to dig deeper into what this play may have to say about identity, self, or race? How does the play complicate our understandings of these theoretical lenses?

21. Although less obviously relevant than Du Bois's or Bruner's theories, Michel Foucault's arguments about self-discipline and self-policing may also lead to new insights about *As the Crow Flies*. Read the play looking for places where the characters seem to have internalized (or escaped) the disciplinary mechanisms of the larger culture. Can you connect these observations to any of the other themes or interpretations you have noted in the play?

Conversation

Wait until you have had a chance to work through your own interpretations of the play before reading this section. Reading other people's interpretations before you have had a chance to form your own surface/depth arguments can often limit—rather than expand—what you see in a play. Create some questions about the text before you read on to see what other critics have argued.

Two critical works have dealt with *As the Crow Flies* in some depth. Una Chaudhuri dedicates a section of her book *Staging Place: The Geography of Modern Drama* to the analysis of *As the Crow Flies*.[2] Chaudhuri begins her analysis by comparing *As the Crow Flies* to Samuel Beckett's *Endgame*, a well-known work of Theater of the Absurd, claiming that both plays depict the final moves in a logic of place and identity that the characters have been playing out for years. Chaudhuri argues that Mrs. Chan and Hannah Carter represent two sides of home that result from the displacements of modern history: Mrs. Chan represents the rejection of home, while Hannah represents home as a prison. Chaudhuri argues that the end of the play validates both Hannah's need for a literal home and the truth of Mrs. Chan's displacement and exile, while P. K.'s return and closing lines indicate a lack of closure and the continuation of the struggle over "home."

[2] Chaudhuri, Una. *Staging Place: The Geography of Modern Drama*. Ann Arbor: U of Michigan P, 1995. 216–22. Print.

Tsui-fen Jiang's article "Disembedding, Deterritorialization, Hybridization in David Henry Hwang's *As the Crow Flies*" discusses three theoretical lenses—disembedding, deterritorialization, and hybridization—and uses these lenses to interpret *As the Crow Flies* as a work of migrant literature.[3] Jiang argues that Mrs. Chan's experiences cause her identity to be disengaged from the physical places she occupies. However, even though Mrs. Chan isolates herself from American culture and experience, this culture still encroaches on her. Jiang argues that the interactions of different cultures in the play give rise to a third, hybrid culture in which Mrs. Chan can find a home.

22. How do your interpretations of the play compare to Chaudhuri's or Jiang's? Do either of these critics help you expand your arguments about the play? Are there any elements of their interpretations that you disagree with? Do you find yourself agreeing with parts of their interpretations but not all of their conclusions?

    If you want to converse with these critics in a formal paper, you should locate and read the actual works of criticism yourself rather than work from these summaries. However, these summaries should be sufficient for class discussion and to see how you might position your interpretation so that it is in conversation with other critics' arguments about this text.

---

[3] Jiang, Tsui-fen. "Disembedding, Deterritorialization, Hybridization in David Henry Hwang's *As the Crow Flies*." *Tamkang Review* 33.3–4 (2003): 177–96. Print.

part 4

CRAFTING YOUR ESSAY

part 4 » CRAFTING YOUR ESSAY

13

Developing a Thesis and Organizing Your Essay

··

When you are asked to write a literary analysis, we hope you will see the assignment as an invitation to participate in the discourse community of literary critics and take your turn developing an extended argument about the meaning or meanings of a text.

The strategies presented in previous chapters will help you discover worthwhile, debatable claims about a text. Once you have made these discoveries, you will need to organize your thoughts into a coherent argument focused on supporting a thesis. This chapter aims to help you craft a good thesis statement and organize a draft while developing your ideas about a text. The next two chapters will address using textual evidence effectively, peer review of drafts, and revision. ■

UNDERSTANDING THE ROLE OF THE THESIS STATEMENT

As explained throughout Chapter 2, a *thesis* is a succinct statement of your most important, overall argument. In a literary analysis, a thesis usually makes a surface/depth argument that indicates how the text is complex. In general, a good thesis statement in literary analysis will answer the question, "On a deeper level, what does this text mean?" or "What does a careful reading of this text uncover?" Example thesis statements include:

> On one level, Ondaatje's "The Cinnamon Peeler" shows a man who desires total ownership and possession of a woman, while at the same time it seems to suggest that this desire is an impossible fantasy. The poem implies that lust is neither as powerful nor as all encompassing as it might first seem.

"The Man to Send Rain Clouds" illustrates how even well-meaning colonizers are unable to fully hear and see the people they wish to help.

Note that both of these thesis statements make debatable arguments that define something complex about the texts. The first thesis makes a surface/depth–contrasting argument showing that the depiction of lust in "The Cinnamon Peeler" is more complex than it at first seems. The second uses a surface/depth–linking argument to claim that "The Man to Send Rain Clouds" illustrates some of the contradictions of colonialism. Note also that while the second example is one sentence long, the first one is two sentences. As you learn to make increasingly complex arguments, you may find that you need multiple sentences to articulate your thesis.

In literary analyses, thesis statements usually appear near the beginning of an essay where they summarize and preview ideas that will be developed and supported in the essay's body. Clear statements of your argument's key claims in a thesis statement and topic sentences help your readers keep your argument in mind and anticipate where it will go. Thus, placing the thesis statement early in an essay allows literary critics to make complex arguments that readers nonetheless find relatively easy to follow.

Your arguments should pique your readers' curiosity—remember that readers should find your main arguments debatable—so foregrounding your thesis early is also a way to interest your readers. Think of your thesis statement as starting a conversation with your readers. When they read your thesis, readers should start asking questions and thinking of counterarguments. In other words, readers should want to respond to your arguments. As a writer and critic, you should try to anticipate these responses and answer them in your essay. If your analysis ultimately satisfies the counterarguments your readers begin to raise when they first encounter your thesis, you will have written a persuasive analysis.

Writing a good thesis statement is not usually a matter of having a single moment of brilliant insight. Most often, a good thesis emerges slowly as critics move back and forth between analyzing a text and organizing their arguments into a coherent whole. We will discuss two main processes literary critics use to develop a thesis statement: freewriting and outlining. Critics using both of these strategies often draft several potential theses and shift between writing a thesis statement, writing the supporting arguments, and analyzing the text. In other words, as you organize your arguments, you will need to return to the discovery process to fill in gaps and make additional connections between various ideas that at first seemed unconnected. In this chapter, we will show you how successful literary critics do this.

ANALYZING THE WELL-ORGANIZED ESSAY

To understand how to develop a thesis, it is useful to look at what a thesis does and how it helps order an essay. On the next few pages, we have reproduced a short analysis from the end of Chapter 4. This essay has a traditional structure for a literary analysis:

- The thesis appears at the end of the first paragraph.
- The paragraphs in the body each develop and support a part of this thesis.
- The final paragraph extends the argument presented in the thesis and answers the question, "What does this poem mean or illustrate?"

You may have been told in previous writing classes that the ideal essay has a five-paragraph structure. Such a structure may be a good model for relatively short, simple arguments. However, more complex arguments often require more sophisticated organizational structures than the five-paragraph essay.

To see how a relatively complex, well-organized essay works, let's do a reverse outline of its arguments. A **reverse outline** is an outline written after you have written an essay. To make a reverse outline of an argumentative essay such as a literary analysis, read through the essay and write down the main argument or arguments of each paragraph. Note the difference between a list of *arguments* and a list of *topics*: a topic is simply a word or phrase that indicates what the paragraph is about, while an argument is a debatable statement that indicates what the paragraph claims.

Let's try this process with the essay titled "Contradictory Desires in Michael Ondaatje's 'The Cinnamon Peeler.'" Go through the essay below and write down the main arguments made in each paragraph.

Contradictory Desires in Michael Ondaatje's "The Cinnamon Peeler"

Michael Ondaatje's "The Cinnamon Peeler" is a poem that provides contradictory images of lust. On one level, the poem shows a man who desires total ownership and possession of a woman, while at the same time it seems to suggest that this desire is an impossible fantasy. The poem implies that lust is neither as powerful nor as all encompassing as it might first seem.

The first half of the poem shows the speaker lusting after total domination of a woman. He imagines leaving a visible trace of himself on her pillow after he has been with her, suggesting that he wants to "mark" her as his own. He further imagines her body will "reek" (5) of his smell, even in a crowded marketplace, showing that he wants everyone to know, without doubt, that she belongs to him. This desire for total domination is perhaps best illustrated by the lines "you will be known among strangers / as the cinnamon peeler's wife" (17–18). These lines show how the speaker wants this woman to be known only by her marital relationship to him. Moreover, this image reveals that he wants his domination of her to be so obvious that even strangers will recognize that she belongs to him.

The speaker's desire for total ownership of this woman is further illustrated in how he divides her body into pieces in the second and third stanza. He refers to her "breasts and shoulders" (5), her "upper thigh" (12), "the crease that cuts your back" (15–16), and "This ankle" (16), suggesting that he sees her as a series of body parts rather than as a whole person. Moreover, he talks about her body the way people often talk about land, describing her "pasture" and how her different parts act as "neighbours" to one another (13–14). These images show how the speaker wants to stake his claim to individual pieces of the woman's body much like a person might stake a claim to a plot of land or other physical piece of property.

However, even while "The Cinnamon Peeler" projects a male fantasy of domination, there are many places in the poem that contradict this fantasy. The very first word of the poem is "if," which shows the reader that the speaker is in reality not a cinnamon peeler and that the domination and possession portrayed in the poem is a fantasy. The ellipses at the end of the first half (26) indicate that this fantasy cannot be maintained. Immediately afterward, the poem abruptly shifts tone and point of view, suggesting an alternate view of their relationship.

The second half of the poem contradicts the fantasy of total ownership depicted in the first half. In the first half of the poem, the speaker tells the woman that his smell completely defines her. The traces of his cinnamon perfume on her body provide guidance for the blind, who can "stumble certain of whom they approach," suggesting that the most important, defining quality of this woman is not anything of her own, but a smell she has acquired from her husband's profession. Moreover, his stamp on her is so strong that it cannot be erased even by a monsoon (8–11), showing that his control over her is stronger than the forces of nature. However, in the second half of the poem, the cinnamon scent is so weak that a short swim is enough to rid her of his perfume and make both of them "blind of smell" (30). This imagery suggests that the man's hold over this woman is temporary and easily washed away. Moreover, we find that the cinnamon peeler has touched other women whose smells overpower his own, further illustrating his inability to completely possess and define a woman. His lack of ownership is further emphasized by the fact that their bodies remain "free" (29) in the water, showing she is independent of him no matter how much he may want to possess her.

The second half of the poem thus illustrates that a single-minded, totalizing lust that marks lovers as belonging to one another is only a fantasy. Images of absence and loss are found in the second half of the poem: his perfume is "missing" (35), she imagines others "left with no trace" (39) and "not spoken to" (40), and she is "blind of smell" (30). Even the opening line of this section emphasizes the temporary nature of their situation by stating, "When we swam once" (27), suggesting that their contact was temporary and in the past. The poem thus seems to indicate that real love is marked by loss and the absence of totalizing and overpowering desire.

Yet, the second half of the poem is not all loss since it is only in this second half that the woman has a voice. Where the first half shows the speaker dominating a woman's obedient body with his lust, the second half shows two independent people cooperating in their desire. The last two lines of the poem are spoken by the woman and she is the one who initiates sexual action by pressing her belly to his hands and commanding him to smell her, thus illustrating her independence. Since we know that her swim has washed away the cinnamon smell, she seems to be commanding the speaker here to smell her as she really is, free of the cinnamon perfume. The ending of the poem suggests that the man does not simply "ride" her bed as in the first stanza but is invited there and implies that true possession requires the freedom and cooperation of a partner.

Work Cited

Ondaatje, Michael. "The Cinnamon Peeler." *Digging into Literature: Strategies for Reading, Analysis, and Writing.* Joanna Wolfe and Laura Wilder. Boston: Bedford/St. Martin's, 2016. 74–76. Print.

A list of arguments in this essay might read:

Para. 1	On one level, the poem shows a man who desires total ownership and possession of a woman, while at the same time it seems to suggest that this desire is an impossible fantasy. The poem implies that lust is neither as powerful nor as all encompassing as it might first seem. (**Thesis**)
Para. 2	The speaker lusts after total domination of a woman.
Para. 3	The speaker's desire for total ownership of this woman is shown in how he talks about her body the way people talk about land.
Para. 4	The first half of the poem is a fantasy that cannot be maintained.
Para. 5	The second half of the poem contradicts the first half by showing the speaker's temporary hold and lack of ownership of this woman.
Para. 6	The second half of the poem uses images of absence and loss to show that totalizing lust is a fantasy.
Para. 7	The second half is not all loss because the woman gains a voice. The ending implies that true possession requires the freedom and cooperation of a partner.

Your list of arguments may be worded differently, but your version should include variations of most of the statements listed. Because this essay is clearly written, the main arguments are easy to pick out, even though the author is making a relatively complex argument.

We believe "Contradictory Desires" is a well-organized essay because it does the following:

Each paragraph of the body is closely connected to the thesis. The figure below shows how each paragraph in the body of the essay develops a part of the claims suggested in the thesis.

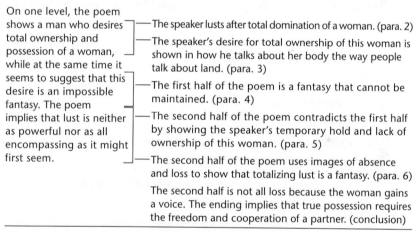

On one level, the poem shows a man who desires total ownership and possession of a woman, while at the same time it seems to suggest that this desire is an impossible fantasy. The poem implies that lust is neither as powerful nor as all encompassing as it might first seem.

— The speaker lusts after total domination of a woman. (para. 2)

— The speaker's desire for total ownership of this woman is shown in how he talks about her body the way people talk about land. (para. 3)

— The first half of the poem is a fantasy that cannot be maintained. (para. 4)

— The second half of the poem contradicts the first half by showing the speaker's temporary hold and lack of ownership of this woman. (para. 5)

— The second half of the poem uses images of absence and loss to show that totalizing lust is a fantasy. (para. 6)

The second half is not all loss because the woman gains a voice. The ending implies that true possession requires the freedom and cooperation of a partner. (conclusion)

Relationship between thesis and arguments in the body of the essay

This figure illustrates how the paragraphs in the body of the essay are closely tied to the thesis:

▸ The first (and most obvious) claim in the thesis is developed in paragraphs 2 and 3.

▸ The second major claim (that the desire for total domination is a fantasy) is taken up by paragraphs 4 and 6.

- ▸ The third major claim of the thesis (lust is not as all encompassing as it might first seem) is developed in paragraphs 5 and 6.
- ▸ The final paragraph concludes the essay not by summing up the arguments that have just been made but by extending the thesis.

Each paragraph of the body focuses on a single argument or pair of arguments. Note how each paragraph is focused on a relatively narrow claim that relates to the overall claim in the thesis. The evidence in these paragraphs helps support the central claim of the paragraph.

Each paragraph builds on the previous paragraphs. The figure below shows how each paragraph builds on the previous one.

THESIS: States Claims 1 & 2 and shows how they are related

Claim 1 asserted and supported
Poem shows desire for total domination

Claim 1 supported and refined with patterns
Total domination shown in land imagery

Claim 1 complicated with surface/depth-contrast
Total domination is a fantasy

Claim 2 introduced
Second half shows lack of domination

Claim 2 supported and refined with patterns
Lack of domination shown in images of absence

CONCLUSION: Redefines thesis to state the meaning of the poem: true possession requires cooperation

Structure of the argument

The essay is ordered by logical progression of the arguments rather than the sequence of the poem. Take a quick look at the essay and note the lines cited. The essay moves from line 5 to lines 17–18 in paragraph 2. We then have lines 5 and 12–16 cited in the third paragraph, and then the fourth paragraph moves between the first line of the poem and line 26. Paragraph 5 jumps between quotes taken from both the beginning of the poem and near the end. Although the essay works its way from the beginning to the end of the poem, it does not limit its organization to follow the exact order of events and lines in the poem. The focus of the essay's organization is on the argument this critic is making about the poem rather than on the poem itself.

Note that line 5 is used as evidence twice, to support two different arguments. While you will want to avoid overusing any one particular piece of evidence since this will reduce the persuasiveness of your argument, it is acceptable occasionally to cite the same evidence more than once. In fact, if you are making complex surface/depth arguments, you may need to do exactly that in order to show how a given line or quotation works on multiple levels.

TOPIC SENTENCES AID RECALL

Research on how readers process texts shows that topic sentences (statements summarizing a paragraph's main argument) help readers recall what they've read because they prepare readers for the ideas that follow.[1] Consequently, when topic sentences begin paragraphs, readers read more quickly and remember more of what they read than when paragraphs lack clear summarizing sentences.

Since information found in a topic sentence is much more likely to be recalled than information appearing elsewhere in a paragraph, writers may

---

[1] See, for example, D'Angelo, Frank J. "The Topic Sentence Revisited." *College Composition and Communication* 37.4 (1986): 431–41. Print.

want to ensure that their most important arguments appear in topic sentences. This helps ensure that readers focus on and remember what is most important to the writer's argument.

Such advice to place key information in topic sentences is particularly important to keep in mind when writing complex arguments that may otherwise be difficult for readers to follow. By preparing readers for subsequent arguments, topic sentences cut down on the work required to make sense of an essay, allowing readers to focus on content.

DEVELOPING A THESIS BY FREEWRITING AND REVERSE OUTLINING

Now that we have analyzed how a well-organized and reasonably complex essay works, let's discuss how you can use reverse outlining in your own writing.

We asked the professor who thought aloud for us while reading "The Man to Send Rain Clouds" about her writing process. She told us that her normal process is to read a story and then immediately freewrite about it. A **freewrite** is an essay draft (or some may call it a pre-draft) in which you quickly write down all your thoughts about a text while they are still fresh in your mind. No editing or censorship goes on during a freewrite—the goal is to get as much quantity down on the page as possible.

This professor told us that, after freewriting about a text, she creates a reverse outline to see what her major arguments are and locate areas that need more development and insight:

> [Y]ou can't expect yourself to write something fabulous the first time out, so you draft and re-draft, do the reverse outline, put it back together, tighten your thesis.
>
> I sometimes get to the point where, in fact, I make myself sit down after I've got a good longer draft going, and then I try to write just a one-paragraph abstract of what the paper is about, because if I can't figure out my argument

in one paragraph, that means I need to do more defining of my thesis and my argument.

And sometimes also writing that paragraph gives me a good idea because I'm forced to make logical connections between the parts of my argument in one paragraph. I can go back and, in fact, reorganize based on that paragraph. It becomes another version of an outline. So if I can make a logical connection in one paragraph, I can go back and reorganize the paper to follow that paragraph.

Here is this professor's initial freewrite with typos and glaring errors omitted (of which there were many—she typed this quickly, and seldom looked at her computer screen while composing). Again, her goal here was to get down as many thoughts as she could, to generate material without judgment to mold into something more graceful later.

FREEWRITE ON "THE MAN TO SEND RAIN CLOUDS"

In Leslie Marmon Silko's story "The Man to Send Rain Clouds," the ambiguity written into the title as to just who that man may be is in fact the central question of the story and one that is answered only by implication. These implications become clear when a careful reader closely tracks the play of perspective in the story; perspective understood on two levels, both as the narrative voice and point of view and related to that, perspective as cultural ways of understanding the world. The narrative voice begins as a fairly neutral third-person omniscient, though objective, narrator who follows the actions of four Laguna characters, Leon, Ken, Teresa, and Louise, as they discover and prepare for burial of the body of their grandfather, Teofilo. These four characters and the briefly mentioned neighbors treat the death of the old man as a matter of course, and while they are not casual in their manner of dealing with Teofilo's death and/or corpse, neither are they dramatic or noisy. In fact the story emphasizes the quietness of the characters (not talking during their dinner, the silent preparation of the body) and their neighbors who as the text says: "The neighbors and clanspeople came quietly to embrace Teofilo's family." This calmness with which the Laguna characters react to Teofilo's death is contrasted by the noise associated with Father Paul, the only non-Laguna character represented in the story. He is represented as hard of hearing in some ways, again both literally and metaphorically. His first communication with Ken and Leon is marked by his misunderstanding of their experience of Death. " 'Did you find old Teofilo?' he asked loudly," as one might when talking to someone who you assume cannot understand you. The conversation ends with Father Paul saying, "I'm glad you understand," when, in fact, he understands nothing. The irony is almost too much here— Father Paul's radical misunderstanding of the Laguna position on death. "Everything is O.K. now" makes evident the ongoing tension between the indigenous peoples' and this outsider/colonizer's voice/ perspective/understanding of things as basic as life and death. This fundamental incompatibility is emphasized near the end of the story when four of the last five paragraphs describe Father Paul's hesitation to bless Teofilo's burial with holy water when he hasn't had a chance to direct the final rites as he "sees" fit. He is however eventually persuaded (though this seems too strong a word for Leon's silent assumption of consent, which Father Paul seems powerless to resist). Father Paul in a frenzy of missed opportunities for conversions soaks the body of Teofilo with holy water thinking perhaps that at least this is one Indian he can make his mark on. What is most striking about these last four out of five paragraphs is the switch to Father Paul's perspective and complete depersonalization of the Laguna characters, namely Leon, Ken, Teresa, and Louise, who do not get names, do not even get individual features, but are instead in Father Paul's eyes reduced to an indistinguishable mass of traits, not even human traits, gloves, hats, scarves, steaming breath. In the last paragraph, Silko gives the control over the story back to one of her Laguna characters, Leon (the lion, a pun on one of the Christian symbols for Jesus perhaps?), and has Leon remark that the holy water has served its purpose as understood not by Father Paul but by the Laguna: it has wet Grandfather's throat so that he may in turn release rain to his descendants and not hoard it for himself. This subtle (even tricky perhaps if Father Paul were asked) appropriation of the symbols of Western imperial culture that seeks to reduce all natives or indigenes to undifferentiated cripples and pagans displayed in a magazine reasserts the native perspective on the landscape, on life, and even on death. Father Paul's loudness, or tone deafness, is reinforced and made to represent his own implication in colonial culture when the narrator tells us that the most remarkable feature of Father Paul's small church is the "[t]win bells from the king of Spain with the last sunlight pouring around them in their tower." Every detail in this quotation bears out in the rest of the story: Father Paul's and by extension Christianity's loud efforts to drown out the noises of indigenous life; their insistence that the colonial mission was in fact a mission of enlightenment (the sun peering through the tower); and the colonizers' obsessive desire to exist both in the colonized sphere but be apart from the colonized sphere (entrenched in their towers).

Exercise

1. Do a reverse outline of the major arguments in this freewrite. Because little attention was given to organization in composing the freewrite and some thoughts are not yet fully formed, your reverse outline should be a list of what you see as the main arguments the writer made or was on the verge of making.

2. To move from this reverse outline to a draft, the writer needs to evaluate the claims listed and assess which are worth pursuing further and which should be abandoned. Which of the arguments you listed do you think should be cut from this writer's next draft? Which should be elaborated? Where should the professor go back to the text and fill in blanks? On what should she do additional research?

3. Is one or more of the claims on your list a candidate for a possible thesis statement for this writer's paper? Has the professor defined the meaning of the text? If so, how?

4. Play around with different sequences for the major claims on your list. Which should be argued first, second, third? Why? (You may even try placing the

claims on separate pieces of paper and moving them around.) Revise your list into an outline that reflects a good order of claims for the writer's next draft.

5. Now try to summarize the main arguments of this freewrite in a coherent paragraph. What does this paragraph suggest about how the body of the essay should be organized?

DEVELOPING A THESIS WITH AN OUTLINING-FIRST STRATEGY

While many scholars begin by freewriting, others like to plan carefully first, taking detailed notes and preparing outlines of their major arguments and topic sentences. By the time these critics start writing connected sentences, they have a good idea of what the thesis and general direction of their essay will be. These scholars work from an outline and often revise the outline as they flesh out their arguments to reflect the new directions that the essay is going.

The professor who thought aloud for us while reading "Morning Song" indicated that she uses such an outlining-first strategy. She takes extensive

Plath—Morning Song
"Empty" Imagery

Baby	Her/others
bald cry	blankly as walls
moth-breath	no more your mother
flickers	cloud
mouth open clean	mirror
clear vowels	effacement at wind
balloons	far sea
nakedness	window square whitens
	and swallows
	shadows (veto)

Shadow =
Faint representation
Prefigure
  • This poem equates motherhood with loss of self.
Voices serve baby
Walls before this statue that shadows them

Cloud dripping away
Cloud effaced by wind

Notes made by professor reading Plath's "Morning Song"

notes on the text, writing, rearranging, and rewriting these notes before starting on the draft. In the following figure, we see her initial notes.

Here is how this professor described her writing process:

PROFESSOR: Typically, I'll start by making a bunch of lists of patterns that I see. In this case, I noticed a pattern of "empty imagery" in the poem. As I was jotting things down I saw that the empty imagery could be grouped into images associated with her, the narrator, and images associated with the baby. So I made two lists.

The lists helped me generate a thesis—"the poem equates motherhood with a loss of self." I'm not entirely happy with that thesis. I think there's more going on in the poem. But it is a starting point. Next, I'd go back and re-read the poem again and start adding new lists and try to come up with more arguments. Then I'd try to put all of those individual arguments together into some kind of more coherent thesis.

Looking at the lists again, I see that the stuff under "baby" seems to be more concrete than the things under the "her" column. The "baby" images are more nouns that you can see or hear while the "her" images are more abstract. I might do something with that.

INTERVIEWER: At what point would you start writing a draft?

PROFESSOR: Oh, not for quite a while. I spend a lot of time taking notes—a huge amount of time. I make all these lists and then go back and re-read and make more lists and jot down arguments all over the place. I usually have several pages of notes. Once I have a bunch of arguments down, I try to make sense of them and put them down in an outline that I work from.

By the time I start writing, I have this list of all these milestones, or signposts, I want to hit in my essay. I won't say the writing is then easy, but I usually have a good sense of where I want to go before I start writing.

I'm not saying that the milestones don't change once I get into the actual details of writing. Sometimes I realize that things I thought were pretty clear-cut aren't really in the text or can't be supported as well as I thought. But I like to at least have a clear direction before I start, even if that direction changes later.

Likewise, another professor we interviewed also works from notes before beginning to draft an essay.

PROFESSOR: If I was doing this for my own work, I actually would take a ridiculous amount of time on this. . . . I would probably come up with three or four claims [containing] declarative statements like, "This poem is about . . ."

I'd see . . . which of those led me to the best reading . . . to the reading that would allow me to account for most of the poem.

For my work with "Coal" [a poem by Audre Lorde], I had a couple of assertions that didn't go anywhere and a couple that seemed to get deeper and deeper as I went. I tried to keep open as many possibilities as possible while I was reading.

INTERVIEWER: How many drafts do you think you would normally end up doing?

PROFESSOR: First I would start with . . . a list that would be an outline of a reading of the poem in the order in which I read it. And then I would probably start typing and rearrange some of those observations.

> I would probably do handwritten notes and then a first draft that I would re-draft again. But I would reorder my thoughts, so that the process of thought that I initially narrated when I took my handwritten notes, I would sort of rearrange it to make the most effective reading, which may, in fact, begin with the end of the poem, rather than the beginning of the poem.

MOVING BETWEEN DRAFTING, ORGANIZING, AND DISCOVERING

All three professors interviewed here move back and forth between making observations about a text, organizing those observations, and drafting their essays. The first professor freewrites and uses a reverse outline to discover the best arguments to include in her essay. The other two both work from notes, creating outlines with "milestones, or signposts" before trying to draft prose.

Despite these different approaches to drafting, all three professors are similar in that they move back and forth between reading the text and drafting and organizing their arguments. Moreover, all three consciously try out multiple arguments before deciding on a thesis. These experienced writers try out a range of ideas because they know that their first attempt at a thesis is usually not their best.

As you begin organizing your own ideas to create a coherent argument, you will find some that are perhaps interesting but that ultimately are dead ends that don't fit into an overall argument and others that need elaboration. You should move between what you have written and the text to try out new ideas as you plan your essay. Even if you work from an outline, you should be open to new ideas that emerge while you write; you can always update your outline as you progress. If you prefer to freewrite, you should be prepared to reorganize your freewriting radically and to abandon some of the text you write. Freewriters should test the quality of a draft's organization by writing summaries or reverse outlines that connect their ideas in a logical fashion.

Exercise

1. Which of the three professors' writing processes sounds most useful or productive to you? Why? Which is most similar to how you currently go about writing?

2. What do you think you will need to change in your writing process to create clearly organized literary analyses with complex arguments?

Review

A well-organized essay demonstrates the following characteristics:

1. Each paragraph in the body of the essay is clearly connected to the thesis.

2. Each paragraph in the body focuses on a single argument or two closely related arguments.

3. Each paragraph builds on the previous paragraphs. In other words, the paragraphs are connected to one another but avoid repeating the same arguments.

4. The essay is ordered by logical progression of the arguments rather than by strictly following the chronological order of the literary text that is the focus of the essay.

We have discussed two strategies that successful critics use to develop essays. Some begin by freewriting and then create a reverse outline of main points. Others spend considerable time taking notes and creating outlines of their major arguments before they begin writing connected prose.

Exercise

Read the following student essay about Rick Bass's story "Antlers" reprinted in Chapter 5 (pp. 110–19) and then answer the questions that follow.

Hunter and Hunted: The Mixture of Animal and Human
in "Antlers"

Rick Bass's short story "Antlers" explores the relationships among a group of people who choose to live close to wild, untamed nature. While there are not many in this rather dispersed community, their relationships with each other, and with nature, are complex, and Bass's depiction of them often raises more questions than it clearly answers. For instance, a reader may be left with many unsettling questions, such as "Is hunting moral?" and "Are humans animals?" It seems like this story enters into contemporary debates on hunting, but it does not provide easy answers. One reason for this may be the surprising similarities between two of its central characters who seem at first glance to be as diametrically opposed to each other as possible: Randy, the lone bowhunter who romantically pursues Suzie, and Suzie, the lone activist against bow hunting who repeatedly rejects Randy. On a close reading, the similarities between Suzie and Randy are so numerous and striking that it becomes difficult not to see Suzie as a hunter, despite her vocal opposition to the practice, and Randy as feeling sympathetic connections with wild animals, despite his willingness to kill them. The effect of this troubling intermixing of qualities of hunter and hunted is, I claim, Bass's way of portraying our deep connection to animal ways of being and surviving.

Throughout "Antlers" it is suggested that Randy's pursuit of Suzie resembles aspects of a hunter seeking his prey, a dynamic that pits these two characters in opposition to each other. Randy seems as relentless in his pursuit of Suzie as he is in his pursuit of elk with a bow. He repeatedly gives her gifts, which seems a way to get close to Suzie as he must to the elk he shoots. His visits to the bar where Suzie serves him would get him as close to her as he needs to be to the elk, "close enough to hear water sloshing in the elk's belly, from where he's just taken a drink from the creek" (113). And Suzie is described as resembling an elk or a deer which would be Randy's prey. Her appearance seems deer-like, with her "sandy red" hair and "high cold cheeks" (112). Furthermore, her perpetual fear of being alone, which she "can't help" and which makes her "jumpy" (118), seems to resemble the instincts of the kind herd animals Randy hunts. In fact, she says her fear of loneliness stems from "no reason" (118), making it seem all the more instinctual and animalistic.

However, "Antlers" also presents Suzie as being hunter-like, and not one who practices the kind of rifle hunting that she seems more tolerant of but the kind of bow hunting that Randy practices and which even he describes as particularly "cruel" (116). Suzie's similarity to a bowhunter is most apparent in the effect she has on the narrator when she first leaves him. The narrator describes the pain of her leaving him in terms that are reminiscent of the effect Randy's arrows have on elk. The narrator says, "When she left, I did not think I would ever eat or drink again. It felt as if my heart had been torn from my chest, as if my lungs were on fire; every breath burned" (112). Even later, when Suzie is with Davey, the narrator says "it felt as if my heart would never heal" (114). The pain that Suzie causes the narrator is one he repeatedly describes as centered in his heart and lungs, which are the same organs that Randy's arrow enters when he shoots a bull elk while the narrator observes: "I saw him shoot an elk, saw the arrow go in behind the bull's shoulder, where the heart and lungs are hidden" (116). Both the narrator and the elk are initially described as being surprised by the pain: the narrator is "caught . . . by surprise" (112), even though he knows Suzie is bound to leave him, and the elk "looked around in wild-eyed surprise" (116) when Randy shot him, aware that danger could sneak up on him from behind. The elk's death is apparently a slow and painful one, with the bull wandering around injured for hours and traveling at least "a half mile away" (116). So much blood slowly came out of the bull that it seemed to the narrator that "surely all of the bull's blood had drained out" (116). While the elk's death is described as being caused by "trauma" (113), it seems that given the way the narrator describes his heartbreak that he, too, has been through a long-lasting traumatic experience, even if emotional rather than physical. And this means that Suzie, the source of his heartache, occupies a position analogous to Randy, the source of the elk's pain. In short, Suzie is more like Randy on this emotional level than she may care to admit.

Suzie's ability to inflict cruel pain is apparent in other aspects of her behavior, too. Although Suzie feels intense compassion for wild animals, her compassion contains elements of cruelty. We see this cruelty when Suzie argues for a petition to ban bow hunting by saying, "Cattle are like city people. Cattle expect, even deserve, what they've got coming. But wild animals are different. Wild animals enjoy life. They live in the woods on purpose. It's cruel to go in after them and kill them" (113). Although Suzie is sympathizing with, and trying to protect, wild animals, her statements about cattle and city people are anything but compassionate. Suzie implies that cattle (and city people) are less valuable than wild animals and deserve death. We also see Suzie's cruelty in her treatment of Randy. Again, because she has such strong sympathy for hunted animals, Suzie rejects Randy, even refusing to thank him for the beautiful handmade gifts he brings her. This treatment shows contempt for Randy's feelings and desires. More than just rejecting a suitor she is uninterested in, Suzie seems to want to cause Randy an emotional pain that hurts as much as the physical pain he inflicts on the elk.

And as much as Suzie may be cruel like a bow hunter in the emotional pain she inflicts on others, Randy can likewise be seen as having much in common with the animals he hunts. His appearance, when hunting, can be seen as more animal than human. He practices his bow hunting "shirtless" (115). When he hunts, he paints his face with "stripes, like a tiger's" (116) and he stops his entirely human habit of smoking (116). Moreover, he describes his need to hunt as primal and instinctive. As he admits to the narrator, "I'm not sure why I do it. . . . I keep doing it. . . . I know it's cruel, but I can't help it. I have to do it" (116). Randy's heightened instincts pertain not only to his ability to hunt exceptionally well but also to his uncanny ability to predict what those with him are thinking. For instance, he explains his hunting instinct to the narrator because he accurately senses that the narrator desires to hear his explanation. As the narrator says, Randy offers his explanation after "reading my mind" (116). The narrator also sees similarities between the brutality of Randy's bow hunting and the ways wild animals hunt. As he says when describing his inclination to defend Randy, "wolves eviscerate their prey; it's a hard life" (112).

Thus, while seemingly locked in an interminable battle of wills, Randy and Suzie have a great deal in common—beginning, perhaps, with their shared stubbornness (her refusal to reconsider bow hunting or Randy in light of his kind gifts, and his refusal to give up bow hunting, even as he knows it is the one impediment keeping him from Suzie). The narrator uses the word "fury" to describe both of them, and the bull elk that Randy shoots, in ways that engage several senses (sight, touch, and scent): Suzie's eyes are "fury-blue" (112), Randy's final glance at the narrator is filled with "a fury I could feel as well as see" (119), and the narrator smells the bull's "fury" (116) just as Randy's arrow enters it. They further share other animalistic qualities, such as their roaming the valley to their own rhythms which do not conform to typical social practices: Suzie "moved through the valley with a rhythm that is all her own" (111), and Randy "keeps his own schedule" (112). The "brutal" and "cruel" pain they inflict on others can be understood as a further shared animal quality if seen from the perspective of the narrator's defense of bow hunting as being similar to the hunting practices of wolves and other wild animals.

But if seen from the perspective of Suzie's stance against bow hunting, Randy and Suzie's cruelty can be seen as a very human quality that separates them from animals. Their cruelty is described in terms of the effects of bow hunting, which is a sport that requires a human-made tool. Not only are both characters described as possessing "fury," but both have "polite masks" that they wear from time to time to contain this fury, and masks are another human invention. Suzie dons hers when serving Randy drinks at the bar. She may be "polite" at such times, "but her face is blank, her smiles stiff" (113). She similarly offers a mute "polite smile" (113) when receiving Randy's gifts. Randy also wears "a polite smile" (118) when he drinks at the bar. The narrator describes Randy as offering "flat looks" that "could mean anything" (118), flat as a mask makes a face look. And finally, when Randy looks at the narrator at the end of the story with extreme fury, "the mask, the polite mask, came back down over him" (119).

On one hand the ways in which these characters are described as being like animals may be interpreted as support for the argument the narrator thinks about making in defense of Randy's bow hunting: we are like animals, and animals hunt brutally; therefore, we, too, should hunt with brutality. But on the other hand, Suzie's heartfelt and moral concern for wild animals, which she may express by her similarities to them and by her targeting only human hunters with the kind of emotional trauma she inflicts, is not so easily dismissed. It seems that Bass's depiction of the ways in which Suzie is like Randy and Randy like Suzie, and the ways in which they are both like animals, running on instinct, and both like humans, living by civilized and polite rules, asks us to consider what may be a true paradox, difficult to unravel: we simultaneously are and are not animals. While Halloween sounds like a fun night of partying in this community, it seems to also provide a sort of needed symbolic outlet, with its "mock battles" (111) between people with real antlers artificially tied to their heads, for the real tensions caused by this paradox of our existence. I don't think Bass gives us a way out of this paradox, but "Antlers" seems to say that we need to face it.

Works Cited

Bass, Rick. "Antlers." Digging into Literature: Strategies for Reading, Analysis, and Writing. Joanna Wolfe and Laura Wilder. Boston: Bedford/St. Martin's 2016. 110–19. Print.

Exercises

1. Create a reverse outline of the arguments in this essay.

2. Analyze the overall structure of the essay by creating diagrams such as those in the figures on pages 271 and 273.

3. Identify the strategies of literary analysis (e.g., surface/depth, patterns) that you see operating in the essay. You can write these in the margins of the essay.

4. How would you describe the strengths and weaknesses of this essay?

For Discussion

1. Compare your reverse outline with those of your classmates. Which of your outlines do you think would be most useful for a writer planning to revise this essay? Why?

2. What weaknesses or gaps in the essay do the reverse outlines reveal? How would you revise to address these flaws?

14

Presenting Textual Evidence Effectively

One of the criteria for a successful literary analysis is that it be supported by textual evidence in the form of quotations, summaries, and paraphrases. In this chapter, we will discuss how to present textual evidence effectively.

It is important to note that there are two types of evidence you will use in your literary analyses. The first is evidence from the primary text (the poem, play, story, novel, or film) you are discussing or analyzing. The second is evidence that comes from outside the text and includes contextual information, theories, and other critics' interpretations. These types of evidence are discussed in Chapters 7–11.

To begin thinking about how to present and use evidence from your primary text effectively, let's take a look at the following short paragraphs about "Everyday Use" and "Antlers," stories reprinted in Chapters 6 and 5. Compare and contrast how these two paragraphs introduce and interpret quotations. Which does a better job presenting the quotations and using them to support a surface/depth argument about the story?

Paragraph 1

Dee's self-realization seems to require that others feel inferior before her. "A dress so loud it hurts my eyes. There are yellows and oranges enough to throw back the light of the sun. I feel my whole face warming from the heat waves it throws out" (35). Even as a teenager, Dee's ego thrived on putting her family down. "She used to read to us without pity; forcing words, lies, other folks' habits, whole lives upon us two, sitting trapped and ignorant underneath her voice. She washed us in a river of make-believe, burned us with a lot of knowledge we didn't necessarily need to know" (133). Dee uses her knowledge and ambition to put others down.

Paragraph 2
Although Suzie appears to be compassionate, she can also be cruel. For instance, she protests hunting by saying that "Cattle are like city people. Cattle expect, even deserve, what they've got coming. But wild animals are different. Wild animals enjoy life. They live in the woods on purpose. It's cruel to go in after them and kill them" (113). This statement draws sharp distinctions between wild animals and domestic ones: while wild animals should be protected, domestic animals deserve to be confined and killed. Suzie's contempt for cattle stands in stark contrast to her compassion toward the deer. Suzie's treatment of Randy is similarly contemptuous. For example, when Randy makes her a beautiful porch swing, Suzie just "smiled a little—a polite smile, which was, in a way, worse than if she had looked angry—and said nothing, not even thank you" before taking the swing away (114). Suzie's refusal to show gratitude in this passage seems calculated to cause Randy pain. Her smile is just a polite cover for her contempt.

Both passages use two quotations to support arguments about character. Both passages also correctly document their quotations. However, most readers find the second example more skillful. Why do you think that is? ∎

THE QUOTATION SANDWICH

Many writers find it useful to think of quotations and other kinds of textual evidence as a metaphorical sandwich in which the quotation is the meat or filling and the text introducing and interpreting the quotation is the bread.

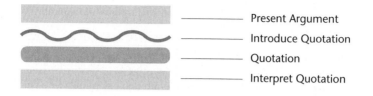

— Present Argument

— Introduce Quotation

— Quotation

— Interpret Quotation

The Quotation Sandwich

Let's discuss each of these steps in detail.

1. Present the argument	State the main argument that the quotation will support, usually a surface/depth argument about the text.
2. Introduce the quotation	Explain where in the text the quotation occurs (who is speaking or what is happening at this point in the text, not the page or line number since this will be given in the citation). Often writers use transitions, such as *for instance* or *for example,* to clearly signal that the quotation will support the main argument.
3. Quote	Include only as much text as is needed to support your argument, then document the page or line numbers.
4. Interpret the quotation	Explain why you find the quotation significant, specifying key words or phrases that support your argument. Often the interpretation will begin with a phrase such as *This description shows* or *This passage emphasizes.* Key words from the main argument are often used in this interpretation to show relevance and build coherence.

Let's examine how the Paragraph 2 on page 290 follows the quotation sandwich:

Although Suzie appears to be compassionate, she —— Present Argument
can also be cruel. *For instance, she protests hunting*
by saying, that "Cattle are like city people. Cattle —— Introduce Quotation
expect, even deserve, what they've got coming.
But wild animals are different. Wild animals enjoy
life. They live in the woods on purpose. It's cruel
to go in after them and kill them" (113). **This** —— Quotation with Page
statement draws sharp distinctions between Number
wild animals and domestic ones: while wild
animals should be protected, domestic animals
deserve to be confined and killed. Suzie's —— Interpret Quotation
contempt for cattle stands in stark contrast to
her compassion toward the deer.

Suzie's treatment of Randy is similarly contemp- —— Main Argument
tuous. *For example, when Randy makes her* —— Introduce Quotation
a beautiful porch swing, Suzie just "smiled a
little—a polite smile, which was, in a way, worse
than if she had looked angry—and said nothing,
not even thank you" before taking the swing away
(114). **Suzie's refusal to show gratitude in this** —— Quotation with Page
passage seems calculated to cause Randy pain. Number
Her smile is just a polite cover for her contempt. —— Interpret Quotation

The annotated figure shows that each of the quotations begins with surface/
depth arguments about Suzie's character. These arguments are followed by
transitions (*for instance, for example*) and information that tells us what is occurring in the story at the time of the quotation. Next is the quotation itself.
Finally, the quotations are restated in ways that emphasize the writer's main
argument—that Suzie is cruel in her compassion.

Note that even though this example contains two substantial quotations,
the majority of the paragraph is the writer's own argument. Contrast this with
the first example, where more than half of the words are direct quotations.

If we were to revise the example about "Everyday Use" to use the quotation sandwich more effectively, our revision might look something like this:

<u>Dee's self-realization seems to require that others feel inferior before her.</u> *For instance, Mama describes the dress Dee wears as* "so loud it hurts my eyes. There are yellows and oranges enough to throw back the light of the sun. I feel my whole face warming from the heat waves it throws out" (35). This description emphasizes the pain Dee's dress causes, which "hurts" Mama's eyes and throws out "heat waves" on a day that is already hot. Thus, the dress Dee wears to express her new self is described in terms of fire that burns those who get too close to her. <u>This tendency to hurt her family with her accomplishments</u> *dates back to her teenage years when Mama describes her as reading* "without pity; forcing words, lies, other folks' habits, whole lives upon us two, sitting trapped and ignorant underneath her voice. She washed us in a river of make-believe, burned us with a lot of knowledge we didn't necessarily need to know" (133). This passage suggests that, as a youth, Dee "burned" her family with her reading and knowledge, just as her dress now seems to burn Mama's eyes and face. Dee seems to use her achievements to make Mama and Maggie feel their inferiority, rather than to help them better their situation.	—— Present Argument —— Introduce Quotation —— Quotation with Page Number —— Interpret Quotation —— Present Argument —— Introduce Quotation —— Quotation with Page Number —— Interpret Quotation

The quotations have been trimmed to better fit the flow of the introductory sentences. After the quotations, the writer has provided interpretations that explain how specific words and phrases in the quotation support the main argument. Key words from the main argument, such as "self" and "inferior," are repeated in order to build coherence and emphasize main ideas.

Note that the proportion of quotation to the writer's text has changed dramatically. The figure below illustrates how quotations overwhelm the writer's argument in the original version. By contrast, the revised version spends proportionately more space developing the writer's argument.

Original

Dee's self-realization seems to require that others feel inferior before her. "A dress so loud it hurts my eyes. There are yellows and oranges enough to throw back the light of the sun. I feel my whole face warming from the heat waves it throws out" (35). Even as a teenager, Dee's ego thrived on putting her family down. "She used to read to us without pity; forcing words, lies, other folks' habits, whole lives upon us two, sitting trapped and ignorant underneath her voice. She washed us in a river of make-believe, burned us with a lot of knowledge we didn't necessarily need to know" (133). Dee uses her knowledge and ambition to put others down.

Revised

Dee's self-realization seems to require that others feel inferior before her. For instance, Mama describes the dress Dee wears as "so loud it hurts my eyes. There are yellows and oranges enough to throw back the light of the sun. I feel my whole face warming from the heat waves it throws out" (35). This description emphasizes the pain Dee's dress causes, which "hurts" Mama's eyes and throws out "heat waves" on a day that is already hot. Thus, the dress Dee wears to express her new self is described in terms of fire that burns those who get too close to her. This tendency to hurt her family with her accomplishments dates back to her teenage years when Mama describes her as reading "without pity; forcing words, lies, other folks' habits, whole lives upon us two, sitting trapped and ignorant underneath her voice. She washed us in a river of make-believe, burned us with a lot of knowledge we didn't necessarily need to know" (133). This passage suggests that, as a youth, Dee "burned" her family with her reading and knowledge, just as her dress now seems to burn Mama's eyes and face. Dee seems to use her achievements to make Mama and Maggie feel their inferiority, rather than to help them better their situation.

In the original version, over half of the paragraph is direct quotation. The revised paragraph gives more attention to developing the writer's argument and intersperses quotations with the writer's own ideas.

GOOD REPETITION *VS.* BAD REPETITION

You may have been told before that repetition in writing is bad and should be avoided. This is true when writers repeat the same ideas multiple times without adding new information or arguments—or when sentence patterns repeat so that all sentences sound identical. Such lack of novelty is what we call bad repetition.

Good repetition, by contrast, occurs when writers add new ideas but repeat key words or phrases to help readers follow their train of thought. As your arguments become more complex, this good repetition becomes increasingly important in making your arguments coherent. For instance, the above revised analysis of "Everyday Use" uses the words "hurt" and "burn" multiple times to explain the quotations. This repetition helps readers connect new evidence to the main idea—in this case, the argument that Dee makes her family feel inferior to increase her own status.

Good repetition can also involve synonyms rather than repetition of an exact word or phrase. Using synonyms, or closely related words and phrases, for main concepts can keep your writing from sounding dull and redundant. For instance, the brief analysis of "Antlers" relies on synonyms for *cruelty* and *cruel*—such as "contempt," "contemptuous," and "calculated to cause him pain"—to develop the writer's main argument that Suzie is cruel.

Exercise

Which of the following student paragraphs contain good use of quotations and which are weak? How would you revise the weak quotations?

1. The speaker in "The Cinnamon Peeler" treats women as objects.

> Here on the upper thigh
> at this smooth pasture
> neighbour to your hair
> or the crease
> that cuts your back. This ankle. (12–16)

He sees women as just a series of body parts. He wants to own his wife just like he might own a car or a house: "You will be known among strangers / as the cinnamon peeler's wife" (17–18).

2. We can easily see the patriarchal nature of the mountain community in "Antlers." "Suzie has sandy red hair, high cold cheeks, and fiery blue eyes. She is short,

no taller than even a short man's shoulders. Suzie's boyfriends have lasted, on average, for three months. No man has ever left her—even the sworn bachelors among us have enjoyed her company. It is always Suzie who goes away from the men first" (112).

3. Father Paul is unable to see and understand the Laguna people clearly. In his house is a missionary magazine with "colored pages full of lepers and pagans" that Father Paul absentmindedly turns "without looking" (33). Although Father Paul may not fully identify with this magazine, it represents a worldview that sharply divides the world into saviors and those who need to be saved. The magazine thus encourages its readers to view non-Christians as generic groups who do not need to be seen as true individuals.

QUOTING *VS.* PARAPHRASING

Whereas a quotation is taken directly from a text, a paraphrase involves restating the text and its events in your own words. It can be difficult to decide when to provide a direct quotation and when to paraphrase. As a general rule of thumb, use direct quotation when the exact wording is important to your argument; use paraphrase when the exact wording is not central.

For instance, the following passage uses direct quotations when paraphrases may have been more appropriate.

Randy's hunting brings out his animalistic characteristics. He removes clothing when hunting, as the narrator tells us, "It was unusual to drive past then and not see him outside, shirtless, perspiring, his cheeks flushed" (115). When he hunts, he paints his face to resemble an animal, as the narrator says, "He'd painted his face in stripes, like a tiger's" (116). His need to hunt is primal and instinctive. He says as much to the narrator after killing an elk:

We sat down beside the elk and admired him, studied him. Randy, who because of the scent did not smoke during the hunting season, at least not until he had his elk, pulled out a pack of cigarettes, shook one out, and lit it.

"I'm not sure why I do it," he said, reading my mind. "I feel kind of bad about it each time I see one like this, but I keep doing

it." He shrugged. I listened to the sound of the creek. "I know it's
cruel, but I can't help it, I have to do it," he said. (116)

The writer of this passage uses three long quotations to tell us that Randy shares
some characteristics with animals. While each quotation provides good textual
evidence to support this claim, all of these long quotation contain extraneous
information that make seeing the pertinent textual evidence difficult. To avoid
this difficulty and make the interpretive argument more persuasive, much of
this information could have been trimmed and paraphrased as follows:

> Randy's hunting brings out his animalistic characteristics. He practices his
> bowhunting "shirtless" (115), and when he hunts, he camouflages his face
> with stripes "like a tiger's" (116), signaling his voyage into the animal world.
> Moreover, he stops smoking for the hunting season (117), further blurring
> the distinction between human and animal. His need to hunt is primal and
> instinctive. As he admits to the narrator, "I'm not sure why I do it. . . . I feel
> kind of bad about it each time I see one like this, but I keep doing it. . . . I
> know it's cruel, but I can't help it, I have to do it" (116).

The modified passage pares down what is directly quoted to the most significant textual evidence. Single words and short phrases like "shirtless" and "like
a tiger's" are placed in quotation marks to signal to readers that these terms are
the exact words the author used, and whatever connotations or sounds these
terms convey is important to understanding the text. The critic places them
in quotation marks not out of a worry that he could be accused of plagiarism
(anyone can use, indeed must use, single words that have previously appeared
elsewhere). Instead, the critic wants to point readers' attention to very specific
aspects of the text, and the quotation marks help him do that.

MECHANICS OF QUOTING

Literary critics have developed and follow several conventions for quoting literary texts that, because they are widely understood in this discourse community,

are good to follow. They allow you to convey a lot of information efficiently. But using these conventions appropriately will take some getting used to. Below are some of the key conventions. Others can be found in the Modern Language Association's *MLA Handbook for Writers of Research Papers,* Seventh Edition and in *Research and Documentation in the Digital Age*, Sixth Edition, by Diana Hacker and Barbara Fister.

▸ **Use the present tense to describe what happens in a literary text.** Follow this convention when paraphrasing a literary text, when setting up each quotation you use by clarifying where in a text it is drawn from, when and describing an author's possible intention or actions. For instance, in the previous two examples (see pp. 296 and 297), even though the narrator of "Antlers" uses the past tense, the critic of the story uses the present tense to describe it. While Bass may have written that Randy "admitted," the critic sets up his final quote with "as he admits."

▸ **When a quotation is longer than four lines of text in your paper, use a special long quotation format.** When a long quotation is necessary, introduce it as described above. But instead of using quotation marks, offset the entire quotation by indenting it one inch from the left (see the figure on p. 299). The quotation is double-spaced like the rest of your paper. A parenthetical citation should appear after the final punctuation mark in your quotation (see the example on pp. 299–300).

▸ **When quoting poetry, use a slash (/) to indicate line breaks.** Place a space before and after the slash, as in this example:

> The speaker of Michael Ondaatje's "The Cinnamon Peeler" tries to disguise the telltale scent that gives away his identity in less bold attempts to touch the woman before they are married. He buries his "hands / in saffron, disguised them / over smoking tar" (23–25).

If you quote more than three lines, use the long format previously described.

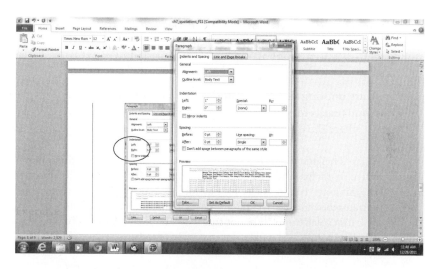

Use the "paragraph" tab in Microsoft Word to indent block quotations by one inch.

▸ **When quoting dialogue between two or more characters in a play, indent by one inch.** Use the same one-inch indentation you would use for any long quotation. Identify each dialogue participant by putting his or her name in all capital letters followed by a period. Indent any additional lines of speech beyond the first by an additional quarter inch, as in this example:

> Identity in David Henry Hwang's *As the Crow Flies* is not fixed, but multiple and fluid. Shortly after Hannah announces that she has another person living inside her, Mrs. Chan responds that such multiple identities are not unusual:
>
> CHAN. So what? So you have two different people.
> HANNAH. That's right. Living inside me.
> CHAN. So what? My uncle had six!
> HANNAH. Six people?

> **CHAN.** Maybe even seven. Who can keep count?
> **HANNAH.** Seven? All in one guy?
> **CHAN.** Way back in China—my second uncle—he had seven, maybe even eight people—inside here. I don't . . . is hard to remember all their name. (245–46)

▸ **If you are quoting text that contains quotation marks in it, use single quotation marks for the internal quote and double quotation marks to signify where the quote you are using begins and ends:**

> Randy's heightened instincts pertain not only to his ability to hunt but also to his uncanny ability to predict what those with him are thinking. For instance, he explains his hunting instinct to the narrator because he accurately senses that the narrator desires to hear his explanation: "'I'm not sure why I do it,' he said, reading my mind" (116).

DOCUMENTING QUOTATIONS AND PARAPHRASES

When you quote from a text, you must give readers information that will allow them to find the passage that you quoted. This gives readers a chance to double-check your interpretation for themselves and make sure that you have not misquoted or taken an author's words out of context.

Different disciplines have different guidelines that they follow for documenting quotations and other evidence. As we mention earlier, literary critics usually follow the documentation guidelines of the Modern Language Association (MLA), a professional organization that brings together literary scholars at conferences and in publications. There are two steps to correctly documenting quotations and paraphrases in MLA:

1. Provide a brief, parenthetical citation in the text itself.
2. Provide a detailed entry in a list of works cited on a separate page at the end of your paper.

You provide an **in-text citation** by referring to the page number that the quote came from (or the line number if from a poem) and, if needed, the name of the author. If the author's name is clear from the context, you only need the page number. The sentence is punctuated after the citation.

> Leslie Marmon Silko's character Father Paul is continually described as lacking vision. Leon perceives Father Paul's eyes as "tired" (32) and when Father Paul sits in his chair, he picks up a missionary magazine and turns the "colored pages full of lepers and pagans without looking at them" (33). These descriptions suggest that Father Paul is unwilling, or perhaps unable, to see the people he serves. He sees the Laguna people for what they represent—pagans to be converted—rather than who they really are.

In this passage, the author of the quotation cited is clear from the context. Thus, the critic only needs to provide the page number of the quotation. If the author is not clear from the context, provide the author's name followed by a space and a page number (indicated by bold face):

> The poem's speaker appears to experience a form of "double-consciousness" (**Du Bois 327**).

When quoting from more than one work by the same author, use the first few words of the title in the in-text citations (boldfaced in the following example), since the author's last name alone will not clarify which text is being quoted or paraphrased:

> In Phillis Wheatley's poems "On Being Brought from Africa to America" and "To the University of Cambridge, in New England," the speaker claims "mercy" (**"On Being" 1; "To the University" 5**) brought her to America. Yet in these same poems we can see Wheatley's speaker accuses America's inhabitants of being far from merciful. "Some" Americans are described as viewing "with scornful eye" (**"On Being" 5**) or as "revilers" who utter unchristian "scorn" (**"To the University" 15**). In these poems Wheatley's speaker speaks from the position of one granted mercy in order to educate her White American readers of their grave potential not only for lack of compassion but also for sin and eternal damnation. This way, Wheatley is able to chastise her powerful audience behind a righteous, religious mask about contemporary racial and social injustices. "To the University of Cambridge, in New England" makes this

dynamic between speaker and audience particularly clear when one considers that the self-described "Ethiop" (28) speaker is addressing the extremely privileged male white students of Harvard University.

Each citation should directly follow the quotation or paraphrase to which it applies so that it is clear to readers what your thoughts and interpretations are and what is evidence drawn from other texts.

The **works cited list** appears at the end of your essay and provides information on every text cited, sorted alphabetically. The basic information you want to include in a Works Cited entry includes the author's name, the title of the work, the year it was published, and where it was published. For the most straightforward Works Cited entry—a book written by a single author—that information is formatted and placed in the following order:

> Last name, First name. *Title of book*. City of publication: Publisher's name, Year of publication. Format.

> Frye, Northrop. *Anatomy of Criticism: Four Essays*. Princeton: Princeton UP, 1957. Print.

When citing texts that have been republished, you need to include information both about the original publication and the republication:

> Wordsworth, William. "The World Is Too Much with Us." 1802. *Digging into Literature: Strategies for Reading, Analysis, and Writing*. Joanna Wolfe and Laura Wilder. Boston: Bedford/St. Martin's, 2016. 156. Print.

The following is an example of a properly formatted "Works Cited" page that has been annotated to draw your attention to important aspects of this format.

Works Cited

Amistad. Dir. Steven Spielberg. DreamWorks, 1997. DVD. Film.

Brooks, Joanna. "The Early American Public Sphere and the Emergence of a Black Print Counterpublic." *The William and Mary Quarterly* 62.1 (2005): 67-92. *JSTOR.* Web. 20 Dec. 2012.

"Redemption." Def. 2a. *The Oxford English Dictionary Online.* 2nd ed. 1989. Web. 21 Dec. 2012.

Wheatley, Phillis. "On Being Brought from Africa to America." *The Norton Anthology of American Literature.* 3rd. ed. Vol. 1. New York: Norton, 1989. 729. Print.

---. "To the University of Cambridge, in New England." *The Norton Anthology of American Literature.* 3rd. ed. Vol. 1. New York: Norton, 1989. 729–730. Print.

Center the title "Works Cited."

Use a hanging indent of .5 inch for entries of multiple lines.

Use 1" margins and double-space, just as you do in the rest of the paper.

Alphabetize the entries.

For multiple entries by the same author, replace the author's name with "---."

Sample "Works Cited" Page

Format the Works Cited entries with a hanging indent (found in the "paragraph" menu of Microsoft Word).

Review

In this chapter, we present some of the key conventions for using textual evidence in your arguments.

Direct quotations are extremely important in literary analyses because they provide the evidence to support your claims and persuade readers to see a text in a new way. But it is unwise to assume quotations can "speak for themselves." You will need to introduce and interpret all the quotations you use. Introducing quotations helps readers understand why different voices beyond your own voice appear in your paper and recollect where in a text, beyond simply the page or line number, a quotation is from. Your clear interpretation of each quotation helps readers see exactly what you see in the text. Because different readers interpret texts in different ways, your explanation of what you want readers to see in a specific passage is crucial.

Paraphrasing the text is useful when the information in the text, rather than the specific wording, is what provides your textual evidence. Instead of providing lots of long quotations, aim to use direct quotations selectively, sometimes even quoting single words or short phrases, to point to specific words because of their connotations or sounds.

Lastly, this chapter provides an overview of some of the key conventions of the MLA style for punctuating and formatting quotations and documenting your sources. These conventions, used widely in the discourse community of literary scholars, convey useful information efficiently but take some getting used to following. Your readers will expect in-text parenthetical citations and a Works Cited page, and this chapter covers some of the basics for preparing them.

15 Revision and Peer Review

There is no denying that analytic academic writing is difficult. You may be surprised to hear that experienced academic writers tend to work harder at their writing—spending more time planning, revising, reflecting, and seeking feedback from others—than do inexperienced ones. Therefore, if your words do not flow immediately or easily onto the pages of your academic essay, you are not necessarily doing anything wrong. Rather, your struggles with analytic academic writing—when you take them seriously and work through them—may very well signal that you are becoming a more expert writer. When you devote significant, regular time and energy to writing, you are behaving like highly experienced and successful writers.

Rather than simply think, write, edit, and submit in a strictly sequential order, experienced writers tend to move back and forth through these activities, looping back around from writing to brainstorming then back to rewriting that is informed by new ideas. Such rewriting is called **revision**: writing informed by seeing the thoughts your words express in a new way.

Planning is central to revision, but writers differ in when and how they plan. Although you may be accustomed to thinking of planning as an activity that just occurs at the beginning of the writing process, experienced writers continually revisit and revise their plans. Moreover, as we pointed out in Chapter 13, experienced writers have different methods of planning: some freewrite first, pouring out ideas, and then meticulously revisit and revise these ideas, while others gradually expand outlines into complete texts. What unites all of these writers is that they reconsider their plans at multiple points during the writing process. Moreover, nearly all experienced writers seek reactions from readers at some point in the writing process, although some prefer to talk about their ideas early in the brainstorming process, while others wait to share a fairly complete draft.

This chapter focuses on various strategies literary critics use to reflect on their drafts and to revise them based on feedback from and conversations they have had with other critics. ■

GLOBAL *VS.* LOCAL REVISION

Students and instructors do not always understand the term *revision* in the same way. Nancy Sommers interviewed first-year college students and more experienced writers about their revision strategies. She found that student writers tended to describe revision as a matter of reconsidering word choices and correcting mistakes. For instance, one typical student told Sommers that when revising:[1]

> I just review every word and make sure that everything is worded right. I see if I am rambling; I see if I can put a better word in or leave one out. Usually when I read what I have written, I say to myself, "that word is so bland or so trite," and then I go [to the] thesaurus.

In general, Sommers found that student writers focused on words when revising. Many students were especially concerned about repeating particular words and phrases and revised primarily to replace such repetitive phrasings with different words. That is, students' revisions were primarily concerned with the question, *Can I find a better word or phrase?*

---

[1] The next four block quotations are from Sommers, Nancy. "Revision Strategies of Student Writers and Experienced Adult Writers." *College Composition and Communication* 31.4 (1980): 378–88. Print.

In contrast to the word-focused student writers, more experienced writers saw revision as a chance to find the form or the shape of their arguments. These expert writers told Sommers:

> [Revising] means taking apart what I have written and putting it back together again. I ask major theoretical questions of my ideas, respond to those questions, and think of proportion and structure, and try to find a controlling metaphor. I find out which ideas can be developed and which should be dropped. I am constantly chiseling and changing as I revise.

> My first draft is usually very scattered. In rewriting, I find the line of argument. After the argument is resolved, I am much more interested in word choice and phrasing.

> I have learned from experience that I need to keep writing a first draft until I figure out what I want to say. Then in a second draft, I begin to see the structure of an argument and how all the various sub-arguments which are buried beneath the surface of all those sentences are related.

For these expert writers, revising involves reconsidering content and organization. They revise in order to clarify their theses, they delete and insert new ideas, they refine arguments and sub-arguments, and they reorder major sections of their essays. Even when they make smaller changes to words or phrases, the changes often affect the overall theses of their essays.

We call the type of revision the expert writers describe **global revision** to distinguish it from the **local revision** students tend to implement. Global revision involves not just small changes to words and phrasing but also substantive changes to the overall content and organization of arguments. We recognize global revision when the changes to an essay would affect our overall summary of its argument.

As you revise your literary analyses, we advise that you move beyond changes that merely affect wording and style and instead experiment with more radical and thorough approaches to revising than you may be used to doing. At first it may seem odd, even frightening, to alter a draft that already looks complete. However, if you are willing to reconsider and change your arguments, you should find the risk of revision yields exciting rewards. Your claims may become more interesting, your evidence stronger, and your arguments more persuasive, even to you.

For Discussion

1. What does the word *revision* mean to you?

2. What is your typical revision process? How does it compare to the student or expert writers' comments on pages 307–8?

Exercise

1. Take a look at the argument on scientific imagery in Sylvia Plath's "Morning Song" on pages 63–64 as it develops from a brainstorming idea to an argument that can be included in an essay:

   ▸ The transcript excerpt on pages 63–64 shows a professor first noting some of this imagery.

   ▸ Question 3 in the exercise on pages 69–70 is a first attempt at articulating this argument.

   ▸ The short essay "Sylvia Plath's 'Morning Song' and the Challenge of Motherly Identity" (pp. 71–72) begins incorporating this argument into an essay.

   What changes does this critic make to the "scientific" argument as it moves from an idea to part of an essay?

2. Now consider the opening to the essay "Competing Parental Philosophies in Sylvia Plath's 'Morning Song'" (pp. 163–64). How has the critic revised the "scientific" argument? Would you characterize this as global or local revision? How does this revision compare to the types of changes you typically make when you revise your essays?

HOW TO REVISE GLOBALLY

Global revision requires thoughtful planning and a willingness to go back to the drawing board and reconsider your thesis and other arguments. There is a very strong link between global revision and the planning and thesis-development strategies we discussed in Chapter 13. In fact, we recommend that you think of revision and planning as parallel activities that you revisit continually throughout the writing process.

One of the best ways to do the rethinking of your argument that global revision requires is to receive feedback from your peers and instructor. We will discuss giving and receiving feedback in detail later in this chapter. However, you also need some techniques to implement this feedback and re-envision your argument from the ground up. We provide three techniques here to help you with this rethinking.

Revision technique 1: Outline or reverse outline

We introduced the reverse outline in Chapter 13 (p. 267). Most experienced writers develop an outline of their main arguments at some point in their writing process. Some writers begin with an outline of their arguments, spending substantial time fleshing out and organizing what they want to say before they start drafting connected prose. Other writers prefer to freewrite or create a very rough draft of their ideas and then construct an outline from this initial draft.

No matter when you create an outline you should try to create an argumentative rather than a topical outline. A **topical outline** is a list of topics you plan to address in your essay, while an **argumentative outline** lists the key arguments and subarguments you need to support. While a topical outline can help you organize informational and other types of texts, an argumentative outline is necessary to help you think through your ideas and develop a complex argument that readers can follow with minimal difficulty.

The figure on page 311 distinguishes between topical and argumentative outlines. The outlines are based on the critical essay "Hunter and Hunted: The Mixture of Animals and Humans in 'Antlers'" on pages 283–88.

Topical Outline	Argumentative Outline
	THESIS: The key characters in "Antlers" are depicted as possessing the qualities of both animals and humans.
I. Thesis	1. Randy's pursuit of Suzie resembles a hunter seeking his prey, a dynamic that pits these two characters in opposition to each other. ▸ Randy pursues Suzie as relentlessly as he pursues elk. ▸ Randy gets close to both Suzie and elk. ▸ Suzie resembles Randy's animal prey.
II. Randy's pursuit of Suzie A. Relentless B. Close proximity C. Suzie animal-like	2. But Suzie is also depicted as being hunter-like in her emotional cruelty toward the narrator. ▸ The way Suzie hurts the narrator is similar to the way a bow hunter kills elk, in the heart and lungs. ▸ The narrator's emotional trauma is similar to an elk's physical trauma when shot.
III. Suzie as hunter A. Effect on narrator B. Long-lasting trauma	3. Suzie's ability to inflict cruelty is also apparent in her views on domestic animals and her treatment of Randy. ▸ She feels domesticated animals and city people deserve what they get. ▸ Her rejection of Randy is aimed to cause emotional pain.
IV. Suzie's cruelty A. Domestic animals and city people B. Randy	4. Randy is depicted as having much in common with the animals he hunts. ▸ He looks like an animal when he hunts. ▸ His animal-like instincts propel his hunting and his ability to sense what others think. ▸ His manner of hunting resembles that of wolves.

(continued)

Topical Outline	Argumentative Outline
V. Randy animal-like A. Appearance B. Instinct C. Read minds	5. Randy and Suzie thus have a lot in common in their being like animals. ‣ They are both very stubborn. ‣ "Fury" is used to describe both them and the elk. ‣ They follow their own, rather than social, rhythms. ‣ Their cruelty makes them like animal hunters.
VI. Randy and Suzie animalistic A. Stubborn B. Fury C. Own rhythms D. Cruel	6. But Randy and Suzie also have several similar human qualities. ‣ Bow hunters use human-made tools. ‣ They both wear "polite masks."
VII. Randy and Suzie human A. Bow B. Mask VIII. Paradox A. Humans hunt B. Human compassion C. Paradox D. Confront truth	7. These seemingly irreconcilable similarities and differences reveal the story to be about our need to confront the paradox that human beings both are and are not animals. ‣ Humans hunt like wild animals. ‣ But humans identify with animals and feel a moral obligation to protect them. ‣ Paradoxically, both these statements are true. ‣ "Antlers" is about our need to confront this truth.

Topical *vs.* Argumentative Outline of "Hunter and Hunted: The Mixture of Animal and Human in 'Antlers'"

The topical outline focuses on the subjects or topics addressed in the essay. It uses a very formal outline format, which you may have been taught previously. It also gives us almost no information that can help us judge whether this essay meets any of the criteria of a literary analysis.

By contrast, the argumentative outline in the second column focuses on the claims and evidence used to support the thesis. We can tell from this outline whether the main arguments are debatable, whether they help define the text's meaning, and whether the essay will help us see the story's complexity.

We can tell whether the sequencing of the arguments and subarguments make sense and we can make judgments about whether a skeptical audience might find the evidence persuasive. The format is casual but informative, and the outline is intended for the writer's own use.

Once you have created an outline of your essay's main arguments, you should begin questioning it to discover logical gaps and inconsistencies, incomplete arguments, claims that need more support, and arguments that need to be dropped. Questions that you might ask of your outline include:

1. Are my arguments interesting and debatable? Would my arguments or evidence point out something new to my readers? Could someone in my class disagree with these arguments?

   If "no," then do you need to:

   - **add new arguments** that readers will find interesting or debatable?
   - **delete an argument** that does not really say anything new or debatable?
   - **move an argument** or a claim that might be "buried" in your draft (e.g., a claim that appears in the middle of a paragraph or in the last paragraph of the essay) to a more prominent position?
   - **replace an argument** with one that better illustrates the text's complexity?
   - **return to the text** to discover new arguments?

2. Do all of my arguments "fit" together? Does each argument build on or extend the previous one?

   If "no," then do you need to:

   - **add a new argument** to help fill in a logical gap?
   - **delete an argument** because it does not fit your overall line of reasoning or repeats an argument you made previously?
   - **move an argument** so that individual claims or subarguments more clearly build on one another?
   - **replace an argument** with one that more precisely communicates what you want to say?
   - **return to the text** to discover new evidence or claims that might help connect or refine your ideas?

3. Are all of my arguments fully supported? Would a skeptical reader find enough evidence here to be persuaded that my argument has merit? Is there any evidence a skeptical reader would question or reject?

If "no," then do you need to:

▸ **add new evidence** to better support your claims?

▸ **delete an argument** because it doesn't have sufficient support—or delete existing evidence that doesn't really support your argument?

▸ **move evidence** so its relationship to the argument it supports is clarified?

▸ **replace your interpretation of the evidence** with one that will help readers better understand how the evidence supports your argument?

▸ **return to the text** to discover new evidence or determine whether there really is sufficient evidence to support your argument?

For instance, the argumentative outline on pages 311–12 for "Hunter and Hunted: The Mixture of Animal and Human in 'Antlers'" reveals some logical weaknesses in the essay. The first bullet under argument 5 ("They are both very stubborn") does not clearly support the claim that Randy and Suzie are like animals. The writer has multiple choices here:

▸ He could replace his interpretation of this evidence with one that offers an explanation for why stubbornness should be seen as an animal quality.

▸ He could simply delete the claim about these characters' shared stubbornness if he can't find a way to make it relevant to his argument.

We might also use this outline to question whether some of the arguments could be moved or introduced later in the essay in order to build toward the most interesting or provocative claims. For instance, the claim that Suzie is in fact like a hunter seems more provocative and arguable than the claim that Randy possesses animal qualities. Switching the order of these two arguments would make the essay progressively build toward its more arguable claims. As a result, readers who have accepted to the essay's earlier claims may be more likely to be persuaded by the essay's later, provocative claims.

For Discussion

Have you used outlines to help you plan and revise your essays? How helpful were these outlines? How do you think you might have used the outlines differently to help you better re-see and change your arguments?

Revision technique 2: One-paragraph summary

Instead of (or in addition to) creating an outline, some writers like to develop a one-paragraph summary of their main arguments. Such a summary is particularly useful for revising longer essays for which an outline listing main arguments can become unwieldy. Two major advantages of writing a summary over an outline is that it requires you to develop transitions between main ideas and it can be useful for checking the overall "flow" or coherence of your argument.

The professor who completed the think-aloud protocols for "The Man to Send Rain Clouds" (in Chapter 7) said she finds such a summary helpful:

> . . . because if I can't figure out my argument in one paragraph, that means I need to do more defining of my thesis and my argument. And sometimes also writing that paragraph gives me a good idea because I'm forced to make logical connections between the parts of my argument in one paragraph. I can go back and, in fact, reorganize based on that paragraph.

A one-paragraph summary of "Hunter and Hunted: The Mixture of Animal and Human in 'Antlers'" might read as follows:

> On the surface it appears that Suzie and Randy, key characters in Rick Bass's "Antlers" who are caught in a story of unrequited love, could not be more different. But in some fundamental ways they are depicted as possessing a similar mixture of animal and human qualities. Indeed, at first glance their differences seem insurmountable, with Randy's pursuit of Suzie resembling a hunter seeking his prey, and Suzie's decision to start a petition to ban bow hunting making her an animal rights activist. But Suzie is also depicted as being hunter-like in her emotional cruelty toward the narrator, domestic animals, "city people," and Randy. And Randy is depicted as having much in common with the animals he

hunts. Randy and Suzie thus have a lot in common in their being like ferocious, wild animals and in their being like hunters and other civilized humans who must wear "polite masks" from time to time. These strong similarities between Randy and Suzie reveal the story to be about our need to confront the paradox that human beings both are and are not animals.

This one-paragraph summary provides the writer with new insights into his ideas because it challenges him to phrase arguments differently and make the connections between various parts of his argument more explicit. For instance, this one-paragraph summary contains the claim that Suzie's decision to start a petition to ban bow hunting makes her an animal rights activist and that this positions her in opposition to Randy as much as her being the animal-like object of his hunt. This argument is implied, but not fully articulated, in the essay. Thus, writing the one-paragraph summary can help the writer articulate connections and find arguments that need to be elaborated in the essay.

As the professor's comments on page 315 emphasize, writing a one-paragraph summary is a good way to reenvision your argument and make logical connections between the various parts of a complex idea. Once these connections have been clarified in the summary, it can serve as a blueprint for organizing the essay itself.

Revision technique 3: Paragraph analysis

Our next revision technique involves working with a draft to evaluate each paragraph carefully in relation to the thesis and then evaluate each sentence's relationship to the paragraph in which it appears.[2] To implement this technique:

1. **Examine each paragraph in relation to the thesis.** Consider each paragraph in your essay, summarize its main argument, and explain to yourself how it relates to the thesis you have developed. Does the paragraph extend or support an argument clearly related to the thesis?

---

[2] This revision technique is adapted from J. Butler and M. Britt, "Investigating Instruction for Improving Revision of Argumentative Essays," *Written Communication* 28.1 (2011): 70–96. Web. 16 June 2011.

If "no," then do you need to:

- **revise** the thesis?
- **delete** the paragraph?
- **replace** the paragraph with one that has a clearer connection to the thesis?

2. **Examine each paragraph in relation to other paragraphs.** Consider each paragraph in your essay and explain to yourself how it relates to the paragraphs that come before it. Does it clearly support or extend the argument in the previous paragraph?

If "no," then do you need to:

- **delete** the paragraph because it repeats or does not clearly connect to the main line of argument?
- **move** the paragraph to a better location in the essay?
- **replace** the paragraph with one that has a clearer connection to the previous paragraph?
- **add** a new paragraph or new material that can help articulate the connection between the two arguments?

3. **Examine each sentence in relation to its paragraph.** After examining each paragraph, look at each sentence in your essay and explain to yourself its function within the paragraph. Is it elaborating or extending the paragraph's main argument, providing evidence, interpreting evidence, or transitioning to a new idea?

If "no," then do you need to:

- **delete** the sentence because it is not clearly related to the paragraph's main argument—or because it is "fluff" that does not add any new ideas?
- **move** the sentence to a better location in the paragraph—or move the sentence to another paragraph altogether?
- **replace** the sentence with one that has a clearer connection to the paragraph's main line of argument?
- **add** a new sentence that can clarify how this sentence relates to other arguments in the paragraph?

Deleting text

Many people find writing so difficult or frustrating that they fervently avoid deleting text that took so long to produce. However, when unrelated passages are left in a text, the reader is taken in too many different directions, and the writing seems uncontrolled and chaotic.

More experienced writers are typically more comfortable than less experienced writers with deleting text. These writers have confidence that they will be able to produce additional text that is just as good as what they are deleting and that better fits their line of argument. One writer Nancy Sommers interviewed had this to say:

> My cardinal rule in revising is never to fall in love with what I have written in a first or second draft. An idea, a sentence, or even a phrase that looks catchy, I don't trust. Part of this idea is to wait awhile. I am much more in love with something after I have written it than I am a day or two later. It is much easier to change anything with time.

As this experienced writer makes clear, giving yourself some time away from your text will increase your willingness to revise and to delete passages that really do not belong. Think of your willingness to delete text as evidence that you are becoming a more mature and thoughtful writer.

And of course, to implement this advice, you cannot wait until right before a deadline to begin a writing project. Another hallmark of experienced writers is their tendency to work on a project in regular, realistic chunks of time that allow for taking breaks, reflecting, and getting feedback.

Exercise

Pick one of your previous essays and analyze it using the three revision strategies described on pages 310–17:

1. Create an argumentative outline of the essay and ask yourself the questions on pages 313–14 about this outline.

2. Create a one-paragraph summary and use it to identify missing connections or unelaborated arguments.

3. Conduct a paragraph-by-paragraph analysis of your essay as on pages 316–17.

Which of these three strategies helped you the most in seeing new ways to revise and improve your original essay?

RECEIVING FEEDBACK: PEER REVIEW AND THE CRITICAL CONVERSATION

In addition to thinking critically about their own texts, experienced critics seek feedback from other writers. In fact, feedback is so important to the writing process that before an essay can be published in a professional journal, it must receive feedback from anonymous reviewers. For this reason, professional academic journals are often referred to as **peer-reviewed publications** in order to emphasize this review process.

A critic who wants to publish a paper in a peer-reviewed journal submits a copy of the paper to the journal editor, who in turn sends it out to other critics who are kept unaware of the author's identity. These critics then write a review of the paper, recommending that it be accepted, revised, or rejected and providing suggestions to help the writer revise. After the editor hears back from the reviewers, the editor makes a final decision on whether the paper should be published in the journal. The reviewers' anonymous responses as well as the editor's own recommendations are then submitted to the author.

If the essay is accepted, the author is still often asked to revise it in response to the reviewers' comments. If the reviewers recommended revision, the author revises the essay and it is again submitted anonymously to the reviewers who will reread it and make a new recommendation to accept, reject, or revise yet again.

For Discussion

1. Why do you think this peer-review process was initiated? What purposes might it serve?

2. Does the peer-review process influence who and what gets "heard" in the critical conversation? How?

3. Do you read an article differently if you know it comes from a peer-reviewed journal?

Writing courses often ask students to act as peer reviewers of their class-mates' essays. However, instead of providing the critically constructive feed-back that is common in the professional peer-review process, student review-ers often refrain from making substantive suggestions for revision. We believe classroom peer review will be more useful and helpful to both writers and reviewers if it more closely resembles the "real-world" practice of scholarly peer review. We encourage you to evaluate your peers' essays in terms of whether or not they would be acceptable for publication in a journal of literary criticism written by and for literature students. Your recommendations to your peers should provide them with advice for meeting the expectations of readers famil-iar with the best arguments students make about literature. Letting your peers know whether you are persuaded by all their arguments—and what it would take to persuade you if you are not—is some of the most useful feedback a writer can receive.

For Discussion

1. What possible benefits might there be for you in helping your classmates participate in the conversation about literature through their writing?

2. What kind of feedback is most helpful to you as you seek to contribute to and be heard in this conversation?

Exercise

The purpose of this exercise is to write a peer review letter to one of your classmates.

Step 1: Swap essays with a classmate.

Step 2: Without holding or picking up a pen or pencil, read your partner's draft through fully one time.

Step 3: Re-read your partner's draft, this time with a pen or pencil in hand to mark the following:

> ‣ **Underline what you identify as the draft's thesis statement**, or the central claim the entire paper seeks to support. Then, to the assess the structure of the argument, perform one of the three global revision techniques described in this chapter.

▸ When you notice one of the strategies of literary analysis that this book discusses (e.g., surface/depth, patterns, opposites, context, etc.), **label the strategy in the margin.**

A note on grammar and spelling: At this point in the writing process, we are not yet at the editing stage. This peer review should be more concerned with the overall structure and effectiveness of the argument. But you may be distracted by misspelled words or have questions about comma usage. You can point out to your partner some editing concerns you spotted (by circling them), but do not set out on a hunt for these types of concerns. We will address these concerns shortly, but first we need to think about more substantive global revision.

Step 4: Once you have completed a second reading, **write a letter addressed to the paper's author** that encourages and helps him/her revise the draft. Try to respond to some of the following prompts about your partner's draft in your letter. Your honest yet diplomatic responses are invaluable. Have confidence in your reading skills and share your opinions of the draft's strengths and weaknesses. If you are confused by or, conversely, persuaded by aspects of the draft, chances are other readers will respond similarly. And remember, if not persuaded by your review of the draft, your partner is not obligated to heed all of your advice.

Your instructor will be looking to see that **your peer review letter is well organized** (it should prioritize the advice you give—what are the most important things the writer should do?) **and supported** (you provide good, specific reasons for the recommendations you make). This review is in many ways also an argument—you need to persuade your readers that your reading has been careful and your recommendations are sound. The following questions may guide your analysis, though to write a well-organized review that prioritizes your recommendations, you need not address these questions in this order.

1. **Thesis:** First, does the thesis make an *interpretive claim*? (The primary purpose of literary critical analysis is to make an argument about meaning or significance.) Second, do you think the thesis is compelling and arguable? In other words, does it make a claim its audience (which includes you and the rest of the class and other literary scholars) might find provocative or illuminating and one that some of us (without given the evidence and reasoning the paper provides) might even want to counterargue? Why or why not?

2. **Strategies of literary analysis:** Which of the strategies of literary analysis that you identified in the margins of the draft do you think are currently being used to the best persuasive effect? (In other words, which of the strategies your partner tries to use are you most impressed by?) Why? Could the writer use one or more of the strategies of literary analysis that we have been discussing to improve this draft? Which? How?

3. **Evidence:** Are the claims made supported with sufficient evidence to be persuasive? Is there evidence that is not discussed here that might be relevant? Which details from the text could be used to further develop ideas presented here? Be specific—you can even point to page or line numbers.

4. **Interpretive analysis:** Is the presented evidence explained, or does your partner occasionally assume that the significance of the evidence to support a claim is self-evident? Where might your partner step in and explain the textual evidence more so that we will be certain to see in it what he/she does?

5. **Complexity:** Does the draft consider complications, implications, and/or potential opposing interpretations? How does the draft treat these complicating factors? How could it treat these factors more effectively or persuasively?

6. **Organization:** Is this a logical order for this paper's argument? How would you describe the logic of the arrangement: does it build toward greater and greater illumination, does it start with a "bang" by placing its most provocative arguments first, or is there some other logic, such as following the temporal sequence of the story? How does this arrangement affect you? Do you get confused or lost, or do you follow easily? How might the arrangement of this draft be improved in revision?

7. What do you think are currently **this draft's two greatest strengths**?

8. What do you think are **this draft's two biggest weaknesses** that the writer should address when revising?

Review

This chapter instructs you on how to make global revisions to your essays. Global revision involves changing content and organization and elaborating on ideas to improve the essay's line of argument. Global revision should be distinguished from local revision that makes changes primarily to improve the phrasing or wording of the essay.

We introduce three strategies to help you see ways to globally revise your essay:

1. Create an argumentative outline of your essay's main arguments.

2. Write a one-paragraph summary of your main arguments.

3. Analyze each paragraph in your essay to assess its relationship to the thesis and its relationship to other paragraphs, and analyze each sentence in your essay to assess whether it is fulfilling a useful function in the paragraph.

In addition, we discuss the peer-review process used in professional journals and encourage you to think of your own classroom peer reviews as serving a similar function for an audience of advanced literature students.

Exercise

Interview someone with more experience than you have writing literary and cultural analyses about his/her process for writing such texts. Consider speaking with another literature professor in your school's English department, a graduate student studying literature, or an undergraduate student soon to graduate with a degree in English.

▸ Ask this person to describe his/her usual process of writing a critical analysis of a text. For instance, how does he/she get started? How much reading does he/she do before starting to write? Does he/she write outlines or multiple drafts? Does he/she seek out reactions to drafts from readers? What are his/her goals in revision? How often, and for how long, does he/she write?

▸ Another useful interview method is to ask for advice on reading and writing. Does this experienced writer have suggestions for less experienced writers? What does this person look for when reading analyses written by other critics? How would he/she describe a "good analytic essay"? Or what mistakes can he/she warn you away from?

Write a summary of your interview for your instructor and plan to share with your class what you thought was your most surprising or more useful finding from this interview.

Appendix: Theoretical Lenses

W. E. B. Du Bois
Of Our Spiritual Strivings   1903

William Edward Burghardt Du Bois (1868–1963) was an American sociologist, civil rights activist, author, and editor. In this excerpt from From The Souls of Black Folk, *which is summarized in Chapter 10, spelling but not punctuation has been modernized.*

Of Our Spiritual Strivings
O water, voice of my heart, crying in the sand,
    All night long crying with a mournful cry,
As I lie and listen, and cannot understand
    The voice of my heart in my side or the voice of the sea,
O water, crying for rest, is it I, is it I?
    All night long the water is crying to me.
Unresting water, there shall never be rest
    Till the last moon droop and the last tide fail,
And the fire of the end begin to burn in the west;
    And the heart shall be weary and wonder and cry like the sea,
All life long crying without avail
    As the water all night long is crying to me.

                       —*Arthur Symons*

1

Between me and the other world there is ever an unasked question: unasked by some through feelings of delicacy; by others through the difficulty of rightly framing it. All, nevertheless, flutter round it. They approach me in a half-hesitant sort of way, eye me curiously or compassionately, and then, instead of saying directly, How does it feel to be a problem? they say, I know an excellent colored man in my town; or, I fought at Mechanicsville; or, Do not these Southern outrages make your blood boil? At these I smile, or am interested, or reduce the boiling to a simmer, as the occasion may require. To the real question, How does it feel to be a problem? I answer seldom a word.

And yet, being a problem is a strange experience—peculiar even for one who has never been anything else, save perhaps in babyhood and in Europe. It is in the early days of rollicking boyhood that the revelation first bursts upon one, all in a day, as it were. I remember well when the shadow swept across me. I was a little thing, away up in the hills of New England, where the dark Housatonic winds between Hoosac and Taghkanic to the sea. In a wee wooden schoolhouse, something put it into the boys' and girls' heads to buy gorgeous visiting-cards—ten cents a package—and exchange. The exchange was merry, till one girl, a tall newcomer, refused my card—refused it peremptorily, with a glance. Then it dawned upon me with a certain suddenness that I was different from the others; or like, mayhap, in heart and life and longing, but shut out from their world by a vast veil. I had thereafter no desire to tear down that veil, to creep through; I held all beyond it in common contempt, and lived above it in a region of blue sky and great wandering shadows. That sky was bluest when I could beat my mates at examination time, or beat them at a footrace, or even beat their stringy heads. Alas, with the years all this fine contempt began to fade; for the worlds I longed for, and all their dazzling opportunities, were theirs, not mine. But they should not keep these prizes, I said; some, all, I would wrest from them. Just how I would do it I could never decide: by reading law, by healing the sick, by telling the wonderful tales that swam in my head—some way. With other black boys the strife was not so fiercely sunny: their youth shrunk into tasteless sycophancy, or into silent hatred of the pale world about them and mocking distrust of everything white; or wasted itself in a bitter cry, Why did God make me an outcast and a stranger in mine own house? The shades of the prison-house closed round about us all: walls strait and stubborn to the whitest, but relentlessly narrow, tall, and unscalable to sons of night who must plod darkly on in resignation, or beat unavailing palms against the stone, or steadily, half hopelessly, watch the streak of blue above.

After the Egyptian and Indian, the Greek and Roman, the Teuton and Mongolian, the Negro is a sort of seventh son, born with a veil, and gifted with second-sight in this American world, a world which yields him no true self-consciousness, but only lets him see himself through the revelation of the other world. It is a peculiar sensation, this double-consciousness, this sense of always looking at one's self through the eyes of others, of measuring one's soul by the tape of a world that looks on in amused contempt and pity. One ever feels his two-ness, an American, a Negro; two souls, two thoughts, two unreconciled strivings; two warring ideals in one dark body, whose dogged strength alone keeps it from being torn asunder.

The history of the American Negro is the history of this strife, this longing to attain self-conscious manhood, to merge his double self into a better and truer self. In this merging he wishes neither of the older selves to be lost. He would not Africanize America, for America has too much to teach the world and Africa. He would not bleach his Negro soul in a flood of white American-ism, for he knows that Negro blood has a message for the world. He simply wishes to make it possible for a man to be both a Negro and an American, without being cursed and spit upon by his fellows, without having the doors of Opportunity closed roughly in his face.

This, then, is the end of his striving: to be a coworker in the kingdom 5 of culture, to escape both death and isolation, to husband and use his best powers and his latent genius. These powers of body and mind have in the past been strangely wasted, dispersed, or forgotten. The shadow of a mighty Negro past flits through the tale of Ethiopia the Shadowy and of Egypt the Sphinx. Throughout history, the powers of single black men flash here and there like falling stars, and die sometimes before the world has rightly gauged their brightness. Here in America, in the few days since Emancipation, the black man's turning hither and thither in hesitant and doubtful striving has often made his very strength to lose effectiveness, to seem like absence of power, like weakness. And yet it is not weakness—it is the contradiction of double aims. The double-aimed struggle of the black artisan—on the one hand to escape white contempt for a nation of mere hewers of wood and drawers of water, and on the other hand to plough and nail and dig for a poverty-stricken horde—could only result in making him a poor craftsman, for he had but half a heart either cause. By the poverty and ignorance of his people, the Negro minister or doctor was tempted toward quackery and demagogy; and by the criticism of the other world, toward ideals that made him ashamed of his lowly tasks. The would-be black *savant* was confronted by the paradox that the knowledge his people needed was a twice-told tale to his white neighbors, while the knowledge which would teach the white world was Greek to his own flesh and blood. The innate love of harmony and beauty that set the ruder souls of his people a-dancing and a-singing raised but confusion and doubt in the soul of the black artist; for the beauty revealed to him was the soul-beauty of a race which his larger audience despised, and he could not articulate the message of another people. This waste of double aims, this seeking to satisfy two unreconciled ideals, has wrought sad havoc with the courage and faith and deeds of ten thousand thousand people—has sent them often wooing false gods and invoking false means of salvation, and at times has even seemed about to make them ashamed of themselves.

Away back in the days of bondage they thought to see in one divine event the end of all doubt and disappointment; few men ever worshipped Freedom with half such unquestioning faith as did the American Negro for two centuries. To him, so far as he thought and dreamed, slavery was indeed the sum of all villainies, the cause of all sorrow, the root of all prejudice; Emancipation was the key to a promised land of sweeter beauty than ever stretched before the eyes of wearied Israelites. In song and exhortation swelled one refrain—Liberty; in his tears and curses the God he implored had Freedom in his right hand. At last it came—suddenly, fearfully, like a dream. With one wild carnival of blood and passion came the message in his own plaintive cadences:—

> "Shout, O children!
> Shout, you're free!
> For God has bought your liberty!"

Years have passed away since then—ten, twenty, forty; forty years of national life, forty years of renewal and development, and yet the swarthy specter sits in its accustomed seat at the Nation's feast. In vain do we cry to this our vastest social problem:—

> "Take any shape but that, and my firm nerves
> Shall never tremble!"

The Nation has not yet found peace from its sins; the freedman has not yet found in freedom his promised land. Whatever of good may have come in these years of change, the shadow of a deep disappointment rests upon the Negro people—a disappointment all the more bitter because the unattained ideal was unbounded save by the simple ignorance of a lowly people.

The first decade was merely a prolongation of the vain search for freedom, the boon that seemed ever barely to elude their grasp—like a tantalizing will-o-the-wisp, maddening and misleading the headless host. The holocaust of

war, the terrors of the Ku Klux Klan, the lies of carpetbaggers, the disorga-
nization of industry, and the contradictory advice of friends and foes, left the
bewildered serf with no new watchword beyond the old cry for freedom. As
the time flew, however, he began to grasp a new idea. The ideal of liberty
demanded for its attainment powerful means, and these the Fifteenth Amend-
ment gave him. The ballot, which before he had looked upon as a visible sign
of freedom, he now regarded as the chief means of gaining and perfecting the
liberty with which war had partially endowed him. And why not? Had not
votes made war and emancipated millions? Had not votes enfranchised the
freedmen? Was anything impossible to a power that had done all this? A mil-
lion black men started with renewed zeal to vote themselves into the kingdom.
So the decade flew away, the revolution of 1876 came, and left the half-free
serf weary, wondering, but still inspired. Slowly but steadily, in the following
years, a new vision began gradually to replace the dream of political power—a
powerful movement, the rise of another ideal to guide the unguided, another
pillar of fire by night after a clouded day. It was the ideal of "book-learning":
the curiosity, born of compulsory ignorance, to know and test the power of the
cabalistic letters of the white man, the longing to know. Here at last seemed to
have been discovered the mountain path to Canaan; longer than the highway
of Emancipation and law, steep and rugged, but straight, leading to heights
high enough to overlook life.

Up the new path the advance guard toiled, slowly, heavily, doggedly; only 10
those who have watched and guided the faltering feet, the misty minds, the dull
understandings, of the dark pupils of these schools know how faithfully, how
piteously, this people strove to learn. It was weary work. The cold statistician
wrote down the inches of progress here and there, noted also where here and
there a foot had slipped or someone had fallen. To the tired climbers, the horizon was ever dark, the mists were often cold, the Canaan was always dim and
far away. If, however, the vistas disclosed as yet no goal, no resting place, little

but flattery and criticism, the journey at least gave leisure for reflection and self-examination; it changed the child of Emancipation to the youth with dawning self-consciousness, self-realization, self-respect. In those somber forests of his striving his own soul rose before him, and he saw himself—darkly as through a veil; and yet he saw in himself some faint revelation of his power, of his mission. He began to have a dim feeling that, to attain his place in the world, he must be himself, and not another. For the first time he sought to analyze the burden he bore upon his back, that deadweight of social degradation partially masked behind a half-named Negro problem. He felt his poverty; without a cent, without a home, without land, tools, or savings, he had entered into competition with rich, landed, skilled neighbors. To be a poor man is hard, but to be a poor race in a land of dollars is the very bottom of hardships. He felt the weight of his ignorance,—not simply of letters, but of life, of business, of the humanities; the accumulated sloth and shirking and awkwardness of decades and centuries shackled his hands and feet. Nor was his burden all poverty and ignorance. The red stain of bastardy, which two centuries of systematic legal defilement of Negro women had stamped upon his race, meant not only the loss of ancient African chastity, but also the hereditary weight of a mass of corruption from white adulterers, threatening almost the obliteration of the Negro home.

A people thus handicapped ought not to be asked to race with the world, but rather allowed to give all its time and thought to its own social problems. But alas! while sociologists gleefully count his bastards and his prostitutes, the very soul of the toiling, sweating black man is darkened by the shadow of a vast despair. Men call the shadow prejudice, and learnedly explain it as the natural defense of culture against barbarism, learning against ignorance, purity against crime, the "higher" against the lower races. To which the Negro cries Amen! and swears that to so much of this strange prejudice as is founded on just homage to civilization, culture, righteousness, and progress, he humbly bows and meekly does obeisance. But before that nameless prejudice that leaps beyond all this he stands helpless, dismayed, and well-nigh speechless; before that personal disrespect and mockery, the ridicule and systematic humiliation, the distortion of fact and wanton license of fancy, the cynical ignoring of the better and the boisterous welcoming of the worse, the all-pervading desire to inculcate disdain for everything black, from Toussaint to the devil—before this there rises a sickening despair that would disarm and discourage any nation save that black host to whom "discouragement" is an unwritten word.

But the facing of so vast a prejudice could not but bring the inevitable self-questioning, self-disparagement, and lowering of ideals which ever accompany repression and breed in an atmosphere of contempt and hate. Whisperings and portents came borne upon the four winds: Lo! we are diseased and dying, cried the dark hosts; we cannot write, our voting is vain; what need of education, since we must always cook and serve? And the Nation echoed and enforced this self-criticism, saying: Be content to be servants, and nothing more; what need of higher culture for half-men? Away with the black man's ballot, by force or fraud—and behold the suicide of a race! Nevertheless, out of the evil came something of good—the more careful adjustment of education to real life, the clearer perception of the Negroes' social responsibilities, and the sobering realization of the meaning of progress.

So dawned the time of Sturm und Drang: storm and stress today rocks our little boat on the mad waters of the world-sea; there is within and without the sound of conflict, the burning of body and rending of soul; inspiration strives with doubt, and faith with vain questionings. The bright ideals of the past—physical freedom, political power, the training of brains and the training of hands—all these in turn have waxed and waned, until even the last grows dim and overcast. Are they all wrong—all false? No, not that, but each alone was oversimple and incomplete—the dreams of a credulous race-childhood, or the fond imaginings of the other world which does not know and does not want to know our power. To be really true, all these ideals must be melted and welded into one. The training of the schools we need today more than ever—the training of deft hands, quick eyes and ears, and above all the broader, deeper, higher culture of gifted minds and pure hearts. The power of the ballot we need in sheer self-defense—else what shall save us from a second slavery? Freedom, too, the long-sought, we still seek—the freedom of life and limb, the freedom to work and think, the freedom to love and aspire. Work, culture, liberty—all these we need, not singly but together, not successively but together, each growing and aiding each, and all striving toward that vaster ideal that swims before the Negro people, the ideal of human brotherhood, gamed through the unifying ideal of Race; the ideal of fostering and developing the traits and talents of the Negro, not in opposition to or contempt for other race, but rather in large conformity to the greater ideals of the American Republic, in order that someday on American soil two world races may give each to each those characteristics both so sadly lack. We the darker ones come even now not altogether empty-handed: there are today no truer exponents of the pure human spirit of the Declaration of Independence than the American Negroes; there is no true American music but the wild sweet melodies of the Negro slave; the American fairy tales and folklore are Indian and African; and, all in all, we black men seem the sole oasis of simple faith and reverence in a dusty desert of dollars and smartness. Will America be poorer if she replace her brutal dyspeptic blundering with light-hearted but determined Negro humility? or her coarse and cruel wit with loving jovial good-humor? or her vulgar music with the soul of the Sorrow Songs?

Merely a concrete test of the underlying principles of the great republic is the Negro Problem, and the spiritual striving of the freedmen's sons is the travail of souls whose burden is almost beyond the measure of their strength, but who bear it in the name of an historic race, in the name of this the land of their fathers' fathers, and in the name of human opportunity.

And now what I have briefly sketched in large outline let me on coming 15 pages tell again in many ways, with loving emphasis and deeper detail, that men may listen to the striving in the souls of black folk.

Jerome Bruner

The Narrative Creation of Self   2003

Jerome Bruner (b. 1915) is a psychologist who developed a theory on how our minds use narrative to construct reality. In "The Narrative Creation of Self," Bruner argues that selfhood is not some independent entity but instead a personal and cultural narrative that we continually create and re-create.

In this essay, Bruner claims that self-making is from both the inside and the outside. The inside is memory, feelings, and beliefs. The outside is based on what others think of us and the many expectations we pick up from our culture. Telling others about ourselves depends on what we think they think we ought to be like. Thus, the self is also other.

One of Bruner's main arguments is that talking about ourselves ironically joins us with others. Although our self-narratives seek to establish independence from the culture in which we live, we are also bound to this culture. In other words, we need culture and others in order to understand ourselves—even as we try to define a self that aims to free itself from this dependency.

This cultural dependence on others' stories influences what we choose to tell about ourselves. We select and choose to remember those events that fit particular self-narratives.

"Self" is a surprisingly quirky idea—intuitively obvious to commonsense, yet notoriously evasive to definition by the fastidious philosopher. The best we seem able to do when asked what it is is to point a finger at our forehead or our chest. Yet, self is common coin: no conversation goes long without its being unapologetically invoked. And the legal code simply takes it for granted when it invokes such legal concepts as "responsibility" and "privacy." So we would do well, then, to have a brief look at what the "self" is that self narratives are supposed to be about.

Is it that there is some essential self inside us that we need to put into words? If that were so, why would we ever need to tell ourselves about ourselves—or why would there be such injunctions as "Know thyself" or "To thine own self be true"? Surely, if our selves were transparent to us, we would have no need to tell ourselves about them. Yet we spend a good deal of time doing just that, either alone, or vicariously at the psychiatrist's, or at confession if we are believers. So what function does such self-telling serve?

The standard twentieth-century answer to this question was, of course, that much of ourselves was unconscious and adroitly defended from our conscious probings by various mechanisms for concealing or distorting it. We needed, as it were, to find ways around these defenses—with the help of a psychoanalyst in interaction with whom we would reenact the past and overcome our resistance to discovering ourselves. Where there was id, now there shall be ego, to paraphrase Freud. Little question that Freud's solution to our puzzle was a brilliant metaphor and that it had profound effects on our image of man (Bruner, 1958).

Yet, we do well to continue our inquiry. Freud's struggle drama of ego, superego, and id, for all its metaphoric brilliance, should not blind us to the unfinished business that remains. And it is to the pursuit of this unfinished business that this chapter is dedicated. More precisely, why do we need to tell stories in order to elucidate what we mean by "self"? Indeed, it is a question that has even come to preoccupy mainstream psychoanalysis itself (Spence, 1982, 1987).*

I begin by proposing boldly that, in effect, there is no such thing as an 5 intuitively obvious and essential self to know, one that just sits there to be portrayed in words. Rather, we constantly construct and reconstruct a self to meet the needs of the situations we encounter, and do so with the guidance of our memories of the past and our hopes and fears for the future.[1] Telling oneself about oneself is rather like making up a story about who and what we are, what has happened, and why we are doing what we are doing.

---

* Documentation style appears as originally published in a variation of MLA style.

It is not that we have to make up these stories from scratch each time. We develop habits. Our self-making stories accumulate over time, even begin to fall into genres. They get out of date, and not just because we grow older or wiser, but because our self-making stories need to fit new circumstances, new friends, new enterprises. Our very memories become victims of our self-making stories. It is not that I can no longer tell you (or myself) the "original, true story" about my desolation in the bleak summer after my father died. Rather, I would be telling you (or myself) a new one about a twelve-year-old "once upon a time." And I could tell it several ways, all of them shaped as much by my life since then as by the circumstances of that long-ago summer. Self-making is a narrative art, and although it is more constrained by memory than fiction, it is uneasily constrained, a matter we come to presently. Self-making, anomalously, is from both the inside and the outside. The inside of it, we like to say in our Cartesian way, is memory, feelings, ideas, beliefs, subjectivity. A part of its insidedness is almost certainly innate and species-specific in origin, like our irresistible sense of continuity over time and place, our postural sense of ourselves, and the like. But much of self-making is based on outside sources as well—on the apparent esteem of others, and on the myriad expectations that we early, even mindlessly, pick up from the culture in which we are immersed. For with respect to those expectations, "the fish will be the last to discover water."

Besides, narrative acts of self-making are typically guided by unspoken, implicit cultural models of what selfhood should be and what it might be—and, of course, what it should not be. Not that we are slaves of culture, as even the most dedicated cultural anthropologists now appreciate (Clifford, 1988; Kuper, 1999). Rather, there are too many possible, ambiguous models of selfhood on offer even in simple or ritualized cultures. Yet, all cultures provide presuppositions and perspectives about selfhood, rather like plot summaries or homilies for telling oneself or others about oneself, ranging from the locative ("A man's home is his castle") to the affectional ("Love thy neighbor as thyself").

But they are not all of a piece, these self-making precepts—like those last two homilies, for example. They leave ample room for maneuver. Self-making is, after all, our principal means for establishing our own uniqueness. And a moment's thought makes plain that our uniqueness comes from distinguishing ourselves from others, which we do by comparing our self-told accounts of ourselves with the accounts that others give us of themselves—which add further ambiguity. For we are forever mindful of the difference between what we tell ourselves about ourselves and what we reveal to others.

Telling others about oneself is, then, no simple matter; it depends on what we think they think we ought to be like. Nor do such calculations end when we come to telling ourselves about ourselves. Our own self-making narratives soon come to reflect what we think others expect us to be like. Without much awareness of it, we develop a decorum for telling ourself about ourself: how to be frank with ourselves, how not to offend others. A thoughtful student of autobiography proposed that self narratives (at least those in the genre of written autobiography) conform to a tacit *pacte autobiographique* governing what constitutes appropriate public self-telling (Lejeune, 1989). We follow some variant of it even when we are only telling ourselves about ourselves. In the process, selfhood becomes res publica, even when talking to ourselves.

It hardly requires a postmodern leap to conclude, then, that self is also other (Ricoeur, 1962). Classicists, interestingly, see this phenomenon even in the ancient world. Did the Roman art of rhetoric, originally designed to aid in arguing convincingly to others, not eventually get turned inward to self-telling? And may that have produced the resoluteness so characteristic of Roman masculinity? (Gunderson, 1999) Who would doubt John Donne any longer that "No man is an islande entyre to himself"? 10

Yet, a haunting question remains. Is there some sort of spiraling effect in all this? Does so private a process as self-making become the sport of the tools and institutions that a culture creates? Take rhetoric as a case in point. It is part of a culture's tool kit for bettering how we convince the other fellow in argument. Eventually, we are told, it was turned inward as an adjunct to self-making, yielding the sharp-minded Roman, clear about who and what he was and what was expected of him. Did that self-certainty shape the Emperor Justinian, pushing him at the peak of his career to cleanse all local ambiguity from the administration of Roman law? Is Empire affected by the long reach of self narratives?

Take another example from antiquity, this one offered by the distinguished Cambridge classicist, Sir Geoffrey Lloyd. He noted, with impressive evidence, that the ancient Greeks were much more confrontational and autonomy-driven in their conduct of life than the then-contemporary Chinese (Lloyd, 1979, 1998, 1999). The Greeks, not the Chinese, invented the "winner-take-all" syllogism for resolving their arguments, whereas the Chinese, surely as gifted mathematically, avoided such showdown procedures like the plague. Showdowns fit Chinese decorum properly. Did their methods of proof make the Greeks even more confrontational, until, as with the rhetoric of the later Romans, it even sharpened their sense of their own selfhood? Do we invent tools to further our cultural bent, and then become servants of those tools, even developing selves to fit?

Americans, it has been said, no longer show as much overt affection toward each other as they used to: men worry that it might be taken as sexual harassment if directed toward women, adults that it might appear like child abuse if toward kids, all of it the side-effect of well-intended prohibitive statutes. A posted notice in one California school district expressly forbids "showing your affections" (on a list of prohibitions that includes "Don't spit" as well!). Will our new guardedness end up obscuring the tender side of selfhood? At least one commentator thinks so (Oxenhandler, 2001). Or does global mobility affect our attachments, our empathy for others? The shape of selfhood is not as private an issue as it once seemed.

Selfhood seems to have become an astonishingly public issue in our times. Endless books tell us how to improve it: how to keep from becoming "divided," narcissistic, isolated, or unsituated. Research psychologists, ordinarily proud of their neutrality, warn us of our "errors" in judging self, that we usually "see" others as guided by enduring beliefs and dispositions while seeing ourselves as more subtly steered by our circumstances—what they call the primary attribution error.

But has not self always been a matter of public, moral concern, even a topic 15 of debate? Self and soul have forever been yin and yang in the Judeo-Christian tradition. Confession of sins and appropriate penance purged the soul—and raised the spirits of one's secular self. Doctrinally, the soul was cursed with original sin, and we know from magisterial works on the history of childhood how important it was to purge that sin from selfhood. Calvin's version of original sin was so compelling that it took Rousseau's (1979) irony and courage to bid it bitter farewell in *Emile*.

But the good self has also been an issue in that perpetual cockpit of secular moral debate called pedagogy. Does education make the spirit more generous by broadening the mind? Does selfhood become the richer by exposure, in Arnold's (1993) classic phrase, to "all that was best" is a society's tradition? Education was *Bildung*, character building, not just subject matter. Hegel (1995) thought he had diagnosed the difficulty: the young (or anybody) had to be inspired to rise above immediate demands by being instructed in the culture's noble history. He went so far as to suggest that pedagogy should "alienate one from the present." Even the allegedly pragmatic Dewey in his time debated the issue of how to create a self fit for a good society (Ryan, 2001).

No generation, it seems, has even been able to heed the advice of the title of Thurber's (1986) little classic of a generation ago, *Leave Your Self Alone!* Am I any freer of value judgments writing about selfhood than anybody before me? I hold the Western liberal view that inviolate selfhood is the base of human freedom, or the rather odd aesthetic view that our selves are among the most impressive works of literary art we human beings create. Surely, I am not above the fray. The only hope I can harbor, perhaps, is that I may help myself become more aware of what the contending values are—and even make the reader so.

Yes, self-making and self-telling are about as public an activity as any private acts can be. And so are the critiques of them.

Why do we naturally portray ourselves through story, so naturally indeed that selfhood itself seems like a product of our own story making? Does the research literature of psychology provide any answers? One gifted psychologist, Neisser, has done us the favor of gathering much of that literature together in several learned volumes containing articles by leading scholars in the field (Neisser, 1993; Neisser & Fivush, 1994; Neisser & Jopling, 1997; Neisser & Winograd, 1988). I have gone back over those volumes with our question in mind, "Why narrative?" Let me condense what I found into a dozen psychological one-liners about selfhood of "The Self."

1. It is teleological, replete with desires, intentions, aspirations, endlessly in pursuit of goals.

2. In consequence, it is sensitive to obstacles: responsive to success or failure, unsteady in handling uncertain outcomes.

3. It responds to its judged successes and failures by altering its aspirations and ambitions and changing its reference group (Bruner, 1991).

4. It relies on selective remembering to adjust the past to the demands of the present and the anticipated future.

5. It is oriented toward "reference groups" and "significant others" who provide the cultural standards by which it judges itself.[2]

6. It is possessive and extensible, adopting beliefs, values, loyalties, even objects as aspects of its own identity.

7. Yet, it seems able to shed these values and possessions as required by circumstances without losing its continuity.

8. It is experientially continuous over time and circumstances, despite striking transformations in its contents and activities.

9. It is sensitive to where and with whom it finds itself in the world.

10. It is accountable and sometimes responsible for formulating itself in words, becoming troubled when words cannot be found.[3]

11. It is moody, affective, labile, and situation sensitive.

12. It is coherence seeking and coherence guarding, eschewing dissonance and contradiction through highly developed psychic procedures.

It is not a very surprising list, hardly counterintuitive in the smallest detail. It 20 becomes somewhat more interesting, though, if you translate it into a set of reminders about how to tell a good story. Something like:

1. A story needs a plot.

2. Plots need obstacles to goal.

3. Obstacles make people reconsider.

4. Tell only about the story-relevant past.

5. Give your characters allies and connections.

6. Let your characters grow.

7. But keep their identity intact.

8. And also keep their continuity evident.

9. Locate your characters in the world of people.

10. Let your characters explain themselves as needed.

11. Let your characters suffer moods.

12. Characters should worry when not making sense.

Should we say, then, that all the psychological research on selfhood has rediscovered the wheel, that all we have learned from it is that most people have learned how to tell passable stories, with themselves as the chief protagonist? That would surely be unjust and, besides, just plain untrue. But we could certainly fault the psychologists responsible for those findings with a failure to tell the dancer from the dance, the medium from the message, or however one puts it. For the self of the psychologists comes out to be little more than a standard protagonist in a standard story of a standard genre. She sets out on some quest, runs into obstacles and has second thoughts about her aims in life, remembers what's needed as needed, has allies and people she cares about, yet grows without losing herself in the process. She lives in a recognizable world, speaks her own mind when she needs to, but is thrown when words fail her, and wonders whether her life makes sense. It can be tragic, comic, a bildungsroman, whatever. Does selfhood require more than a reasonably well-wrought story, a story whose continuing episodes tie together (like continued stories generally, or like lines of precedent in the law)?

Maybe we're faced with another chicken-and-egg puzzle. Is our sense of selfhood the *fons et origio* of storytelling, or is it the human gift of narrative that endows selfhood with the shape it has taken? But perhaps that oversimplifies. There is an old adage in linguistics that "thinking is for speaking"—that we come to think in a certain way in order to say it in the language we have learned to use, which hardly means that *all* thinking is shaped just for the sake of talking. Slobin (2000), a gifted scholar and a seasoned student of how language and thought influence each other, put it well:

> . . . one cannot verbalize experience without taking a perspective, and . . . the language being used often favors particular perspectives. The world does not present "events" to be encoded in language. Rather, in the process of speaking or writing, experiences are filtered through language into verbalized events.

Selfhood can surely be thought of as one of those verbalized events, a kind of metaevent that provides coherence and continuity to the scramble of experience. But it is not just language per se but narrative that shapes its use—particularly its use in self-making. Is it so surprising? Physicists come to think in those scrawls they put on the blackboard for each other. Musicians are so adept at thinking musically that (to cite a sometimes cellist in his orchestra), the conductor Dmitri Miropoulos would, in rehearsal, hum his way backward through a passage to get to where he felt the orchestra's playing had gone off! Are we any less adept in those acts of retrospect by which we try to decide whether, after all, "this is the kind of person I really mean to be"?

Most people never get around to composing a full-scale autobiography. Self-telling, rather, is mostly provoked by episodes related to some longer term concern. Although linked to or provoked by particular happenings, it ordinarily presupposes those longer term, larger scale concerns—much as history writing where the *annales* record of particular events is already somehow determined or shaped by a more encompassing *chronique*, which itself bears the stamp of an overarching *histoire*. An account of a battle takes for granted the existence of a war which takes for granted the even larger notion of competitive nation-states and a world order.

No autobiography is completed, only ended. No autobiographer is free of 25 questions about which self his autobiography is about, composed from what perspective, for whom. The one we actually write is only one version, one way of achieving coherence. Autobiography turns even a seasoned writer into doppelganger—and turns its readers into sleuths. How can any version of an autobiography strike a balance between what one actually was and what one might have been? And we play games with ourselves about this would-be balance. A writer friend and neighbor of mine, a gifted journalist engaged in writing an autobiography as was I, responded to my doubts with: "No problem for me; I am faithful to memory." Yet she was renowned locally as a delicious fabulist who, in the words of a witty fellow townsman, "could make a shopping trip to Skibbereen sound like a visit to ancient Rome itself." Like her, we are forever balancing what was with what might have been—and, in the main, mercifully unaware of how we do it.

Literally, autobiography, for all its pitfalls, has much to teach us about what we leave implicit in our more spontaneous, episode-linked, briefer self-accounts. It can even provide hints about a writer's cryptophilosophical notion of what a self is! And that is no idle question.

A recent book highlights this point vividly—Olney's thoughtful *Memory and Narrative: The Weave of Life-Writing* (1998). Olney is particularly concerned with the rise and fall of the narrative form in self-accounting, and with why, in recent times, it has begun losing its allure for literary autobiographers, even if they cannot escape it in their more spontaneous and episodic self-telling.

Four famous life-writers come under his scrutiny, their work extending over more than a millennium, starting with St. Augustine, whose *Confessions* virtually pioneered the autobiographical genre in the fourth century, and ending with Samuel Beckett. Augustine saw his as a search for his true life, his true self, and conceived of autobiography as a quest for true memory, for reality. For Augustine, one's true life is that which has been given us by God and Providence, and narrative's inherent and unique orderliness reflects the natural form of memory, the form truest to Providence-given being. True memory mirrors the real world, and Augustine accepted narrative as its medium. His was a "narrative realism" and the Self that emerges is the gift of Revelation, leavened by Reason.

Contrast Giambattista Vico in the seventeenth century, next on Olney's historical trajectory. Vico's reflections on the powers of mind itself led him to cock his eye at Augustine's narrative realism. For him, a life is crafted by the mental acts of those who live it, not by an act of God. Its story-likeness is of our doing, not God's. Vico was perhaps the first radical constructivist, though he was protected by a rationalism that guarded him from the skepticism usually associated with that radical stance.

Enter Jean-Jacques Rousseau a century later, who, alerted by Vico's reflec- 30 tions and emboldened by the new skepticism of his own revolutionary times, set out to raise new doubts about Augustine's stable and innocent narrative realism. Rousseau's *Confessions* are laced with high-spirited skepticism. Yes, acts-of-mind, not Providence, shape an autobiography, but Rousseau also poked fun at our acts-of-mind—their passionate follies and vanity-serving uses. Life stories for Rousseau became rather more like social games than quests for some higher truth, and that may be one reason he had little patience with notions like original sin. He turned Vico's respect for reason into a somewhat rueful and impious skepticism.

Jump two centuries now to Samuel Beckett and our own times. Beckett was at one with Vico's reasoned rejection of Augustine's narrative realism and even more in sympathy with Rousseau's wry skepticism. But he explicitly rejected narrative as reflecting that inherent order of life. Indeed, he denied the very notion that there is any inherent order. His was a thoroughgoing factionalism, his mission to free life-writing (as well as literature) of its narrative straitjacket. Life is problematic, not to be shackled in conventional genres. So even his somewhat autobiographical dramas, like *Waiting for Godot*, pose problems rather than answer them. For him, the road was better than the inn: let one be not lulled by the illusion of narrative.

Each—Augustine, Vico, Rousseau, and Beckett—is a child of his historical time, each cultivating a fresh image of childhood and rejecting what for him was a stale one. For Augustine, at the start, self was the product of revelation—guided narrative, revealing what God had wrought; by the time we reach Beckett, a millennium later, the self-told narrative was a mere *façon d'écrire*, a man-made noose strangling the imagination. But for each of them, the issue of selfhood, its nature and origin, were matters of deep and debatable concern, a concern that seems not to have diminished over a millennium, although issues changed drastically. Why did Thomas à Kempis call his account of true monastic selfhood the *Imitation Christi*? Was he pushing Augustinian narrative realism, proposing Christ's depiction of the serving self as the true model? And were the monks and nuns of his time convinced that their selves were truly imitations of Christ's? Reading Thomas with modern eyes, one even senses that he is rather like a recruiter glorifying the kind of selfhood that might lure novices into the monastic life—or justify staying in it. The contrast implied throughout his stirring little book is of the selfish, secular self. And so it seems to be the case for all disquisitions about selfhood. In some indirect way, they are also advertisements about the right selfhood, each age with its own version of the competition.

So it is, also, with Virginia Woolf's metaphoric "room of one's own," her new feminist appeal for a change in women's conceptions of their selfhood. Was Jack Kerouac's *On the Road* turned to reducing the teleological intensity in his generation's style of self-telling and self-making?

Olney's account of the great innovations in conceptions of selfhood is brilliant. One regrets only that he did not explore more fully the struggles his heroic authors suffered in their times—Augustine's against Christian blind faith, Rousseau's against an oppressive *ancien regime*, Vico's against the spirit of the Enlightenment, and Beckett's against literary realism. The four of them obviously shaped new images of selfhood. But their images, indeed, no image of selfhood ever gains a monopoly.

We would do well to inquire why this is so. 35

A self-making narrative is something of a balancing act. It must, on the one hand, create a conviction of autonomy, that one has a will of one's own, a certain freedom of choice, a degree of possibility. However, it must also relate one to a world of others—to friends and family, to institutions, to the past, to reference groups. But there is an implicit commitment to others in relating oneself to others that, of course, limits our autonomy. We seem virtually unable to live without both, autonomy and commitment, and our lives strive to balance the two. So do the self-narratives we tell ourselves.

Not everyone succeeds. Take one Christopher McCandless, a twenty-three-year-old whose dead body was found several years ago in a deserted bus in the Alaska wilderness. Some autobiographical fragments showed up among his meager possessions, and they tell the story of a "radically autonomous identity gone wrong" (Eakin, 1999). "Dealing with things on his own" was his ideal, and he translated Thoreau's injunction, "simplify, simplify," to mean he should depend on nobody, strive for unfettered autonomy. And his self-narrative fit this formula: at the end of his days, he was living in remote Alaska entirely on edible plants, and after three months he died of starvation. Shortly before his death, he went to the trouble of taking a self-portrait, the film of which was found in his camera. In it the young man is seated, with one hand raised and holding in the other a block-letter note on which he has written, "I have had a happy life and Thank the Lord. Goodbye and may God Bless All." On a plywood-covered window of the deserted bus that became his last refuge, he scratched this message: "Two Years He walks the Earth . . . Ultimate Freedom. An Extremist. An Aesthetic Voyager Whose Home is *The Road* . . . No Longer To Be Poisoned By Civilization He Flees, And Walks Alone Upon the Land To Become Lost in the Wild."

In the end, even poor Christopher McCandless felt some commitment to others, his commitment offered, mind you, as an act of free will. As he lay alone, starving to death, he still felt impelled to offer God's blessings to those he had spurned—an act of grace, a balancing act. Then, perhaps nostalgically, perhaps bitterly, he died. Was he victim or victor in his own story? A generation ago, the great Vladimir Propp (Bruner, 1958) demonstrated how characters and events in folk stories serve as functions in narrative plots: they do not exist on their own. What function did poor Christopher McCandless's final act play in his story, and how did he tell it to himself?

I once knew a young doctor, disillusioned with the humdrum of private practice, who, on hearing about the organization *Médecins sans Frontières*, began reading their literature and raising money for them at his county medical association meetings. Finally, he himself spent two years doctoring in Africa. On his return, I asked him if he had changed. "Yes," he said, "my life's more all of a piece now." All of a piece? Scattered over two continents? Yes, for now my physician friend is not only practicing medicine back where he'd started, but researching the roiling history of the town he'd left to go off to Africa, better to find the sources of his discontent, to reconcile his autonomy with his commitment to a town that he is making part of the wider world he had longed for. In doing so, has he created a viable Self? He has even enlisted the local town fathers as his allies in the effort!

So how indeed does one balance autonomy and commitment in one's sense 40 of self—let alone making it all of a piece? I had studied that question as a psychologist in the usual indirect way we psychologists do, and dutifully contributed my chapter to one of those Neisser volumes mentioned earlier. But somehow the balance comes out more plainly in just ordinary conversation. So I have been asking people about it casually when the topic seemed right— friends, people with whom I work, acquaintances with whom I have become familiar. I simply ask them outright about themselves whenever the topic of balancing seems natural. One was a third-year law student, a young woman who was deeply committed to child advocacy in support of parents during child-related litigation. I had met her at a conference and asked her how she had gotten into that work, which seemed to suit her to a T. She said she would send me an e-mail, and here in effect is what it said:

> It was in some ways inadvertent. I had graduated from college on the West Coast with a B.A. in English and Creative Writing, and didn't want to go into education or publishing, etc. but did want to do something . . . to better the lives of poor children. By a peculiar turn of circumstances (too long and boring to go into) I fell into an internship with the Community Legal Aid Society in a middle-sized city back East, where I worked closely with an attorney who was representing parents (often with mental disabilities) in abuse and neglect cases. I was immediately drawn to the work. Most of all, I was astounded by the strength of these parents in the face of tremendous environmental adversity, but also by the way their voices were heard by no one. When they encountered someone (the attorney I worked with, myself) who

was truly interested in listening to them, they often weren't able to trust the relationship and this in turn interfered with effective [legal] representation. Having done a lot of my own work "finding my voice" and learning firsthand the healing, even transformative power of being in relationship with someone who really listened, I felt very connected to these parents, despite our differences in background, etc. So, in the end, it is a continuation of my very deep, very personal interest. . . .

Both the doctor and the child advocate had reached impasses: bored and discontented, going on and on with foreseeable duties to fulfill previously established commitments. Medical school, then internship, then small-town private practice. The well-brought-up daughter of literary bent, on to college, on into teaching high school English. Both were on trajectories shaped by conventional commitment, early commitment. Neither was in material need; they did not have to continue. Both foresaw the next step too clearly, as if possibility had been closed off by the sheer predictability of what lay ahead.

Commitment under these conditions is a narrative reminiscent of law stories. It is dominated by precedent—obligations in one's own life. Medical graduates go on to internships and then into practice—with hometown practice perhaps providing an off-the-track fillip. Circumstances change. The balancing act between commitment and autonomy no longer satisfies as the range of possibilities narrow. One's self narrative seems lacking in those imagined possible worlds that imagination generates—and that novelists and dramatists cultivate.

We can think of these times in life in several ways that are familiar. For example, we can think of them as akin to times at which things are ripe for a landmark decision by a court of law. And, like landmark decisions, where a prior doctrinal principle is expanded to take account of new conditions, turning points in a life honor an old aspiration in a new way. Medical care is not just for the safe and hometown familiars, but for the deprived and beleaguered beyond a horizon one had not realized existed earlier. Or one gives one's more developed voice to those who need it in their defense, not just to those who would routinely find it on their own. Or poor Christopher McCandless: if self-sufficiency is good, then total self-sufficiency is its epitome. Or one can conceive of turning points in one's self-telling as rather like a self-generated peripéteia, one's previously coping with trouble having now generated trouble of its own.

The bald fact of the matter is that one rarely encounters autobiographies, whether written or spontaneously told in interview, that are without turning points. And they are almost always accompanied by some such remark as "I became a new woman," or "I found a new voice," or "It was a new me after I walked out." Are they an integral part of growing up—like the Sturm und Drang of adolescence? Perhaps, although they certainly are not a product of youth, for turning points occur often later in life, particularly as retirement approaches. It may well be that Erikson's (1966) renowned "life stages," marked by a shift in concern from autonomy to competence to intimacy and then to continuity, provide stage settings for our autobiographical turning points.

Some cultures seem to provide for them ritually, as *rites de passage*, and they are often sufficiently painful or taxing to get the idea across. A Kung Bushman boy is put through a painful ceremonial (including fresh ashes rubbed into fresh gashes in his cheeks, tomorrow's proud scars of manhood) designed to mark his passage out of childhood. Now he is fit to be a hunter, ready to reject the ways of childhood. He is even taken on a hunt soon after, and much hoopla is made about his role in killing the giraffe, or whatever gets snagged on the hunt. The rite of passage not only encourages but legitimates change.[4]

But it is only in *rites de passage* (or in Erikson's life stages) that turning points are conventionalized. Self-narrating (if I may be permitted to say it again) is from the outside in as well as from the inside out. When circumstances ready us for change, we turn to others who have lived through one, become open to new trends and new ways of looking at oneself in the world. We read novels with new interest, go to demos, listen with a more open ear. Lawyers bored with the routines of mergers and copyright infringement suits pay new attention to what the Civil Liberties Union is up to. A rising and discontented Jane Fonda, on her own testimony, begins reading the "new" feminist literature to help her understand a divorce through which she has just suffered. And, indeed, feminism itself offers changing versions of a woman's selfhood: from feminine consciousness in a Willa Cather or Katherine Mansfield to the protest feminism of a Simone de Beauvoir or Germaine Greer to today's activist "equality" feminists.

Self-making through self-narrating is restless and endless. It is probably more so now than ever before. It is a dialectical process, a balancing act. And despite our self-assuring homilies about people never changing, they do. They rebalance their autonomy and their commitments, most usually in a form that honors what they were before. The decorum of self-making keeps most of us from the sorts of wild adventure in self-making that brought Christopher McCandless down.

What is there to say in conclusion about the narrative art of self-making?

Sigmund Freud (1956), in an interesting book too seldom read, remarked that we are rather like a "cast of characters" in a novel or play. Novelists and playwrights, he remarked, construct their works of art by decomposing their own interior cast of characters, putting them on stage or on the page to work out their relations with each other. Those characters can also be heard in the pages of any autobiography. Perhaps it is a literary exaggeration to call our multiple inner voices "characters." But they are there to be heard, trying to come to terms with each other, sometimes at loggerheads. An extensive self-making narrative will try to speak for them all, but we know already that there is no single all-purpose story that can do that. To whom are you telling it, and to what end? Besides, we are too Hamlet-like to make it all-of-a-piece—too torn between the familiar and the possible.

None of which seems to discourage us. We go on, constructing ourselves through narrative. Why is narrative so essential, why do we need it for self-definition? Although I turn to that question at the end, let me make one simple point now. The narrative gift is as distinctively human as our upright posture and our opposable thumb and forefinger. It seems to be our "natural" way of using language for characterizing those ever-present deviations from the ex-pected state of things that characterizes living in a human culture. None of us knows the just-so evolutionary story of its rise and survival. But what we do know is that it is irresistible as our way of making sense of human interaction.

I have argued that it is through narrative that we create and re-create self-hood, that self is a product of our telling and not some essence to be delved for in the recesses of subjectivity. There is now evidence that without the capacity to make stories about ourselves, there would be no such thing as selfhood. So let me offer the evidence that exists on this point.

There is a neurological disorder called *dysnarrativia* (Eakin, 1999), a severe impairment in the ability to tell or understand stories. It is associated with neuropathies like Korsakov's or Alzheimer's syndrome. But it is more than an impairment of memory about the past, which is itself highly disruptive of one's sense of self as Sacks's (1973) work made plain. In Korsakov's syndrome par-ticularly, where affect as well as memory is severely impaired, selfhood virtually vanishes. Sacks describes one of his severe Korsakov patients as "scooped out, de-souled" (Sacks, 1987).

One of the most characteristic symptoms in such cases is an almost complete loss of ability to read other minds, to tell what others might have been thinking, feeling, even seeing. They seem to have lost a sense of self, but also a sense of other. An astute critic of autobiography, Paul John Eakin, commenting on this literature, took this evidence as further proof that selfhood is profoundly relational, that self, as noted earlier, is also other. These are the patients who suffer what I referred to earlier as dysnarrativia.

The emerging view seems to be that dysnarrativia is deadly for selfhood. Eakin (1999) cited the conclusion of an unpublished paper by Young and Saver (1995): "Individuals who have lost the ability to construct narratives have lost their selves." The construction of selfhood, it seems, cannot proceed without a capacity to narrate.

Once we are equipped with that capacity, then we can produce a selfhood 55 that joins us with others, that permits us to hark back selectively to our past while shaping ourselves for the possibilities of an imagined future. But the self-told narratives that make and remake our selves are ones we gain from the culture in which we live. However much we may rely on a functioning brain to achieve our selfhood, we are virtually from the start expressions of the culture that nurtures us. But culture itself is a dialectic, replete with alternative narratives about what self is or might be. And the stories we tell to create ourselves reflect that dialectic.

References

Arnold, M. (1993). *Culture and anarchy and other writings.* New York: Cambridge University Press.

Bruner, J. (1958). The Freudian conception of man. *Daedalus*, 8, 77–84.

Clifford, J. (1988). *The predicament of culture.* Cambridge: Harvard University Press.

Eakin, P. J. (1999). *How our lives become stories: Making selves.* Ithaca, NY: Cornell University Press.

Erikson, E. (1966). Eight ages of man. *International Journal of Psychiatry*, 2, 281–300.

Freud, S. (1956). *Delusion and dream: An interpretation in the light of psychoanalysis of Gradiva, a novel by Wilhelm Jensen* (P. Reiff, Ed.). Boston: Beacon Press.

Gunderson, E. (1999). *Staging masculinity: The rhetoric of performance in the Roman world.* Ann Arbor: University of Michigan Press.

Hegel, G. W. F. (1995). *Lectures on natural rights and political science.* Berkeley: University of California Press.

Kuper, A. (1999). *Culture: The anthropologist's account.* Cambridge: Harvard University Press.

Lejeune, P. (1989). *On autobiography.* Minneapolis: University of Minnesota Press.

Lloyd, G. E. R. (1979). *Magic, reason, and experience.* Cambridge: Cambridge University Press.

Lloyd, G. E. R. (1998). Lecture at the University of Toronto.

Lloyd, G. E. R. (1999). *Science, folklore, and ideology.* Indianapolis: Hackett.

Neisser, U., & Fivush, R. (1994). *The remembered self: Accuracy and construction in the life narrative.* New York: Cambridge University Press.

Neisser, U., & Jopling, D. (1997). *The conceptual self in context: Culture, self-understanding.* New York: Cambridge University Press.

Neisser, U. (Ed.). (1993). *The perceived self.* New York: Cambridge Press.

Neisser, U., & Winograd, E. (1988). (Eds.) *Remembering reconsidered.* Cambridge: Cambridge University Press.

Olney, J. (1998). *Memory and narrative: The weave of life writing.* Chicago: University of Chicago Press.

Oxenhandler, N. (2001). *The eros of parenthood.* New York: St. Martin's Press.

Ricoeur, P. (1962). *Oneself as another.* Chicago: University of Chicago Press.

Rousseau, J. J. (1979). *Emile: or, On education.* New York: Basic Books.

Ryan, A. (2001). Schools: the price of "progress" (a review of Diane Ravitch's *Left Back: A century of failed school reforms*) in the *New York Review of Books*, 48(3), 22, 18ff.

Sacks, O. (1973). *Awakenings.* London: Duckworth.

Sacks, O. (1987). *The man who mistook his wife for a hat and other clinical tales.* New York: Harpers.

Schweder, R. (2000). The psychology of practice and the practice of three psychologies. *Asian Journal of Social Psychology*, 3, 207–222.

Slobin, D. E. (2000). Verbalized events: A dynamic approach to linguistic relativity and determinism. *Current Issues in Linguistic Theory*, 198, p. 107.

Spence, D. (1982). *Narrative truth and historical truth: meaning and interpretation in psychoanalysis.* New York: Norton.

Spence, D. (1987). *The Freudian metaphor: Toward paradigm change in psychoanalysis.* New York: Norton.

Thurber, J. (1986). *The works of James Thurber: Complete and unabridged.* New York: Longmeadow Press.

Wang, Q. (2001). Culture effects of adults' earliest childhood recollection and self-description. *Journal of Personality and Social Psychology.*

Young, K., & Saver, J. L (1995, December). *The neurology of narrative.* Paper presented at Modern Languages Association Convention, New York.

Endnotes

1. Plainly, there are certain "features" of selfhood that are innate: for example, we locate ourselves posturally at the "zero point" of personal space and time, something we share with most mammals. But we rise above that primitive identity almost from the start. Even as young children, we master "Peekaboo" and then go on, once language begins, to the mastery of such daunting tasks as deictic reference: when I say *here* it means something near me; when you use it, it means something near to you. My here is your there, a self-switcher found nowhere else in the animal kingdom. How the primitive, postural, and preconceptual self is transformed into a conceptual self is interestingly discussed in Neisser, 1993.

2. The anthropologist Richard Shweder argued (on comparative evidence) that there seem to be three normative or "ethical" criteria by which human beings, whatever their culture, judge themselves and others. He spoke of them as relating to "the ethics of autonomy, the ethics of community, and the ethics of divinity": each has its particularized expression in different cultures, with each given different weightings. So, for example, more communitarian Asian cultures differ strikingly from more autonomy-oriented Western cultures, with even the earliest autobiographical memories of Chinese adults containing more community-related self-judging episodes than do the early memories of Americans, the latter tending to remember more episodes related to autonomy (Shweder, 2000). The data on early autobiographical memories is to be found in Wang (2001).

3. While self-telling ordinarily proceeds in ordinary language, ordinary language also sports the genres and fashions of its time. Has the so-called "inward turn" of the novel pulled self-telling inward? Or what of the lexical "self explosion" in seventeenth-century England, replete with new reflexive compounds like *self-conscious, self-reliant, self-possessed,* and the like? Did those words appear in response to a turbulent century of Hobbes and Locke, Cromwell's Puritan uprising, two Stuart kings dethroned, the Glorious Revolution? Did the spate of reflexive compounds appear in response to change in the world, and did it alter the way people looked at and told about themselves?

4. Inadvertent trauma often produces disruptive and profound turning points in self-narrative, but they are in sharp contrast to the communally supported orderly change of the *rite de passage*. Trauma typically alienates and isolates those who have suffered it. Victims of rape, for example, are often so consumed by self-blame and guilt that they can scarcely face their community. They are gently aided by group therapy with other victims, in the course of which they discover that their fellow victims suffer the same sense of isolation as they do.

∾ NOW PRACTICE ON YOUR OWN

1. Re-read Langston Hughes's "Theme for English B" (p. 203) with Bruner's theories in mind. How does using Bruner as a theoretical lens affect what you focus on in the poem? Try writing a short, three-paragraph analysis that uses Bruner's ideas of selfhood as a lens for interpreting "Theme for English B." Do not worry about reflecting back on the theory (part two of the theoretical lens strategy) for now. Instead, focus on showing how Hughes's poem "matches" some of Bruner's ideas.

2. In Alice Walker's "Everyday Use," (p. 131) Dee reinvents herself after going to college. How might Bruner's ideas about self-narration help us understand the story Dee is constructing out of her life? Although the story focuses on Dee, Mama is actually the narrator of the story. How might Bruner's theory help us understand the self narrative Mama creates through her interactions with her two daughters and the culture around her?

3. In Sylvia Plath's "Morning Song," (p. 41) the speaker struggles with defining her self-identity after the birth of her child. How might Bruner's theories of selfhood help us better understand the complexities in this poem—or place the dilemma the speaker is facing in a larger cultural context? How might this specific conflict over a motherly self help us better understand how our identities are bound to other people and our culture?

Michel Foucault

From *Discipline and Punish* 1975

Michel Foucault (1926–1984) was a French historian whose theories have become widely influential in literary criticism, particularly in the school of New Historicism. Foucault's influential book Discipline and Punish *begins with a puzzle: how is it that, in the span of less than a hundred years, public torture came to be wholly replaced with incarceration as the primary means of state punishment? For Foucault, the birth of the prison in late–eighteenth–century Europe parallels an overall shift in Western society toward normalization—or the tendency to describe human behavior in terms of what is considered normal and what is considered deviant.*

In the section of this book titled "Panopticism," which we include below, Fou-cault focuses on the role surveillance plays in enforcing "normal" behavior. Foucault uses the quarantine system used in France during the plague to demonstrate how inspection and surveillance came to be seen as a social good. The quarantine system helped pave the way for other forms of surveillance. Such surveillance eventually became so normal that people internalized it and began policing themselves.

For Foucault, this kind of self-policing is best exemplified in prisons in the shape of panopticons. A panopticon has a central tower from which a supervisor may observe inmates. Each inmate is isolated in a cell with a window facing the tower but unable to see the supervisor. Thus, inmates never know if they are actually being observed, but feel they may be observed at any time. This creates a mental state of feeling permanently visible. This mental state, more than the actual surveil-lance itself, regulates the inmates' behavior.

Foucault suggests that modern society is like the panopticon. We experience a feeling of permanent visibility that stops us from performing most deviant behavior. Thus, our governments and institutions no longer need to enforce power directly, but rely on us to police ourselves. Such self-policing has become a part of normal, everyday life.

This idea that others are watching, judging, and waiting to punish us for bad behavior affects our behavior at the most basic, subconscious levels. For most people, "normal" means behaving in ways that our social institutions deem acceptable. Those who do not follow these social rules are classified as deviants. Our social in-stitutions function as a kind of panopticon and power and discipline are a seamless part of everyday life.

1. The body of the condemned

On 2 March 1757 Damiens the regicide was condemned "to make the *amende honorable* before the main door of the Church of Paris," where he was to be "taken and conveyed in a cart, wearing nothing but a shirt, holding a torch of burning wax weighing two pounds"; then, "in the said cart, to the Place de Grève, where, on a scaffold that will be erected there, the flesh will be torn from his breasts, arms, thighs and calves with red-hot pincers, his right hand, holding the knife with which he committed the said parricide, burnt with sulfur, and, on those places where the flesh will be torn away, poured molten lead, boiling oil, burning resin, wax and sulfur melted together and then his body drawn and quartered by four horses and his limbs and body consumed by fire, reduced to ashes. and his ashes thrown to the winds" (*Pièces originates . . .,* 372–4).

"Finally, he was quartered," recounts the *Gazette d'Amsterdam* of 1 April 1757. "This last operation was very long, because the horses used were not accustomed to drawing; consequently, instead of four, six were needed; and when that did not suffice, they were forced, in order to cut off the wretch's thighs, to sever the sinews and hack at the joints. . . ."

"It is said that, though he was always a great swearer, no blasphemy escaped his lips; but the excessive pain made him utter horrible cries, and he often repeated: 'My God, have pity on me! Jesus, help me!' The spectators were all edified by the solicitude of the parish priest of St. Paul's who despite his great age did not spare himself in offering consolation to the patient."

Bouton, an officer of the watch, left us his account:

"The sulfur was lit, but the flame was so poor that only the top skin of the hand was burnt, and that only slightly. Then the executioner, his sleeves rolled up, took the steel pincers, which had been especially made for the occasion, and which were about a foot and a half long, and pulled first at the calf of the right leg, then at the thigh, and from there at the two fleshy parts of the right arm; then at the breasts. Though a strong, sturdy fellow, this executioner found it so difficult to tear away the pieces of flesh that he set about the same spot two or three times, twisting the pincers as he did so, and what he took away formed at each part a wound about the size of a six-pound crown piece.

"After these tearings with the pincers, Damiens, who cried out profusely, though without swearing, raised his head and looked at himself; the same executioner dipped an iron spoon in the pot containing the boiling potion, which he poured liberally over each wound. Then the ropes that were to be harnessed to the horses were attached with cords to the patient's body; the horses were then harnessed and placed alongside the arms and legs, one at each limb.

Monsieur le Breton, the clerk of the court, went up to the patient several times and asked him if he had anything to say. He said he had not; at each torment, he cried out, as the damned in hell are supposed to cry out, 'Pardon, my God! Pardon, Lord.' Despite all this pain, he raised his head from time to time and looked at himself boldly. The cords had been tied so tightly by the men who pulled the ends that they caused him indescribable pain. Monsieur le Breton went up to him again and asked him if he had anything to say; he said no. Several confessors went up to him and spoke to him at length; he willingly kissed the crucifix that was held out to him; he opened his lips and repeated: 'Pardon, Lord.'

The horses tugged hard, each pulling straight on a limb, each horse held by an executioner. After a quarter of an hour, the same ceremony was repeated and finally, after several attempts, the direction of the horses had to be changed, thus: those at the arms were made to pull toward the head, those at the thighs towards the arms, which broke the arms at the joints. This was repeated several times without success. He raised his head and looked at himself. Two more horses had to be added to those harnessed to the thighs, which made six horses in all. Without success.

Finally, the executioner, Samson, said to Monsieur le Breton that there was no way or hope of succeeding, and told him to ask their Lordships if they wished him to have the prisoner cut into pieces. Monsieur le Breton, who had come down from the town, ordered that renewed efforts be made, and this was done; but the horses gave up and one of those harnessed to the thighs fell to the ground. The confessors returned and spoke to him again. He said to them (I heard him): 'Kiss me, gentlemen.' The parish priest of St. Paul's did not dare to, so Monsieur de Marsilly slipped under the rope holding the left arm and kissed him on the forehead. The executioners gathered round and Damiens told them not to swear, to carry out their task and that he did not think ill of them; he begged them to pray to God for him, and asked the parish priest of St. Paul's to pray for him at the first mass.

After two or three attempts, the executioner Samson and he who had used the pincers each drew out a knife from his pocket and cut the body at the thighs instead of severing the legs at the joints; the four horses gave a tug and carried off the two thighs after them, namely, that of the right side first,

10

the other following; then the same was done to the arms, the shoulders, the armpits, and the four limbs; the flesh had to be cut almost to the bone, the horses pulling hard carried off the right arm first and the other afterwards.

When the four limbs had been pulled away, the confessors came to speak to him; but his executioner told them that he was dead, though the truth was that I saw the man move, his lower jaw moving from side to side as if he were talking. One of the executioners even said shortly afterwards that when they had lifted the trunk to throw it on the stake, he was still alive. The four limbs were untied from the ropes and thrown on the stake set up in the enclosure in line with the scaffold, then the trunk and the rest were covered with logs and faggots, and fire was put to the straw mixed with this wood.

. . . In accordance with the decree, the whole was reduced to ashes. The last piece to be found in the embers was still burning at half-past ten in the evening. The pieces of flesh and the trunk had taken about four hours to burn. The officers of whom I was one, as also was my son, and a detachment of archers remained in the square until nearly eleven o'clock.

There were those who made something of the fact that a dog had lain the day before on the grass where the fire had been, had been chased away several times, and had always returned. But it is not difficult to understand that an animal found this place warmer than elsewhere" (quoted in Zevaes, 201–14).

Eighty years later, Léon Faucher drew up his rules "for the House of young prisoners in Paris":

"**Art. 17.** The prisoners' day will begin at six in the morning in winter and at five in summer. They will work for nine hours a day throughout the year. Two hours a day will be devoted to instruction. Work and the day will end at nine o'clock in winter and at eight in summer.

Art. 18. *Rising.* At the first drum-roll, the prisoners must rise and dress in silence, as the supervisor opens the cell doors. At the second drum-roll, they must be dressed and make their beds. At the third, they must line up and proceed to the chapel for morning prayer. There is a five-minute interval between each drum-roll.

Art. 19. The prayers are conducted by the chaplain and followed by a moral or religious reading. This exercise must not last more than half an hour.

Art. 20. *Work.* At a quarter to six in the summer, a quarter to seven in winter, the prisoners go down into the courtyard where they must wash their hands and faces, and receive their first ration of bread. Immediately afterwards, they form into work-teams and go off to work, which must begin at six in summer and seven in winter.

Art. 21. *Meal.* At ten o'clock the prisoners leave their work and go to the refectory; they wash their hands in their courtyards and assemble in divisions. After the dinner, there is recreation until twenty minutes to eleven.

Art. 22. *School.* At twenty minutes to eleven, at the drum-roll, the prisoners form into ranks, and proceed in divisions to the school. The class lasts two hours and consists alternately of reading, writing, drawing, and arithmetic. 20

Art. 23. At twenty minutes to one, the prisoners leave the school, in divisions, and return to their courtyards for recreation. At five minutes to one, at the drum-roll, they form into work teams.

Art. 24. At one o'clock they must be back in the workshops: they work until four o'clock.

Art. 25. At four o'clock the prisoners leave their workshops and go into the courtyards where they wash their hands and form into divisions for the refectory.

Art. 26. Supper and the recreation that follows it last until five o'clock: the prisoners then return to the workshops.

Art. 27. At seven o'clock in the summer, at eight in winter, work stops; 25 bread is distributed for the last time in the workshops. For a quarter of an hour one of the prisoners or supervisors reads a passage from some instructive or uplifting work. This is followed by evening prayer.

Art. 28. At half-past seven in summer, half-past eight in winter, the prisoners must be back in their cells after the washing of hands and the inspection of clothes in the courtyard; at the first drum-roll, they must undress, and at the second get into bed. The cell doors are closed and the supervisors go the rounds in the corridors, to ensure order and silence" (Faucher, 274–82).

We have, then, a public execution and a timetable. They do not punish the same crimes or the same type of delinquent. But they each define a certain penal style. Less than a century separates them. It was a time when, in Europe and in the United States, the entire economy of punishment was redistributed. It was a time of great "scandals" for traditional justice, a time of innumerable projects for reform. It saw a new theory of law and crime, a new moral or political justification of the right to punish; old laws were abolished, old customs died out. Modern codes were planned or drawn up: Russia, 1769; Prussia, 1780; Pennsylvania and Tuscany, 1786; Austria, 1788; France, 1791, Year IV, 1808, and 1810. It was a new age for penal justice.

Among so many changes, I shall consider one: the disappearance of torture as a public spectacle. Today we are rather inclined to ignore it; perhaps, in its time, it gave rise to too much inflated rhetoric; perhaps it has been attributed too readily and too emphatically to a process of "humanization," thus dispensing with the need for further analysis. And, in any case, how important is such a change, when compared with the great institutional transformations, the formulation of explicit, general codes and unified rules of procedure; with the almost universal adoption of the jury system, the definition of the essentially corrective character of the penalty, and the tendency, which has become increasingly marked since the nineteenth century, to adapt punishment to the individual offender? Punishment of a less immediately physical kind, a certain discretion in the art of inflicting pain, a combination of more subtle, more subdued sufferings, deprived of their visible display, should not all this be treated as a special case, an incidental effect of deeper changes? And yet the fact remains that a few decades saw the disappearance of the tortured, dismembered, amputated body, symbolically branded on face or shoulder, exposed alive or dead to public view. The body as the major target of penal repression disappeared.

By the end of the eighteenth and the beginning of the nineteenth century, the gloomy festival of punishment was dying out, though here and there it flickered momentarily into life. In this transformation, two processes were at work. They did not have quite the same chronology or the same raison d'être. The first was the disappearance of punishment as a spectacle. The ceremonial of punishment tended to decline; it survived only as a new legal or administrative practice. The *amende honorable* was first abolished in France in 1791, then again in 1830 after a brief revival; the pillory was abolished in France in 1789 and in England in 1837. The use of prisoners in public works, cleaning city streets or repairing the highways, was practiced in Austria, Switzerland, and certain of the United States, such as Pennsylvania. These convicts, distinguished by their "infamous dress" and shaven heads, "were brought before the public. The sport of the idle and the vicious, they often become incensed and naturally took violent revenge upon the aggressors. To prevent them from returning injuries which might be inflicted on them, they were encumbered with iron collars and chains to which bombshells were attached, to be dragged along while they performed their degrading service, under the eyes of keepers armed with swords, blunderbusses, and other weapons of destruction" (Roberts Vaux, *Notices*, 21, quoted in Teeters, 1937, 24). This practice was abolished practically everywhere at the end of the eighteenth or the beginning of the nineteenth century. The public exhibition of prisoners was maintained in France in 1831, despite violent criticism—"a disgusting scene," said Réal (cf. Bibliography); it was finally abolished in April 1848. While the chain gang, which had dragged convicts across the whole of France, as far as Brest and Toulon, was replaced in 1837 by inconspicuous black-painted cell-carts, punishment had gradually ceased to be a spectacle. And whatever theatrical elements it still retained were now downgraded, as if the functions of the penal ceremony were gradually ceasing to be understood, as if this rite that "concluded the crime" was suspected of being in some undesirable way linked with it. It was as if the punishment was thought to equal, if not to exceed, in savagery the crime itself, to accustom the spectators to a ferocity from which one wished to divert them, to show them the frequency of crime, to make the executioner resemble a criminal, judges murderers, to reverse roles at the last moment, to make the tortured criminal an object of pity or admiration. As early as 1764, Beccaria remarked: "The murder that is depicted as a horrible crime is repeated in cold blood, remorselessly" (Beccaria, 101). The public execution is now seen as a hearth in which violence bursts again into flame.

Punishment, then, will tend to become the most hidden part of the penal 30 process. This has several consequences: it leaves the domain of more or less everyday perception and enters that of abstract consciousness; its effectiveness is seen as resulting from its inevitability, not from its visible intensity; it is the certainty of being punished and not the horrifying spectacle of public punishment that must discourage crime; the exemplary mechanics of punishment changes its mechanisms. As a result, justice no longer takes public responsibility for the violence that is bound up with its practice. If it too strikes, if it too kills, it is not as a glorification of its strength, but as an element of itself that it is obliged to tolerate, that it finds difficult to account for. The apportioning of blame is redistributed: in punishment-as-spectacle a confused horror spread from the scaffold, it enveloped both executioner and condemned; and, although it was always ready to invert the shame inflicted on the victim into pity or glory, it often turned the legal violence of the executioner into shame. Now the scandal and the light are to be distributed differently; it is the conviction itself that marks the offender with the unequivocally negative sign: the publicity has shifted to the trial, and to the sentence; the execution itself is like an additional shame that justice is ashamed to impose on the condemned man; so it keeps its distance from the act, tending always to entrust it to others, under the seal of secrecy. It is ugly to be punishable, but there is no glory in punishing. Hence that double system of protection that justice has set up between itself and the punishment it imposes. Those who carry out the penalty tend to become an autonomous sector; justice is relieved of responsibility for it by a bureaucratic concealment of the penalty itself. It is typical that in France the administration of the prisons should for so long have been the responsibility of the Ministry of the Interior, while responsibility for the *bagnes*, for penal servitude in the convict ships and penal settlements, lay with the Ministry of the Navy or the Ministry of the Colonies. And beyond this distribution of roles operates a theoretical disavowal: do not imagine that the sentences that we judges pass are activated by a desire to punish; they are intended to correct, reclaim, "cure"; a technique of improvement represses, in the penalty, the strict expiation of evildoing, and relieves the magistrates of the demeaning task of punishing. In modern justice and on the part of those who dispense it there is a shame in punishing, which does not always preclude zeal. This sense of shame is constantly growing: the psychologists and the minor civil servants of moral orthopedics proliferate on the wound it leaves.

The disappearance of public executions marks therefore the decline of the spectacle; but it also marks a slackening of the hold on the body. In 1787, in an address to the Society for Promoting Political Enquiries, Benjamin Rush remarked: "I can only hope that the time is not far away when gallows, pillory, scaffold, flogging, and wheel will, in the history of punishment, be regarded as the marks of the barbarity of centuries and of countries and as proofs of the feeble influence of reason and religion over the human mind" (Teeters, 1935, 30). Indeed, sixty years later, Van Meenen, opening the second penitentiary congress, in Brussels, recalled the time of his childhood as of a past age: "I have seen the ground strewn with wheels, gibbets, gallows, pillories; I have seen hideously stretched skeletons on wheels" (*Annales de la Charité*, 529–30). Branding had been abolished in England (1834) and in France (1832); in 1820, England no longer dared to apply the full punishment reserved for traitors (Thistlewood was not quartered). Only flogging still remained in a number of penal systems (Russia, England, Prussia). But, generally speaking, punitive practices had become more reticent. One no longer touched the body, or at least as little as possible, and then only to reach something other than the body itself. It might be objected that imprisonment, confinement, forced labor, penal servitude, prohibition from entering certain areas, deportation—which have occupied so important a place in modern penal systems—are "physical" penalties: unlike fines, for example, they directly affect the body. But the punishment-body relation is not the same as it was in the torture during public executions. The body now serves as an instrument or intermediary: if one intervenes upon it to imprison it, or to make it work, it is in order to deprive the individual of a liberty that is regarded both as a right and as property. The body, according to this penalty, is caught up in a system of constraints and privations, obligations and prohibitions. Physical pain, the pain of the body itself, is no longer the constituent element of the penalty. From being an art of unbearable sensations punishment has become an economy of suspended rights. If it is still necessary for the law to reach and manipulate the body of the convict, it will be at a distance, in the proper way, according to strict rules, and with a much "higher" aim. As a result of this new restraint, a whole army of technicians took over from the executioner, the immediate anatomist of pain: warders, doctors, chaplains, psychiatrists, psychologists, educationalists; by their very presence near the prisoner, they sing the praises that the law needs: they reassure it that the body and pain are not the ultimate objects of its punitive faction. Today a doctor must watch over those condemned to death, right up to the last moment—thus juxtaposing himself as the agent of welfare, as the alleviator of pain, with the official whose task it is to end life. This is worth thinking about. When the moment of execution approaches, the patients are injected with tranquillizers. A utopia of judicial reticence: take away life, but prevent the patient from feeling it; deprive the prisoner of all rights, but do not inflict pain; impose penalties free of all pain. Recourse to psychopharmacology and to various physiological "disconnectors," even if it is temporary, is a logical consequence of this "non-corporal" penality.

The modern rituals of execution attest to this double process: the disappearance of the spectacle and the elimination of pain. The same movement has affected the various European legal systems, each at its own rate: the same death for all—the execution no longer bears the specific mark of the crime or the social status of the criminal; a death that lasts only a moment—no torture must be added to it in advance, no further actions performed upon the corpse; an execution that affects life rather than the body. There are no longer any of those long processes in which death was both retarded by calculated interruptions and multiplied by a series of successive attacks. There are no longer any of those combinations of tortures that were organized for the killing of regicides, or of the kind advocated, at the beginning of the eighteenth century, by the anonymous author of *Hanging not Punishment Enough* (1701), by which the condemned man would be broken on the wheel, then flogged until he fainted, then hung up with chains, then finally left to die slowly of hunger. There are no longer any of those executions in which the condemned man was dragged along on a hurdle (to prevent his head smashing against the cobblestones), in which his belly was opened up, his entrails quickly ripped out, so that he had time to see them, with his own eyes, being thrown on the fire; in which he was finally decapitated and his body quartered. The reduction of these "thousand deaths" to strict capital punishment defines a whole new morality concerning the act of punishing.

[. . .]

3. Panopticism

The following, according to an order published at the end of the seventeenth century, were the measures to be taken when the plague appeared in a town.

First, a strict spatial partitioning: the closing of the town and its outlying districts, a prohibition to leave the town on pain of death, the killing of all stray animals; the division of the town into distinct quarters, each governed by an intendant. Each street is placed under the authority of a syndic, who keeps it under surveillance; if he leaves the street, he will be condemned to death. On the appointed day, everyone is ordered to stay indoors: it is forbidden to leave on pain of death. The syndic himself comes to lock the door of each house from the outside; he takes the key with him and hands it over to the intendant of the quarter; the intendant keeps it until the end of the quarantine. Each family will have made its own provisions; but, for bread and wine, small wooden canals are set up between the street and the interior of the houses, thus allowing each person to receive his ration without communicating with the suppliers and other residents; meat, fish, and herbs will be hoisted up into the houses with pulleys and baskets. If it is absolutely necessary to leave the house, it will be done in turn, avoiding any meeting. Only the intendants, syndics, and guards will move about the streets and also, between the infected houses, from one corpse to another, the "crows," who can be left to die: these are "people of little substance who carry the sick, bury the dead, clean, and do many vile and abject offices." It is a segmented, immobile, frozen space. Each individual is fixed in his place. And, if he moves, he does so at the risk of his life, contagion, or punishment.

Inspection functions ceaselessly. The gaze is alert everywhere: "A considerable 35 body of militia, commanded by good officers and men of substance," guards at the gates, at the town hall and in every quarter to ensure the prompt obedience of the people and the absolute authority of the magistrates, "as also to observe all disorder, theft, and extortion." At each of the town gates there will be an observation post; at the end of each street sentinels. Every day, the intendant visits the quarter in his charge, inquires whether syndics have carried out their tasks, whether the inhabitants have anything to complain of; they "observe their actions." Every day, too, the syndic goes into the street for which he is responsible, stops before each house: gets all the inhabitants to appear at windows (those who live overlooking the courtyard will be allocated a window looking onto the street at which no one but they may show themselves); he calls each of them by name; informs himself as to the state of each and every one of them—"in which respect the inhabitants will be compelled to speak the truth under pain of death"; if someone does not appear at the window, the syndic must ask why: "In this way he will find out easily enough whether dead or sick are being concealed." Everyone locked up in his cage, everyone at his window, answering to his name and showing himself when asked—it is the great review of the living and dead.

This surveillance is based on a system of permanent registration: reports from the syndics to the intendants, from the intendants to the magistrates or mayor. At the beginning of the "lock up," the role of each of the inhabitants present in the town is laid down, one by one; this document bears "the name, age, sex of everyone, notwithstanding his condition": a copy is sent to the intendant of the quarter, another to the office of the town hall, another to enable the syndic to make his daily roll call. Everything that may be observed during the course of the visits—deaths, illnesses, complaints, irregularities—is noted down and transmitted to the intendants and magistrates. The magistrates have complete control over medical treatment; they have appointed a physician in charge; no other practitioner may treat, no apothecary prepare medicine, no confessor visit a sick person without having received from him a written note "to prevent anyone from concealing and dealing with those sick of the contagion unknown to the magistrates." The registration of the pathological must be constantly centralized. The relation of each individual to his disease and to his death passes through the representatives of power, the registration they make of it, the decisions they take on it.

Five or six days after the beginning of the quarantine, the process of purifying the houses one by one is begun. All the inhabitants are made to leave; in each room "the furniture and goods" are raised from the ground or suspended from the air; perfume is poured around the room; after carefully sealing the windows, doors, and even the keyholes with wax, the perfume is set alight.

Finally, the entire house is closed while the perfume is consumed; those who have carried out the work are searched, as they were on entry, "in the presence of the residents of the house, to see that they did not have something on their persons as they left that they did not have on entering." Four hours later, the residents are allowed to reenter their homes.

This enclosed, segmented space, observed at every point, in which the individuals are inserted in a fixed place, in which the slightest movements are supervised, in which all events are recorded, in which an uninterrupted work of writing links the center and periphery, in which power is exercised without division, according to a continuous hierarchical figure, in which each individual is constantly located, examined, and distributed among the living beings, the sick, and the dead—all this constitutes a compact model of the disciplinary mechanism. The plague is met by order; its function is to sort out every possible confusion: that of the disease, which is transmitted when bodies are mixed together; that of the evil, which is increased when fear and death overcome prohibitions. It lays down for each individual his place, his body, his disease and his death, his well-being, by means of an omnipresent and omniscient power that subdivides itself in a regular, uninterrupted way even to the ultimate determination of the individual, of what characterizes him, of what belongs to him, of what happens to him. Against the plague, which is a mixture, discipline brings into play its power, which is one of analysis. A whole literary fiction of the festival grew up around the plague: suspended laws, lifted prohibitions, the frenzy of passing time, bodies mingling together without respect, individuals unmasked, abandoning their statutory identity and the figure under which they had been recognized, allowing a quite different truth to appear. But there was also a political dream of the plague, which was exactly its reverse: not the collective festival, but strict divisions; not laws transgressed, but the penetration of regulation into even the smallest details of everyday life through the mediation of the complete hierarchy that assured the capillary functioning of power; not masks that were put on and taken off, but the assignment to each individual of his "true" name, his "true" place, his "true" body, his "true" disease. The plague as a form, at once real and imaginary, of disorder had as its medical and political correlative discipline. Behind the disciplinary mechanisms can be read the haunting memory of "contagions," of the plague, of rebellions, crimes, vagabondage, desertions, people who appear and disappear, live and die in disorder.

If it is true that the leper gave rise to rituals of exclusion, which to a certain extent provided the model for and general form of the great Confinement, then the plague gave rise to disciplinary projects. Rather than the massive, binary division between one set of people and another, it called for multiple separations, individualizing distributions, an organization in depth of surveillance and control, an intensification and a ramification of power. The leper was caught up in a practice of rejection, of exile-enclosure; he was left to his doom in a mass among which it was useless to differentiate; those sick of the plague were caught up in a meticulous tactical partitioning in which individual differentiations were the constricting effects of a power that multiplied, articulated, and subdivided itself; the great confinement on the one hand; the correct training on the other. The leper and his separation; the plague and its segmentations. The first is marked; the second analyzed and distributed. The exile of the leper and the arrest of the plague do not bring with them the same political dream. The first is that of a pure community, the second that of a disciplined society. Two ways of exercising power over men, of controlling their relations, of separating out their dangerous mixtures. The plague-stricken town, traversed throughout with hierarchy, surveillance, observation, writing; the town immobilized by the functioning of an extensive power that bears in a distinct way over all individual bodies—this is the utopia of the perfectly governed city. The plague (envisaged as a possibility at least) is the trial in the course of which one may define ideally the exercise of disciplinary power. In order to make rights and laws function according to pure theory, the jurists place themselves in imagination in the state of nature; in order to see perfect disciplines functioning, rulers dreamt of the state of plague. Underlying disciplinary projects the image of the plague stands for all forms of confusion and disorder; just as the image of the leper, cut off from all human contact, underlies projects of exclusion.

They are different projects, then, but not incompatible ones. We see them coming slowly together, and it is the peculiarity of the nineteenth century that it applied to the space of exclusion of which the leper was the symbolic inhabitant (beggars, vagabonds, madmen, and the disorderly formed the real population) the technique of power proper to disciplinary partitioning. Treat "lepers" as "plague victims," project the subtle segmentations of discipline onto the confused space of internment, combine it with the methods of analytical distribution proper to power, individualize the excluded, but use procedures of individualization to mark exclusion—this is what was operated regularly by disciplinary power from the beginning of the nineteenth century in the psychiatric asylum, the penitentiary, the reformatory, the approved school, and, to some extent, the hospital. Generally speaking, all the authorities exercising individual control function according to a double mode; that of binary division and branding (mad/sane; dangerous/harmless; normal/abnormal); and that of coercive assignment, of differential distribution (who he is; where he must be; how he is to be characterized; how he is to be recognized; how a constant surveillance is to be exercised over him in an individual way, etc.). On the one hand, the lepers are treated as plague victims; the tactics of individualizing disciplines are imposed on the excluded; and, on the other hand, the universality of disciplinary controls makes it possible to brand the "leper" and to bring into play against him the dualistic mechanisms of exclusion. The constant division between the normal and the abnormal, to which every individual is subjected, brings us back to our own time, by applying the binary branding and exile of the leper to quite different objects; the existence of a whole set of techniques and institutions for measuring, supervising, and correcting the abnormal brings into play the disciplinary mechanisms to which the fear of the plague gave rise. All the mechanisms of power which, even today, are disposed around the abnormal individual, to brand him and to alter him, are composed of those two forms from which they distantly derive.

Bentham's *Panopticon* is the architectural figure of this composition. We know the principle on which it was based: at the periphery, an annular building; at the center, a tower; this tower is pierced with wide windows that open onto the inner side of the ring; the peripheric building is divided into cells, each of which extends the whole width of the building; they have two windows, one on the inside, corresponding to the windows of the tower; the other, on the outside, allows the light to cross the cell from one end to the other. All that is needed, then, is to place a supervisor in a central tower and to shut up in each cell a madman, a patient, a condemned man, a worker, or a schoolboy. By the effect of backlighting, one can observe from the tower, standing out precisely against the light, the small captive shadows in the cells of the periphery. They are like so many cages, so many small theaters, in which each actor is alone, perfectly individualized and constantly visible. The panoptic mechanism arranges spatial unities that make it possible to see constantly and to recognize immediately. In short, it reverses the principle of the dungeon; or rather of its three functions—to enclose, to deprive of light, and to hide—it preserves only the first and eliminates the other two. Full lighting and the eye of a supervisor capture better than darkness, which ultimately protected. Visibility is a trap.

To begin with, this made it possible—as a negative effect—to avoid those compact, swarming, howling masses that were to be found in places of confinement, those painted by Goya or described by Howard. Each individual, in his place, is securely confined to a cell from which he is seen from the front by the supervisor; but the side walls prevent him from coming into contact with his companions. He is seen, but he does not see; he is the object of information, never a subject in communication. The arrangement of his room, opposite the central tower, imposes on him an axial visibility; but the divisions of the ring, those separated cells, imply a lateral invisibility. And this invisibility is a guarantee of order; If the inmates are convicts, there is no danger of a plot, an attempt at collective escape, the planning of new crimes for the future, bad reciprocal influences; if they are patients, there is no danger of contagion; if they are madmen, there is no risk of their committing violence upon one another; if they are schoolchildren, there is no copying, no noise, no chatter, no waste of time; if they are workers, there are no disorders, no theft, no coalitions, none of those distractions that slow down the rate of work, make it less perfect, or cause accidents. The crowd, a compact mass, a locus of multiple exchanges, individualities merging together, a collective effect, is abolished and replaced by a collection of separated individualities. From the point of view of the guardian, it is replaced by a multiplicity that can be numbered and supervised; from the point of view of the inmates, by a sequestered and observed solitude (Bentham, 60–64).

Hence the major effect of the Panopticon: to induce in the inmate a state of conscious and permanent visibility that assures the automatic functioning of power. So to arrange things that the surveillance is permanent in its effects, even if it is discontinuous in its action; that the perfection of power should tend to render its actual exercise unnecessary; that this architectural apparatus should be a machine for creating and sustaining a power relation independent of the person who exercises it; in short, that the inmates should be caught up in a power situation of which they are themselves the bearers. To achieve this, it is at once too much and too little that the prisoner should be constantly observed by an inspector: too little, for what matters is that he knows himself to be observed; too much, because he has no need in fact of being so. In view of this, Bentham laid down the principle that power should be visible and unverifiable. Visible: the inmate will constantly have before his eyes the tall outline of the central tower from which he is spied upon. Unverifiable: the inmate must never know whether he is being looked at at any one moment, but he must be sure that he may always be so. In order to make the presence or absence of the inspector unverifiable, so that the prisoners, in their cells, cannot even see a shadow, Bentham envisaged not only venetian blinds on the windows of the central observation hall, but, on the inside, partitions that intersected the hall at right angles and, in order to pass from one quarter to the other, not doors but zigzag openings; for the slightest noise, a gleam of light, a brightness in a half-opened door would betray the presence of the guardian. The Panopticon is a machine for dissociating the see/being seen dyad: in the peripheric ring, one is totally seen, without ever seeing; in the central tower, one sees everything without ever being seen.

It is an important mechanism, for it automatizes and disindividualizes power. Power has its principle not so much in a person as in a certain concerted distribution of bodies, surfaces, lights, gazes; in an arrangement whose internal mechanisms produce the relation in which individuals are caught up. The ceremonies, the rituals, the marks by which the sovereign's surplus power was manifested are useless. There is a machinery that assures dissymmetry, disequilibrium, difference. Consequently, it does not matter who exercises power. Any individual, taken almost at random, can operate the machine: in the absence of the director, his family, his friends, his visitors, even his servants (Bentham, 45). Similarly, it does not matter what motive animates him: the curiosity of the indiscreet, the malice of a child, the thirst for knowledge of a philosopher who wishes to visit this museum of human nature, or the perversity of those who take pleasure in spying and punishing. The more numerous those anonymous and temporary observers are, the greater the risk for the inmate of being surprised and the greater his anxious awareness of being observed. The Panopticon is a marvelous machine which, whatever use one may wish to put it to, produces homogeneous effects of power.

A real subjection is born mechanically from a fictitious relation. So it is not 45
necessary to use force to constrain the convict to good behavior, the madman
to calm, the worker to work, the schoolboy to application, the patient to the
observation of the regulations. Bentham was surprised that panoptic institutions could be so light: there were no more bars, no more chains, no more
heavy locks; all that was needed was that the separations should be clear and
the openings well arranged. The heaviness of the old "houses of security," with
their fortress-like architecture, could be replaced by the simple, economic
geometry of a "house of certainty." The efficiency of power, its constraining
force have, in a sense, passed over to the other side—to the side of its surface of
application. He who is subjected to a field of visibility, and who knows it, assumes
responsibility for the constraints of power; he makes them play spontaneously
upon himself; he inscribes in himself the power relation in which he simultaneously plays both roles; he becomes the principle of his own subjection. By
this very fact, the external power may throw off its physical weight; it tends to
the non-corporal; and, the more it approaches this limit, the more constant,
profound, and permanent are its effects: it is a perpetual victory that avoids any
physical confrontation and which is always decided in advance.

Bentham does not say whether he was inspired, in his project, by Le Vaux's
menagerie at Versailles: the first menagerie in which the different elements are
not, as they traditionally were, distributed in a park (Loisel, 104–7). At the center was an octagonal pavilion which, on the first floor, consisted of only a single
room, the king's salon; on every side large windows looked out onto seven cages
(the eighth side was reserved for the entrance), containing different species of
animals. By Bentham's time, this menagerie had disappeared. But one finds in
the program of the Panopticon a similar concern with individualizing observation, with characterization and classification, with the analytical arrangement
of space. The Panopticon is a royal menagerie; the animal is replaced by man,
individual distribution by specific grouping, and the king by the machinery

of a furtive power. With this exception, the Panopticon also does the work of a naturalist. It makes it possible to draw up differences: among patients, to observe the symptoms of each individual, without the proximity of beds, the circulation of miasmas, the effects of contagion confusing the clinical tables; among schoolchildren, it makes it possible to observe performances (without there being any imitation or copying), to map aptitudes, to assess characters, to draw up rigorous classifications, and, in relation to normal development, to distinguish "laziness and stubbornness" from "incurable imbecility"; among workers, it makes it possible to note the aptitudes of each worker, compare the time he takes to perform a task, and if they are paid by the day, to calculate their wages (Bentham, 60–64).

So much for the question of observation. But the Panopticon was also a laboratory; it could be used as a machine to carry out experiments, to alter behavior, to train or correct individuals. To experiment with medicines and monitor their effects. To try out different punishments on prisoners, according to their crimes and character, and to seek the most effective ones. To teach different techniques simultaneously to the workers, to decide which is the best. To try out pedagogical experiments—and in particular to take up once again the well-debated problem of secluded education, by using orphans. One would see what would happen when, in their sixteenth or eighteenth year, they were presented with other boys or girls; one could verify whether, as Helvetius thought, anyone could learn anything; one would follow "the genealogy of every observable idea"; one could bring up different children according to different systems of thought, making certain children believe that two and two do not make four or that the moon is a cheese, then put them together when they are twenty or twenty-five years old; one would then have discussions that would be worth a great deal more than the sermons or lectures on which so much money is spent; one would have at least an opportunity of making discoveries in the domain of metaphysics. The Panopticon is a privileged place for experiments on men, and for analyzing with complete certainty the transformations that may be obtained from them. The Panopticon may even provide an apparatus for supervising its own mechanisms. In this central tower, the director may spy on all the employees that he has under his orders: nurses, doctors, foremen, teachers, wardens; he will be able to judge them continuously, alter their behavior, impose upon them the methods he thinks best; and it will even be possible to observe the director himself. An inspector arriving unexpectedly at the center of the Panopticon will be able to judge at a glance, without anything being concealed from him, how the entire establishment is functioning. And, in any case, enclosed as he is in the middle of this architectural mechanism, is not the director's own fate entirely bound up with it! The incompetent physician who has allowed contagion to spread, the incompetent prison governor or workshop manager will be the first victims of an epidemic or a revolt. " 'By every tie I could devise,' said the master of the Panopticon, 'my own fate had been bound up by me with theirs' " (Bentham, 177). The Panopticon functions as a kind of laboratory of power. Thanks to its mechanisms of observation, it gains in efficiency and in the ability to penetrate into men's behavior; knowledge follows the advances of power, discovering new objects of knowledge over all the surfaces on which power is exercised.

The plague-stricken town, the panoptic establishment—the differences are important. They mark, at a distance of a century and a half, the transformations of the disciplinary program. In the first case, there is an exceptional situation: against an extraordinary evil, power is mobilized; it makes itself everywhere present and visible; it invents new mechanisms; it separates, it immobilizes, it partitions; it constructs for a time what is both a counter-city and the perfect society; it imposes an ideal functioning, but one that is reduced, in the final analysis, like the evil that it combats, to a simple dualism of life and death: that which moves brings death, and one kills that which moves. The Panopticon, on the other hand, must be understood as a generalizable model of functioning; a way of defining power relations in terms of the everyday life of men. No doubt Bentham presents it as a particular institution, closed in upon itself. Utopias, perfectly closed in upon themselves, are common enough. As opposed to the ruined prisons, littered with mechanisms of torture, to be seen in Piranese's engravings, the Panopticon presents a cruel, ingenious cage. The fact that it should have given rise, even in our own time, to so many variations, projected or realized, is evidence of the imaginary intensity that it has possessed for almost two hundred years. But the Panopticon must not be understood as a dream building: it is the diagram of a mechanism of power reduced to its ideal form; its functioning, abstracted from any obstacle, resistance, or friction, must be represented as a pure architectural and optical system: it is in fact a figure of political technology that may and must be detached from any specific use.

It is polyvalent in its applications; it serves to reform prisoners, but also to treat patients, to instruct schoolchildren, to confine the insane, to supervise workers, to put beggars and idlers to work. It is a type of location of bodies in space, of distribution of individuals in relation to one another, of hierarchical organization, of disposition of centers and channels of power, of definition of the instruments and modes of intervention of power, which can be implemented in hospitals, workshops, schools, prisons. Whenever one is dealing with a multiplicity of individuals on whom a task or a particular form of behavior must be imposed, the panoptic schema may be used. It is—necessary modifications apart—applicable "to all establishments whatsoever, in which, within a space not too large to be covered or commanded by buildings, a number of persons are meant to be kept under inspection" (Bentham, 40; although Bentham takes the penitentiary house as his prime example, it is because it has many different functions to fulfill—safe custody, confinement, solitude, forced labor, and instruction).

In each of its applications, it makes it possible to perfect the exercise of power. It does this in several ways: because it can reduce the number of those who exercise it, while increasing the number of those on whom it is exercised. Because it is possible to intervene at any moment and because the constant pressure acts even before the offenses, mistakes, or crimes have been committed.

Because, in these conditions, its strength is that it never intervenes, it is exercised spontaneously and without noise, it constitutes a mechanism whose effects follow from one another. Because, without any physical instrument other than architecture and geometry, it acts directly on individuals; it gives "power of mind over mind." The panoptic schema makes any apparatus of power more intense: it assures its economy (in material, in personnel, in time); it assures its efficacy by its preventative character, its continuous functioning, and its automatic mechanisms. It is a way of obtaining from power "in hitherto unexampled quantity," "a great and new instrument of government . . . ; its great excellence consists in the great strength it is capable of giving to any institution it may be thought proper to apply it to" (Bentham, 66).

It's a case of "it's easy once you've thought of it" in the political sphere. It can in fact be integrated into any function (education, medical treatment, production, punishment); it can increase the effect of this function, by being linked closely with it; it can constitute a mixed mechanism in which relations of power (and of knowledge) may be precisely adjusted, in the smallest detail, to the processes that are to be supervised; it can establish a direct proportion between "surplus power" and "surplus production." In short, it arranges things in such a way that the exercise of power is not added on from the outside, like a rigid, heavy constraint, to the functions it invests, but is so subtly present in them as to increase their efficiency by itself increasing its own points of contact. The panoptic mechanism is not simply a hinge, a point of exchange between a mechanism of power and a function; it is a way of making power relations function in a function, and of making a function function through these power relations. Bentham's preface to *Panopticon* opens with a list of the benefits to be obtained from his "inspection-house": "*Morals reformed—health preserved—industry invigorated—instruction diffused—public burthens lightened—*Economy seated, as it were, upon a rock—the gordian knot of the Poor-Laws not cut, but untied—all by a simple idea in architecture!" (Bentham, 39).

Furthermore, the arrangement of this machine is such that its enclosed nature does not preclude a permanent presence from the outside: we have seen that anyone may come and exercise in the central tower the functions of surveillance, and that, this being the case, he can gain a clear idea of the way in which the surveillance is practiced. In fact, any panoptic institution, even if it is as rigorously closed as a penitentiary, may without difficulty be subjected to such irregular and constant inspections: and not only by the appointed inspectors, but also by the public; any member of society will have the right to come and see with his own eyes how the schools, hospitals, factories, prisons function. There is no risk, therefore, that the increase of power created by the panoptic machine may degenerate into tyranny; the disciplinary mechanism will be democratically controlled, since it will be constantly accessible "to the great tribunal committee of the world." This Panopticon, subtly arranged so that an observer may observe, at a glance, so many different individuals, also enables everyone to come and observe any of the observers. The seeing machine was once a sort of dark room into which individuals spied; it has become a transparent building in which the exercise of power may be supervised by society as a whole.

The panoptic schema, without disappearing as such or losing any of its properties, was destined to spread throughout the social body; its vocation was to become a generalized function. The plague-stricken town provided an exceptional disciplinary model: perfect, but absolutely violent; to the disease that brought death, power opposed its perpetual threat of death; life inside it was reduced to its simplest expression; it was, against the power of death, the meticulous exercise of the right of the sword. The Panopticon, on the other hand, has a role of amplification; although it arranges power, although it is intended to make it more economic and more effective, it does so not for power itself, nor for the immediate salvation of a threatened society: its aim is to strengthen the social forces—to increase production, to develop the economy, spread education, raise the level of public morality; to increase and multiply.

How is power to be strengthened in such a way that, far from impeding progress, far from weighing upon it with its rules and regulations, it actually facilitates such progress? What intensifier of power will be able at the same time to be a multiplier of production? How will power, by increasing its forces, be able to increase those of society instead of confiscating them or impeding them? The Panopticon's solution to this problem is that the productive increase of power can be assured only if, on the one hand, it can be exercised continuously in the very foundations of society, in the subtlest possible way, and if, on the other hand, it functions outside these sudden, violent, discontinuous forms that are bound up with the exercise of sovereignty. The body of the king, with its strange material and physical presence, with the force that he himself deploys or transmits to some few others, is at the opposite extreme of this new physics of power represented by panopticism; the domain of panopticism is, on the contrary, that whole lower region, that region of irregular bodies, with their details, their multiple movements, their heterogeneous forces, their spatial relations; what are required are mechanisms that analyze distributions, gaps, series, combinations, and which use instruments that render visible, record, differentiate and compare: a physics of a relational and multiple power, which has its maximum intensity not in the person of the king, but in the bodies that can be individualized by these relations. At the theoretical level, Bentham defines another way of analyzing the social body and the power relations that traverse it; in terms of practice, he defines a procedure of subordination of bodies and forces that must increase the utility of power while practicing the economy of the prince. Panopticism is the general principle of a new "political anatomy" whose object and end are not the relations of sovereignty but the relations of discipline.

The celebrated, transparent, circular cage, with its high tower, powerful 55 and knowing, may have been for Bentham a project of a perfect disciplinary institution; but he also set out to show how one may "unlock" the disciplines and get them to function in a diffused, multiple, polyvalent way throughout

the whole social body. These disciplines, which the classical age had elaborated in specific, relatively enclosed places—barracks, schools, workshops—
and whose total implementation had been imagined only at the limited and
temporary scale of a plague-stricken town, Bentham dreamt of transforming
into a network of mechanisms that would be everywhere and always alert,
running through society without interruption in space or in time. The panoptic arrangement provides the formula for this generalization. It programs,
at the level of an elementary and easily transferable mechanism, the basic
functioning of a society penetrated through and through with disciplinary
mechanisms.

[. . .]

What is now imposed on penal justice as its point of application, its "useful" object, will no longer be the body of the guilty man set up against the
body of the king; nor will it be the juridical subject of an ideal contract; it
will be the disciplinary individual. The extreme point of penal justice under
the *Ancien Régime* was the infinite segmentation of the body of the regicide:
a manifestation of the strongest power over the body of the greatest criminal,
whose total destruction made the crime explode into its truth. The ideal point
of penality today would be an indefinite discipline: an interrogation without
end, an investigation that would be extended without limit to a meticulous
and ever more analytical observation, a judgement that would at the same time
be the constitution of a file that was never closed, the calculated leniency of
a penalty that would be interlaced with the ruthless curiosity of an examination, a procedure that would be at the same time the permanent measure of
a gap in relation to an inaccessible norm and the asymptotic movement that
strives to meet in infinity. The public execution was the logical culmination of
a procedure governed by the Inquisition. The practice of placing individuals
under "observation" is a natural extension of a justice imbued with disciplinary
methods and examination procedures. Is it surprising that the cellular prison,

with its regular chronologies, forced labor, its authorities of surveillance and registration, its experts in normality, who continue and multiply the functions of the judge, should have become the modern instrument of penality? Is it surprising that prisons resemble factories, schools, barracks, hospitals, which all resemble prisons?

∾ **NOW PRACTICE ON YOUR OWN**

1. The characters in Rick Bass's story "Antlers" (p. 111) retreat to a remote valley in the mountains to escape the pressures and problems of modern life. In what ways do these characters seem to have successfully escaped the surveillance that Foucault claims defines modern society? In what ways do they bring the Panopticon's gaze and the self-policing it entails into the valley with them?

2. In the southern United States, power has historically been located with white authorities who define rules, control institutions, and enforce punishments. In what ways do the characters in "Everyday Use" (p. 131) seem to have internalized the norms of southern white power structures? How might we see white institutions and power structures regulating the thoughts and behaviors of these characters? How might we define Dee's relationship with the Panopticon of white authority?

3. In Louise Glück's poem "Gretel in Darkness" (p. 59), Gretel has clearly been traumatized by the events she has lived through. But she has also witnessed several women being punished for their deviant behavior. How might re-reading "Gretel in Darkness," looking for acts of punishment, surveillance, or self-policing, lead us to new interpretations of this poem?

Annette Kolodny
Unearthing Herstory
1975

Ecocriticsm is a relatively new movement in critical theory that examines the relationship between literature, humans, and the environment. Annette Kolodny's book The Lay of the Land, *from which this selection is taken, is a feminist, ecocritical analysis of how the American landscape has been portrayed in literature and art.*

Kolodny (b. 1941) describes a fantasy that she calls the "pastoral impulse"—or a tendency to view wild, unoccupied landscapes as maternal Gardens of Eden that will nourish and provide for human inhabitants. Kolodny argues that this pastoral fantasy was enabled by a tendency to describe the land in feminine terms. We see this tendency in clichés such as "Mother Earth," "the Motherland," or "virgin territories." The pastoral impulse is based on the fantasy that wild landscapes were virgin territories waiting for men to occupy them.

Kolodny claims that the pastoral impulse is a uniquely American fantasy because American history is tied up with the exploration and conquest of new land. In this fantasy, seeking out new lands allowed the heroic American male a way to escape the burdens and pressures of modern civilization.

However, there is a paradox in the pastoral impulse: once the virgin land becomes occupied and cultivated, she is no longer virgin. In pursuing the pastoral fantasy, the early settlers destroyed their own dream because once wilderness had been conquered, it was no longer wilderness. By occupying their imagined Garden of Eden, the early settlers destroyed (or even "raped") it, turning it into the same civilized world they were trying to escape.

> You don't know what you've got 'til it's gone,
> They paved Paradise and put up a parking lot.
>
> —*Joni Mitchell, "Big Yellow Taxi"*

For the brief space of perhaps two weeks at the end of May 1969, a small plot of deserted ground just south of the University of California campus at Berkeley dominated headlines and news broadcasts across the country. That such an apparently local incident as the "Battle for People's Park" could so quickly and so effectively capture a nation's attention suggests that it had touched off a resonant chord in the American imagination. If the various legal, political, moral, and ecological issues involved in the controversy are as confused and confusing today as they were in 1969, they do at least all seem to cohere around a single unifying verbal image that appeared in almost all of the leaflets, handbills, and speeches printed during the uproar:

> The earth is our Mother
>   the land
> The University put a fence around
>   the land-our Mother.[1]

In what has since been partially paved over and designated a parking lot, the advocates of People's Park dared fantasize a natural maternal realm, in which human children happily working together in the spontaneous and unalienated labor of planting and tilling might all be "sod brothers."[2] So powerful was the fantasy, in fact, that many seriously believed that, armed "with sod, lots of flowers, and spirit," those evicted from the park might return and "ask our brothers in the [National] Guard to let us into our park."[3]

If the wished-for fraternity with the National Guard was at least erratically realized, the return to "the land—our Mother," the place, they insisted, "where our souls belong,"[4] was thwarted completely. The disposition of the land through "proper channels"—including city council and university officials— was characterized variously as "the rape of People's Park" or, more graphically, as a case of "The University . . . /fucking with our land."[5] For many, hurt and angered at the massive repression their fantasy had engendered, People's Park became "a mirror in which our society may see itself," a summing up of American history: "We have constituted ourselves socially and politically to conquer and transform nature."[6]

In fact, the advocates of People's Park had asserted another version of what is probably America's oldest and most cherished fantasy: a daily reality of harmony between man and nature based on an experience of the land as essentially feminine—that is, not simply the land as mother but the land as woman, the total female principle of gratification—enclosing the individual in an environment of receptivity, repose, and painless and integral satisfaction.[7] Such imagery is archetypal wherever we find it; the soul's home, as the People's Park Committee leaflet and three hundred years of American writing before it had asserted, is that place where the conditions of exile—from Eden or from some primal harmony with the Mother—do not obtain; it is a realm of nurture, abundance, and unalienated labor within which all men are truly brothers. In short, the place America had long promised to be, ever since the first explorers declared themselves virtually "ravisht with the . . . pleasant land" and described the new continent as a "Paradise with all her Virgin Beauties."[8] The human, and decidedly feminine, impact of the landscape became a staple of the early promotional tracts, inviting prospective settlers to inhabit "valleyes and plaines streaming with sweete Springs, like veynes in a naturall bodie," and to explore "hills and mountaines making a sensible proffer of hidden treasure, never yet searched."[9]

As a result, along with their explicit hopes for commercial, religious, and political gains, the earliest explorers and settlers in the New World can be said to have carried with them a "yearning for paradise." When they ran across people living in what seemed to them "the manner of the golden age," and found lands where "nature and liberty affords us that freely, which in England we want, or it costeth us dearely," dormant dreams found substantial root.[10] When, for instance, Arthur Barlowe's account of his "First Voyage Made to the Coasts of America . . . Anno 1584," described the Indian women who greeted him and his men as uniformly beautiful, gracious, cheerful, and friendly, with the wife of the king's brother taking "great pains to see all things ordered in the best manner she could, making great haste to dress some meat for us to eat," he initiated a habit of mind that came to see the Indian woman as a kind of emblem for a land that was similarly entertaining the Europeans "with all love and kindness and . . . as much bounty." Not until the end of the seventeenth century, when the tragic contradictions inherent in such experience could no longer be ignored, were the Indian women depicted more usually as

5

hag-like, ugly, and immoral. The excitement that greeted John Rolfe's marriage to Pocahontas, in April of 1614, may have been due to the fact that it served, in some symbolic sense, as a kind of objective correlative for the possibility of Europeans actually possessing the charms inherent in the virgin continent. Similarly, the repeated evocation of the new continent as "some delicate garden abounding with all kinds of odoriferous flowers," and the sometimes strident insistence that early explorers had "made a Garden upon the top of a Rockie Ile . . . that grew so well,"[11] tantalizes with the suggestion that the garden may in fact be "an abstraction of the essential femininity of the terrain." Paul Shepard undoubtedly has a point when he claims that "we have yet to recognize the full implication of the mother as a primary landscape,"[12] especially since, as psychiatrist Joel Kovel has argued, "the life of the body and the experiences of infancy, . . . are the reference points of human knowledge and the bedrock of the structures of culture."[13]

If the initial impulse to experience the New World landscape, not merely as an object of domination and exploitation, but as a maternal "garden," receiving and nurturing human children, was a reactivation of what we now recognize as universal mythic wishes, it had one radically different facet: *this* paradise really existed, "Whole" and "True," its many published descriptions boasting "*the proofe* of the present benefit this Countrey affords"[14] (italics mine). All the descriptions of wonderful beasts and strangely contoured humans notwithstanding, the published documents from explorers assured the reader of the author's accuracy and unimpeachable reliability. No mere literary convention this; an irrefutable fact of history (the European discovery of America) touched every word written about the New World with the possibility that the ideally beautiful and bountiful terrain might be lifted forever out of the canon of pastoral convention and invested with the reality of daily experience. In some sense, the process had already begun, as explorer after explorer claimed to have "personally . . . with diligence searched and viewed these countries" before concluding them to be "the fairest, frute fullest, and pleasauntest of all the worlde."[15] Eden, Paradise, the Golden Age, and the idyllic garden, in short, all the backdrops for European literary pastoral, were subsumed in the image of an America promising material ease without labor or hardship, as opposed to the grinding poverty of previous European existence; a frank, free affectional life in which all might share in a primal and noncompetitive fraternity; a resurrection of the lost state of innocence that the adult abandons when he joins the world of competitive self-assertion; and all this possible because, at the deepest psychological level, the move to America was experienced as the daily reality of what has become its single dominating metaphor: regression from the cares of adult life and a return to the primal warmth of womb or breast in a feminine landscape. And when America finally produced a pastoral literature of her own, that literature hailed the essential femininity of the terrain in a way European pastoral never had, explored the historical consequences of its central metaphor in a way European pastoral had never dared, and, from the first, took its metaphors as literal truths. The traditional mode had embraced its last and possibly its most uniquely revitalizing permutation.

As Joel Kovel points out, of course, "It is one thing to daydream and conjure up wishful images of the way things ought to be in order that one's instinctually-based fantasies may come true"; at the time of America's discovery, this had become the province of European pastoral. "It is quite another matter, and a more important one in cultural terms,"[16] he continues, to begin experiencing those fantasies as the pattern of one's daily activity—as was the case in sixteenth- and seventeenth-century America. For only if we acknowledge the power of the pastoral impulse to shape and structure experience can we reconcile the images of abundance in the early texts with the historical evidence of starvation, poor harvests, and inclement weather.[17] To label such an impulse as "mere fantasy" in order to dismiss it ignores the fact that fantasy is a particular way of relating to the world, even, as R. D. Laing suggests, "part of, sometimes the essential part of, the meaning or sense . . . implicit in action."[18] In 1630 Francis Higginson, "one of the ministers of Salem," claimed that "Experience doth manifest that there is hardly a more healthfull place to be found in the World" and boasted that "since I came hither . . . I thanke God I have had perfect health, and . . . whereas beforetime I cloathed my self with double cloathes and thicke Wastcoats to keepe me warme, even in the Summer time, I doe now goe as thin clad as any, onely wearing a light Stuffe Cassocke upon my Shirt and Stuffe Breeches and one thickness without Linings."[19] The fact that he died the next year of pneumonia, or, as Governor Dudley phrased it, "of a feaver," in no way negates what the good minister claimed his "Experience doth manifest." American pastoral, unlike European, holds at its very core the promise of fantasy as daily reality. Implicit in the call to emigrate, then, was the tantalizing proximity to a happiness that had heretofore been the repressed promise of a better future, a call to act out what was at once a psychological and political revolt against a culture based on toil, domination, and self-denial.

But not many who emigrated yearning for pastoral gratifications shared Higginson's "Experience." Colonization brought with it an inevitable paradox: the success of settlement depended on the ability to master the land, transforming the virgin territories into something else—a farm, a village, a road, a canal, a railway, a mine, a factory, a city, and finally, an urban nation. As a result, those who had initially responded to the promise inherent in a feminine landscape were now faced with the consequences of that response: either they recoiled in horror from the meaning of their manipulation of a naturally generous world, accusing one another, as did John Hammond in 1656, of raping and deflowering the "naturall fertility and comelinesse," or, like those whom Robert Beverley and William Byrd accused of "slothful Indolence," they succumbed to a life of easeful regression, "spung[ing] upon the Blessings of a warm Sun, and a fruitful Soil" and "approach[ing] nearer to the Description of Lubberland than any other."[20] Neither response, however, obviated the fact that the despoliation of the land appeared more and more an inevitable consequence of human habitation—any more than it terminated the pastoral impulse itself. The instinctual drive embedded in the fantasy, which had first impelled men to emigrate, now impelled them both to continue pursuing the fantasy in daily life, and, when that failed, to codify it as part of the culture's shared dream life, through art—there for all to see in the paintings of Cole and Audubon, in the fictional "letters" of Crevecoeur, the fallacious "local color" of Irving's Sleepy Hollow, and finally, the northern and southern contours clearly distinguished, in the Leatherstocking novels of James Fenimore Cooper and in the Revolutionary War romances of William Gilmore Simms. "Thus," as Joel Kovel argues, "the decisive symbolic elements [of a culture's history] will be those that represent not only repressed content, but ego activity as well."[21]

Other civilizations have undoubtedly gone through a similar history, but at a pace too slow or in a time too ancient to be remembered. Only in America has the entire process remained within historical memory, giving Americans the unique ability to see themselves as the willful exploiters of the very land that had once promised an escape from such necessities. With the pastoral impulse neither terminated nor yet wholly repressed, the entire process—the dream and its betrayal, and the consequent guilt and anger—in short, the knowledge of what we have done to our continent, continues even in this century, as Gary Snyder put it, "eating at the American heart like acid."[22] How much better might things have turned out had we heeded the advice of an earlier American poet Charles Hansford who probably wrote the following lines about the middle of the eighteenth century:

> To strive with Nature little it avails.
> Her favors to improve and nicely scan
> Is all that is within the reach of Man.
> Nature is to befollow'd, and not forc'd,
> For, otherwise, our labor will be lost. [23]

From accounts of the earliest explorers onward, then, a uniquely American pastoral vocabulary began to show itself, releasing and emphasizing some facets of the traditional European mode and all but ignoring others. At its core lay a yearning to know and to respond to the landscape as feminine, a yearning that I have labeled as the uniquely American "pastoral impulse." Obviously, such an impulse must at some very basic level stem from desires and tensions that arise when patterns from within the human mind confront an external reality of physical phenomena. But the precise psychological and linguistic processes by which the mind imposes order or even meaning onto the phenomena— these have yet to be understood. Let us remember, however, that gendering the land as feminine was nothing new in the sixteenth century; Indo-European languages, among others, have long maintained the habit of gendering the physical world and imbuing it with human capacities. What happened with the discovery of America was the revival of that linguistic habit on the level of personal experience; that is, what had by then degenerated into the dead conventions of self-consciously "literary" language, hardly attended to, let alone explored, suddenly, with the discovery of America, became the vocabulary of everyday reality. Perhaps, after all, the world is really gendered, in some subtle way we have not yet quite understood. Certainly, for William Byrd, topography and anatomy were at least analogous, with "a Single Mountain [in the Blue Ridge range], very much resembling a Woman's breast" and a "Ledge that stretch't away to the N.E. . . . [rising] in the Shape of a Maiden's Breast."[24]

Or, perhaps, the connections are more subtle still: was there perhaps a need to experience the land as a nurturing, giving maternal breast because of the threatening, alien, and potentially emasculating terror of the unknown? Beautiful, indeed, that wilderness appeared—but also dark, uncharted, and prowled by howling beasts. In a sense, to make the new continent Woman was already to civilize it a bit, casting the stamp of human relations upon what was otherwise unknown and untamed. But, more precisely still, just as the impulse for emigration was an impulse to begin again (whether politically, economically, or religiously), so, too, the place of that new beginning was, in a sense, the new Mother, her adopted children having cast off the bonds of Europe, "where mother-country acts the step-dame's part."[25] If the American continent was to become the birthplace of a new culture and, with it, new and improved human possibilities, then it was, in fact as well as in metaphor, a womb of generation and a provider of sustenance. Hence, the heart of American pastoral—the only pastoral in which metaphor and the patterns of daily activity refuse to be separated.

Notes

1. Poem credited to Book Jones, printed in a leaflet issued in Berkeley during the last week of May 1969, by the People's Park Committee (hereafter cited as "People's Park Committee leaflet"). For one of the better detailed accounts of this event, see Sheldon Wolin and John Schaar, "Berkeley: The Battle of People's Park," *New York Review of Books*, 19 June 1969, pp. 24–31. A full collection of pamphlets, leaflets, and newspaper articles about People's Park is available in the Bancroft Library, University of California, Berkeley.

2. A red and black sign printed with the words "sod brother" appeared on shop windows and doors in the south campus area to identify their owners as sympathetic to the demands for a People's Park. The words were also lettered on windows and doors of private homes and became a means of protection from damage by angry and frustrated demonstrators.

3. "People's Park Committee leaflet." While most of the law enforcement groups brought into the area were regarded with hostility both by the student and local communities, the National Guard, which bivouacked on park grounds for two weeks, were more cordially tolerated. Rumors flew that guardsmen were watering the plants behind the fence, and both the underground and establishment local press frequently printed photographs of guardsmen accepting flowers from demonstrators.

4. "People's Park Committee leaflet."

5. Joanna Gewertz, "culturevulture," *Berkeley Monitor*, 31 May 1969, p. 3, "People's Park Committee leaflet."

6. Quoted from leaflet entitled "Ecology and Politics in America," distributed 26–27 May 1969, in Berkeley, by American Federation of Teachers locals 1474 and 1795.

7. The Freudian argument for this approach, with which I only partly concur, but by which my remarks are influenced, is best put forth by Herbert Marcuse, *Eros and Civilization* (1955, reprint ed. New York: Random House, Vintage Books, 1961), pp. 246–47.

8. Robert Johnson, "Nova Britannia: Offering Most Excellent fruites by Planting In Virginia. Exciting all such as be well affected to further the same" (London, 1609), p.11; Robert Mountgomry, "A Discourse Concerning the design'd Establishment of a New Colony To The South of Carolina In The Most delightful Country of the Universe" (London, 1717), p. 6. Both papers are in *Tracts and Other Papers, Relating Principally to the Origin, Settlement, And Progress of the Colonies in the North America, From The Discovery Of The Country To The Year 1776*, comp. Peter Force, 3 vols. (Washington, D.C., 1836–38), vol. 1 (hereafter cited as *Force's Tracts*). All of the papers in *Force's Tracts* are paginated separately.

9. Johnson, "Nova Britannia," p. 11, in *Force's Tracts,* vol. 1.

10. "The First Voyage Made To The Coasts Of America With Two Barks, Wherein Were Captains M. Philip Amadas And M. Arthur Barlowe Who Discovered Part Of The Country Now Called Virginia, Anno 1584. Written By One Of The Said Captains [probably Barlowe, who kept the daily record], And Sent To Sir Walter Raleigh, Knight, At Whose Charge And Direction The Said Voyage Was Set Forth," in *Explorations, Descriptions, and Attempted Settlements of Carolina, 1584–1590*, ed. David Leroy Corbitt (Raleigh: State Department of Archives and History, 1948), pp. 19–20 (hereafter cited as *Explorations of Carolina*); John Smith, "A Description of New England; or, The Observations, and Discoveries of Captain John Smith (Admirall of that Country) in the North of America, in the year of our Lord 1614" (London, 1616), p. 21, in *Force's Tracts*, vol. 2.

11. [M. Arthur Barlowe], "The First Voyage Made to the Coasts of America," in *Explorations of Carolina*, pp. 19, 13; Smith, "A Description of New England," p. 9, in *Force's Tracts*, vol. 2.

12. Paul Shepard, *Man in the Landscape* (New York: Alfred A. Knopf, 1967), pp. 108, 98.

13. Joel Kovel, *White Racism* (New York: Random House, Pantheon Books, 1970), p. 7.

14. Smith, "A Description of New England," title page, in *Force's Tracts*, vol. 2.

15. Richard Hakluyt, "Discourse of Western Planting . . . 1584," in *The Original Writings and Correspondence of the Two Richard Hakluyts*, ed. E. G. R. Taylor, 2d ser. (London: Hakluyt Society, 1935), 77:222 (hereafter cited as *Hakluyt Correspondence*). Hakluyt's note identifies "the work alluded to" as John Ribault's "*The whole and true discouerye of Terra Florida* . . . Prynted at London . . . 1563."

16. Kovel, *White Racism*, p. 99.

17. Most of the original settlers of Jamestown died of either disease or starvation, while only about half of the Pilgrims who landed at Plymouth in December 1620 survived the first winter; of the 900 settlers led by Winthrop to Massachusetts Bay, 200 died during the first year. Howard Mumford Jones has surveyed these materials and pointed out that "it took many years for investors and home officials to learn that you could not found a plantation by dumping a few men on a New World shore. . . . A high percentage of sickness and death accompanied the process of acclimatization" (*O strange New World* [1952; reprint ed. London Chatto & Windus, 1965], p. 277.

18. R. D. Laing, *The Politics of Experience* (New York: Random House, Pantheon Books, 1967), pp. 14–15.

19. Thomas Dudley, "Gov. Thomas Dudley's Letter To The Countess of Lincoln, March, 1631," p. 10, in *Force's Tracts*, vol. 2; Francis Higginson, "New-Englands Plantation; or, A short And True Description of the Commodities And Discommodities of that Countrey" (London, 1630), pp. 9, 10, in *Force's Tracts*, vol. 1.

20. John Hammond, "Leah and Rachel; or, The Two Fruitfull Sisters Virginia and Maryland," in *Narratives of Early Maryland, 1633–1684*, ed. Clayton Colman Hall (New York: Charles Scribner's Sons, 1910), p. 300; Robert Beverley, *The History and Present State of Virginia*, ed. Louis B. Wright (Chapel Hill: University of North Carolina Press, 1947), p. 319; William Byrd, *William Byrd's Histories of the Dividing Line Betwixt Virginia and North Carolina*, ed. William K. Boyd (Raleigh: North Carolina Historical Commission, 1929), p. 92(*H*). Both the *History* and the *Secret History of the Dividing Line* are printed *en face* in this edition, so that corresponding incidents appear on opposite pages; I have distinguished quotes from the *History* and the *Secret History* by placing a parenthetical *H* after page numbers from the first and *SH* after page numbers from the second. The *Secret History* is printed here for the first time, from the original manuscript probably composed about 1728 or shortly thereafter. According to Boyd's introduction, "As the *History of the Dividing Line* is

twice the length of *The Secret History*, it is logical to believe that the latter was the first to be composed and that as the title indicates, it was intended only for a select few, and that the *History of the Dividing Line* was written at a later date for a wider audience. Supporting such a conclusion are letters of Byrd written in 1736 and 1737" (p. xv). We might also note that among other differences, the *Secret History* contains but one unfavorable criticism of the North Carolinians, whereas such criticism is a dominant feature of the *History*. The *History* gives more description of the land and the surveying party's responses to it, while the *Secret History* emphasizes the personal relations between the members of the survey team and includes numerous reflections on women and sex. Both *Histories* emphasize eating and give comparatively few details of the business of surveying.

21. Kovel, *White Racism*, p. 99. For a fuller discussion, see chap. 5, "The Symbolic Matrix," pp. 93–105.

22. Gary Snyder, *Earth House Hold* (New York: New Direction, 1969), p. 119.

23. Charles Hansford, "My Country's Worth," in *The Poems of Charles Hansford*, ed. James A. Services and Carl R. Dolmetsch (Chapel Hill: University of North Carolina Press, 1961), p. 52. Probably born about 1685, Hansford lived in York Country, Virginia, and was by trade a blacksmith; when he died, in 1761, he left in manuscript several poems which he called "A Clumsey Attempt of an Old Man to turn Some of his Serious Thoughts into Verse." The poems are printed here for the first time, with titles supplied by the editors.

24. Byrd, *Histories of the Dividing Line*, pp. 214(*H*), 249(*SH*).

25. Philip Freneau, "To Crispin O'Conner, A Back-Woodsman," in *The Poems of Philip Freneau, Poet of the American Revolution*, ed. Fred Lewis Pattee, 3 vols. (Princeton, N.J.: University Library, 1902–7), 3:74–75. The poem was first published in 1792; the text is from the 1809 edition of Freneau's collected *Poems*. Unless otherwise noted, all quotations from Freneau's poems are from the Pattee edition.

☙ NOW PRACTICE ON YOUR OWN

1. Re-read William Wordsworth's poem "The World Is Too Much with Us" (p. 156). Even though this is a British poem, how might we see the pastoral impulse functioning in it? Does looking at the poem through Kolodny's theories reveal any interpretations you didn't see the first time you read it?

2. How might Kolodny's theory of the pastoral impulse help you reinterpret the characters or setting of Rick Bass's "Antlers" (p. 111)? How would you describe the relationship between each of the main characters and the natural world of the valley? Does Bass's story offer us a way to reinterpret the American tendency to see wilderness in specifically feminine terms?

3. Leslie Marmon Silko's "The Man to Send Rain Clouds" (p. 29) is a story about indigenous Americans and thus might offer a counterpart to the pastoral impulse. How does the Laguna view of Nature and the land seem to differ from the pastoral impulse Kolodny defines?

4. How might Kolodny's theories about the relationship between women and the land help you develop new interpretations of Michael Ondaatje's "The Cinnamon Peeler" (p. 74)? Do you see elements of the pastoral impulse in this poem? How might the poem in some ways resist the pastoral impulse?

Acknowledgments *(continued)*

Jerome Bruner. "The Narrative Creation of Self" and "Notes." From *Making Stories* by Jerome Bruner. Copyright © 2002 by Jerome Bruner. Reprinted by permission of Farrar, Straus & Giroux, LLC.

Michel Foucault. Excerpts from "The Body of the Condemned" and "Panopticism" from *Discipline and Punish* by Michel Foucault. English translation copyright © 1977 by Alan Sheridan (New York: Pantheon). Originally published in French as "Surveiller et Punir." Copyright © 1975 by Éditions Gallimard. Reprinted by permission of Georges Borchardt, Inc., for Éditions Gallimard.

Louise Glück. "Gretel in Darkness." From *The First Four Books of Poems* by Louise Glück. Copyright © 1968, 1971, 1972, 1973, 1974, 1975, 1976, 1977, 1978, 1979, 1980, 1985, 1995 by Louise Glück. Reprinted by permission of HarperCollins Publishers.

Langston Hughes. "Theme for English B." From *The Collected Poems of Langston Hughes* by Langston Hughes, edited by Arnold Rampersad with David Roessel, Associate Editor. Copyright © 1994 by The Estate of Langston Hughes. Used by permission of Harold Ober Associates Incorporated and by permission of Alfred A. Knopf, an imprint of the Knopf Doubleday Publishing Group, a division of Random House LLC. All rights reserved. Any third party use of this material, outside of this publication, is prohibited. Interested parties must apply directly to Random House LLC for permission.

David Henry Hwang. *As the Crow Flies* and excerpt from preface to play (p. 94). From *Between Worlds: Contemporary Asian-American Plays*, edited by Misha Berson. New York: Theatre Communications Group. Copyright © 1985 by David Henry Hwang. Reprinted with the permission of Paradigm.

Annette Kolodny. "Unearthing Herstory: An Introduction." From *The Lay of the Land: Metaphor as Experience and History in American Life and Letters*

Index

steps for using, 42–46
surface (literal) meaning in, 42–45
symbol-hunting and, 53
theoretical lens strategy using, 207–208, 211–212
time and sequence using, 98–100
title meaning using, 100–101
writing persuasively using, 47–51
surface (literal) reading of text, 42–45
audience perception of, 42
contrasting strategy in, 50–51
deeper meaning connected to, 52–53
dictionaries and other tools for, 43
linking strategy in, 48–49
literal meanings in, 42–43
theoretical lens strategy using, 207
"thinking aloud" technique for, 43–45
"Sylvia Plath's 'Morning Song' and the Challenge of Motherly Identity" (sample essay), 71–72

symbol-hunting, 53
interpretative claims using, 24, 53
synopses
definition of, 202
sample of, 204–206
theoretical lens strategy using, 202–203

Tenniel, John, 19
text, 8–9
Theater of the Absurd, 259
"Theme for English B" (Hughes)
text of, 203–204
theoretical lens strategy applied to, 202, 207–210, 211–212, 213–216
theoretical lens strategy, 199–219
applying, 202–206
brainstorming using, 207–210
choosing theoretical lens in, 207
common words and phrases in, 213
context strategy *versus*, 202
definition of, 199
delayed thesis in, 213
examples of, 199–201, 213–216

finding theoretical texts for, 217–218
parts to, 201
possible theoretical texts for, 218, 325–398
relationship between theoretical and primary text in, 201–202
steps in using, 207–208
surface meaning in, 208
writing persuasively using, 211–213
theoretical text, 200
finding, 217–218
relationship between primary text and, 201–202, 208, 212
theoretical lens strategy example of use of, 202–206, 213
theory
definition of, 199
theoretical lens strategy's use of, 199–200
thesis
definition of, 24, 265
interpretative claims in, 15
questions about text answered by, 24
text evidence supporting, 19, 23